Codex 5½/0106

Renault 5 Owners Workshop Manual

A K Legg LAE MIMI

Models covered
Renault 5 models, including special/limited editions,
Van and GT Turbo
956 cc, 1108 cc, 1237 cc, 1397 cc & 1721 cc petrol
engines

Covers most mechanical features of Extra Van
Does not cover 1390 cc petrol engine models with single-point fuel
injection, or Diesel engine models

(1219-9U5)

ABCDE
FGHIJ
KLMNO

2

D1429062

Haynes Publishing Group
Sparkford Nr Yeovil
Somerset BA22 7JJ England

Haynes Publications, Inc
861 Lawrence Drive
Newbury Park
California 91320 USA

Acknowledgements

Thanks are due to Champion Spark Plug who supplied the illustrations showing spark plug conditions, to Holt Lloyd Limited who supplied the illustrations showing bodywork repair, and to Duckhams Oils who provided lubrication data. Certain other illustrations are the copyright of Renault Limited (UK) and are used with their permission. Thanks are also due to Sykes-Pickavant Limited who provided some of the workshop tools and to all those people at Sparkford who helped in the production of this manual.

© **Haynes Publishing Group 1992**

A book in the **Haynes Owners Workshop Manual Series**

Printed by J. H. Haynes & Co. Ltd., Sparkford, Nr Yeovil, Somerset BA22 7JJ, England

ISBN 1 85010 880 3

British Library Cataloguing in Publication Data
A catalogue record for this book is available from the British Library

We take great pride in the accuracy of information given in this manual, but vehicle manufacturers make alterations and design changes during the production run of a particular vehicle of which they do not inform us. No liability can be accepted by the authors or publishers for loss, damage or injury caused by any errors in, or omissions from, the information given.

Restoring and Preserving our Motoring Heritage

Few people can have had the luck to realise their dreams to quite the same extent and in such a remarkable fashion as John Haynes, Founder and Chairman of the Haynes Publishing Group.

Since 1965 his unique approach to workshop manual publishing has proved so successful that millions of Haynes Manuals are now sold every year throughout the world, covering literally thousands of different makes and models of cars, vans and motorcycles.

A continuing passion for cars and motoring led to the founding in 1985 of a Charitable Trust dedicated to the restoration and preservation of our motoring heritage. To inaugurate the new Museum, John Haynes donated virtually his entire private collection of 52 cars.

Now with an unrivalled international collection of over 210 veteran, vintage and classic cars and motorcycles, the Haynes Motor Museum in Somerset is well on the way to becoming one of the most interesting Motor Museums in the world.

A 70 seat video cinema, a cafe and an extensive motoring bookshop, together with a specially constructed one kilometre motor circuit, make a visit to the Haynes Motor Museum a truly unforgettable experience.

Every vehicle in the museum is preserved in as near as possible mint condition and each car is run every six months on the motor circuit.

Enjoy the picnic area set amongst the rolling Somerset hills. Peer through the William Morris workshop windows at cars being restored, and browse through the extensive displays of fascinating motoring memorabilia.

From the 1903 Oldsmobile through such classics as an MG Midget to the mighty 'E' Type Jaguar, Lamborghini, Ferrari Berlinetta Boxer, and Graham Hill's Lola Cosworth, there is something for everyone, young and old alike, at this Somerset Museum.

Haynes Motor Museum

Situated mid-way between London and Penzance, the Haynes Motor Museum is located just off the A303 at Sparkford, Somerset (home of the Haynes Manual) and is open to the public 7 days a week all year round, except Christmas Day and Boxing Day.

Contents

Spark plug condition and bodywork repair colour pages between pages 32 and 33

Renault 5TL (three-door)

About this manual

Its aim

The aim of this manual is to help you get the best value from your vehicle. It can do so in several ways. It can help you decide what work must be done (even should you choose to get it done by a garage), provide information on routine maintenance and servicing, and give a logical course of action and diagnosis when random faults occur. However, it is hoped that you will use the manual by tackling the work yourself. On simpler jobs it may even be quicker than booking the car into a garage and going there twice, to leave and collect it. Perhaps most important, a lot of money can be saved by avoiding the costs a garage must charge to cover its labour and overheads.

The manual has drawings and descriptions to show the function of the various components so that their layout can be understood. Then the tasks are described and photographed in a step-by-step sequence so that even a novice can do the work.

Its arrangement

The manual is divided into twelve Chapters, each covering a logical sub-division of the vehicle. The Chapters are each divided into Sections, numbered with single figures, eg 5; and the Sections into paragraphs (or sub-sections), with decimal numbers following on from the Section they are in, eg 5.1, 5.2, 5.3 etc.

It is freely illustrated, especially in those parts where there is a detailed sequence of operations to be carried out. There are two forms of illustration: figures and photographs. The figures are numbered in sequence with decimal numbers, according to their position in the Chapter – eg Fig. 6.4 is the fourth drawing/illustration in Chapter 6. Photographs carry the same number (either individually or in related groups) as the Section or sub-section to which they relate.

There is an alphabetical index at the back of the manual as well as a contents list at the front. Each Chapter is also preceded by its own individual contents list.

References to the 'left' or 'right' of the vehicle are in the sense of a person in the driver's seat facing forwards.

Unless otherwise stated, nuts and bolts are removed by turning anti-clockwise, and tightened by turning clockwise.

Vehicle manufacturers continually make changes to specifications and recommendations, and these, when notified, are incorporated into our manuals at the earliest opportunity.

We take great pride in the accuracy of information given in this manual, but vehicle manufacturers make alterations and design changes during the production run of a particular vehicle of which they do not inform us. No liability can be accepted by the authors or publishers for loss, damage or injury caused by any errors in, or omissions from, the information given.

Introduction to the new Renault 5

Available in France from late 1984 and the UK from February 1985 the new Renault 5 incorporates many innovations compared with its forerunner. Front-wheel drive is retained, but with a transverse engine and gearbox instead of the in-line previous arrangement. This has not only improved front wheel traction owing to a greater concentration of weight over the wheels, but has also resulted in additional interior space. Many components both mechanical and body have been subjected to weight saving in order to improve economy and performance, one example being the gearbox which is now of light alloy instead of cast iron. The MacPherson strut front suspension replaces the previous torsion bar and wishbone type, and the bodywork incorporates improved aerodynamics giving it a sleeker look.

A choice of 956 cc, 1108 cc and 1397 cc overhead valve engines is available, ranging from 42 brake horse power to 115 brake horse power for the Turbo version. A 1721 cc overhead cam engine became available in 1987: this and other later model changes are covered in Chapter 12.

The car is quite conventional in design and the DIY home mechanic should find most work straightforward.

General dimensions, weights and capacities

For information applicable to later models, see Supplement at end of manual

Dimensions

Overall length:
  Three-door .... 3591 mm (141.4 in)
  Five-door .... 3651 mm (143.7 in)
Overall width .... 1584 mm (62.4 in)
Overall height:
  Non-Turbo .... 1397 mm (55.0 in)
  Turbo .... 1367 mm (53.8 in)
Ground clearance .... 120 mm (4.7 in)
Track:
  Front .... 1320 mm (52.0 in)
  Rear .... 1290 mm (50.8 in)
Wheelbase:
  Three-door .... 2400 mm (94.5 in)
  Five-door .... 2460 mm (96.9 in)
Turning circle (between kerbs) .... 9800 mm (385.8 in)

Weights

Kerb weight:
  TC .... 710 kg (1565 lb)
  TL (three-door) .... 730 kg (1609 lb)
  TL (five-door) .... 735 kg (1620 lb)
  GTL (three-door) .... 740 kg (1631 lb)
  GTL (five-door) .... 745 kg (1642 lb)
  TS .... 720 kg (1587 lb)
  Auto (three-door) .... 770 kg (1698 lb)
  Auto (five-door) .... 775 kg (1709 lb)
  TSE .... 755 kg (1664 lb)
  GT Turbo .... 830 kg (1830 lb)
Maximum roof rack weight .... 60 kg (132 lb)
Maximum towing weight:
  TC .... 550 kg (1213 lb)
  TL .... 650 kg (1433 lb)
  GTL, TS and TSE .... 750 kg (1653 lb)
  Auto .... 450 kg (992 lb)
  GT Turbo .... 800 kg (1764 lb)

Capacities

Engine oil (excluding filter):
  Non-Turbo .... 3.0 litre (5.3 Imp pt)
  Turbo .... 3.7 litre (6.5 Imp pt)
Oil filter:
  Non-Turbo .... 0.50 litre (0.9 Imp pt)
  Turbo .... 0.25 litre (0.4 Imp pt)

	Steel filler plug	Plastic filler plug
Manual gearbox:		
Four-speed units	3.25 litre (5.72 Imp pt)	2.75 litre (4.84 Imp pt)
Five-speed units	3.40 litre (5.98 Imp pt)	2.90 litre (5.10 Imp pt)

Automatic transmission (refill after draining) .... 2.0 litre (3.52 Imp pt)
Cooling system (total) .... 5.5 litre (9.7 Imp pt)
Fuel tank:
  Non-Turbo .... 43.0 litre (9.5 Imp gal)
  Turbo – main .... 43.0 litre (9.5 Imp gal)
  Turbo – auxiliary .... 7.0 litre (1.54 Imp gal)

Jacking and towing

To change a wheel, remove the spare wheel and jack, apply the handbrake and chock the wheel diagonally opposite the one to be changed. On automatic transmission models, place the selector lever in P. Make sure that the car is located on firm level ground and then slightly loosen the wheel bolts with the brace provided. Locate the jack head in the jacking point nearest to the wheel to be changed and raise the jack using the other end of the brace. When the wheel is clear of the ground remove the bolts (and trim) and lift off the wheel. Fit the spare wheel using two diagonally opposite wheelbolts and moderately tighten them, then locate the large holes of the trim over them and fit the two remaining wheelbolts. This trim is only fitted to steel wheels and has two large and two small holes to allow prior fitting of two bolts. Lower the car and then tighten the bolts fully. With the spare wheel in position, remove the chock and stow the jack and tools.

When jacking up the car to carry out repair or maintenance tasks position the jack as follows:

If the front of the car is to be raised, position the jack head under a stout wooden beam placed transversely across the underside of the car and in contact with the front subframe side rails. Supplement the jack with axle stands which can be placed under the subframe or under the load bearing members of the underbody.

To raise the rear of the car, jack up each side in turn with the jack head positioned under the load bearing underbody members adjacent to the rear suspension bearing brackets.

To raise the side of the car place a block of wood under the side sill and located centrally under the front door. Place the jack head in contact with the block and raise the car. Shape the wooden blocks as necessary to avoid damaging the sill edges and supplement the jack with axle stands positioned under the jacking points. Never work under, around or near a raised car unless it is adequately supported in at least two places with axle stands or suitable sturdy blocks.

The car may be towed for breakdown recovery purposes only using the towing eyes positioned at the front and rear of the vehicle. These eyes are intended for traction loads only and must not be used for lifting the car either directly or indirectly. If the car is equipped with automatic transmission the following precautions must be observed if the vehicle is to be towed. Preferably a front end suspended tow should be used. If this is not possible, add an extra 2 litres (3.5 Imp pints) of the specified automatic transmission fluid to the transmission. The car may now be towed for a maximum of 30 miles (48 km) at a speed not exceeding 18 mph (30 kph). The selector lever must be in the N position during the tow. Drain off the surplus transmission fluid on completion of the tow.

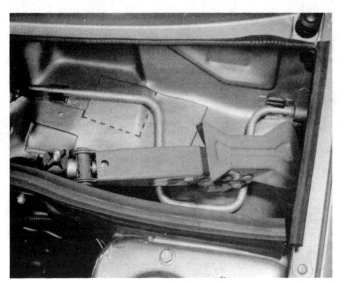

Jack and brace location

Turn nut (A) to lower spare wheel

Spare wheel carrier retaining hook

8

On steel wheels two wheel bolts can be fitted before fitting the trim

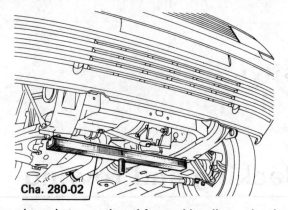

Cha. 280-02

Use a beam between the subframe side rails to raise the front of the car

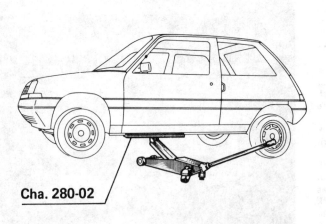

Cha. 280-02

Raising the side of the car

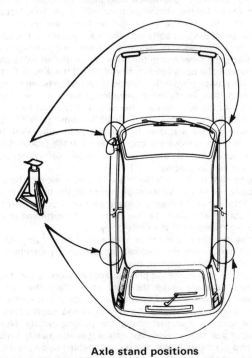

Axle stand positions

Front towing eye

Rear towing eye

Buying spare parts and vehicle identification numbers

For information applicable to later models, see Supplement at end of manual

Buying spare parts

Spare parts are available from many sources, for example: Renault garages, other garages and accessory shops, and motor factors. Our advice regarding spare parts is as follows:

Officially appointed Renault garages: These will be the best source of parts which are peculiar to your car and are otherwise not generally available (eg, complete cylinder heads, internal gearbox components, badges, interior trim etc). It is also the only place at which you should buy parts if your car is still under warranty; non-Renault components may invalidate the warranty. To be sure of obtaining the correct parts it will always be necessary to give the storeman your car's vehicle identification number, and if possible to take the old part along for positive identification. Remember that many parts are available on a factory exchange scheme – any parts returned should always be clean! It obviously makes good sense to go straight to the specialists on your car for this type of part as they are best equipped to supply you.

Other garages and accessory shops – These are often very good places to buy materials and components needed for the maintenance of your car (eg, oil filters, spark plugs, bulbs, fan belts, oils and greases, touch-up paint, filler paste etc). They also sell general accessories, usually have convenient opening hours, charge lower prices and can often be found not far from home.

Motor factors – Good factors will stock all of the more important components which wear out relatively quickly (eg, clutch components, pistons, valves, exhaust systems, brake cylinders/pipes/hoses/seals/shoes and pads etc). Motor factors will often provide new or reconditioned components on a part exchange basis – this can save a considerable amount of money.

Vehicle identification numbers

Modifications are a continuing and unpublicised process in vehicle manufacture quite apart from their major model changes. Spare parts manuals and lists are compiled on a numerical basis, the individual vehicle numbers being essential for correct identification of the component required.

When ordering parts it will usually be necessary to quote the numbers on the oval plate under all circumstances and often those on the manufacturer's plate. If engine or gearbox parts are being ordered the engine plate or gearbox plate numbers will be needed. The paint code may be required if the colour of the car is not easily described. All these numbers with the exception of those on the gearbox plate are located in readily visible places in the engine compartment. The gearbox plate is affixed to the transmission housing. The vehicle type numbers and corresponding details are as follows – a C prefix indicates a three-door version and a B prefix indicates a five-door version.

Type	Engine code	Engine capacity	Model
C 400	C1C	956 cc	TC
C/B 401	C1E	1108 cc	TL
C/B 402	C1J	1397 cc	GTL
C/B 403	C2J	1397 cc	TS,TSE, Auto
C 405	C1J	1397 cc	GT Turbo

The oval plate may also be positioned on the front right-hand side of the engine compartment

A *Oval plate*
B *Manufacturer's plate*
C *Engine number plate*
D *Paint code*

General repair procedures

Whenever servicing, repair or overhaul work is carried out on the car or its components, it is necessary to observe the following procedures and instructions. This will assist in carrying out the operation efficiently and to a professional standard of workmanship.

Joint mating faces and gaskets

Where a gasket is used between the mating faces of two components, ensure that it is renewed on reassembly, and fit it dry unless otherwise stated in the repair procedure. Make sure that the mating faces are clean and dry with all traces of old gasket removed. When cleaning a joint face, use a tool which is not likely to score or damage the face, and remove any burrs or nicks with an oilstone or fine file.

Make sure that tapped holes are cleaned with a pipe cleaner, and keep them free of jointing compound if this is being used unless specifically instructed otherwise.

Ensure that all orifices, channels or pipes are clear and blow through them, preferably using compressed air.

Oil seals

Whenever an oil seal is removed from its working location, either individually or as part of an assembly, it should be renewed.

The very fine sealing lip of the seal is easily damaged and will not seal if the surface it contacts is not completely clean and free from scratches, nicks or grooves. If the original sealing surface of the component cannot be restored, the component should be renewed.

Protect the lips of the seal from any surface which may damage them in the course of fitting. Use tape or a conical sleeve where possible. Lubricate the seal lips with oil before fitting and, on dual lipped seals, fill the space between the lips with grease.

Unless otherwise stated, oil seals must be fitted with their sealing lips toward the lubricant to be sealed.

Use a tubular drift or block of wood of the appropriate size to install the seal and, if the seal housing is shouldered, drive the seal down to the shoulder. If the seal housing is unshouldered, the seal should be fitted with its face flush with the housing top face.

Screw threads and fastenings

Always ensure that a blind tapped hole is completely free from oil, grease, water or other fluid before installing the bolt or stud. Failure to do this could cause the housing to crack due to the hydraulic action of the bolt or stud as it is screwed in.

When tightening a castellated nut to accept a split pin, tighten the nut to the specified torque, where applicable, and then tighten further to the next split pin hole. Never slacken the nut to align a split pin hole unless stated in the repair procedure.

When checking or retightening a nut or bolt to a specified torque setting, slacken the nut or bolt by a quarter of a turn, and then retighten to the specified setting.

Locknuts, locktabs and washers

Any fastening which will rotate against a component or housing in the course of tightening should always have a washer between it and the relevant component or housing.

Spring or split washers should always be renewed when they are used to lock a critical component such as a big-end bearing retaining nut or bolt.

Locktabs which are folded over to retain a nut or bolt should always be renewed.

Self-locking nuts can be reused in non-critical areas, providing resistance can be felt when the locking portion passes over the bolt or stud thread.

Split pins must always be replaced with new ones of the correct size for the hole.

Special tools

Some repair procedures in this manual entail the use of special tools such as a press, two or three-legged pullers, spring compressors etc. Wherever possible, suitable readily available alternatives to the manufacturer's special tools are described, and are shown in use. In some instances, where no alternative is possible, it has been necessary to resort to the use of a manufacturer's tool and this has been done for reasons of safety as well as the efficient completion of the repair operation. Unless you are highly skilled and have a thorough understanding of the procedure described, never attempt to bypass the use of any special tool when the procedure described specifies its use. Not only is there a very great risk of personal injury, but expensive damage could be caused to the components involved.

Tools and working facilities

Introduction

A selection of good tools is a fundamental requirement for anyone contemplating the maintenance and repair of a motor vehicle. For the owner who does not possess any, their purchase will prove a considerable expense, offsetting some of the savings made by doing-it-yourself. However, provided that the tools purchased meet the relevant national safety standards and are of good quality, they will last for many years and prove an extremely worthwhile investment.

To help the average owner to decide which tools are needed to carry out the various tasks detailed in this manual, we have compiled three lists of tools under the following headings: *Maintenance and minor repair, Repair and overhaul,* and *Special.* The newcomer to practical mechanics should start off with the *Maintenance and minor repair* tool kit and confine himself to the simpler jobs around the vehicle. Then, as his confidence and experience grow, he can undertake more difficult tasks, buying extra tools as, and when, they are needed. In this way, a *Maintenance and minor repair* tool kit can be built-up into a *Repair and overhaul* tool kit over a considerable period of time without any major cash outlays. The experienced do-it-yourselfer will have a tool kit good enough for most repair and overhaul procedures and will add tools from the *Special* category when he feels the expense is justified by the amount of use to which these tools will be put.

It is obviously not possible to cover the subject of tools fully here. For those who wish to learn more about tools and their use there is a book entitled *How to Choose and Use Car Tools* available from the publishers of this manual.

Maintenance and minor repair tool kit

The tools given in this list should be considered as a minimum requirement if routine maintenance, servicing and minor repair operations are to be undertaken. We recommend the purchase of combination spanners (ring one end, open-ended the other); although more expensive than open-ended ones, they do give the advantages of both types of spanner.

Combination spanners - 10, 11, 12, 13, 14, 15, 16 & 17 mm
Adjustable spanner - 9 inch
Engine sump/gearbox drain plug key
Spark plug spanner (with rubber insert)
Spark plug gap adjustment tool
Set of feeler gauges
Brake bleed nipple spanner
Screwdriver - 4 in long x 1/4 in dia (flat blade)
Screwdriver - 4 in long x 1/4 in dia (cross blade)
Combination pliers - 6 inch
Hacksaw (junior)
Tyre pump
Tyre pressure gauge
Oil can
Fine emery cloth (1 sheet)
Wire brush (small)
Funnel (medium size)

Repair and overhaul tool kit

These tools are virtually essential for anyone undertaking any major repairs to a motor vehicle, and are additional to those given in the *Maintenance and minor repair* list. Included in this list is a comprehensive set of sockets. Although these are expensive they will be found invaluable as they are so versatile - particularly if various drives are included in the set. We recommend the ½ in square-drive type, as this can be used with most proprietary torque wrenches. If you cannot afford a socket set, even bought piecemeal, then inexpensive tubular box spanners are a useful alternative.

The tools in this list will occasionally need to be supplemented by tools from the *Special* list.

Sockets (or box spanners) to cover range in previous list
Reversible ratchet drive (for use with sockets)
Extension piece, 10 inch (for use with sockets)
Universal joint (for use with sockets)
Torque wrench (for use with sockets)
'Mole' wrench - 8 inch
Ball pein hammer
Soft-faced hammer, plastic or rubber
Screwdriver - 6 in long x 5/16 in dia (flat blade)
Screwdriver - 2 in long x 5/16 in square (flat blade)
Screwdriver - 1 1/2 in long x 1/4 in dia (cross blade)
Screwdriver - 3 in long x 1/8 in dia (electricians)
Pliers - electricians side cutters
Pliers - needle nosed
Pliers - circlip (internal and external)
Cold chisel - 1/2 inch
Scriber
Scraper
Centre punch
Pin punch
Hacksaw
Valve grinding tool
Steel rule/straight-edge
Allen keys (inc. splined/Torx type if necessary)
Selection of files
Wire brush (large)
Axle-stands
Jack (strong trolley or hydraulic type)

Special tools

The tools in this list are those which are not used regularly, are expensive to buy, or which need to be used in accordance with their manufacturers' instructions. Unless relatively difficult mechanical jobs are undertaken frequently, it will not be economic to buy many of these tools. Where this is the case, you could consider clubbing together with friends (or joining a motorists' club) to make a joint purchase, or borrowing the tools against a deposit from a local garage or tool hire specialist.

The following list contains only those tools and instruments freely available to the public, and not those special tools produced by the vehicle manufacturer specifically for its dealer network. You will find occasional references to these manufacturers' special tools in the text of this manual. Generally, an alternative method of doing the job without the vehicle manufacturers' special tool is given. However, sometimes, there is no alternative to using them. Where this is the case and the relevant tool cannot be bought or borrowed, you will have to entrust the work to a franchised garage.

Valve spring compressor
Piston ring compressor
Balljoint separator
Universal hub/bearing puller
Impact screwdriver
Micrometer and/or vernier gauge
Dial gauge
Stroboscopic timing light

Dwell angle meter/tachometer
Universal electrical multi-meter
Cylinder compression gauge
Lifting tackle
Trolley jack
Light with extension lead

Buying tools

For practically all tools, a tool factor is the best source since he will have a very comprehensive range compared with the average garage or accessory shop. Having said that, accessory shops often offer excellent quality tools at discount prices, so it pays to shop around.

There are plenty of good tools around at reasonable prices, but always aim to purchase items which meet the relevant national safety standards. If in doubt, ask the proprietor or manager of the shop for advice before making a purchase.

Care and maintenance of tools

Having purchased a reasonable tool kit, it is necessary to keep the tools in a clean serviceable condition. After use, always wipe off any dirt, grease and metal particles using a clean, dry cloth, before putting the tools away. Never leave them lying around after they have been used. A simple tool rack on the garage or workshop wall, for items such as screwdrivers and pliers is a good idea. Store all normal wrenches and sockets in a metal box. Any measuring instruments, gauges, meters, etc, must be carefully stored where they cannot be damaged or become rusty.

Take a little care when tools are used. Hammer heads inevitably become marked and screwdrivers lose the keen edge on their blades from time to time. A little timely attention with emery cloth or a file will soon restore items like this to a good serviceable finish.

Working facilities

Not to be forgotten when discussing tools, is the workshop itself. If anything more than routine maintenance is to be carried out, some form of suitable working area becomes essential.

It is appreciated that many an owner mechanic is forced by circumstances to remove an engine or similar item, without the benefit of a garage or workshop. Having done this, any repairs should always be done under the cover of a roof.

Wherever possible, any dismantling should be done on a clean, flat workbench or table at a suitable working height.

Any workbench needs a vice: one with a jaw opening of 4 in (100 mm) is suitable for most jobs. As mentioned previously, some clean dry storage space is also required for tools, as well as for lubricants, cleaning fluids, touch-up paints and so on, which become necessary.

Another item which may be required, and which has a much more general usage, is an electric drill with a chuck capacity of at least $5/16$ in (8 mm). This, together with a good range of twist drills, is virtually essential for fitting accessories such as mirrors and reversing lights.

Last, but not least, always keep a supply of old newspapers and clean, lint-free rags available, and try to keep any working area as clean as possible.

Spanner jaw gap comparison table

Jaw gap (in)	Spanner size
0.250	$1/4$ in AF
0.276	7 mm
0.313	$5/16$ in AF
0.315	8 mm
0.344	$11/32$ in AF; $1/8$ in Whitworth
0.354	9 mm
0.375	$3/8$ in AF
0.394	10 mm
0.433	11 mm
0.438	$7/16$ in AF
0.445	$3/16$ in Whitworth; $1/4$ in BSF
0.472	12 mm
0.500	$1/2$ in AF
0.512	13 mm
0.525	$1/4$ in Whitworth; $5/16$ in BSF
0.551	14 mm
0.563	$9/16$ in AF
0.591	15 mm
0.600	$5/16$ in Whitworth; $3/8$ in BSF
0.625	$5/8$ in AF
0.630	16 mm
0.669	17 mm
0.686	$11/16$ in AF
0.709	18 mm
0.710	$3/8$ in Whitworth; $7/16$ in BSF
0.748	19 mm
0.750	$3/4$ in AF
0.813	$13/16$ in AF
0.820	$7/16$ in Whitworth; $1/2$ in BSF
0.866	22 mm
0.875	$7/8$ in AF
0.920	$1/2$ in Whitworth; $9/16$ in BSF
0.938	$15/16$ in AF
0.945	24 mm
1.000	1 in AF
1.010	$9/16$ in Whitworth; $5/8$ in BSF
1.024	26 mm
1.063	$1 1/16$ in AF; 27 mm
1.100	$5/8$ in Whitworth; $11/16$ in BSF
1.125	$1 1/8$ in AF
1.181	30 mm
1.200	$11/16$ in Whitworth; $3/4$ in BSF
1.250	$1 1/4$ in AF
1.260	32 mm
1.300	$3/4$ in Whitworth; $7/8$ in BSF
1.313	$1 5/16$ in AF
1.390	$13/16$ in Whitworth; $15/16$ in BSF
1.417	36 mm
1.438	$1 7/16$ in AF
1.480	$7/8$ in Whitworth; 1 in BSF
1.500	$1 1/2$ in AF
1.575	40 mm; $15/16$ in Whitworth
1.614	41 mm
1.625	$1 5/8$ in AF
1.670	1 in Whitworth; $1 1/8$ in BSF
1.688	$1 11/16$ in AF
1.811	46 mm
1.813	$1 13/16$ in AF
1.860	$1 1/8$ in Whitworth; $1 1/4$ in BSF
1.875	$1 7/8$ in AF
1.969	50 mm
2.000	2 in AF
2.050	$1 1/4$ in Whitworth; $1 3/8$ in BSF
2.165	55 mm
2.362	60 mm

Conversion factors

Length (distance)

Inches (in)	X	25.4	= Millimetres (mm)	X	0.0394	= Inches (in)
Feet (ft)	X	0.305	= Metres (m)	X	3.281	= Feet (ft)
Miles	X	1.609	= Kilometres (km)	X	0.621	= Miles

Volume (capacity)

Cubic inches (cu in; in³)	X	16.387	= Cubic centimetres (cc; cm³)	X	0.061	= Cubic inches (cu in; in³)
Imperial pints (Imp pt)	X	0.568	= Litres (l)	X	1.76	= Imperial pints (Imp pt)
Imperial quarts (Imp qt)	X	1.137	= Litres (l)	X	0.88	= Imperial quarts (Imp qt)
Imperial quarts (Imp qt)	X	1.201	= US quarts (US qt)	X	0.833	= Imperial quarts (Imp qt)
US quarts (US qt)	X	0.946	= Litres (l)	X	1.057	= US quarts (US qt)
Imperial gallons (Imp gal)	X	4.546	= Litres (l)	X	0.22	= Imperial gallons (Imp gal)
Imperial gallons (Imp gal)	X	1.201	= US gallons (US gal)	X	0.833	= Imperial gallons (Imp gal)
US gallons (US gal)	X	3.785	= Litres (l)	X	0.264	= US gallons (US gal)

Mass (weight)

Ounces (oz)	X	28.35	= Grams (g)	X	0.035	= Ounces (oz)
Pounds (lb)	X	0.454	= Kilograms (kg)	X	2.205	= Pounds (lb)

Force

Ounces-force (ozf; oz)	X	0.278	= Newtons (N)	X	3.6	= Ounces-force (ozf; oz)
Pounds-force (lbf; lb)	X	4.448	= Newtons (N)	X	0.225	= Pounds-force (lbf; lb)
Newtons (N)	X	0.1	= Kilograms-force (kgf; kg)	X	9.81	= Newtons (N)

Pressure

Pounds-force per square inch (psi; lbf/in²; lb/in²)	X	0.070	= Kilograms-force per square centimetre (kgf/cm²; kg/cm²)	X	14.223	= Pounds-force per square inch (psi; lbf/in²; lb/in²)
Pounds-force per square inch (psi; lbf/in²; lb/in²)	X	0.068	= Atmospheres (atm)	X	14.696	= Pounds-force per square inch (psi; lbf/in²; lb/in²)
Pounds-force per square inch (psi; lbf/in²; lb/in²)	X	0.069	= Bars	X	14.5	= Pounds-force per square inch (psi; lbf/in²; lb/in²)
Pounds-force per square inch (psi; lbf/in²; lb/in²)	X	6.895	= Kilopascals (kPa)	X	0.145	= Pounds-force per square inch (psi; lbf/in²; lb/in²)
Kilopascals (kPa)	X	0.01	= Kilograms-force per square centimetre (kgf/cm²; kg/cm²)	X	98.1	= Kilopascals (kPa)
Millibar (mbar)	X	100	= Pascals (Pa)	X	0.01	= Millibar (mbar)
Millibar (mbar)	X	0.0145	= Pounds-force per square inch (psi; lbf/in²; lb/in²)	X	68.947	= Millibar (mbar)
Millibar (mbar)	X	0.75	= Millimetres of mercury (mmHg)	X	1.333	= Millibar (mbar)
Millibar (mbar)	X	0.401	= Inches of water (inH₂O)	X	2.491	= Millibar (mbar)
Millimetres of mercury (mmHg)	X	0.535	= Inches of water (inH₂O)	X	1.868	= Millimetres of mercury (mmHg)
Inches of water (inH₂O)	X	0.036	= Pounds-force per square inch (psi; lbf/in²; lb/in²)	X	27.68	= Inches of water (inH₂O)

Torque (moment of force)

Pounds-force inches (lbf in; lb in)	X	1.152	= Kilograms-force centimetre (kgf cm; kg cm)	X	0.868	= Pounds-force inches (lbf in; lb in)
Pounds-force inches (lbf in; lb in)	X	0.113	= Newton metres (Nm)	X	8.85	= Pounds-force inches (lbf in; lb in)
Pounds-force inches (lbf in; lb in)	X	0.083	= Pounds-force feet (lbf ft; lb ft)	X	12	= Pounds-force inches (lbf in; lb in)
Pounds-force feet (lbf ft; lb ft)	X	0.138	= Kilograms-force metres (kgf m; kg m)	X	7.233	= Pounds-force feet (lbf ft; lb ft)
Pounds-force feet (lbf ft; lb ft)	X	1.356	= Newton metres (Nm)	X	0.738	= Pounds-force feet (lbf ft; lb ft)
Newton metres (Nm)	X	0.102	= Kilograms-force metres (kgf m; kg m)	X	9.804	= Newton metres (Nm)

Power

Horsepower (hp)	X	745.7	= Watts (W)	X	0.0013	= Horsepower (hp)

Velocity (speed)

Miles per hour (miles/hr; mph)	X	1.609	= Kilometres per hour (km/hr; kph)	X	0.621	= Miles per hour (miles/hr; mph)

*Fuel consumption**

Miles per gallon, Imperial (mpg)	X	0.354	= Kilometres per litre (km/l)	X	2.825	= Miles per gallon, Imperial (mpg)
Miles per gallon, US (mpg)	X	0.425	= Kilometres per litre (km/l)	X	2.352	= Miles per gallon, US (mpg)

Temperature

Degrees Fahrenheit = (°C x 1.8) + 32   Degrees Celsius (Degrees Centigrade; °C) = (°F - 32) x 0.56

*It is common practice to convert from miles per gallon (mpg) to litres/100 kilometres (l/100km), where mpg (Imperial) x l/100 km = 282 and mpg (US) x l/100 km = 235

Safety first!

Professional motor mechanics are trained in safe working procedures. However enthusiastic you may be about getting on with the job in hand, do take the time to ensure that your safety is not put at risk. A moment's lack of attention can result in an accident, as can failure to observe certain elementary precautions.

There will always be new ways of having accidents, and the following points do not pretend to be a comprehensive list of all dangers; they are intended rather to make you aware of the risks and to encourage a safety-conscious approach to all work you carry out on your vehicle.

Essential DOs and DON'Ts

DON'T rely on a single jack when working underneath the vehicle. Always use reliable additional means of support, such as axle stands, securely placed under a part of the vehicle that you know will not give way.

DON'T attempt to loosen or tighten high-torque nuts (e.g. wheel hub nuts) while the vehicle is on a jack; it may be pulled off.

DON'T start the engine without first ascertaining that the transmission is in neutral (or 'Park' where applicable) and the parking brake applied.

DON'T suddenly remove the filler cap from a hot cooling system – cover it with a cloth and release the pressure gradually first, or you may get scalded by escaping coolant.

DON'T attempt to drain oil until you are sure it has cooled sufficiently to avoid scalding you.

DON'T grasp any part of the engine, exhaust or catalytic converter without first ascertaining that it is sufficiently cool to avoid burning you.

DON'T allow brake fluid or antifreeze to contact vehicle paintwork.

DON'T syphon toxic liquids such as fuel, brake fluid or antifreeze by mouth, or allow them to remain on your skin.

DON'T inhale dust – it may be injurious to health (see *Asbestos* below).

DON'T allow any spilt oil or grease to remain on the floor – wipe it up straight away, before someone slips on it.

DON'T use ill-fitting spanners or other tools which may slip and cause injury.

DON'T attempt to lift a heavy component which may be beyond your capability – get assistance.

DON'T rush to finish a job, or take unverified short cuts.

DON'T allow children or animals in or around an unattended vehicle.

DO wear eye protection when using power tools such as drill, sander, bench grinder etc, and when working under the vehicle.

DO use a barrier cream on your hands prior to undertaking dirty jobs – it will protect your skin from infection as well as making the dirt easier to remove afterwards; but make sure your hands aren't left slippery. Note that long-term contact with used engine oil can be a health hazard.

DO keep loose clothing (cuffs, tie etc) and long hair well out of the way of moving mechanical parts.

DO remove rings, wristwatch etc, before working on the vehicle – especially the electrical system.

DO ensure that any lifting tackle used has a safe working load rating adequate for the job.

DO keep your work area tidy – it is only too easy to fall over articles left lying around.

DO get someone to check periodically that all is well, when working alone on the vehicle.

DO carry out work in a logical sequence and check that everything is correctly assembled and tightened afterwards.

DO remember that your vehicle's safety affects that of yourself and others. If in doubt on any point, get specialist advice.

IF, in spite of following these precautions, you are unfortunate enough to injure yourself, seek medical attention as soon as possible.

Asbestos

Certain friction, insulating, sealing, and other products – such as brake linings, brake bands, clutch linings, torque converters, gaskets, etc – contain asbestos. *Extreme care must be taken to avoid inhalation of dust from such products since it is hazardous to health.* If in doubt, assume that they *do* contain asbestos.

Fire

Remember at all times that petrol (gasoline) is highly flammable. Never smoke, or have any kind of naked flame around, when working on the vehicle. But the risk does not end there – a spark caused by an electrical short-circuit, by two metal surfaces contacting each other, by careless use of tools, or even by static electricity built up in your body under certain conditions, can ignite petrol vapour, which in a confined space is highly explosive.

Always disconnect the battery earth (ground) terminal before working on any part of the fuel or electrical system, and never risk spilling fuel on to a hot engine or exhaust.

It is recommended that a fire extinguisher of a type suitable for fuel and electrical fires is kept handy in the garage or workplace at all times. Never try to extinguish a fuel or electrical fire with water.

Note: *Any reference to a 'torch' appearing in this manual should always be taken to mean a hand-held battery-operated electric lamp or flashlight. It does NOT mean a welding/gas torch or blowlamp.*

Fumes

Certain fumes are highly toxic and can quickly cause unconsciousness and even death if inhaled to any extent. Petrol (gasoline) vapour comes into this category, as do the vapours from certain solvents such as trichloroethylene. Any draining or pouring of such volatile fluids should be done in a well ventilated area.

When using cleaning fluids and solvents, read the instructions carefully. Never use materials from unmarked containers – they may give off poisonous vapours.

Never run the engine of a motor vehicle in an enclosed space such as a garage. Exhaust fumes contain carbon monoxide which is extremely poisonous; if you need to run the engine, always do so in the open air or at least have the rear of the vehicle outside the workplace.

If you are fortunate enough to have the use of an inspection pit, never drain or pour petrol, and never run the engine, while the vehicle is standing over it; the fumes, being heavier than air, will concentrate in the pit with possibly lethal results.

The battery

Never cause a spark, or allow a naked light, near the vehicle's battery. It will normally be giving off a certain amount of hydrogen gas, which is highly explosive.

Always disconnect the battery earth (ground) terminal before working on the fuel or electrical systems.

If possible, loosen the filler plugs or cover when charging the battery from an external source. Do not charge at an excessive rate or the battery may burst.

Take care when topping up and when carrying the battery. The acid electrolyte, even when diluted, is very corrosive and should not be allowed to contact the eyes or skin.

If you ever need to prepare electrolyte yourself, always add the acid slowly to the water, and never the other way round. Protect against splashes by wearing rubber gloves and goggles.

When jump starting a car using a booster battery, for negative earth (ground) vehicles, connect the jump leads in the following sequence: First connect one jump lead between the positive (+) terminals of the two batteries. Then connect the other jump lead first to the negative (–) terminal of the booster battery, and then to a good earthing (ground) point on the vehicle to be started, at least 18 in (45 cm) from the battery if possible. Ensure that hands and jump leads are clear of any moving parts, and that the two vehicles do not touch. Disconnect the leads in the reverse order.

Mains electricity and electrical equipment

When using an electric power tool, inspection light etc, always ensure that the appliance is correctly connected to its plug and that, where necessary, it is properly earthed (grounded). Do not use such appliances in damp conditions and, again, beware of creating a spark or applying excessive heat in the vicinity of fuel or fuel vapour. Also ensure that the appliances meet the relevant national safety standards.

Ignition HT voltage

A severe electric shock can result from touching certain parts of the ignition system, such as the HT leads, when the engine is running or being cranked, particularly if components are damp or the insulation is defective. Where an electronic ignition system is fitted, the HT voltage is much higher and could prove fatal.

Routine maintenance

For modifications, and information applicable to later models, see Supplement at end of manual

Maintenance is essential for ensuring safety and desirable for the purpose of getting the best in terms of performance and economy from your car. Over the years the need for periodic lubrication has been greatly reduced if not totally eliminated. This has unfortunately tended to lead some owners to think that because no such action is required the items either no longer exist, or will last forever. This is certainly not the case; it is essential to carry out regular visual examination as comprehensively as possible in order to spot any possible defects at an early stage before they develop into major expensive repairs.

The following service schedules are a list of the maintenance requirements and the intervals at which they should be carried out. Where applicable these procedures are covered in greater detail throughout this manual, near the beginning of each Chapter.

Every 250 miles (400 km) or weekly – whichever comes first

Check the engine oil level and top up if necessary (Chapter 1, Sec 2)
Check the coolant level in the expansion tank and top up if necessary (Chapter 2, Sec 2)
Check the brake fluid level in the master cylinder reservoir and top up if necessary (Chapter 8, Sec 2)
Check the operation of all interior and exterior lamps, wipers and washers (Chapter 11, Sec 3)
Check, and if necessary top up, the washer reservoir adding a screen wash such as Turtle Wax High Tech Screen Wash
Check and adjust the tyre pressures (Chapter 9, Sec 29)
Visually examine the tyres for wear or damage (Chapter 9, Sec 29)
Clean the windscreen and windows
Clean the headlamps

Every 6000 miles (10 000 km) or six months – whichever comes first

Change the engine oil (Chapter 1, Sec 2)
Check the gearbox/automatic trasmission oil level and top up if necessary (Chapter 6, Secs 2 and 18)
Check and adjust the idling speed (Chapter 3, Secs 15 and 38)
Renew the spark plugs (Chapter 4, Secs 10 and 20)
Check condition of contact breaker points where fitted and clean or renew (Chapter 4, Secs 3 and 4)

Check the water pump/alternator drivebelt for condition and tension and adjust if necessary (Chapter 2, Sec 12)
Check and if necessary top up the electrolyte level in the battery (except on maintenance-free type) (chapter 11, Sec 3)
Check the operation of all equipment checking for oil, water and fuel leaks
Check the exhaust system for leaks and deterioration (Chapter 3, Sec 20)
Check the driveshaft rubber bellows for damage and leaks (Chapter 7, Sec 2)
Check bodywork for damage and deterioration (Chapter 10, Sec 2)

Every 12 000 miles (20 000 km) or 12 months – whichever comes first

In addition to the 6000 mile service

Renew the oil filter (Chapter 1, Sec 2)
Renew the air filter (Chapter 3, Sec 3)
Check and if necessary adjust the valve clearances (Chapter 1, Sec 47)
Check disc pad and brake shoe lining wear without removing components (ie using inspection hole for rear brakes) (Chapter 8, Secs 3 and 6)
Lubricate all door hinges and locks (Chapter 10, Sec 6)

Every 30 000 miles (50 000 km)

In addition to the 6000 mile service.

Change the gearbox/automatic transmission oil (Chapter 6, Secs 2 or 20)
Renew the fuel filter (in-line type) (Chapter 3, Sec 28)
Check and adjust the idling mixture (Chapter 3, Secs 15 and 38)
Check disc pad and brake shoe lining wear by removing (Chapter 8, Secs 3 and 6)
Renew the brake fluid (Chapter 8, Sec 18)
Renew the brake servo air filter (Chapter 8, Sec 25)
Check suspension and steering components for condition and wear (Chapter 9, Sec 2)
Check and if necessary adjust the front wheel alignment (Chapter 9, Sec 28)

Every 40 000 miles (60 000 km)

Change the antifreeze (Chapter 2, Secs 2, 3, 4, 5 and 6)

View of engine compartment (GTL, 1397 cc model)

1 Battery (low-maintenance)
2 Washer reservoir
3 Brake vacuum servo unit
4 Accelerator cable
5 Speedometer cable
6 Fuel supply pipe
7 Bonnet lock
8 Crankcase ventilation hoses
9 Hot air stove for automatic temperature control air cleaner
10 Rear engine mounting
11 Electronic ignition computer module
12 Wheel brace
13 Jack
14 Front suspension strut upper mounting
15 Lower suspension arm inner pivot
16 Driveshaft
17 Clutch cable
18 Headlamp bulb connector
19 Coolant expansion tank
20 Earthing braid
21 Radiator filler cap
22 Engine/gearbox mounting
23 Electric cooling fan and motor
24 Ignition timing marks and inspection hole
25 In-line fuel filter
26 Fuel pump
27 Radiator
28 Engine oil level dipstick
29 Radiator cooling fan thermostatic switch
30 Distributor
31 Top hose
32 Alternator
33 Drivebelt
34 Front sidelamp retaining spring
35 Oval plate
36 Top hose bleed screw
37 Choke cable
38 Engine oil filler cap
39 Heater hose bleed screws
40 Throttle return spring
41 Carburettor
42 Brake fluid reservoir
43 Earthing cable

View of front underside of car (GTL, 1397 cc model)

1 Steering gear
2 Gearchange rod
3 Exhaust intermediate section
4 Exhaust front pipe
5 Subframe mounting
6 Anti-roll bar
7 Track rod end
8 Driveshaft inner joint
9 Front suspension lower balljoint
10 Front lower suspension arm
11 Brake caliper
12 Horn
13 Engine oil drain plug
14 Radiator location grommet
15 Engine-to-gearbox steady rod
16 Radiator
17 Front towing eye
18 Gearbox drain plug
19 Anti-roll bar mounting on lower suspension arm
20 Front subframe

View of rear underside of car (GTL, 1397 cc model)

1 Rear towing eye
2 Exhaust rear mounting
3 Brake pressure regulating valve
4 Spare wheel carrier and hook
5 Spare wheel
6 Rear bumper mounting
7 Fuel tank filler neck
8 Rear shock absorber lower mounting
9 Rear brake backplate
10 Connecting hose
11 Rear suspension trailing arm
12 Rear suspension bearing bracket
13 Rear axle
14 Fuel tank
15 Rigid brake hydraulic pipe
16 Flexible brake hydraulic hoses
17 Handbrake cables
18 Anti-roll bar
19 Exhaust intermediate mounting
20 Exhaust intermediate section
21 Rear jacking pad
22 Handbrake cable mounting bracket
23 Exhaust rear section

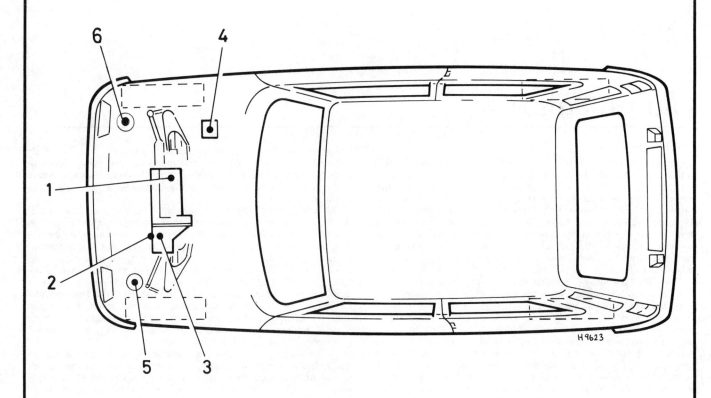

H 9623

Recommended lubricants and fluids

Component or system	Lubricant type/specification	Duckhams recommendation
1 Engine	Multigrade engine oil, viscosity SAE 15W/40, 15W/50, 20W/40, or 20W/50	Duckhams Hypergrade
2 Manual gearbox Non-Turbo models Turbo models	 Gear oil, viscosity SAE 80W Gear oil, viscosity SAE 75W/90S	 Duckhams Hypoid 80S Duckhams Hypoid 75W/90S
3 Automatic transmission	Dexron type ATF	Duckhams Uni-Matic or D-Matic
4 Brake fluid reservoir	Hydraulic fluid to SAE J1703F, DOT 3, or DOT 4	Duckhams Universal Brake and Clutch Fluid
5 Cooling system	Ethylene glycol based antifreeze	Duckhams Universal Antifreeze and Summer Coolant
6 Power steering	Dexron type ATF	Duckhams Uni-Matic or D-Matic

Fault diagnosis

Introduction

The vehicle owner who does his or her own maintenance according to the recommended schedules should not have to use this section of the manual very often. Modern component reliability is such that, provided those items subject to wear or deterioration are inspected or renewed at the specified intervals, sudden failure is comparatively rare. Faults do not usually just happen as a result of sudden failure, but develop over a period of time. Major mechanical failures in particular are usually preceded by characteristic symptoms over hundreds or even thousands of miles. Those components which do occasionally fail without warning are often small and easily carried in the vehicle.

With any fault finding, the first step is to decide where to begin investigations. Sometimes this is obvious, but on other occasions a little detective work will be necessary. The owner who makes half a dozen haphazard adjustments or replacements may be successful in curing a fault (or its symptoms), but he will be none the wiser if the fault recurs and he may well have spent more time and money than was necessary. A calm and logical approach will be found to be more satisfactory in the long run. Always take into account any warning signs or abnormalities that may have been noticed in the period preceding the fault – power loss, high or low gauge readings, unusual noises or smells, etc – and remember that failure of components such as fuses or spark plugs may only be pointers to some underlying fault.

The pages which follow here are intended to help in cases of failure to start or breakdown on the road. There is also a Fault Diagnosis Section at the end of each Chapter which should be consulted if the preliminary checks prove unfruitful. Whatever the fault, certain basic principles apply. These are as follows:

Verify the fault. This is simply a matter of being sure that you know what the symptoms are before starting work. This is particularly important if you are investigating a fault for someone else who may not have described it very accurately.

Don't overlook the obvious. For example, if the vehicle won't start, is there petrol in the tank? (Don't take anyone else's word on this particular point, and don't trust the fuel gauge either!) If an electrical fault is indicated, look for loose or broken wires before digging out the test gear.

Cure the disease, not the symptom. Substituting a flat battery with a fully charged one will get you off the hard shoulder, but if the underlying cause is not attended to, the new battery will go the same way. Similarly, changing oil-fouled spark plugs for a new set will get you moving again, but remember that the reason for the fouling (if it wasn't simply an incorrect grade of plug) will have to be established and corrected.

Don't take anything for granted. Particularly, don't forget that a 'new' component may itself be defective (especially if it's been rattling round in the boot for months), and don't leave components out of a fault diagnosis sequence just because they are new or recently fitted. When you do finally diagnose a difficult fault, you'll probably realise that all the evidence was there from the start.

Electrical faults

Electrical faults can be more puzzling than straightforward mechanical failures, but they are no less susceptible to logical analysis if the basic principles of operation are understood. Vehicle electrical wiring exists in extremely unfavourable conditions – heat, vibration and chemical attack – and the first things to look for are loose or corroded connections and broken or chafed wires, especially where the wires pass through holes in the bodywork or are subject to vibration.

All metal-bodied vehicles in current production have one pole of the battery 'earthed', ie connected to the vehicle bodywork, and in nearly all modern vehicles it is the negative (–) terminal. The various electrical components – motors, bulb holders etc – are also connected to earth, either by means of a lead or directly by their mountings. Electric current flows through the component and then back to the battery via the bodywork. If the component mounting is loose or corroded, or if a good path back to the battery is not available, the circuit will be incomplete and malfunction will result. The engine and/or gearbox are also earthed by means of flexible metal straps to the body or subframe; if these straps are loose or missing, starter motor, generator and ignition trouble may result.

Assuming the earth return to be satisfactory, electrical faults will be due either to component malfunction or to defects in the current supply. Individual components are dealt with in Chapter 11. If supply wires are broken or cracked internally this results in an open-circuit, and the easiest way to check for this is to bypass the suspect wire temporarily with a length of wire having a crocodile clip or suitable connector at each end. Alternatively, a 12V test lamp can be used to verify the presence of supply voltage at various points along the wire and the break can be thus isolated.

If a bare portion of a live wire touches the bodywork or other earthed metal part, the electricity will take the low-resistance path thus formed back to the battery: this is known as a short-circuit. Hopefully a short-circuit will blow a fuse, but otherwise it may cause burning of the insulation (and possibly further short-circuits) or even a fire. This is why it is inadvisable to bypass persistently blowing fuses with silver foil or wire.

Spares and tool kit

Most vehicles are supplied only with sufficient tools for wheel changing; the *Maintenance and minor repair* tool kit detailed in *Tools and working facilities*, with the addition of a hammer, is probably sufficient for those repairs that most motorists would consider attempting at the roadside. In addition a few items which can be fitted without too much trouble in the event of a breakdown should be carried. Experience and available space will modify the list below, but the following may save having to call on professional assistance:

Spark plugs, clean and correctly gapped
HT lead and plug cap – long enough to reach the plug furthest from the distributor
Distributor rotor, condenser and contact breaker points (if applicable)
Drivebelt(s) – emergency type may suffice
Spare fuses
Set of principal light bulbs
Tin of radiator sealer and hose bandage
Exhaust bandage
Roll of insulating tape
Length of soft iron wire
Length of electrical flex
Torch or inspection lamp (can double as test lamp)
Battery jump leads

Tow-rope
Ignition water dispersant aerosol
Litre of engine oil
Sealed can of hydraulic fluid
Emergency windscreen
Worm drive clips

If spare fuel is carried, a can designed for the purpose should be used to minimise risks of leakage and collision damage. A first aid kit and a warning triangle, whilst not at present compulsory in the UK, are obviously sensible items to carry in addition to the above.

When touring abroad it may be advisable to carry additional spares which, even if you cannot fit them yourself, could save having to wait while parts are obtained. The items below may be worth considering:

Clutch and throttle cables
Cylinder head gasket
Alternator brushes
Fuel pump repair kit
Tyre valve core

One of the motoring organisations will be able to advise on availability of fuel etc in foreign countries.

Carrying a few spares can save a long walk!

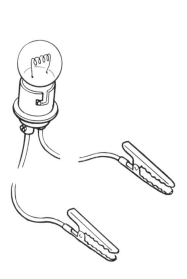

Simple test lamp is useful for tracing electrical faults

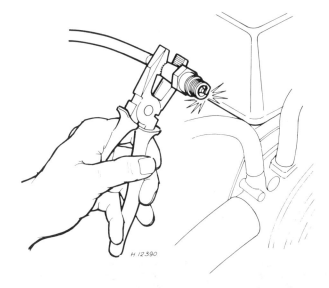

Crank engine and check for spark. Note use of insulated tool

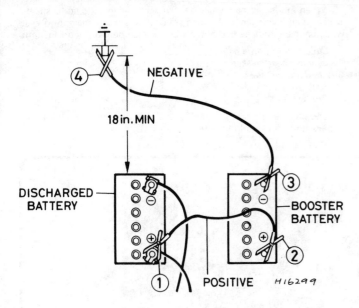

Jump start lead connections for negative earth vehicles – connect leads in order shown

Engine will not start

Engine fails to turn when starter operated

Flat battery (recharge, use jump leads, or push start)
Battery terminals loose or corroded
Battery earth to body defective
Engine earth strap loose or broken
Starter motor (or solenoid) wiring loose or broken
Automatic transmission selector in wrong position, or inhibitor switch faulty
Ignition/starter switch faulty
Major mechanical failure (seizure)
Starter or solenoid internal fault (see Chapter 11)

Starter motor turns engine slowly

Partially discharged battery (recharge, use jump leads, or push start)
Battery terminals loose or corroded
Battery earth to body defective
Engine earth strap loose
Starter motor (or solenoid) wiring loose
Starter motor internal fault (see Chapter 11)

Starter motor spins without turning engine

Flat battery
Starter motor pinion sticking on sleeve
Flywheel gear teeth damaged or worn
Starter motor mounting bolts loose

Engine turns normally but fails to start

Damp or dirty HT leads and distributor cap (crank engine and check for spark) – try moisture dispersant such as Holts Wet Start
Dirty or incorrectly gapped distributor points (if applicable)
No fuel in tank (check for delivery at carburettor)
Excessive choke (hot engine) or insufficient choke (cold engine)
Fouled or incorrectly gapped spark plugs (see Chapter 4)
Other ignition system fault (see Chapter 4)
Other fuel system fault (see Chapter 3)
Poor compression (see Chapter 1)
Major mechanical failure (eg camshaft drive)

Engine fires but will not run

Insufficient choke (cold engine)
Air leaks at carburettor or inlet manifold
Fuel starvation (see Chapter 3)
Ignition fault (see Chapter 4)

Engine cuts out and will not restart

Engine cuts out suddenly – ignition fault

Loose or disconnected LT wires
Wet HT leads or distributor cap (after traversing water splash)
Coil or condenser failure if applicable (check for spark)
Other ignition faults (see Chapter 4)

Engine misfires before cutting out – fuel fault

Fuel tank empty
Fuel pump defective or filter blocked (check for delivery)
Fuel tank filler vent blocked (suction will be evident on releasing cap)
Carburettor needle valve sticking
Carburettor jets blocked (fuel contaminated)
Other fuel system fault (see Chapter 3)

Engine cuts out – other causes

Serious overheating
Major mechanical failure (eg camshaft drive)

Engine overheats

Ignition (no-charge) warning light illuminated

Slack or broken drivebelt – retension or renew (Chapter 2)

Ignition warning light not illuminated

Coolant loss due to internal or external leakage (see Chapter 2)
Thermostat defective
Low oil level
Brakes binding
Radiator clogged externally or internally
Electric cooling fan not operating correctly
Engine waterways clogged
Ignition timing incorrect or automatic advance malfunctioning
Mixture too weak

Note: *Do not add cold water to an overheated engine or damage may result*

Low engine oil pressure

Gauge reads low or warning light illuminated with engine running

Oil level low or incorrect grade
Defective gauge or sender unit
Wire to sender unit earthed
Engine overheating
Oil filter clogged or bypass valve defective
Oil pressure relief valve defective
Oil pick-up strainer clogged
Oil pump worn or mountings loose
Worn main or big-end bearings

Note: *Low oil pressure in a high-mileage engine at tickover is not necessarily a cause for concern. Sudden pressure loss at speed is far more significant. In any event, check the gauge or warning light sender before condemning the engine.*

Engine noises

Pre-ignition (pinking) on acceleration

Incorrect grade of fuel

Ignition timing incorrect
Distributor faulty or worn
Worn or maladjusted carburettor
Excessive carbon build-up in engine

Whistling or wheezing noises

Leaking vacuum hose
Leaking carburettor or manifold gasket
Blowing head gasket

Tapping or rattling

Incorrect valve clearances
Worn valve gear

Worn timing chain or belt
Broken piston ring (ticking noise)

Knocking or thumping

Unintentional mechanical contact (eg fan blades)
Worn drivebelt
Peripheral component fault (generator, water pump etc)
Worn big-end bearings (regular heavy knocking, perhaps less under load)
Worn main bearings (rumbling and knocking, perhaps worsening under load)
Piston slap (most noticeable when cold)

Chapter 1 Engine

For modifications, and information applicable to later models, see Supplement at end of manual

Contents

Specifications

To avoid conversion inaccuracies, most specifications are given in metric values only, as specified by the manufacturers

General

Type	Four-cylinder, in-line, overhead valve			
Firing order	1 – 3 – 4 – 2 (No 1 cylinder at flywheel end)			
Designation	**C1C**	**C1E**	**C1J**	**C2J**
Bore	65.0 mm	70.0 mm	76.0 mm	76.0 mm
Stroke	72.0 mm	72.0 mm	77.0 mm	77.0 mm
Capacity	956 cc	1108 cc	1397 cc	1397 cc
Compression ratio	9.7 : 1	9.5 : 1	9.25:1*	9.25:1

* Turbo models 7.9:1

Crankshaft

Number of main bearings	5
Main journal diameter	54.795 mm
Main journal minimum regrind diameter	54.545 mm
Crankpin journal diameter	43.98 mm
Crankpin journal minimum regrind diameter	43.73 mm
Crankshaft endfloat	0.05 to 0.23 mm

Connecting rods

Small end side-play	0.31 to 0.57 mm

Cylinder liners and pistons

	C1C and C1E	C1J and C2J
Liner protrusion	0.04 to 0.12 mm	0.02 to 0.09 mm (less seal)
Liner base seal type	Excelnyl	O-ring
Liner base seal thickness		1.15 to 1.35 mm
Blue	0.08 mm	
Red	0.10 mm	
Green	0.12 mm	
Piston fitted direction	Arrow on crown towards flywheel	
Gudgeon pin fit in piston	Hand push-fit	
Gudgeon pin fit in connecting rod	Interference	

Piston rings

Number	Three (two compression, one oil control)	
Piston ring end gaps	Supplied pre-set	
Thickness:	**C1E**	**C1C, C1J and C2J**
Top compression	2.0 mm	1.75 mm
No 2 compression	2.0 mm	2.0 mm
Oil control ring	3.5 mm	4.0 mm

Camshaft

Number of bearings	4
Endfloat	0.05 to 0.12 mm

Valves

Seat angle	45°	
Valve guides:		
Bore diameter in cylinder head (nominal)	11.0 mm	
Fitted height above valve seat:	**C1C and C1E**	**C1J and C2J**
Inlet	26.5 mm	30.5 mm
Exhaust	26.2 mm	25.2 mm
Valve springs:		
Free length	42 mm	

Valve timing
at valve clearances of 0.35 mm (inlet), 0.50 mm (exhaust):

	Inlet opens	Inlet closes	Exhaust opens	Exhaust closes
C1C and C1E	12° BTDC	48° ABDC	52° BBDC	8° ATDC
C1J and auto. C2J	12° BTDC	56° ABDC	56° BBDC	12° ATDC
Manual C2J	12° BTDC	62° ABDC	65° BBDC	25° ATDC

Valve clearances (except C1J Turbo):	
Cold – inlet	0.15 mm (0.006 in)
Cold – exhaust	0.20 mm (0.008 in)
Hot – inlet	0.18 mm (0.007 in)
Hot – exhaust	0.25 mm (0.010 in)

Valve clearances (C1J Turbo):	
Cold – inlet	0.20 mm (0.008 in)
Cold – exhaust	0.25 mm (0.010 in)
Hot	Not specified

Cylinder head

Maximum permitted warp	0.05 mm
Maximum permitted refacing cut	0.5 mm

Lubrication system

Oil type/specification	Multigrade engine oil, viscosity SAE 15W/40, 15W/50, 20W/40, or 20W/50 (Duckhams Hypergrade)
Oil filter type:	
Non-Turbo models	Champion F101
Turbo models	Champion F124
Oil pump:	
Gear-to-body clearance	0.2 mm (maximum)
System pressure:	
Idling	0.7 bar (minimum)
Running (at 4000 rpm)	3.5 bar (maximum)

Torque wrench settings

	Nm	lbf ft
Cylinder head bolts	60	44
Rocker shaft pedestal nuts and bolts	20	15
Main bearing cap bolts	65	48
Big-end bearing cap nuts:		
C1C and C1E	35	26
C1J and C2J	45	33
Flywheel retaining bolts	50	37
Torque converter driveplate retaining bolts	70	52
Camshaft sprocket retaining bolt	30	22
Engine mounting nuts and bolts	40	30
Crankshaft pulley retaining bolt	110	81

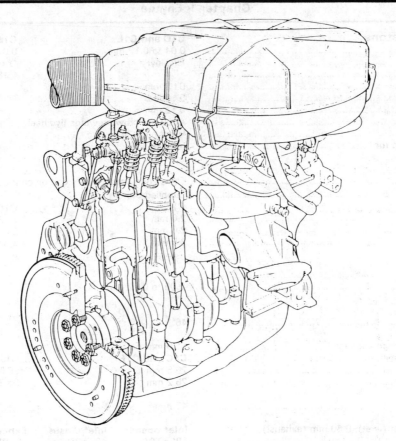

Fig. 1.1 Cut-away view of the C1E and C1C engine (Sec 1)

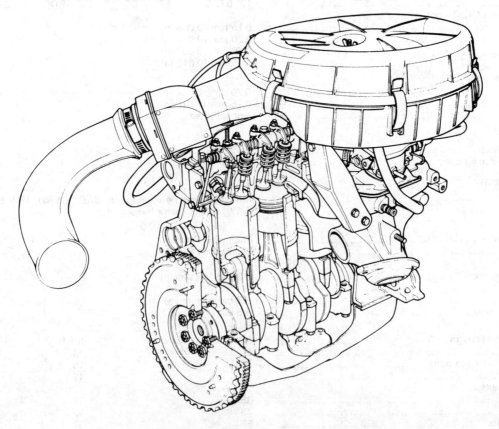

Fig. 1.2 Cut-away view of the C1J engine (Sec 1)

C2J engine has different carburettor and manifolds.

1 General description

The engines are of four-cylinder, in-line overhead valve type, mounted transversely in the front of the car. Apart from the cylinder liner bore diameter, the crankshaft stroke and minor detail differences, all engine types are virtually identical in design and construction.

The cast iron cylinder block is of the replaceable wet liner type. The crankshaft is supported within the cylinder block on five shell type main bearings. Thrust washers are fitted at the centre main bearing to control crankshaft endfloat.

The connecting rods are attached to the crankshaft by horizontally split shell type big-end bearings, and to the pistons by interference fit gudgeon pins. The aluminium alloy pistons are of the slipper type and are fitted with three piston rings, two compression rings and a scraper type oil control ring.

The camshaft is chain driven from the crankshaft and operates the rocker arms via pushrods. The inlet and exhaust valves are each closed by a single valve spring and operate in guides pressed into the cylinder head. The valves are actuated directly by the rocker arms.

A semi-closed crankcase ventilation system is employed, and crankcase gases are drawn from the rocker cover via a hose to the air cleaner and inlet manifold.

Lubrication is provided by a gear type oil pump driven from the camshaft and located in the crankcase. Engine oil is fed through an externally mounted full-flow filter to the engine oil gallery, and then to the crankshaft, camshaft and rocker shaft bearings. A pressure relief valve is incorporated in the oil pump.

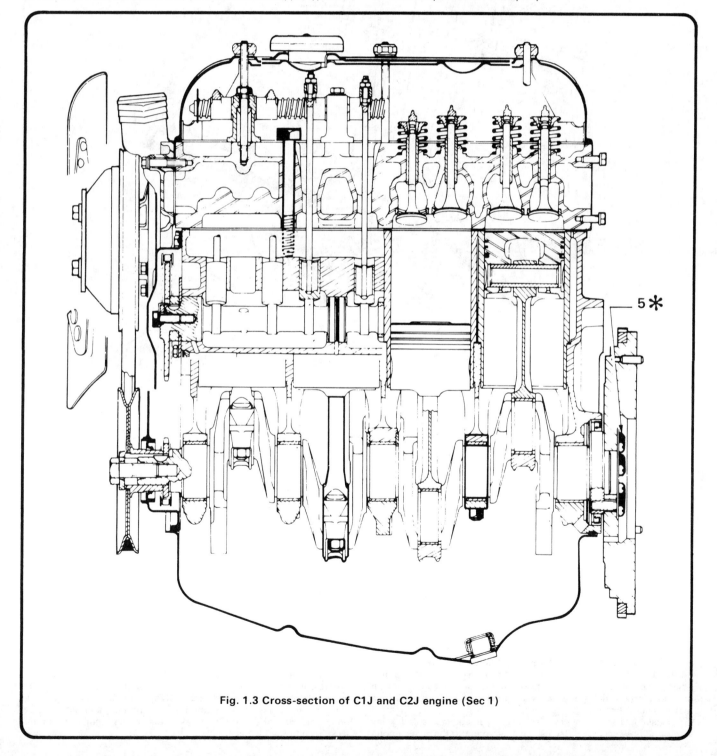

Fig. 1.3 Cross-section of C1J and C2J engine (Sec 1)

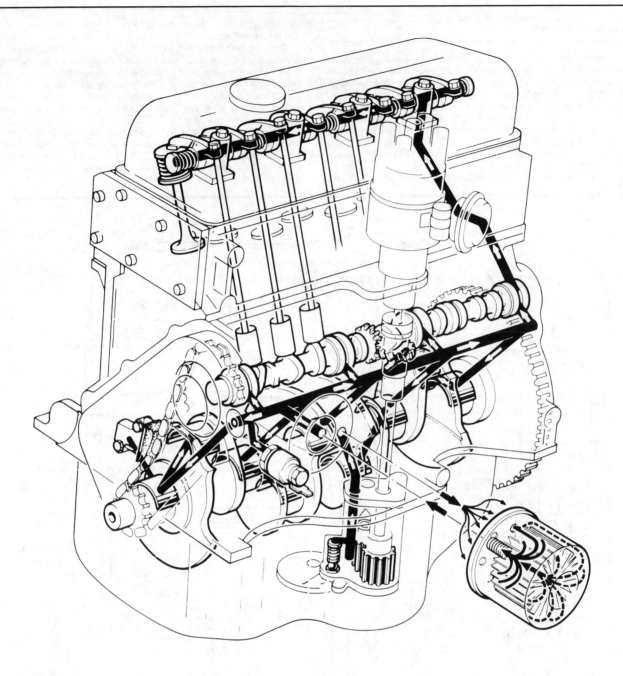

Fig. 1.4 Engine lubrication system (Sec 1)

2 Routine maintenance

At the intervals specified in the Routine Maintenance section in the front of the manual carry out the following procedures.

1 Check the engine oil level with the car on a level surface and the engine cold. Remove the dipstick and wipe it clean then fully insert it and withdraw it again. The oil level should be on the Maximum notch on the dipstick except during the running-in period of a new engine when it should be half way between the minimum and maximum notches. Top up the level if necessary, through the filler neck in the rocker cover (photos).

2 Visually inspect the engine joint faces, gaskets and seals for any sign of oil or water leaks. Pay particular attention to the areas around the rocker cover, cylinder head, timing cover and sump joint faces. Rectify any leaks by referring to the appropriate Sections of this Chapter.

3 Place a suitable container beneath the oil drain plug on the sump. Unscrew the plug and allow the oil to drain (photo). Refit and tighten the plug after draining, then refill the engine with the correct grade and quantity of oil.

4 Move the bowl to the front of the engine, under the oil filter. Using a strap wrench, or filter removal tool, slacken the filter and then unscrew it from the engine and discard. Wipe the mating face on the cylinder block with a rag and then lubricate the seal of a new filter using clean engine oil. Screw the filter into position and tighten it by hand only, do not use any tools. With the engine running, check for leaks around the filter seal.

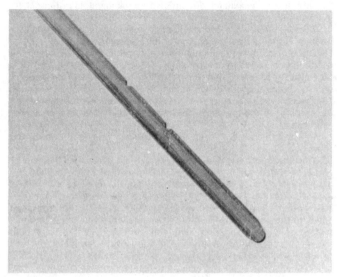

2.1A Showing the engine oil level notches on the dipstick

2.1B Topping-up the engine oil level

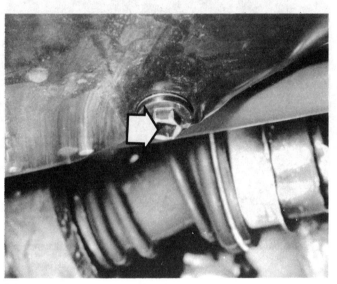

2.3 Engine oil drain plug on the sump

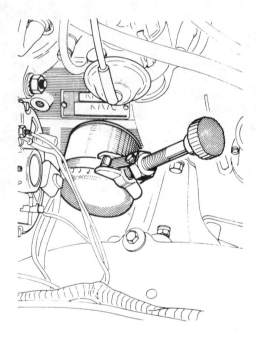

Fig. 1.5 Using a special tool to remove the oil filter (Sec 2)

3 Major operations possible with the engine in the car

The following operations can be carried out without having to remove the engine from the car:

(a) Removal and refitting of the cylinder head
(b) Removal and refitting of the timing cover, chain and gears
(c) Removal and refitting of the sump
(d) Removal and refitting of the connecting rods, pistons and liner assemblies
(e) Removal and refitting of the oil pump
(f) Renewal of the engine mountings

4 Major operations requiring engine removal

The following operations can only be carried out after removal of the engine from the car:

(a) Removal and refitting of the camshaft
(b) Removal and refitting of the crankshaft and main bearings

(c) Removal and refitting of the flywheel
(d) Removal and refitting of the crankshaft rear oil seal

5 Methods of engine removal

The engine is removed upwards and out of the engine compartment. Although it is possible to remove the engine together with the gearbox or transmission, subframe and front suspension downwards this method involves additional work only worthwhile when changing a bodyshell or carrying out similar major procedures.

The engine may be removed on its own or in unit with the gearbox or transmission except in the case of 1986 on automatic transmission models, where it must be removed together with the transmission, then separated on the bench. (Also see Chapter 12).

6 Engine – removal without gearbox or automatic transmission

1   Disconnect both battery leads with reference to Chapter 11.
2   Remove the bonnet as described in Chapter 10.
3   Remove the radiator as described in Chapter 2.
4   Remove the air cleaner or inlet duct as applicable with reference to Chapter 3.
5   On Turbo models remove the anti-percolation device with reference to Chapter 3.
6   Remove the starter motor as described in Chapter 11.
7   Unscrew the nut and remove the engine earth strap from the body.
8   Disconnect the throttle cable, choke cable and vacuum pipe from the carburettor with reference to Chapter 3.
9   Disconnect the wire (brown) from the temperature gauge sender unit at the water pump.
10 Disconnect the brake servo hose from the inlet manifold.
11 Disconnect the two heater hoses from the water pump, remove the bracket from the rocker cover, and tie the hoses to one side.
12 Disconnect the fuel supply and return pipes (photo).

13 Disconnect the exhaust downpipe from the manifold or turbocharger with reference to Chapter 3.
14 Remove the water pump/alternator drivebelt as described in Chapter 2, then adjust the alternator fully against the engine.
15 Disconnect the HT lead and where applicable the LT leads from the distributor and oil level sensor wires.
16 Raise the car on a ramp or jack up the front of the car and support on axle stands. Apply the handbrake.
17 Unscrew the retaining bolts and remove the steady rod connecting the gearbox to the engine. Note the position of the distance spacer (photos).
18 Unscrew the bolts and lift off the cover plate at the base of the gearbox bellhousing (photo).
19 Turn the crankshaft as necessary until the notch on the flywheel or torque converter is in line with the TDC timing mark on the bellhousing timing scale. Make a reference mark on the cylinder block in line with the TDC mark for use when the engine has been removed.
20 Undo the bolt and remove the washer securing the crankshaft pulley to the pulley hub. To lock the engine while the bolt is undone, firmly apply the handbrake and engage top gear. On cars with automatic transmission, wedge a screwdriver between the starter ring

6.12 The fuel supply and return pipes below the water pump. Note cylinder block coolant drain plug (arrowed)

6.17A Engine-to-gearbox steady rod at engine, showing distance spacer

6.17B Engine-to-gearbox steady rod on gearbox

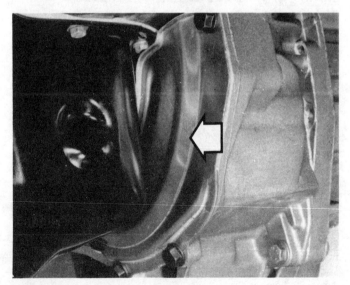

6.18 Flywheel (or driveplate) cover plate

gear teeth and the bellhousing through the starter motor aperture. With the pulley bolt removed, lift off the pulley and withdraw the pulley hub by carefully levering it off using two screwdrivers.

21 Where fitted remove the ignition angular position sensor from the bellhousing with reference to Chapter 4.

22 On automatic transmission models rotate the crankshaft as necessary to provide access, and undo the bolts or nuts securing the torque converter to the driveplate. Retain the torque converter in position on the transmission, using a flat strip of metal secured to the bellhousing with one of the coverplate bolts.

23 Undo all the bellhousing-to-engine retaining bolts accessible from under the car.

24 Place a jack with an interposed block of wood under the gearbox or transmission and just take the weight of the unit.

25 Attach a suitable hoist or crane to the engine using chains or rope slings, or by attaching the chains or ropes to the engine lifting brackets. Raise the hoist to just take the weight of the engine.

26 Undo all the bellhousing-to-engine retaining bolts accessible from above and additionally the two nuts, one each side of the engine. To provide sufficient clearance for engine removal, both these studs must be removed. To do this lock two nuts together on the exposed threads and undo the studs using the innermost nut.

27 Unscrew the bottom nut from the right-hand engine mounting. Alternatively remove the two bolts from the mounting.

28 Raise the engine and gearbox or transmission very slightly and withdraw the engine from the gearbox or transmission bellhousing. The engine may be tight owing to the locating dowels. Check that the right-hand driveshaft joints are not pulled apart.

29 Move the engine as far as possible to the right until it is completely clear of the gearbox or transmission and then lift the engine slowly, turning it as necessary to clear any obstructions. As soon as the engine is high enough, swing it over the front body panel and lower the engine to the floor.

7 Engine – removal with gearbox or automatic transmission

1 Disconnect both battery leads with reference to Chapter 11.
2 Remove the bonnet as described in Chapter 10.
3 Remove the radiator as described in Chapter 2.
4 Drain the gearbox oil or fluid as described in Chapter 6.
5 Remove the air cleaner or inlet duct as applicable with reference to Chapter 3.
6 On Turbo models remove the anti-percolation device with reference to Chapter 3.
7 Where fitted remove the ignition module or transistor assistance unit with reference to Chapter 4.

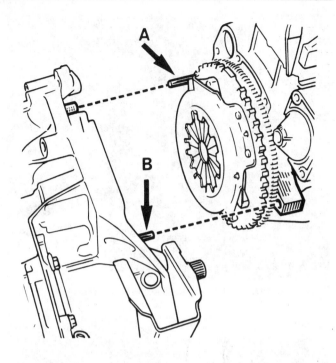

Fig. 1.6 Remove studs A and B to provide clearance for engine removal (Sec 6)

8 Disconnect the wiring to the reversing lamp switch on the gearbox at the connector.
9 On manual gearbox models disconnect the clutch cable with reference to Chapter 5.
10 Disconnect the main engine wiring harness connector near the expansion tank location (photo).
11 Unscrew the nut and remove the engine earth straps from the body (photos).
12 Disconnect the speedometer cable from the gearbox with reference to Chapter 11.
13 Disconnect the throttle cable, choke cable and vacuum pipe from the carburettor with reference to Chapter 3.
14 Disconnect the wire (brown) from the temperature gauge sender unit at the water pump.
15 Disconnect the brake servo hose from the inlet manifold.

7.10 Main engine wiring harness connector

7.11A Earth strap located near the expansion tank

7.11B Earth strap located on the right-hand bulkhead

16 Disconnect the two heater hoses from the water pump, remove the bracket from the rocker cover, and tie the hoses to one side.
17 Press out the grommet and pull the battery positive lead through the bulkhead (photo).
18 Disconnect and plug the fuel supply and return pipes.
19 Disconnect the exhaust downpipe from the manifold or turbocharger with reference to Chapter 3.
20 Remove the water pump/alternator drivebelt as described in Chapter 2, then adjust the alternator fully against the engine.
21 Disconnect the LT and HT leads from the ignition coil where necessary, also the oil level sensor wiring.
22 Raise the car on a ramp or jack up the front of the car and support on axle stands. Apply the handbrake.
23 Remove the splash shield from under the subframe (photos).
24 If a manual gearbox is fitted, slide back the rubber cover and undo the nut and bolt securing the gearchange rod to the gearbox fork control shaft. Slide the rod off the shaft and recover the distance sleeve.
25 If automatic transmission is fitted, disconnect the transmission selector control rod from the bracket and bellcrank. Also disconnect the wiring and hoses as necessary with reference to Chapter 6 and disconnect the fluid cooler pipes.
26 On Turbo models unbolt and remove the engine steady bar.

7.17 Pull the positive battery lead through the bulkhead

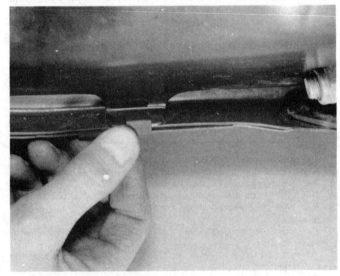

7.23A Engine splash shield side clip

7.23B Engine splash shield rear screw

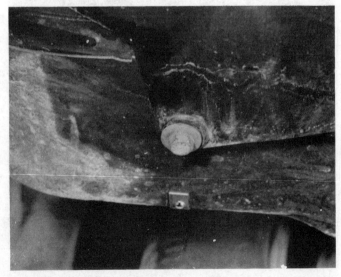

7.23C Engine splash shield front bolt

Are your plugs trying to tell you something?

Normal.
Grey-brown deposits, lightly coated core nose. Plugs ideally suited to engine, and engine in good condition.

Heavy Deposits.
A build up of crusty deposits, light-grey sandy colour in appearance.
Fault: Often caused by worn valve guides, excessive use of upper cylinder lubricant, or idling for long periods.

Lead Glazing.
Plug insulator firing tip appears yellow or green/yellow and shiny in appearance.
Fault: Often caused by incorrect carburation, excessive idling followed by sharp acceleration. Also check ignition timing.

Carbon fouling.
Dry, black, sooty deposits.
Fault: over-rich fuel mixture.
Check: carburettor mixture settings, float level, choke operation, air filter.

Oil fouling.
Wet, oily deposits. Fault: worn bores/piston rings or valve guides; sometimes occurs (temporarily) during running-in period.

Overheating.
Electrodes have glazed appearance, core nose very white – few deposits. Fault: plug overheating. Check: plug value, ignition timing, fuel octane rating (too low) and fuel mixture (too weak).

Electrode damage.
Electrodes burned away; core nose has burned, glazed appearance. Fault: pre-ignition. Check: for correct heat range and as for 'overheating'.

Split core nose.
(May appear initially as a crack). Fault: detonation or wrong gap-setting technique. Check: ignition timing, cooling system, fuel mixture (too weak).

WHY DOUBLE COPPER IS BETTER FOR YOUR ENGINE.

Unique Trapezoidal Copper Cored Earth Electrode — 50% Larger Spark Area — Copper Cored Centre Electrode

Champion Double Copper plugs are the first in the world to have copper core in both centre <u>and</u> earth electrode. This innovative design means that they run cooler by up to 100°C – giving greater efficiency and longer life. These double copper cores transfer heat away from the tip of the plug faster and more efficiently. Therefore, Double Copper runs at cooler temperatures than conventional plugs giving improved acceleration response and high speed performance with no fear of pre-ignition.

TRAPEZOIDAL COPPER CORED EARTH ELECTRODE
NEW TRAPEZOIDAL COPPER CORED EARTH ELECTRODE / CONVENTIONAL SOLID NICKEL ALLOY EARTH ELECTRODE
50% INCREASE IN SPARK AREA

EARTH ELECTRODE TEMPERATURE VS ENGINE SPEED
SOLID NICKEL EARTH ELECTRODE
COPPER CORED EARTH ELECTRODE
TEMPERATURE / ENGINE SPEED

Champion Double Copper plugs also feature a unique trapezoidal earth electrode giving a 50% increase in spark area. This, together with the double copper cores, offers greatly reduced electrode wear, so the spark stays stronger for longer.

  FASTER COLD STARTING

 FOR UNLEADED OR LEADED FUEL

 ELECTRODES UP TO 100°C COOLER

 BETTER ACCELERATION RESPONSE

 LOWER EMISSIONS

 50% BIGGER SPARK AREA

THE LONGER LIFE PLUG

Plug Tips/Hot and Cold.
Spark plugs must operate within well-defined temperature limits to avoid cold fouling at one extreme and overheating at the other.
Champion and the car manufacturers work out the best plugs for an engine to give optimum performance under all conditions, from freezing cold starts to sustained high speed motorway cruising.
Plugs are often referred to as hot or cold. With Champion, the higher the number on its body, the hotter the plug, and the lower the number the cooler the plug.

Plug Cleaning
Modern plug design and materials mean that Champion no longer recommends periodic plug cleaning. Certainly don't clean your plugs with a wire brush as this can cause metal conductive paths across the nose of the insulator so impairing its performance and resulting in loss of acceleration and reduced m.p.g.
However, if plugs are removed, always carefully clean the area where the plug seats in the cylinder head as grit and dirt can sometimes cause gas leakage.
Also wipe any traces of oil or grease from plug leads as this may lead to arcing.

CHAMPION

DOUBLE COPPER

This photographic sequence shows the steps taken to repair the dent and paintwork damage shown above. In general, the procedure for repairing a hole will be similar; where there are substantial differences, the procedure is clearly described and shown in a separate photograph.

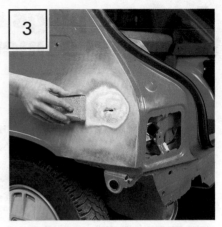

First remove any trim around the dent, then hammer out the dent where access is possible. This will minimise filling. Here, after the large dent has been hammered out, the damaged area is being made slightly concave.

Next, remove all paint from the damaged area by rubbing with coarse abrasive paper or using a power drill fitted with a wire brush or abrasive pad. 'Feather' the edge of the boundary with good paintwork using a finer grade of abrasive paper.

Where there are holes or other damage, the sheet metal should be cut away before proceeding further. The damaged area and any signs of rust should be treated with Turtle Wax Hi-Tech Rust Eater, which will also inhibit further rust formation.

For a large dent or hole mix Holts Body Plus Resin and Hardener according to the manufacturer's instructions and apply around the edge of the repair. Press Glass Fibre Matting over the repair area and leave for 20-30 minutes to harden. Then ...

... brush more Holts Body Plus Resin and Hardener onto the matting and leave to harden. Repeat the sequence with two or three layers of matting, checking that the final layer is lower than the surrounding area. Apply Holts Body Plus Filler Paste as shown in Step 5B.

For a medium dent, mix Holts Body Plus Filler Paste and Hardener according to the manufacturer's instructions and apply it with a flexible applicator. Apply thin layers of filler at 20-minute intervals, until the filler surface is slightly proud of the surrounding bodywork.

For small dents and scratches use Holts No Mix Filler Paste straight from the tube. Apply it according to the instructions in thin layers, using the spatula provided. It will harden in minutes if applied outdoors and may then be used as its own knifing putty.

Use a plane or file for initial shaping. Then, using progressively finer grades of wet-and-dry paper, wrapped round a sanding block, and copious amounts of clean water, rub down the filler until glass smooth. 'Feather' the edges of adjoining paintwork.

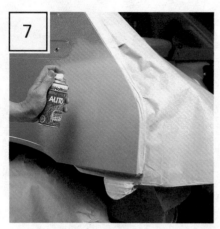

Protect adjoining areas before spraying the whole repair area and at least one inch of the surrounding sound paintwork with Holts Dupli-Color primer.

Fill any imperfections in the filler surface with a small amount of Holts Body Plus Knifing Putty. Using plenty of clean water, rub down the surface with a fine grade wet-and-dry paper – 400 grade is recommended – until it is really smooth.

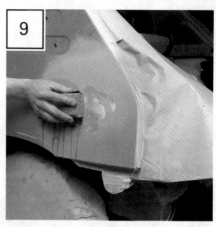

Carefully fill any remaining imperfections with knifing putty before applying the last coat of primer. Then rub down the surface with Holts Body Plus Rubbing Compound to ensure a really smooth surface.

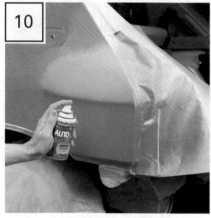

Protect surrounding areas from overspray before applying the topcoat in several thin layers. Agitate Holts Dupli-Color aerosol thoroughly. Start at the repair centre, spraying outwards with a side-to-side motion.

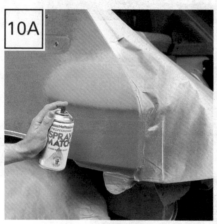

If the exact colour is not available off the shelf, local Holts Professional Spraymatch Centres will custom fill an aerosol to match perfectly.

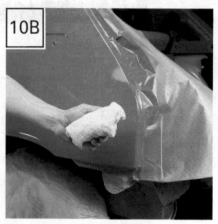

To identify whether a lacquer finish is required, rub a painted unrepaired part of the body with wax and a clean cloth.

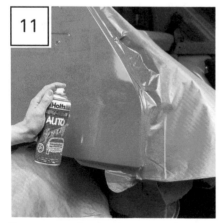

If no traces of paint appear on the cloth, spray Holts Dupli-Color clear lacquer over the repaired area to achieve the correct gloss level.

The paint will take about two weeks to harden fully. After this time it can be 'cut' with a mild cutting compound such as Turtle Wax Minute Cut prior to polishing with a final coating of Turtle Wax Extra.

When carrying out bodywork repairs, remember that the quality of the finished job is proportional to the time and effort expended.

27 Remove both front wheels.

28 From under the car drive out the roll pin securing the right-hand driveshaft inner joint to the differential stub shaft. Note that the roll pin is in fact two roll pins, one inside the other.

29 Unscrew the bolts securing the left-hand driveshaft inner joint bellows and retaining plate to the side of the gearbox or transmission.

30 Unscrew and remove the bolts securing the right-hand suspension strut to the upper part of the stub axle carrier noting that the bolt heads are facing forward. Pull the stub axle carrier to disconnect it from the stub shaft taking care not to damage the bellows, and support it in this position without straining the flexible brake hose.

31 Unbolt the left-hand brake caliper with reference to Chapter 8 and tie it to one side.

32 Disconnect the left-hand steering track rod from the stub axle carrier with reference to Chapter 9.

33 Unscrew and remove the bolts securing the left-hand suspension strut to the upper part of the stub axle carrier noting that the bolt heads are facing forward. Pull the stub axle carrier to disconnect the inner joint from the differential and support it in this position.

34 Unscrew the nut from the rear engine mounting and where fitted, remove the small support bracket (photos).

35 Remove the shield from the left-hand side of the engine compartment (photo).

36 Check that all cables and pipes have been disconnected then attach a hoist and take the weight of the engine and gearbox.

37 Unscrew the nuts and bolts from the left, right and front engine mountings.

38 Slowly lift the engine and gearbox or transmission assembly, moving it around as necessary to clear all obstructions. When high enough, lift it over the front body panel and lower the unit to the ground (photo).

39 If the car is to be moved refit the stub axle carriers to the struts and fit the wheels.

8 Engine – separation from manual gearbox or automatic transmission

1 With the assembly removed from the car disconnect the wiring harness from the alternator, oil pressure switch and starter and remove it.

2 Unscrew the retaining bolts and lift off the cover plate at the base of the transmission bellhousing.

3 Turn the crankshaft as necessary until the notch on the flywheel or torque converter is in line with the TDC timing mark on the bellhousing

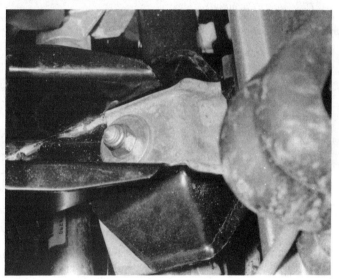

7.34A Rear engine mounting

7.34B Rear engine mounting with nut and bracket removed

7.35 Engine compartment left-hand side splash shield

7.38 Lifting the engine and gearbox assembly from the car

timing scale. Now make a reference mark on the cylinder block in line with the flywheel or torque converter notch. This will provide a useful reference because, once the gearbox or transmission is removed, the timing marks go with it, and it then becomes difficult to determine the TDC position of the engine.

4   If automatic transmission is fitted, undo the bolts or nuts securing the torque converter to the driveplate. Using a strip of metal as a suitable bracket, retain the torque converter on the transmission by securing the bracket to one of the cover plate bolt holes.

5   Undo the support bracket bolt and the three bellhousing bolts securing the starter motor in position. Lift off the starter noting the location of the dowel in one of the bolt holes.

6   Undo the two bolts securing the steady rod to the engine and gearbox or transmission. Lift off the rod, noting the location of the distance spacer.

7   Undo the bolts and the two nuts securing the engine to the gearbox or transmission bellhousing. Support the engine then withdraw the gearbox or transmission from it (photo).

8.7 Separating the gearbox from the engine

9   Engine dismantling – general

1   If possible mount the engine on a stand for the dismantling procedure, but, failing this, support it in an upright position with blocks of wood placed under each side of the sump or crankcase.

2   Drain the oil into a suitable container before cleaning the engine or major dismantling.

3   Cleanliness is most important, and if the engine is dirty it should be cleaned with paraffin or a suitable solvent while keeping it in an upright position.

4   Avoid working with the engine directly on a concrete floor, as grit presents a real source of trouble.

5   As parts are removed, clean them in a paraffin bath. However, do not immerse parts with internal oilways in paraffin as it is difficult to remove, usually requiring a high pressure hose. Clean oilways with nylon pipe cleaners.

6   It is advisable to have suitable containers to hold small items, as this will help when reassembling the engine and also prevent possible losses.

7   Always obtain complete sets of gaskets when the engine is being dismantled, but retain the old gaskets with a view to using them as a pattern to make a replacement if a new one is not available. Note that in many instances a gasket is not used, but instead the joints are sealed with an RTV sealant. It is recommended that a tube of CAF 4/60 THIXO paste, obtainable from Renault dealers be obtained as it is specially formulated for this purpose.

8   When possible, refit nuts, bolts and washers in their location after

being removed, as this helps to protect the threads and will also be helpful when reassembling the engine.

9   Retain serviceable components in order to compare them with the new parts supplied.

10   The operations described in this Chapter are a step by step sequence, assuming that the engine is to be completely dismantled for major overhaul or repair. Where an operation can be carried out with the engine in the car, the dismantling necessary to gain access to the component concerned is described separately.

10   Ancillary components – removal

With the engine separated from the gearbox or transmission the externally-mounted ancillary components, as given in the following list, can be removed. In most cases removal is straightforward, but further information will be found in the relevant Chapters.

Inlet and exhaust manifolds and carburettor, also Turbo components where applicable (Chapter 3)
Fuel pump, except on Turbo models (Chapter 3)
Alternator (Chapter 11)
Spark plugs (Chapter 4)
Distributor (Chapter 4)
Water pump (Chapter 2)
Clutch (Chapter 5)
Oil filter (Section 2 of this Chapter)
Engine front mounting bracket (Section 22 of this Chapter)
Fuel supply and return pipes

11   Cylinder head – removal with engine in car

1   Disconnect both battery leads with reference to Chapter 11.

2   Refer to Chapter 2 and drain the cooling system.

3   Remove the air cleaner or inlet duct as applicable with reference to Chapter 3.

4   On Turbo models remove the anti-percolation device and turbo-charger with reference to Chapter 3.

5   Disconnect the HT leads at the spark plugs, release the distributor cap retaining clips or screws and remove the cap and leads.

6   Disconnect the lead at the water temperature gauge sender on the water pump.

7   Slacken the alternator mountings and adjustment arm bolt, push the alternator in towards the engine and slip the drivebelt off the three pulleys. Undo the bolt securing the alternator adjustment arm to the water pump and swing the alternator clear of the engine (photo).

11.7 Undo the bolt (A) and remove the alternator adjustment arm from the pump at (B)

8   Release the hose clips and remove the two heater hoses from the water pump (photo). Also remove the support bracket from the rocker cover.

9   Release the hose clip and remove the radiator top hose from the water pump (photo).

10 Disconnect the throttle cable, choke cable and vacuum pipe from the carburettor with reference to Chapter 3.

11 Disconnect the brake servo hose from the inlet manifold (photo).

12 Undo the nut and washer on the inlet manifold and on the cylinder block and lift off the heat shield where fitted.

13 Disconnect the fuel inlet pipe and the crankcase ventilation hose at the carburettor (photo).

14 Disconnect the distributor LT lead (where applicable) at the wiring connector.

15 Undo the bolt and release the retaining clip securing the cable and hose guide to the side of the cylinder head.

16 Undo the two bolts and withdraw the tension springs securing the exhaust front section to the manifold.

17 Undo the nuts and remove the rocker cover, complete with gasket, from the cylinder head (photo).

18 Undo the two bolts and two nuts securing the rocker shaft pedestals to the cylinder head (photo). Lift the rocker shaft assembly upwards and off the two studs.

11.8 Disconnect the heater hoses ...

11.9 ... and the radiator top hose at the water pump

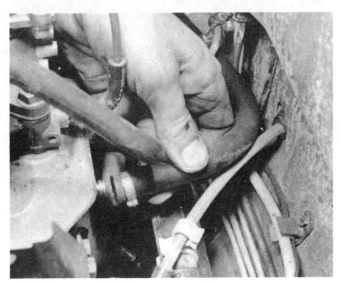

11.11 Disconnect the brake servo vacuum hose

11.13 Disconnect the fuel inlet pipe at the carburettor

11.17 Undo the nuts and lift off the rocker cover

11.18 Undo the nuts and bolts arrowed and withdraw the rocker shaft assembly

11.19 Take out the pushrods and keep them in order

19 Lift out each of the pushrods in turn using a twisting action to release them from their cam followers (photo). Keep them in strict order of removal by inserting them in a strip of cardboard having eight numbered holes punched in it. Note that No 1 should be the pushrod nearest the flywheel.

20 Slacken all the cylinder head retaining bolts half a turn at a time in the reverse order to that shown in Fig. 1.28. When the tension has been relieved remove all the bolts, with the exception of the centre bolt on the distributor side.

21 Using a hide or plastic mallet, tap each end of the cylinder head so as to pivot the head around the remaining locating bolt and unstick the gasket. Do not attempt to lift the head until the gasket has been unstuck, otherwise the cylinder liner seal at the base of each liner will be broken, allowing water and foreign matter to enter the sump.

22 After unsticking the cylinder head from the gasket, remove the remaining bolt and lift the head, complete with water pump, manifolds and carburettor, off the engine (photo). **Note** the crankshaft must not be rotated with the head removed, otherwise the liners will be displaced. If it is necessary to turn the engine (eg to clean the piston crowns), use bolts with suitable washers screwed into the top of the block to retain the liners (photo 35.11).

12 Cylinder head – removal with engine on the bench

The procedure for removing the cylinder head with the engine on the bench is similar to that for removal when the engine is in the car, with the exception of disconnecting the controls and services. Refer to Section 11 and follow the procedure given in paragraphs 7, 12 and 15, then 17 to 22.

13 Cylinder head – dismantling

1 Extract the circlip from the end of the rocker shaft, then remove the springs, rockers arms and pedestals, keeping each component in its original fitted sequence.

2 Remove the valves from the cylinder head. Compress each spring in turn, with a valve spring compressor until the collets can be removed. Release the compressor and remove the spring, spring retainer and thrust washer.

3 If, when the valve spring compressor is screwed down, the valve spring retaining cap refuses to free to expose the split collet, do not continue to screw down on the compressor, but gently tap the top of the tool directly over the cap with a light hammer. At the same time hold the compressor firmly in position with one hand to avoid it jumping off.

11.22 Free the cylinder head from the gasket then lift the head, complete with manifolds and water pump, off the engine

4 It is essential that the valves are kept in their correct sequence unless they are so badly worn that they are to be renewed. Numbering from the flywheel end of the cylinder head, exhaust valves are 1-4-5-8 and inlet valves 2-3-6-7.

5 The valve springs and collets should also be kept in their correct sequence as the inlet and exhaust valve components differ.

14 Sump – removal

1 If the sump is to be removed with the engine in the car, first carry out the following operations:

   (a) Jack up the front of the car and support on axle stands, remove the splash shield, the unscrew the two bolts, noting the position of the spacer, and remove the engine steady rod

   (b) Undo the bolts and remove the flywheel or torque converter cover plate from the bellhousing

   (c) Drain the engine oil

   (d) Where fitted, disconnect the two wires at the oil level sensor on the front face of the sump

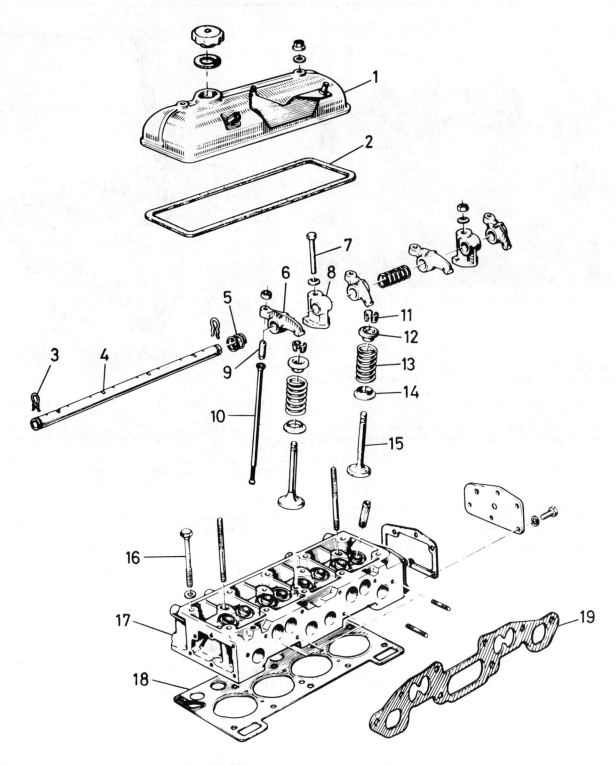

Fig. 1.7 Exploded view of the cylinder head components (Sec 13)

1 Rocker cover	8 Pedestal	14 Washer
2 Gasket	9 Adjuster	15 Valve
3 Circlip	10 Pushrod	16 Cylinder head bolt
4 Rocker shaft	11 Split collet	17 Cylinder head
5 Spring	12 Retainer	18 Cylinder head gasket
6 Rocker	13 Spring	19 Manifold gasket
7 Bolt		

14.2 Undo the retaining bolts and remove the sump

2   Undo and remove the bolts securing the sump to the crankcase (photo). Tap the sump with a hide or plastic mallet to break the seal between sump flange and crankcase, and remove the sump. Note that on some models a gasket is not used, only a sealing compound. On Turbo models it is necessary to remove the right-hand engine mounting first, and to do this the engine must be lifted approximately 10.0 cm (4.0 in) using a hoist and chain (Fig. 1.8) and having removed the air filter.

15 Oil pump – removal

1   If the oil pump is to be removed with the engine in the car, first remove the sump, as described in the previous Section.
2   Undo the retaining bolts (photo) and withdraw the oil pump from the crankcase and drivegear.

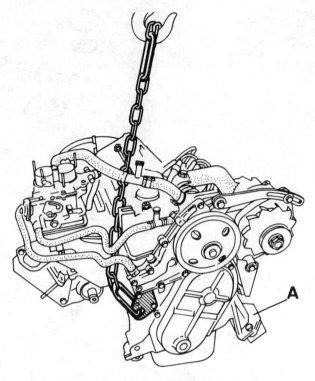

Fig. 1.8 Chain position for lifting the Turbo engine for sump removal (Sec 14)

A   Right-hand engine mounting

16 Timing cover, gears and chain – removal

1   If the engine is in the car, first carry out the following operations:

   (a) *Remove the alternator drivebelt*
   (b) *Remove the sump*

2   If the engine is in the car, rotate the crankshaft until the notch in the flywheel or torque converter is aligned with the TDC mark on the bellhousing timing scale (photo), and the distributor rotor is pointing towards the No 1 cylinder HT lead segment in the cap.

15.2 Undo the retaining bolts and withdraw the oil pump

16.2 Flywheel notch (arrowed) aligned with TDC mark on the bellhousing timing scale

16.3 Lock the starter ring gear using a strip of angle iron

16.4 A puller may be needed to remove the crankshaft pulley hub

3   Using a socket or spanner, undo the crankshaft pulley retaining bolt. If the engine is in the car lock the starter ring gear to prevent the engine turning using a wide-bladed screwdriver between the ring gear teeth and the crankcase or apply the handbrake and engage top gear. If the engine is out of the car the ring gear can be locked using a strip of angle iron engaged with the dowel bolt (photo).

4   With the bolt removed, lift off the pulley and withdraw the pulley hub. If the hub is tight, carefully lever it off using two screwdrivers or use a two- or three-legged puller (photo).

5   Undo the nuts and bolts securing the timing cover to the cylinder block and carefully prise the timing cover off using a screwdriver to release the sealant. Note that a gasket is not used on all models.

6   If the engine is out of the car, rotate the crankshaft by means of the flywheel or torque converter driveplate until No 1 piston is returned to TDC, and the timing marks on the crankshaft and camshaft sprockets are towards each other. If the cylinder head has been removed, make sure that the cylinder liners are retained with bolts and washers, as

described in Section 35, otherwise the liners will be displaced when the crankshaft is rotated.

7   Observe the components of the timing chain tensioner, noting that one of three types may be fitted. These are; a mechanical tensioner, identifiable by its coil tensioning spring; a hydraulic tensioner with manual presetting, identifiable by the small bolt on the side of the tensioner body; a hydraulic tensioner with automatic presetting identifiable by the absence of a small bolt on the side of the tensioner body.

8   To remove the mechanical tensioner, undo the retaining bolt using an Allen key, hold the tensioner slipper and spring end together and withdraw the assembly from the cylinder block.

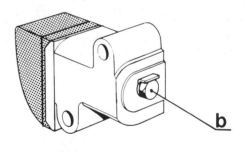

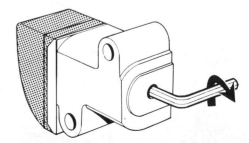

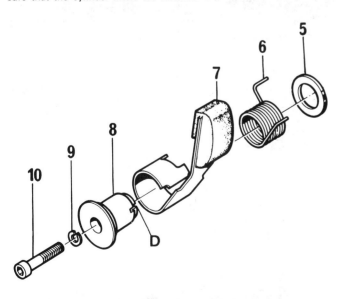

Fig. 1.9 Mechanical timing chain tensioner components (Sec 16)

5	Washer	8	Collar
6	Spring	9	Washer
7	Slipper arm	10	Retaining bolt

Fig. 1.10 Hydraulic timing chain tensioner with manual presetting (Sec 16)

Remove bolt (b) and turn slipper piston clockwise using an Allen key to retract the tensioner slipper

9   If an hydraulic tensioner with manual presetting is fitted, bend up the locktab and unscrew the small bolt on the side of the tensioner body. Insert a suitable Allen key into the bolt hole and engage the Allen key with the end of the slipper piston. Turn the key clockwise to retract the tensioner slipper. Now undo the two retaining bolts, lift off the tensioner and recover the spacer plate located behind the tensioner body. Removal of the tensioner with automatic presetting follows the same procedure, except that the piston cannot be retracted manually and must be held in compression by hand as the tensioner is removed.

10 Bend back the locktab then undo and remove the camshaft sprocket retaining bolt.

11 Withdraw the camshaft and crankshaft sprockets, complete with chain, using two screwdrivers to lever the sprockets off if they are tight (photo).

12 With the sprockets and chain removed, check that the Woodruff key in the end of the crankshaft is a tight fit in its groove, but if not, remove it now and store it safely to avoid the risk of it dropping out and getting lost.

17 Camshaft and followers – removal

1   Using a suitable bolt screwed into the distributor drivegear, or a length of tapered dowel rod, extract the drivegear from the distributor aperture.

2   Withdraw the camshaft followers from the top of the cylinder block, keeping them in strict order of removal (photo).

3   Undo and remove the two bolts securing the camshaft retaining plate to the cylinder block and carefully withdraw the camshaft from its location (photo).

18 Liners, pistons and connecting rods – removal

1   If the engine is in the car, first carry out the following operations:

   (a) *Remove the sump*
   (b) *For easier access, remove the oil pump*
   (c) *Remove the cylinder head (not necessary if only the big-end bearings are to be removed)*

2   Rotate the crankshaft so that No 1 big-end cap (nearest the flywheel) is at the lowest point of its travel. If the big-end cap and rod are not already numbered, mark them with a centre punch on the side opposite the camshaft (rear facing side of engine when in the car). Mark both the cap and rod in relation to the cylinder liner they operate in, noting that No 1 is nearest the flywheel end of the engine.

16.11 Removing the timing chain and sprockets

17.2 Withdraw the cam followers and keep them in order

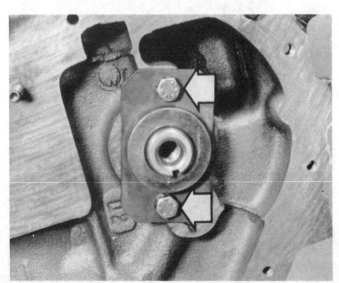

17.3 Undo the bolts (arrowed) and withdraw the camshaft

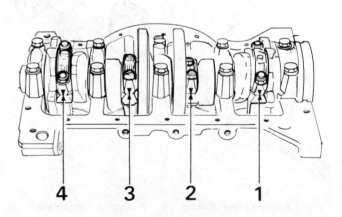

4   3   2   1

Fig. 1.11 Mark the big-end bearing caps and connecting rods before removal (Sec 18)

3 Undo and remove the big-end bearing cap nuts and withdraw the cap, complete with shell bearing from the connecting rod. If only the bearing shells are being attended to, push the connecting rod up and off the crankpin and remove the upper bearing shell. Keep the bearing shells and cap together in their correct sequence if they are to be refitted.

4 Remove the liner clamps and withdraw the liner together with piston and connecting rod, from the top of the cylinder block. Mark the liners using masking tape, so that they may be refitted in their original locations.

5 Push the connecting rod up and remove the piston and rod from the liner.

6 Now repeat these operations on the remaining three liner, piston and connecting rod assemblies.

19 Flywheel or torque converter driveplate – removal

1 Lock the crankshaft using a strip of angle iron between the ring gear teeth and the engine dowel bolt, or a block of wood between one of the crankshaft counterweights and the crankcase.

2 Mark the flywheel or driveplate in relation to the crankshaft, undo the retaining bolts and withdraw the unit.

20 Crankshaft and main bearings – removal

1 Identification numbers should be cast onto the base of each main bearing cap (photo), but if not, number the cap and crankcase using a centre punch, as was done for the connecting rods and caps.

2 Undo and remove the main bearing cap retaining bolts and withdraw the caps, complete with bearing shells. Withdraw the oil dipstick tube first after undoing the bolts at No 2 bearing cap (photo).

3 Carefully lift the crankshaft from the crankcase (photo).

4 Remove the thrust washers at each side of the centre main bearing, then remove the bearing shell upper halves from the crankcase. Place each shell with its respective bearing cap.

21 Crankshaft rear oil seal – renewal

1 With the engine removed from the car and separated from the gearbox or automatic transmission (if these units were removed with it), remove the flywheel or torque converter driveplate.

2 Clean the area around the crankshaft rear oil seal, then use a screwdriver to prise it from the block and bearing cap.

3 Wipe clean the oil seal recess. Dip the new oil seal in clean engine oil and carefully install it over the crankshaft rear journal. Take great care not to damage the delicate lip of the seal and make sure that the seal open face is towards the engine.

4 Using a tube of suitable diameter, a block of wood or the old seal, install the new seal squarely into its location until the outer face is flush with the block and bearing cap. If the original seal has worn a groove in the journal, drive the seal in a further 3 mm (0.12 in).

5 Refit the flywheel and the engine, as described in the applicable Sections of this Chapter.

22 Engine mountings – renewal

Front mountings

1 Place a jack and an interposed block of wood under the sump if the right-hand mounting is to be removed, or under the gearbox or transmission if the left-hand mounting is to be removed. Raise the jack to just take the weight of the engine and gearbox or automatic transmission.

20.1 Identification number on main beading cap

20.2 The oil dipstick tube is secured to No 2 main bearing cap

20.3 Crankshaft removal

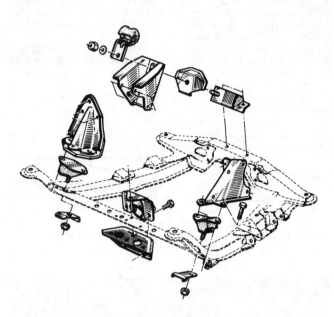

22.2 Engine rubber mounting-to-subframe retaining nut

Fig. 1.12 Engine/gearbox mounting and brackets (Sec 22)

2   Undo the nut securing the rubber mounting to the subframe from below, and remove the flat washer (photo).
3   Undo the two nuts and bolts securing the rubber mounting to the engine/gearbox or automatic transmission mounting brackets. Undo the bolts securing the bracket to the engine, gearbox or transmission, lift off the bracket and withdraw the rubber mounting (photos).
4   Refitting is the reverse sequence to removal.

Rear mounting
5   Disconnect the battery negative terminal and remove the air cleaner, as described in Chapter 3.
6   Place a jack beneath the gearbox or transmission with an interposed block of wood and just take the weight of the unit.
7   Undo the nut and remove the washer securing the rubber mounting to the gearbox or automatic transmission mounting bracket.
8   Undo the two bolts securing the mounting rear support bracket to the subframe, slide out the bracket and withdraw the rubber mounting.
9   Refitting is the reverse sequence to removal.

22.3A Front right-hand engine mounting bracket

22.3B Front left-hand engine/gearbox mounting

22.3C Front left-hand engine/gearbox mounting with bracket removed

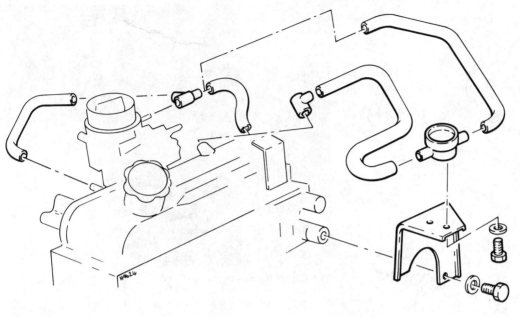

Fig. 1.13 Crankcase ventilation hose layout for C1C, C1E and non-Turbo C1J engines (Sec 23)

23 Crankcase ventilation system – description

The layout of the crankcase ventilation system according to engine type is shown in the accompanying illustrations.

When the engine is idling, or under partial load conditions, the high depression in the inlet manifold draws the crankcase fumes (diluted by air from the air cleaner) through the calibrated restrictor and into the combustion chambers.

The system ensures that there is always a partial vacuum in the crankcase, and so prevents pressure which could cause oil contamination, fume emission and oil leakage past seals.

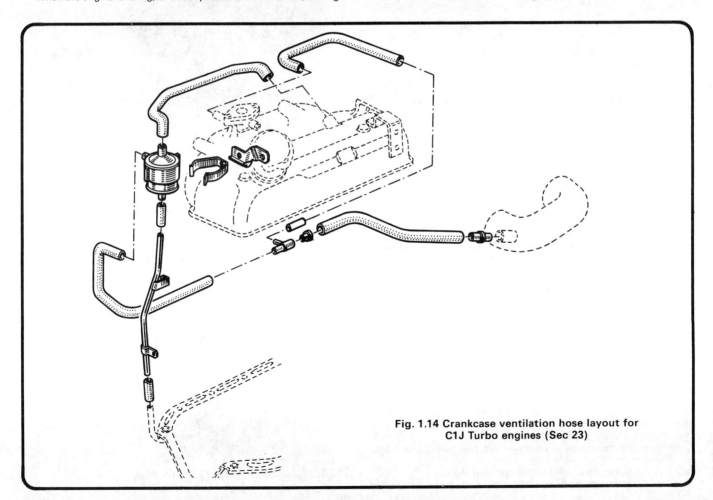

Fig. 1.14 Crankcase ventilation hose layout for C1J Turbo engines (Sec 23)

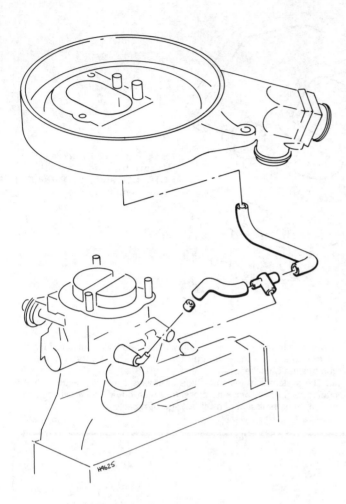

Fig. 1.15 Crankcase ventilation hose layout for
C2J engines (Sec 23)

25.1 Lift off the oil pump cover

25.2A Remove the pressure relief valve ball seat and ball ...

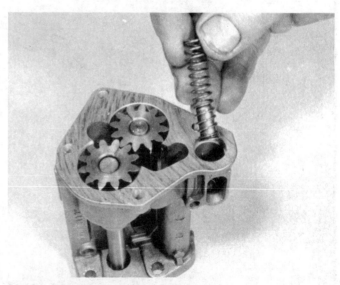

25.2B ... followed by the spring and spring seat

On C1J Turbo engines a one-way valve is fitted on the inlet
manifold to prevent the crankcase being pressurised when the
turbocharger is in operation, however the system still operates in a
reduced capacity by feeding fumes into the inlet system upstream of
the turbocharger.

24 Examination and renovation – general

With the engine completely stripped, clean all components and
examine them for wear. Each part should be checked and, where
necessary, renewed or renovated as described in the following
Sections. Renew main and big-end shell bearings as a matter of
course, unless you know that they have had little wear and are in
perfect condition.

25 Oil pump – examination and renovation

1   Undo the four retaining bolts and lift off the pump cover (photo),
taking care not to lose the oil pressure relief valve components which
may be ejected under the action of the spring.
2   Remove the pressure relief valve ball seat, ball, spring and spring
seat from the pump body (photos).
3   Lift out the idler gear, and the drivegear and shaft.
4   Clean the components and carefully examine the gears, pump body

and relief valve ball and seat for any signs of scoring or wear. Renew the pump if these conditions are apparent.

5   If the components appear serviceable, measure the clearance between the pump body and the gears using a feeler blade (photo). If the clearance exceeds the specified amount, the pump must be renewed.

6   If the pump is satisfactory, reassemble the components in the order of removal, fill the pump with oil and refit the cover.

25.5 Check the gear-to-body clearance using feeler gauges

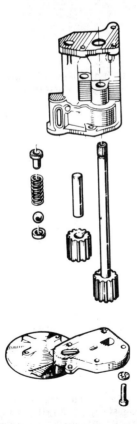

Fig. 1.16 Exploded view of the oil pump components (Sec 25)

26 Crankshaft and main bearings – examination and renovation

1   Examine the bearing surfaces of the crankshaft for scatches or scoring and, using a micrometer, check each journal and crankpin for ovality. Where this is found to be in excess of 0.0254 mm, the crankshaft will have to be reground and undersize bearings fitted.

2   Crankshaft regrinding should be carried out by a suitable engineering works, who will normally supply the matching undersize main and big-end shell bearings.

3   If the crankshaft endfloat is more than the maximum specified amount, new thrust washers should be fitted to the centre main bearing; these are usually supplied together with the main and big-end bearings on a reground crankshaft.

27 Cylinder liners and crankcase – examination and renovation

1   Examine the liners for taper, ovality, scoring and scratches. If a ridge is found at the top of the bore on the thrust side, the bores are worn. The owner will have a good indication of the bore wear prior to dismantling the engine or on removing the cylinder head. Excessive oil consumption accompanied by blue smoke from the exhaust is a sure sign of worn bores and piston rings.

2   Measure the bore diameter just under the ridge with an internal micrometer and compare it with the diameter at the bottom of the bore, which is not subject to wear. If the difference between the two measurements exceeds 0.20 mm then it will be necessary to fit oversize pistons and rings or obtain new piston and liner assemblies. Contrary to popular belief the liners can be rebored if necessary and fitted with oversize pistons.

3   The liners should also be checked for cracking.

4   If the bores are only slightly worn, special oil control rings can be fitted which will restore compression and stop the engine burning oil. Several different types are available and the manufacturer's instructions concerning their fitting must be followed closely.

5   If new pistons only are being fitted and the bores have not been reground, it is essential to slightly roughen the hard glaze on the sides of the bores with fine glasspaper to enable the new piston rings to bed in properly.

6   Examine the crankcase for cracks and leaks, then clean the oil galleries and waterways using a piece of wire.

7   Note that if new piston and liner assemblies have been obtained, each piston is matched to its respective liner and they must not be interchanged.

8   Whether new liners or the original components are being refitted, new liner base seals will be required. On the 1397 cc engine the base seals are in the form of a rubber O-ring. On the 956 cc and 1108 cc engines the seals are a flat ring type gasket of special material and are available in three sizes colour-coded blue, red or green. The three sizes are necessary so that the liner protrusion can be accurately set.

9   To check the liner protrusion, first ensure that the sealing area at the base of the liner and in the cylinder block is perfectly clean.

10 Place a blue seal on each liner (956 cc and 1108 cc engines only, liners on 1397 cc engines should have no seal for this check) and place the liner firmly in position in the cylinder block. If previously used liners are being checked, place them in their correct locations. If new liners are being fitted they may initially be placed in any location, but keep their respective matched pistons together with them. With the liners in place, the flats on liners 1 and 2 must be towards each other and the flats on liners 3 and 4 must be towards each other also.

11 Lay a straight-edge across the top of the liner and measure the gap between the straight-edge and the top of the cylinder block (photo). This is the liner protrusion and must be within the tolerance given in the Specifications. If not, try a red seal or green seal.

12 On 956 cc, 1108 cc and 1397 cc engines the liner height variation must be checked, but only if new liners are being fitted. The liner height variation is the difference in cylinder liner protrusion between one liner and the next. The liner must be arranged so that the one with the greatest protrusion becomes No 1 and all the others are stepped down in order so that the one with the least protrusion becomes No 4. This is checked in the same way as for liner protrusion described previously. The base seals must be in position for this check on 956 cc

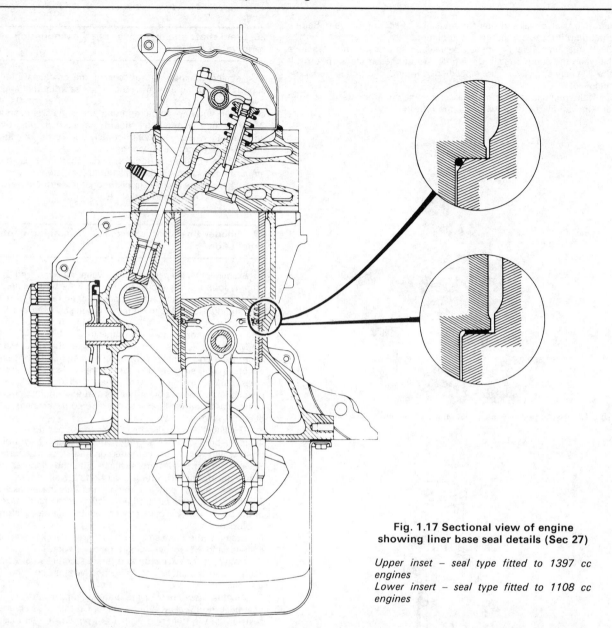

Fig. 1.17 Sectional view of engine showing liner base seal details (Sec 27)

Upper inset – seal type fitted to 1397 cc engines
Lower insert – seal type fitted to 1108 cc engines

27.11 Measuring the cylinder liner protrusion

and 1108 cc engines, but not on 1397 cc engines. Recheck that liner protrusion remains within tolerance. Also make sure when moving a liner from one position to another that its matched piston stays with it.
13 Having finally selected the correct location for each liner, identify the liner and its piston with a number 1 to 4 to identify the assembly to be fitted to each location on reassembly.

28 Piston and connecting rod assemblies – examination and renovation

1   Examine the pistons for ovality, scoring and scratches, and for wear of the piston ring grooves.
2   If the pistons or connecting rods are to be renewed it is necessary to have this work carried out by a Renault dealer or suitable engineering works who will have the necessary tooling to remove the gudgeon pins.
3   If new rings are to be fitted to the original pistons, expand the old rings over the top of the pistons (photo). The use of two or three old feeler blades will be helpful in preventing the rings dropping into empty grooves.
4   Before fitting the new rings, ensure that the ring grooves in the piston are free of carbon by cleaning them using an old ring. Break the ring in half to do this.

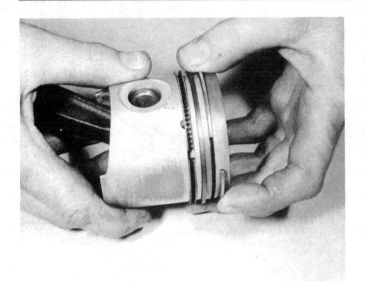

28.3 Remove the piston rings from the top of the pistons

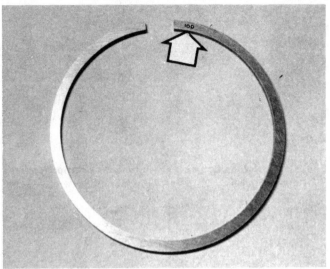

28.5 The word TOP (arrowed) indicates the second compression ring upper face

5 Install the new rings by fitting them over the top of the piston, starting with the oil control scraper ring. Note that the second compression ring is tapered and must be fitted with the word TOP uppermost (photo).
6 With all the rings in position, space the ring gaps at 120° to each other.
7 Note that, if new piston and liner assemblies have been obtained, each piston is matched to its respective liner and they must not be interchanged.

29 Camshaft and followers – examination and renovation

1 Examine the camshaft bearing surfaces, cam lobes and skew gear for wear ridges, pitting, scoring or chipping of the gear teeth. Renew the camshaft if any of these conditions are apparent.

2 If the camshaft is serviceable, temporarily refit the sprocket and secure with the retaining bolt. Using a feeler gauge measure the clearance between the camshaft retaining plate and the outer face of the bearing journal. If the clearance exceeds the specified dimension, renew the retaining plate. To do this, remove the sprocket and draw off the plate and retaining collar using a suitable puller. Fit the new plate and a new collar using a hammer and tube to drive the collar into position.
3 Examine the condition of the camshaft bearings, and if renewal is necessary have this work carried out by a Renault dealer or engineering works.
4 Inspect the cam followers for wear ridges and pitting of their camshaft lobe contact faces, and for scoring on the sides of the follower body. Light scuff marks and side discolouration are normal, but there should be no signs of scoring or ridges. If the followers show signs of wear, renew them. Note that they must all be renewed if a new camshaft is being fitted.

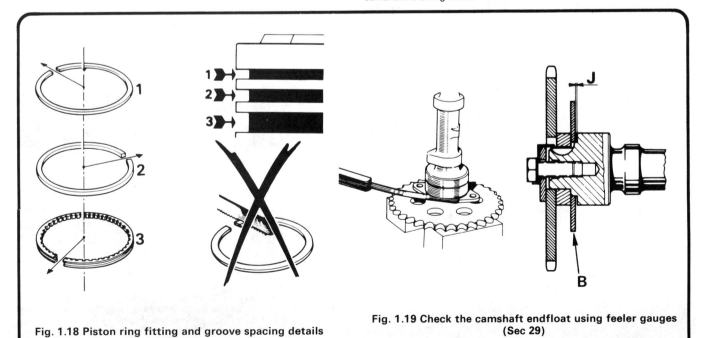

Fig. 1.18 Piston ring fitting and groove spacing details (Sec 28)

Fig. 1.19 Check the camshaft endfloat using feeler gauges (Sec 29)

B   Camshaft retaining plate   J   Specified endfloat

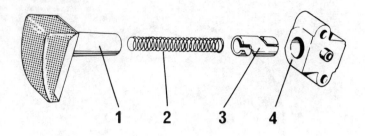

**Fig. 1.20 Hydraulic timing chain tensioner components
(Sec 30)**

1 Piston with tensioner   3 Sleeve
   slipper   4 Tensioner body
2 Spring

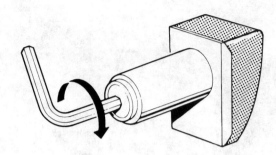

**Fig. 1.21 Using an Allen key to lock the sleeve in the hydraulic
tensioner with automatic presetting (Sec 30)**

30 Timing cover, gears and chain – examination and renovation

1 Examine all the teeth on the camshaft and crankshaft sprockets. If these are 'hooked' in appearance, renew the sprockets.

2 If a mechanical chain tensioner is fitted, examine the chain contact pad and renew the tensioner assembly if the pad is heavily scored.

3 If a hydraulic tensioner is fitted, dismantle the components by taking them apart on the automatic presetting type (photo), or by releasing the slipper piston (turn it anti-clockwise with an Allen key) on the manual presetting type. Examine the piston, spring, sleeve and tensioner body bore for signs of scoring and renew if evident. Also renew the tensioner if the chain contact pad is heavily scored.

4 If the hydraulic tensioner is serviceable, lubricate the components and reassemble. On the manual presetting type, retain the slipper piston in the retracted position by turning it clockwise with an Allen key. On the automatic presetting type, lock the sleeve in the slipper piston first by turning it clockwise with an Allen key, then slide this assembly into the tensioner body (photo). Avoid pressing the slipper now or the sleeve will be released and the whole assembly will fly apart.

5 Renew the oil seal in the timing cover by driving out the old seal using a suitable drift and then install the new seal using a large socket or block of wood (photo).

30.3 Hydraulic timing chain tensioner with automatic presetting

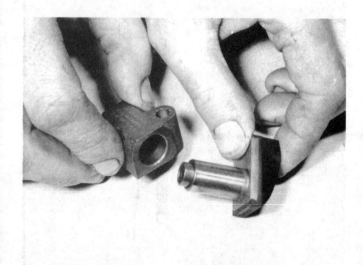

30.4 Refitting the locked sleeve and slipper piston assembly on the automatic presetting hydraulic tensioner

30.5 Use a socket or tube to renew the timing cover oil seal

31 Flywheel or torque converter driveplate – examination and renovation

1 Examine the flywheel for scoring of the clutch face and for wear or chipping of the ring gear teeth. If the clutch face is scored, the flywheel may be machined until flat, but renewal is preferable. If the ring gear is worn or damaged it may be renewed separately, but this job is best left to a Renault dealer or engineering works. The temperature to which the new ring gear must be heated for installation is critical and, if not done accurately, the hardness of the teeth will be destroyed.
2 Check the torque converter driveplate carefully for signs of distortion or any hairline cracks around the bolt holes or radiating outwards from the centre.

32 Cylinder head and pistons – decarbonizing, valve grinding and renovation

1 The operation will normally only be required at comparatively high mileages. However, if persistent pinking occurs and performance has deteriorated, even though the engine adjustments are correct, decarbonizing and valve grinding may be required.
2 With the cylinder head removed, use a scraper to remove the carbon from the combustion chambers and ports. Remove all traces of gasket from the cylinder head surface, then wash it thoroughly with paraffin.
3 Use a straight-edge and feeler blade to check that the cylinder head surface is not distorted. If it is, it must be resurfaced by a suitably equipped engineering works.
4 If the engine is still in the car, clean the piston crowns and cylinder bore upper edges, but make sure that no carbon drops between the pistons and bores. To do this, locate two of the pistons at the top of their bores and seal off the remaining bores with paper and masking tape. Press a little grease between the two pistons and their bores to collect any carbon dust; this can be wiped away when the piston is lowered. To prevent carbon build-up, polish the piston crown with metal polish, but remove all traces of polish afterwards.
5 Examine the heads of the valves for pitting and burning, especially the exhaust valve heads. Renew any valve which is badly burnt. Examine the valve seats at the same time. If the pitting is very slight, it can be removed by grinding the valve heads and seats together with coarse, then fine grinding paste.
6 Where excessive pitting has occurred, the valve seats must be recut or renewed by a suitably equipped engineering works.
7 Valve grinding is carried out as follows: Place the cylinder head upside down on a bench with a block of wood at each end to give clearance for the valve stems.
8 Smear a trace of coarse carborundum paste on the seat face and press a suction grinding tool onto the valve heads. With a semi-rotary action, grind the valve head to its seat, lifting the valve occasionally to redistribute the grinding paste. When a dull matt even surface is produced on both the valve seat and the valve, wipe off the paste and repeat the process with fine carborundum paste. A light spring placed under the valve head will greatly ease this operation. When a smooth unbroken ring of light grey matt finish is produced on both the valve and seat, the grinding operation is complete.
9 Scrape away all carbon from the valve head and stem, and clean away all traces of grinding compound. Clean the valves and seats with a paraffin-soaked rag, then wipe with a clean rag.
10 If the valve guides are worn, indicated by a side-to-side motion of the valve, new guides must be fitted. To do this, use a suitable mandrel to press the worn guides downwards and out through the combustion chamber. Press the new guides into the cylinder head in the same direction until they are at the specified fitted height.
11 Examine the pushrods and rocker shaft assembly for wear, and renew them as necessary.

33 Engine reassembly – general

1 To ensure maximum life with minimum trouble from a rebuilt engine, not only must everything be correctly assembled, but it must also be spotlessly clean. All oilways must be clear, and locking washers

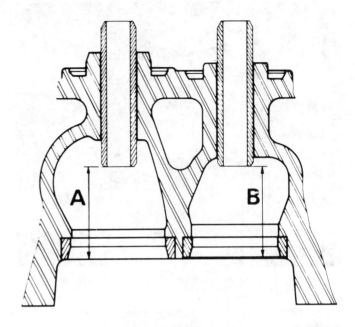

Fig. 1.22 Valve guide fitted height dimensions (Sec 32)

A Inlet   *B Exhaust*

and spring washers must be fitted where indicated. Oil all bearings and other working surfaces thoroughly with engine oil during assembly.
2 Before assembly begins, renew any bolts or studs with damaged threads and have all new components at hand ready for assembly.
3 Gather together a torque wrench, oil can, clean rags and a set of engine gaskets, together with a new oil filter. A tube of RTV sealing compound will also be required for the joint faces that are fitted without gaskets. It is recommended that CAF 4/60 THIXO paste, obtainable from Renault dealers is used, as it is specially formulated for this purpose.

34 Crankshaft and main bearings – refitting

1 Clean the backs of the bearing shells and the bearing recesses in both the cylinder block and main bearing caps.
2 Press the bearing shells without oil holes into the caps, ensuring that the tag on the shell engages in the notch in the cap.
3 Press the bearing shells with the oil holes into the recesses in the cylinder block. If all five shells have two oil holes they may be fitted into any location. If two of the shells only have one oil hole, these must be fitted to journals No 1 and 3 (No 1 journal being nearest the flywheel). Fit the remaining shells to any of the three remaining locations.
4 If the original main bearing shells are being re-used these must be refitted to their original locations in the block and caps.
5 Using a little grease, stick the thrust washers to each side of the centre main bearing journal in the block (photo). Ensure that the oilway grooves on each thrust washer face outwards.
6 Lubricate the lips of a new crankshaft oil seal and carefully slip it over the end of the crankshaft. Do this carefully as the seal lips are very delicate. Ensure that the open side of the seal faces the engine.
7 Liberally lubricate each bearing shell in the cylinder block and lower the crankshaft into position (photo).
8 Fit the bearing caps in their numbered, or previously noted locations, so that the bearing shell locating notches in the cap and block are both on the same side (photo).
9 Fit the main bearing cap retaining bolts and make sure that the dipstick tube is in position with its bracket located under the No 2 bearing cap retaining bolt.
10 Tighten the bolts until they are moderately tight, but before

34.5 Fit the thrust washers with their oilway grooves (arrowed) facing outwards

34.7 Lubricate the bearing shells, then lower the crankshaft into place

tightening No 1 bearing cap position the oil seal so that its face is 3.0 mm (0.12 in) inset from the outer face of the block and bearing cap. This will ensure that its sealing lip does not bear on the worn section of the journal.

11 Check that the crankshaft is free to turn and then tighten the main bearing retaining bolts to the specified torque (photo).

12 Check the crankshaft endfloat using feeler gauges inserted between the thrust washers and the side of the bearing journal (photo). If new thrust washers have been fitted the endfloat should be in accordance with the dimension given in the Specifications. If the original washers have been refitted and the endfloat is excessive, new thrust washers must be fitted. These are obtainable in a number of oversizes.

13 Finally check that the crankshaft turns reasonably freely without any tight spots.

35 Liners, pistons and connecting rods – refitting

1 If the liner protrusion and liner height variation have not already been checked, do this now using the procedure described in Section 27, before proceeding further.

34.8 Fit the bearing caps and retaining bolts ...

34.11 ... and tighten the bolts to the specified torque

34.12 Measure the crankshaft endfloat using feeler gauges

2 Lay the four liners face down in a row on the bench, in their correct order. Turn them as necessary so that the flats on the edges of liners 1 and 2 are towards each other, and the flats on liners 3 and 4 are towards each other also.

3 Lubricate the pistons and piston rings then lay each piston and connecting rod assembly with its respective liner.

4 Starting with assembly No 1, make sure that the piston rings are still spaced out at 120° to each other and clamp the piston rings using a piston ring compressor.

5 Insert the piston and connecting rod assembly into the bottom of the liner ensuring that the arrow on the piston crown faces the flywheel end of the engine (photos). In other words, if the liners are laid out as described, the arrow should face away from the other liners. Using a block of wood or hammer handle against the end of the connecting rod, tap the piston into the liner until the top of the piston is approximately 25 mm (1.0 in) away from the top of the liner.

6 Repeat this procedure for the remaining three piston and liner assemblies.

7 Turn the crankshaft so that No 1 crankpin is at the bottom of its travel.

8 Press the upper half of the big-end shell in the connecting rod and press the lower half into the cap (photo). Ensure that the tags on the shells engage with the notches on the cap and rod.

9 With the liner base seal in position, place No 1 liner, piston and connecting rod assembly into its location in the cylinder block (photo). Ensure that the arrow on the piston crown faces the flywheel end of the engine and the flat on the liner is positioned as described previously.

10 Liberally lubricate the crankpin journal, pull the connecting rod down and engage it with the crankpin. Check that the marks made on the cap and rod during removal are opposite the camshaft side of the engine then refit the cap and retaining nuts. The notches for the bearing shell tags in the cap and rod must be together. Tighten the connecting rod cap retaining nut to the specified torque (photos).

11 With the liner piston and connecting rod assembly installed, retain the liner using a bolt and washer screwed into the cylinder head bolt holes. This will prevent damage to the base seal due to displacement of the liner as the engine is turned (photo).

12 Repeat the foregoing procedures for the remaining piston and liner assemblies, turning the crankshaft each time to make sure it is free.

13 If the engine is in the car, refit the oil pump, sump and cylinder head.

35.5A Check that the arrow on the piston crown will face the flywheel when installed ...

35.5B ... then fit the piston-connecting rod assembly to the liner

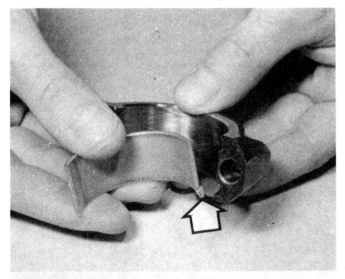

35.8 Fit the bearing shells with their tags (arrowed) engaged with the cap and rod notches

35.9 Fit the liner, piston and connecting rod assemblies

35.10A Fit the bearing caps to their respective connecting rods ...

35.10B ... and tighten the retaining nuts to the specified torque

35.11 Retain the liners using washers, nuts and bolts

36 Camshaft and followers – refitting

1   Lubricate the camshaft bearings and carefully insert the camshaft from the timing gear end of the engine (photo).
2   Refit the retaining plate bolts and tighten them. Check that the camshaft rotates smoothly.
3   Lubricate the cam followers and insert them into their original bores in the cylinder lock.

37 Flywheel or torque converter driveplate – refitting

1   Clean the flywheel and crankshaft faces, then fit the flywheel or driveplate making sure that any previously made marks are aligned.
2   Apply a few drops of thread locking compound to the retaining bolt threads, fit the bolts and tighten them in a diagonal sequence to the specified torque (photo).

36.1 Refitting the camshaft

37.2 Use a thread locking compound on the flywheel bolts

38 Timing cover, gears and chain – refitting

1 Refit the Woodruff key to the crankshaft groove and then tap the crankshaft sprocket into position. Ensure that the timing mark on the sprocket is on the side facing away from the engine.

2 If the engine is in the car, turn the crankshaft until the timing notch on the flywheel or torque converter is in line with the TDC mark on the bellhousing timing scale (photo 16.2). If the engine is out of the car, turn the crankshaft until Nos 1 and 4 pistons are at the very top of their travel.

3 Temporarily place the camshaft sprocket in position and turn the camshaft so that the timing marks on the sprocket faces are facing each other, and coincide with an imaginary line joining the crankshaft and camshaft centres, then remove the camshaft sprocket.

4 Fit the timing chain to the camshaft sprocket, position the sprocket in its approximate fitted position and locate the chain over the crankshaft sprocket. Position the camshaft sprocket on the camshaft and check that the marks are still aligned when there is an equal amount of slack on both sides of the chain.

5 Refit the camshaft sprocket retaining bolt using a new locktab and tighten the bolt to the specified torque. Bend up the locktabs to retain the bolt.

6 If a mechanical tensioner is fitted, place it in position and locate the spring ends in the block and over the slipper arm. Refit the retaining bolt and tighten it securely with an Allen key.

7 If a hydraulic tensioner is fitted, first position the spacer on the cylinder block and retain it in place using a little grease (photo).

8 Locate the tensioner body over the plate then refit and tighten the retaining bolts (photo). If the tensioner is of the manual presetting type, release the slipper piston by turning it anti-clockwise using an Allen key inserted in the end of the tensioner body. With the piston released, refit the small bolt to the tensioner body and secure with a new locktab. If the tensioner is of the automatic presetting type, push the slipper piston in and then release it. The piston should spring out automatically under spring pressure.

9 Ensure that the mating faces of the timing cover are clean and dry with all traces of old sealant removed and a new oil seal in place in the timing cover.

10 If there are no locating dowels for the timing cover, a gasket must

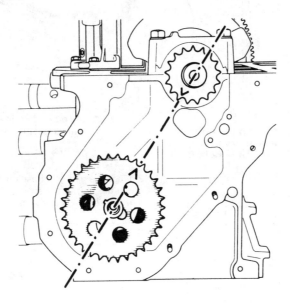

Fig. 1.23 Correct alignment of crankshaft and camshaft
sprocket timing marks (Sec 38)

38.7 Fit the hydraulic tensioner spacer ...

38.8 ... followed by the tensioner

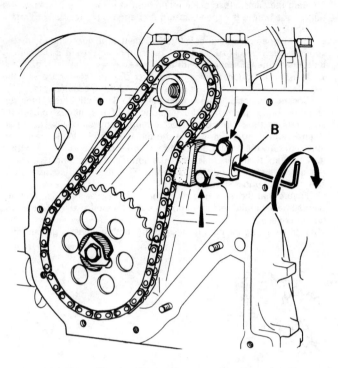

Fig. 1.24 Secure the hydraulic tensioner with the bolts (arrowed), then, if the tensioner has manual presetting, release the piston using an Allen key inserted in hole B (Sec 38)

Fig. 1.25 Apply a bead of sealant paste to the timing cover and sump before fitting (Secs 38 and 40)

be fitted. Locate the gasket on the cylinder block then fit the timing cover inserting the bolts loosely. Oil the pulley hub and temporarily fit it on the end of the crankshaft so that the timing cover is positioned correctly then tighten the cover bolts.

11 Where locating dowels are fitted, apply a bead of CAF 4/60 THIXO paste to the timing cover joint face then position the cover over the dowels and the two studs. Refit the nuts and retaining bolts then progressively tighten them in a diagonal sequence (photo).

12 Lubricate the crankshaft pulley hub and carefully slide it onto the end of the crankshaft (photo).

13 Place the pulley in position, refit the retaining bolt and washer and tighten the bolt to the specified torque (photos).

14 If the engine is in the car, refit the sump and alternator drivebelt.

39 Oil pump – refitting

1 Enter the oil pump shaft into its location in the cylinder block and, if the engine is in the car, engage the shaft with the distributor drivegear (photo).

2 Push the pump up into contact with the block, then refit and tighten the three retaining bolts. Note that a gasket is not used.

3 If the engine is in the car, refit the sump.

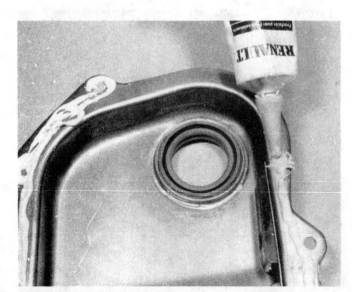

38.11 Applying CAF 4/60 THIXO paste to the timing cover

38.12 Refit the crankshaft pulley hub ...

38.13A ... followed by the pulley ...

38.13B ... and retaining bolt

40 Sump – refitting

1   Check that the mating faces of the sump and cylinder block are perfectly clean and dry.
2   Check if rubber seals are fitted between the sump and Nos 1 and 5 main bearing caps. This is the case on Turbo models and certain other models.
3   Apply a uniform bead of CAF 4/60 THIXO paste to the sump in accordance with Fig. 1.25 or 1.26, ensuring that a liberal quantity of the paste is used at the corners. Where rubber seals are fitted leave the areas shown in Fig. 1.26 clear of paste.
4   Where applicable fit the rubber seals to Nos 1 and 5 main bearing caps.
5   Place the sump in position then refit the retaining bolts (photo). Tighten the bolts progressively and in a diagonal sequence.

39.1 Refitting the oil pump

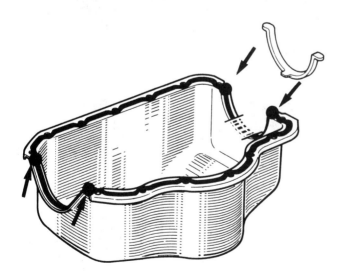

Fig. 1.26 Do not apply sealant to the shaded area if rubber seals are fitted to the end main bearing caps (Sec 40)

Note: *some models have a rubber seal at the timing chain end*

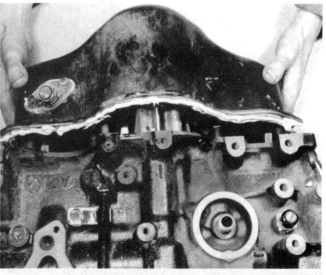

40.5 Place the sump in position and secure with the retaining bolts

6   If the engine is in the car, refit the engine steady rod, the flywheel or
torque converter cover plate and, where fitted, the two wires to the
engine oil level sensor. Refill the engine with the specified grade of oil.
On Turbo models refit the right-hand engine mounting and air filter.
Finally refit the splash shield and lower the car to the ground.

41 Cylinder head – reassembly and refitting

1   Lubricate the stems of the valves and insert them into their original
locations. If new valves are being fitted, insert them into the locations
to which they have been ground (photo).
2   Working on the first valve, fit the thrust washer to the cylinder head,
followed by the valve spring and retainer. Note that the spring should
be fitted with the end where the coils are closest towards the cylinder
head (photos).
3   Compress the valve spring and locate the split collets in the recess
in the valve stem. Note that the collets are different for the inlet and
exhaust valves (photos), the latter type having two curved collars.
Release the compressor, then repeat the procedure on the remaining
valves.

41.1 Insert the valves into their guides

41.2A Fit the thrust washer ...

41.2B ... followed by the spring and retainer

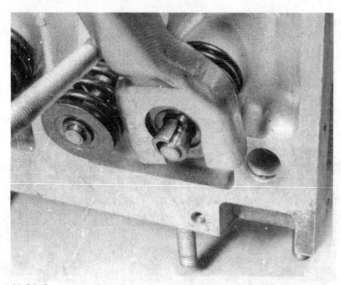

41.3A Compress the valve spring and locate the split collets ...

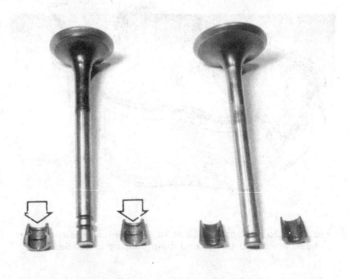

41.3B ... noting that those for the exhaust valves (arrowed) have
two curved collars

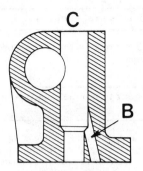

Fig. 1.27 Sectional view of the rocker pedestal (C) with oil hole (B) which must be fitted at the flywheel end of the shaft assembly (Sec 41)

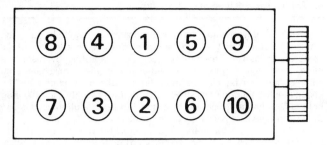

Fig. 1.28 Cylinder head tightening sequence (Sec 41)

4   With all the valves installed, place the cylinder head flat on the bench and, using a hammer and interposed block of wood, tap the end of each valve stem to settle the components.

5   Oil the rocker shaft, then reassemble the springs, rocker arms and pedestals in the reverse order to removal, and finally fit the circlip. Check that the bolt holes in the pedestals are aligned with the recesses in the rocker shaft, and that the pedestal with the oilway (where applicable) is fitted at the flywheel end.

6   Remove the cylinder liner clamps, if fitted, and make sure that the faces of the cylinder head and the cylinder block are perfectly clean. Lay a new gasket on the cylinder block with the words 'Haut-Top' uppermost (photo). Do not use any kind of jointing compound.

7   Lower the cylinder head into position, insert the cylinder head bolts, and tighten them to the specified torque in the sequence shown in Fig. 1.28 (photos).

8   Install the pushrods in their original locations (photo).

9   Lower the rocker shaft assembly onto the cylinder head, making sure that the adjusting ball-ends locate in the pushrods. Install the spring washer (convex side uppermost), nuts and bolts, and tighten them to the specified torque (photo).

10 Adjust the valve clearances, as described in Section 47 to the cold setting (see Specifications).

11 If the engine is in the car refit the controls, cables and services using the reverse of the removal procedure described in Section 11, but bearing in mind the following points:

(a) Tighten the exhaust front section to manifold retaining bolts so that the tension springs are coil-bound, then loosen them 1¹/₂ turns each
(b) Adjust the choke and accelerator cables, as described in Chapter 3
(c) Adjust the drivebelt tension, as described in Chapter 2
(d) Refill the cooling system, as described in Chapter 2

41.6 Place the gasket in position

41.7A Lower the cylinder head onto the gasket and ...

41.7B ... fit the retaining bolts and tighten in the correct sequence to the specified torque

41.8 Install the pushrods in their original locations

41.9 Refit the rocker shaft assembly

42 Distributor drivegear – refitting

1   Using a ring spanner on the crankshaft pulley bolt, turn the crankshaft until No 1 piston (flywheel end) is at the top of its compression stroke. This position can be established by placing a finger over No 1 plug hole and rotating the crankshaft until compression can be felt; continue turning the crankshaft until the piston reaches the top of its stroke. Use a screwdriver through the plug hole to feel the movement of the piston, but be careful not to damage the piston crown or plug threads in the cylinder head.
2   Without moving the crankshaft, position the drivegear so that its slots are at the 2 o'clock and 8 o'clock positions with the larger offset side facing away from the engine (photo).
3   Now lower the drivegear into mesh with the camshaft and oil pump driveshaft. As the gear meshes with the camshaft it will rotate anti-clockwise and should end up with its slot at right angles to the crankshaft centreline and with the larger offset towards the flywheel. It will probably be a tooth out on the first attempt and will take two or three attempts to get it just right (Fig. 1.29 and photo).

42.2 Fit the distributor drivegear ...

42.3 ... so that the slot is at right-angles to the crankshaft centreline with its larger offset side facing the flywheel when fitted

43 Ancillary components – refitting

Refer to Section 10 and refit the listed components with reference to the Chapters indicated.

44 Engine – attachment to manual gearbox or automatic transmission

Refer to Section 8 and attach the engine using the reverse of the removal procedure. Apply a trace of molybdenum disulphide grease to the end of the gearbox input shaft or torque converter locator before fitting.

45 Engine – refitting

Refitting the engine, either on its own or complete with manual gearbox or automatic transmission, is a reverse of the removal procedures contained in Sections 6 and 7. In addition bear in mind the following points:

(a) Tighten the exhaust front section-to-manifold retaining bolts so that the tension springs are coil-bound, then loosen them $1^1/_2$ turns each
(b) Refill the cooling system with reference to Chapter 2
(c) Adjust the choke and accelerator cables with reference to Chapter 3
(d) If the drivebelt was removed, adjust its tension with reference to Chapter 2
(e) Where applicable, refill the gearbox or automatic transmission with oil, as described in Chapter 6, and the engine, as described in Section 2 of this Chapter

46 Engine – adjustments after major overhaul

1   With the engine and gearbox refitted to the car, make a final check to ensure that everything has been reconnected and that no rags or tools have been left in the engine compartment.
2   Make sure that the oil and water levels are topped up and then start the engine; this may take a little longer than usual as the fuel pump and carburettor float chamber may be empty.

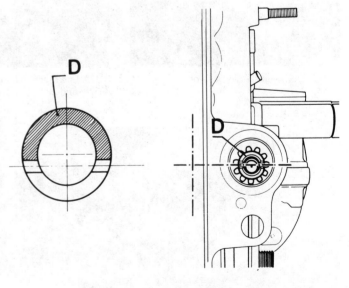

Fig. 1.29 Fitted position of distributor drivegear (Sec 42)

D = Larger offset side

3   As soon as the engine starts, watch for the oil pressure light to go out and check for any oil, fuel or water leaks. Don't be alarmed if there are some odd smells and smoke from parts getting hot and burning off oil deposits.

4   Allow the engine to run for approximately 20 minutes then switch it off and allow it to cool for at least $2^{1}/2$ hours. Remove the rocker cover and re-torque the cylinder head bolts in the sequence shown in Fig. 1.28. Slacken each bolt in turn, half a turn then retighten it to the specified torque before moving on to the next bolt. After retightening, adjust the valve clearances again, as described in Section 47.

5   If new pistons, rings or crankshaft bearings have been fitted the engine must be run-in for the first 500 miles (800 km). Do not exceed 45 mph (72 kph), operate the engine at full throttle or allow it to labour in any gear.

47 Valve clearances – adjustment

1   If the engine is in the car, remove the air cleaner or inlet duct as applicable as described in Chapter 3.

2   Detach the crankcase ventilation hose at the rocker cover and disconnect the throttle linkage return spring (photo).

3   Mark the spark plug HT lead locations and withdraw them from the spark plugs. Remove the distributor cap retaining screws or clips, and move the cap and leads to one side.

4   Undo the nuts securing the rocker cover in place, tap the cover lightly to free it then manipulate it off the studs.

5   Number the valves 1 to 8 from the flywheel end of the engine then, using a ring spanner on the crankshaft pulley bolt, turn the engine in a clockwise direction until No 8 valve is fully open (ie spring compressed).

6   Insert a feeler blade of the correct thickness for an exhaust valve (see Specifications) between the end of No 1 valve stem and the rocker arm, then adjust the rocker arm ball-end (after loosening the locknut) until the feeler blade is a firm sliding fit (photo). Tighten the locknut and recheck the adjustment, then repeat the procedure on the remaining seven valves in the following sequence.

Valve open	Valve to adjust
No 8 ex	*No 1 ex*
No 6 in	*No 3 in*
No 4 ex	*No 5 ex*
No 7 in	*No 2 in*
No 1 ex	*No 8 ex*
No 3 in	*No 6 in*
No 5 ex	*No 4 ex*
No 2 in	*No 7 in*

7   On completion, refit the rocker cover using a new gasket (photo). If the engine is in the car refit the disconnected components using the reverse of the removal sequence.

47.2 Throttle linkage return spring attachment on rocker cover

47.6 Adjusting the valve clearances

47.7 Refit the rocker cover using a new gasket

Fault diagnosis overleaf

48 Fault diagnosis – engine

Symptom	Reason(s)
Engine fails to start	Discharged battery
	Loose battery connection
	Loose or broken ignition leads
	Moisture on spark plugs, distributor cap, or HT leads
	Incorrect spark plug gaps
	Cracked distributor cap or rotor
	Other ignition system fault
	Dirt or water in carburettor
	Empty fuel tank
	Faulty fuel pump
	Other fuel system fault
	Faulty starter motor
	Low cylinder compressions
Engine idles erratically	Inlet manifold air leak
	Leaking system head gasket
	Worn rocker arms, timing chain or sprockets
	Worn camshaft lobes
	Faulty fuel pump
	Incorrect valve clearances
	Loose crankcase ventilation hoses
	Carburettor adjustment incorrect
	Uneven cylinder compressions
Engine misfires	Spark plugs worn or incorrectly gapped
	Dirt or water in carburettor
	Carburettor adjustment incorrect
	Burnt out valve
	Leaking cylinder head gasket
	Distributor cap cracked
	Incorrect valve clearances
	Uneven cylinder compressions
	Worn carburettor
Engine stalls	Carburettor adjustment incorrect
	Inlet manifold air leak
	Ignition timing incorrect
Excessive oil consumption	Worn pistons, cylinder bores or piston rings
	Valve guides and valve stems worn
	Oil leaking from rocker cover, timing cover, engine gaskets or oil seals
Engine backfires	Carburettor adjustment incorrect
	Ignition timing incorrect
	Incorrect valve clearances
	Inlet manifold air leak
	Sticking valve

Chapter 2 Cooling system

For modifications, and information applicable to later models, see Supplement at end of manual

Contents

Specifications

System type .... Pressurised with belt-driven pump, front-mounted crossflow radiator with expansion tank, electric cooling fan, and thermostat

Thermostat opening temperature .... 83°C or 86°C (181°F or 187°F) depending on model

Water pump/alternator drivebelt tension .... 4 mm (0.16 in)

Coolant type .... Ethylene glycol based antifreeze (Duckhams Universal Antifreeze and Summer Coolant)

System capacity (total) .... 5.5 litre (9.7 Imp pint)

1 General description

The cooling system is of the pressurised type consisting of a belt-driven pump, aluminium crossflow radiator, expansion tank, electric cooling fan and a thermostat located in the radiator top hose.

The system functions as follows: Cold coolant in the bottom of the radiator right-hand tank passes through the bottom hose to the water pump where it is pumped around the cylinder block and head passages. After cooling the cylinder bores, combustion surfaces and valve seats, the coolant reaches the underside of the thermostat, which is initially closed, and is diverted through passages in the water pump to the heater and carburettor hose outlets. After passing through the heater matrix and through passages in the carburettor body, the coolant is returned to the water pump. When the engine is cold the thermostat remains closed and the coolant circulates only through the engine, heater and carburettor. When the coolant reaches a predetermined temperature, the thermostat opens and the coolant passes through the top hose and back to the radiator. As the coolant circulates through the radiator it is cooled by the inrush of air when the car is in forward motion. Airflow is supplemented by the action of the electric cooling fan when necessary. Upon reaching the bottom right-hand side of the radiator, the coolant is now cooled and the cycle is repeated.

When the engine is at normal operating temperature the coolant expands and some of it is displaced into the expansion tank. This coolant collects in the tank and is returned to the radiator when the system cools.

The electric cooling fan mounted behind the radiator is controlled by a thermostatic switch located in the radiator side tank. At a predetermined coolant temperature the switch contacts close, thus actuating the fan.

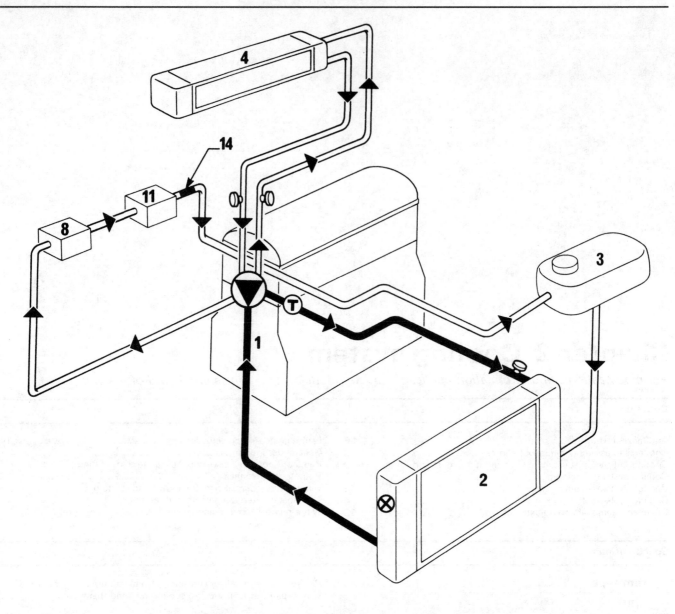

Fig. 2.1 Diagram of cooling system on Turbo models (Sec 1)

1	Engine	3	Expansion tank (constant	4	Heater matrix	11	Carburettor base

1   Engine
2   Radiator
3   Expansion tank (constant
     flow type on Turbo models
     only)
4   Heater matrix
8   Inlet manifold
11 Carburettor base
14 3.5 mm jet
T = Thermostat in top hose

2   Routine maintenance

At the intervals specified in the Routine Maintenance section in the front of the manual carry out the following procedures.
1   With the engine and coolant cold, check the level in the system and if necessary top up to the maximum mark on the expansion tank (photo). With a sealed type cooling system, topping-up should only be necessary at very infrequent intervals. If this is not the case and frequent topping-up is required, it is likely there is a leak in the system. Check all hoses and joint faces for any straining or actual wetness, and rectify if necessary. If no leaks can be found it is advisable to have the system pressure tested as the leak could possibly be internal. It is a good idea to keep a check on the engine oil level as a serious internal leak can often cause the level in the sump to rise, thus confirming suspicions.
2   Carefully inspect all the hoses, hose clips and visible joint gaskets of the system for cracks, corrosion, deterioration or leakage. Renew

any hoses and clips that are suspect and also renew any gaskets, if necessary.
3   Carefully inspect the condition of the drivebelt and renew it if there is any sign of cracking or fraying, using the procedure described in Section 12. Check and adjust the tension of the belt, as described in the same Section.
4   Drain, flush and refill the cooling system with a new antifreeze mixture as described in Sections 3, 4 and 5.

3   Cooling system – draining

Note: *The hose clips fitted in manufacture are not intended to be re-used. They are released by prising up their tabs (ratchet type) or by unwinding the tensioning key ('sardine can' type). As a last resort they may be cut off, at risk of damaging the hose. Obtain new worm drive* *hose clips before draining the cooling system.*

1   It is preferable to drain the cooling system when the engine is cold. If the engine is hot the pressure in the system must be released before attempting to drain the system. Place a cloth over the pressure cap of the expansion tank and slowly unscrew the cap. Wait until the pressure has escaped and then remove the cap.

2   Raise and support the front of the vehicle. Remove the engine splash shield for access to the bottom of the radiator.

3   Place a suitable container beneath the right-hand side of the radiator. Slacken the hose clip and carefully ease the bottom hose off the radiator outlet. Allow the coolant to drain into the container.

4   Now position the container beneath the cylinder block drain plug located on the crankshaft pulley end of the engine, below the water pump. Unscrew the plug and drain the coolant into the container. (The drain plug may be seen in Chapter 1, photo 6.12.)

5   If the system needs to be flushed after draining, refer to the next Section, otherwise refit the drain plug and secure the bottom hose to the radiator. Use a new hose clip if necessary.

4   Cooling system – flushing

1   With time the cooling system may gradually lose its efficiency as the radiator core becomes choked with rust, scale deposits from the water and other sediment.

2   To flush the system, first drain the coolant, as described in the previous Section.

3   Remove the radiator filler cap, insert a hose through the filler neck and allow water to circulate through the radiator until it runs clear from the bottom outlet. If, after a reasonable period, the water still does not run clear, the radiator should be flushed with a good proprietary cleaning system such as Holts Radflush or Holts Speedflush.

4   To flush the engine and the remainder of the system, disconnect the top hose at the water pump, place a hose in the outlet and allow water to circulate until it runs clear from the bottom hose. Also flush the expansion tank and hoses.

5   In severe cases of contamination the radiator should be reverse-flushed. To do this, first remove it from the car, as described in Section 7, invert it and insert a hose in the bottom outlet. Continue flushing until clear water runs from the top hose outlet.

6   The use of chemical cleaners should only be necessary as a last resort. The regular renewal of corrosion inhibiting antifreeze should prevent severe contamination of the system. Note that as the radiator is of aluminium it is important not to use caustic soda or alkaline compounds to clean it.

5   Cooling system – filling

1   Refit the cylinder block drain plug, radiator bottom hose and any other hoses removed if the system has just been flushed.

2   Unclip the expansion tank from its location and tie it up, as high as the hose will allow, on the open bonnet.

3   Open the bleed screws located on the top hose, heater hose(s) and where applicable the hose to the carburettor (photos).

4   Remove the plug and gasket from the top left-hand side of the

radiator then fill the radiator with the appropriate mixture of water and antifreeze (see Section 6). Refit the gasket and tighten the plug.

5   Fill the rest of the cooling system by pouring the coolant in the expansion tank. Close each bleed screw in turn as soon as a continuous flow of coolant can be seen flowing from it. Fill the expansion tank to the maximum mark (MAXI) then fit the pressure cap.

6   Refit the expansion tank in its correct location.

7   Run the engine at 1500 rpm (ie a fast idle speed) until it reaches the normal operating temperature, then switch it off and allow it to cool.

8   With the engine cold check the level in the expansion tank and if necessary top it up to the MAXI mark.

6   Antifreeze mixture

1   The antifreeze should be renewed at regular intervals. This is necessary not only to maintain the antifreeze properties, but also to prevent corrosion which would otherwise occur as the corrosion inhibitors become progressively less effective.

2   Always use a good quality ethylene glycol based antifreeze which is suitable for use in mixed cooling systems.

3   Before adding fresh antifreeze the cooling system should be completely drained, preferably flushed, and all hoses checked for security and condition.

4   Follow the antifreeze manufacturer's recommendations as to concentration, but generally a 50% solution of antifreeze will give protection down to $-40°C$ ($-40°F$) and a 33% solution will give protection down to $-20°C$ ($-4°F$). Do not allow the concentration of antifreeze in the system to fall below 25% regardless of the temperature or time of year.

5   After filling with antifreeze, a label should be attached to the radiator stating the type and concentration of antifreeze used and the date installed. Any subsequent topping-up should be made with the same type and concentration of antifreeze.

6   **Do not** use engine antifreeze in the screen washer system as it will cause damage to the vehicle paintwork. Screen washer antifreeze is available from most accessory shops.

7   Radiator – removal, inspection, cleaning and refitting

1   Disconnect the battery negative terminal and then drain the cooling system, as described in Section 3.

2   Slacken the hose clip and detach the top hose from the radiator.

3   Release the retaining clip and detach the expansion tank hose from the outlet beneath the filler cap.

4   Disconnect the two wires from the thermostatic switch on the right-hand side of the radiator (photo).

5   Disconnect the cooling fan wires at the two-pin connector (photo). Where fitted, unscrew the transmission oil cooler unions.

6   Lift up the large wire retaining clip at the top, move the radiator towards the engine and lift it upwards to disengage the two lower retaining pegs (photos). Withdraw the radiator, complete with cooling fan assembly, from the engine compartment.

2.1 Topping-up coolant level

5.3A Bleed screw located in the top hose

5.3B Bleed screws located in the heater hoses

7.4 Wiring on the radiator thermostatic switch

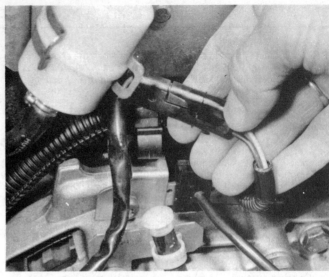

7.5 Cooling fan wiring connector

7.6A Radiator top retaining clip

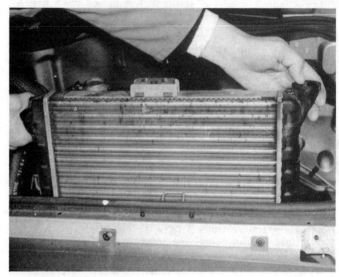

7.6B Removing the radiator

7.6C Radiator lower retaining peg

7.6D Location grommet for the radiator lower retaining peg

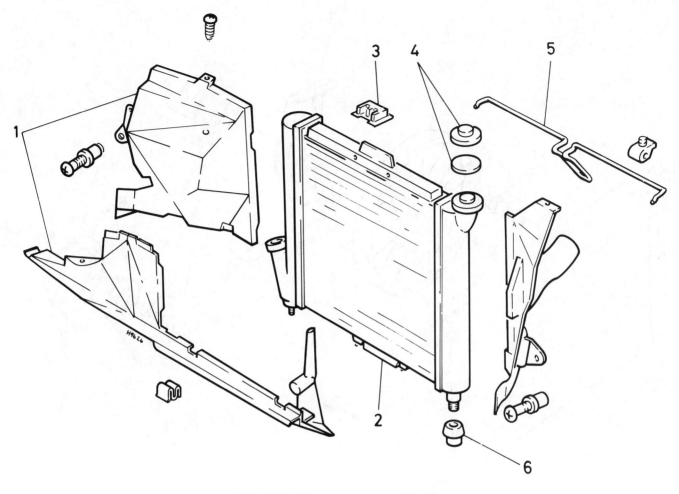

Fig. 2.2 Radiator components (Sec 7)

1	Cowling	3	Mounting rubber (upper)	5	Retaining clip
2	Radiator	4	Plug and gasket	6	Mounting rubber (lower)

7   Minor leaks from the radiator can be cured using Holts Radweld. Extensive damage should be repaired by a specialist or the unit exchanged for a new or reconditioned radiator. Clear the radiator matrix of flies and small leaves with a soft brush, or by hosing.

8   If the radiator is to be left out of the car for more than 48 hours, special precautions must be taken to prevent the brazing flux used during manufacture from reacting with the chloride elements remaining from the coolant. This reaction could cause the aluminium core to oxidize causing leakage. To prevent this, either flush the radiator thoroughly with clean water, dry with compressed air and seal all outlets, or refill the radiator with coolant and temporarily plug all outlets.

9   Refitting the radiator is the reverse sequence to removal. Fill the cooling system, as described in Section 5, and on automatic transmission models top up the fluid, as described in Chapter 6.

8   Cooling fan assembly – removal and refitting

1   Remove the radiator as described in Section 7.

2   According to model the fan assembly bracket is either bolted or riveted to the radiator (photo). In the latter case the rivets must be drilled out to remove the bracket.

3   Unscrew the nut and slide the fan off the motor shaft noting which way round it is fitted.

8.2 Cooling fan assembly mounting bolts on the radiator

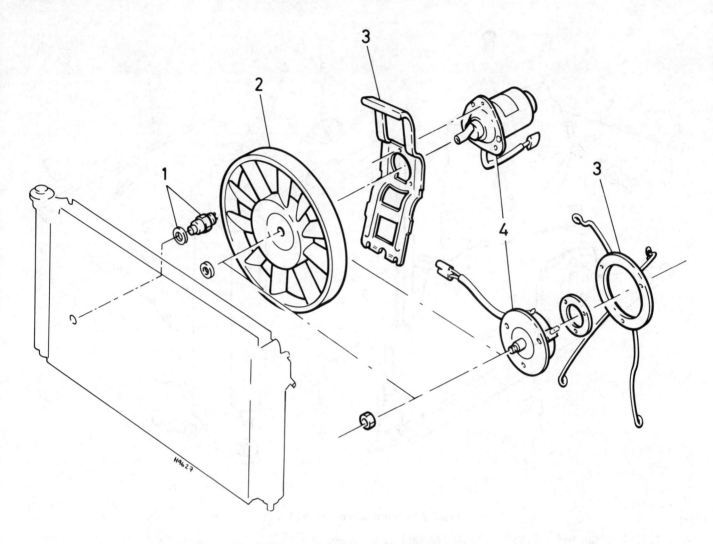

Fig. 2.3 Cooling fan components (Sec 8)

1 *Thermostatic switch and*
   washer
2 *Fan*

3 *Mounting bracket (alternative*
   types)
4 *Motor (alternative types)*

4 Separate the motor from the bracket by drilling out the rivets.
5 If the motor is faulty it must be renewed as it is not possible to obtain spare parts.
6 Refitting is a reversal of removal using new rivets where required.

9 Cooling fan thermostatic switch – testing, removal and refitting

1 If the thermostatic switch, located on the right-hand side of the radiator, develops a fault it is most likely to fail open circuit. This will result in the fan motor remaining stationary even though the coolant may reach boiling point.
2 To test for a faulty thermostatic switch, disconnect the two switch wires and join them together with a suitable length of wire. If the fan now operates with the ignition switched on, the thermostatic switch is proved faulty and must be renewed.
3 To remove the switch, disconnect the battery negative terminal and drain the cooling system, as described in Section 3.
4 Disconnect the two wires and then unscrew the switch from the radiator. Remove the washer (photo).
5 Refitting is the reverse sequence to removal. Refill the cooling system, as described in Section 5, after refitting the switch.

9.4 Cooling fan thermostatic switch

10 Thermostat – removal, testing and refitting

1 The thermostat is located in the end of the radiator top hose at the water pump and is retained by a hose clip (photo).
2 To remove the thermostat, first unscrew the expansion tank filler cap. If the engine is hot, place a cloth over the cap and unscrew it slowly allowing all the pressure to escape before removing the cap completely.
3 Place a suitable container beneath the radiator bottom hose outlet. Disconnect the bottom hose and drain approximately 1 litre (1.76 pints) of the coolant. Reconnect the bottom hose and tighten the clip.
4 Slacken the two clips on the radiator top hose adjacent to the water pump. Detach the hose from the pump outlet and withdraw the thermostat from the hose (photo).
5 To test whether the unit is serviceable, suspend it on a string in a saucepan of cold water together with a thermometer. Heat the water and note the temperature at which the thermostat begins to open. Continue heating the water until the thermostat is fully open and then remove it from the water.

6 The temperature at which the thermostat should start to open is stamped on the unit. If the thermostat does not start to open at the specified temperature, does not fully open in boiling water or does not fully close when removed from the water, then it must be discarded and a new one fitted.
7 Refitting the thermostat is the reverse sequence to removal, but make sure that the thermostat bleed hole is in the slot on the end of the water pump outlet. After fitting, fill the cooling system, with reference to Section 5.

11 Water pump – removal and refitting

Note: *Water pump failure is indicated by water leaking from the gland at the front of the pump, or by rough and noisy operation. This is usually accompanied by excessive play of the pump spindle which can be checked by moving the pulley from side to side. Repair or overhaul of a faulty pump is not possible, as internal parts are not available separately. In the event of failure a replacement pump must be obtained. However if the gasket between the two halves of the water pump is the cause of a leak, it can be renewed.*
1 Disconnect the battery negative terminal and then refer to Section 3 and drain the cooling system.
2 Refer to Section 12 and remove the drivebelt.
3 Undo the bolt securing the alternator adjusting arm to the pump body, remove the bolt and swing the arm clear (photo).
4 Slacken the hose clips and disconnect the hoses from the pump (photos).
5 Disconnect the lead from the coolant temperature switch on top of the pump body (photo).
6 Undo and remove the bolts securing the water pump to the cylinder head. Access to the bolt behind the pulley can be gained by inserting a socket bar through a hole in the pulley (photo).
7 With all the bolts removed, withdraw the pump from the cylinder head (photos). If it is stuck, strike it sharply with a plastic or hide mallet.
8 If necessary unbolt the water pump halves and prise them apart taking care not to damage the mating surfaces (photos).
9 Remove all traces of gasket from the surfaces of the water pump and cylinder head.
10 Refitting is a reversal of removal, but use new gaskets. Adjust the drivebelt tension as described in Section 12, and refill the cooling system as described in Section 5.

10.1 Thermostat retaining clip

10.4 View of the thermostat in the top hose

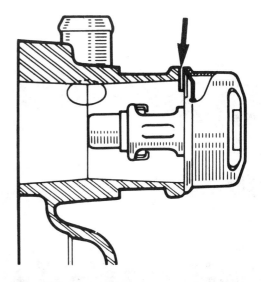

Fig. 2.4 Align the thermostat bleed hole with the pump outlet slot (arrowed) (Sec 10)

11.3 Removing the alternator adjusting arm from the water pump

11.4A Disconnecting the top hose

11.4B Disconnecting the bottom hose

11.4C Heater hoses (1) and carburettor base return hose (2) on the water pump

11.4D Carburettor base feed hose on the water pump

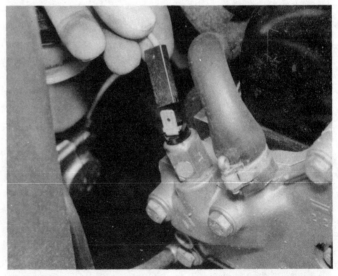

11.5 Disconnecting the lead from the coolant temperature switch

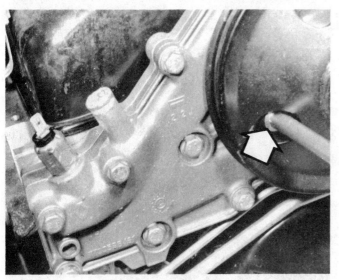

11.6 One of the water pump mounting bolts is located behind the pulley

11.7A Removing the water pump from the cylinder head

11.7B Water pump removed from the engine

11.8A Water pump half securing bolts on the rear of the pump

11.8B The two halves of the water pump separated

12 Drivebelt – renewal and adjustment

1　The drivebelt should be checked and if necessary re-tensioned at regular intervals (see Routine Maintenance). It should be renewed if it shows any signs of fraying or deterioration.
2　To remove the drivebelt, slacken the nuts at the alternator pivot mounting and at the adjustment arm.
3　Move the alternator towards the engine and slip the drivebelt off the three pulleys.
4　Fit the new drivebelt over the pulleys then lever the alternator away from the engine until it is just possible to deflect the belt using moderate finger pressure by 4 mm (0.16 in) at a point midway between the water pump and crankshaft pulleys (photo). The alternator must only be levered at the drive end bracket.
5　Hold the alternator in this position and tighten the adjusting arm bolt and nut followed by the pivot mounting nut.
6　Run the engine for approximately ten minutes and then recheck the tension.

13 Temperature gauge sensor – removal and refitting

1　Unscrew the expansion tank filler cap. If the engine is hot, place a cloth over the cap and unscrew it slowly allowing all the pressure to escape before removing the cap completely.
2　Place a suitable container beneath the radiator bottom hose outlet. Disconnect the bottom hose and drain approximately 1 litre (1.76 pints) of the coolant. Reconnect the hose and tighten the clip.

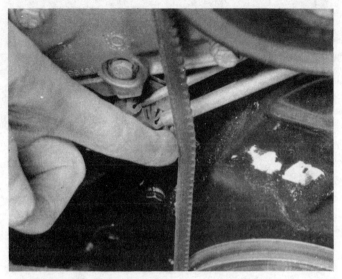

12.4 Checking the drivebelt tension

3　Disconnect the lead at the sensor, located on top of the water pump. Unscrew the sensor from its location.
4　Refitting is the reverse sequence to removal. Fill the cooling system, as described in Section 5, on completion.

14 Fault diagnosis – cooling system

Symptom	Reason(s)
Overheating	Low coolant level (this may be the result of overheating for other reasons)
	Drivebelt slipping or broken
	Radiator blockage (internal or external), or grille restricted
	Thermostat defective
	Ignition timing incorrect
	Carburettor maladjustment
	Faulty cooling fan thermostatic switch
	Faulty cooling fan
	Blown cylinder head gasket (combustion gases in coolant)
	Water pump defective
	Expansion tank pressure cap faulty
	Brakes binding
Overcooling	Thermostat missing, defective or wrong heat range
Water loss – external	Loose hose clips
	Perished or cracked hoses
	Radiator core leaking
	Heater matrix leaking
	Expansion tank pressure cap leaking
	Boiling due to overheating
	Water pump leaking
	Core plug leaking
Water loss – internal	Cylinder head gasket blown
	Cylinder head cracked or warped
	Cylinder block cracked
Corrosion	Infrequent draining and flushing
	Incorrect antifreeze mixture or inappropriate type
	Combustion gases contaminating coolant

Chapter 3 Fuel and exhaust systems

For modifications, and information applicable to later models, see Supplement at end of manual

Contents

Specifications

Part 1: Non-Turbo models

Air cleaner
Type .... Automatic or manual air temperature control with renewable paper element

Application:
   956 cc and 1108 cc .... Champion W191
   1397 cc .... Champion W145

Fuel filter .... Champion L101

Fuel pump .... Mechanical, driven by camshaft

Fuel tank capacity .... 43.0 litre (9.5 Imp gal)

Carburettor
Type .... Single or dual throat downdraught
Application:
   C1C, 956 cc engine .... Zenith 32 IF 2*
   C1E, 1108 cc engine .... Solex 32 BIS* or Zenith 32 IF 2 **
   C1J, 1397 cc engine .... Solex 32 BIS** or Zenith 32 IF 2 ***
   C2J, 1397 cc engine .... Weber 32 DRT

Carburettor data

Zenith 32 IF 2:

	V10508*	V10509**	V10511***
Type identification number:			
Venturi	21	23	24
Main jet	100	122	124
Idling jet	52	54	55
Air compensating jet	90 x 160	80 x 180	90 x 160
Pneumatic enrichment jet	50	80	80
Accelerator pump stroke	27.8 mm (1.10 in)	28.3 mm (1.11 in)	28.3 mm (1.11 in)
Accelerator pump jet	45	45	50
Accelerator pump delivery tube setting	58.0 mm (2.284 in)	6.0 mm (2.362 in)	58.0 mm (2.284 in)
Needle valve	1.25	1.25	1.25
Float height dimension	13.65 mm (0.537 in)	13.65 mm (0.537 in)	13.65 mm (0.537 in)
Auxiliary jet	60	70	110
Auxiliary jet tube setting	6.0 mm (0.236 in)	6.0 mm (0.236 in)	6.0 mm (0.236 in)
Defuming valve setting	2.0 mm (0.079 in)	2.0 mm (0.079 in)	2.0 mm (0.079 in)
Initial throttle opening (fast idle)	0.9 mm (0.035 in)	0.8 mm (0.032 in)	0.85 mm (0.034 in)
Idling speed	700 ± 25 rpm	625 ± 50 rpm	650 ± 25 rpm
CO mixture	1 ± 0.5%	1 ± 0.5%	1 ± 0.5%

Solex 32 BIS:

	836*	849**
Type identification number		
Venturi	23	24
Main jet	110	112.5
Air compensating jet	145	155
Idling jet	42	40
Enrichener	50	60
Needle valve	1.3	1.6
Accelerator pump jet	40	40
Initial throttle opening (fast idle)	0.7 mm (0.028 in)	0.75 mm (0.030 in)
Defuming valve setting	3.0 ± 0.5 mm	3.0 ± 0.5 mm
	(0.118 ± 0.02 in)	(0.118 ± 0.002 in)
Idling speed	625 ± 50 rpm	650 ± 25 rpm
CO mixture	1 ± 0.5%	1 ± 0.5%

Weber 32 DRT

	Primary	Secondary
Venturi	23	24
Main jet	107	105
Air compensating jet	220	135
Idling jet	47	70
Emulsifier	F58	F56
Needle valve	1.75	
Float height dimension	8.0 mm (0.315 in)	
Float travel dimension	13.0 mm (0.512 in)	
Accelerator pump jet	50	
Initial throttle opening (fast idle)	0.75 mm (0.030 in)	
Choke flap pneumatic part opening setting	3.5 mm (0.138 in)	
Defuming valve throttle opening	0.3 mm (0.012 in)	
Idling speed	700 ± 25 rpm	
CO mixture	1.5 ± 0.5%	

Torque wrench settings

	Nm	lbf ft
Exhaust pipe section clamp	40	30
Manifold retaining nuts	30	22
Fuel gauge sender unit ring nut	30	22

Part 2: Turbo models

Air cleaner

Type .... Automatic air temperature control with renewable paper element
Application .... Champion W109

Fuel filter .... Champion L203

Fuel pump

Type .... Electric, roller cell
Delivery .... 60 litre per hour at pressure of 2.5 bar

Fuel tank capacity

Main .... 43.0 litre (9.5 Imp gal)
Auxiliary .... 7.0 litre (1.54 Imp gal)

Fuel pressure regulator pressure at idling .... 275 ± 25 mbar

Anti-percolation thermostatic switch
temperature range .... 95 to 89°C (203 to 192°F)

Turbocharger

Type .... Garret T2
Boost pressure .... 680 ± 30 mbar at 3500 rpm or 700 ± 30 mbar at 5500 rpm

Safety switch operating pressure .... 1100 ± 50 mbar

Carburettor

Type .... Single throat downdraught, sealed
Application:
    C1J (suffix 782), 1397 cc engine .... Solex 32 DIS

Carburettor data

Solex 32 DIS:

	854	931
Type identification number	25	115
Venturi	120	115
Main jet	125	135
Air compensating jet	45	46
Idling jet	100	80
Enrichener	1.7	1.7
Needle valve..	40	40
Accelerator pump jet	5 mm (0.20 in)	5 mm (0.20 in)
Accelerator pump stroke	0.75 mm (0.03 in) or 20°	0.75 mm (0.03 in) or 20°
Initial throttle opening (fast idle)	6.4 mm (0.25 in)	2.7 mm (0.11 in)
Pneumatic part-opening setting	650 ± 50 rpm	700 ± 50 rpm
Idling speed	$1.0 {+0.5 \atop -0}$ %	1.5 ± 0.5%
CO mixture		

Torque wrench settings .... As non-Turbo models

Part 1: Non-turbo models

1 General description

The fuel system consists of a fuel tank mounted under the rear of the car, mechanical fuel pump and a single or dual throat downdraught carburettor.

The mechanical fuel pump is separated by an eccentric on the camshaft and is mounted on the forward facing side of the cylinder block. The air cleaner contains a disposable paper filter element and incorporates a flap valve air temperature control system. This system allows cold air from the air cleaner main intake spout, or warm air from the exhaust manifold stove, to enter the air cleaner via a secondary intake according to the positon of the flap valve. Depending on model, the flap valve may be either manually-controlled by a two position selector on the side of the air cleaner body, or automatically-controlled by a temperature sensitive wax capsule located in the intake spout.

Carburettors may be of Zenith, Solex or Weber manufacture according to model. All types incorporate a water-heated lower body to improve fuel atomization, particularly when the engine is cold. Mixture enrichment for cold starting is by a manually-operated choke control on all models.

The exhaust system consists of three push-fit sections secured with circular clamps. and a cast iron exhaust manifold. A spring-loaded semi ball and socket joint is used to connect the exhaust front pipe section to the manifold and to provide a certain degree of flexibility, thus catering for engine and exhaust system movement. A silencer is fitted to the tailpipe section of all models, with an additional silencer incorporated in the intermediate section of certain versions. The system is suspended throughout its length on rubber block type mountings.

Warning: *Many of the procedures in this Chapter entail the removal of fuel pipes and connections which may result in some fuel spillage. Before carrying out any operation on the fuel system, refer to the precautions given in Safety First! at the beginning of this manual and follow them implicitly. Petrol is a highly dangerous and volatile liquid, and the precautions necessary when handling it cannot be overstressed.*

2 Routine maintenance

At the intervals specified in the Routine Maintenance section in the front of the manual carry out the following procedures.

1 With the car over a pit, raised on a vehicle lift or securely supported on axle stands, carefully inspect the underbody fuel pipes, hoses and unions for chafing, leaks and corrosion. Renew any pipes that are severely pitted with corrosion or in any way damaged. Renew any hoses that show signs of cracking or other deterioration.

2 Check the fuel tank for leaks, for any signs of damage, and the security of the mountings.

3 Check the exhaust system condition, as described in Section 20.

4 From within the engine compartment, check the security of all fuel hose attachments and inspect them for chafing, kinks, leaks or deterioration.

5 Clean the fuel filter in the fuel pump, as described in Section 4, and, where fitted, renew the additional filter in the pump outlet pipe (photo). Ensure that this filter is fitted with the arrows stamped on the filter body pointing in the direction of fuel flow.

2.5 In-line fuel filter in the fuel pump outlet pipe

6 Renew the air cleaner paper filter element, as described in Section 3. On models with a manually-operated air temperature control, set the control or inlet tube to the summer or winter position according to season. On models with automatically-operated air cleaner air temperature control, check the operation of the flap valve, as described in Section 3.

7 Check the operation of the accelerator and choke control linkage and lubricate the linkage, cables and accelerator pedal pivot with a few drops of engine oil.

8 Check the carburettor idle speed and mixture settings and adjust, if necessary, as described in Section 15.

3 Air cleaner and filter element – removal and refitting

1 If a 'throw-away' type air cleaner is fitted (Fig. 3.1), disconnect the inlet duct then release the straps and lift the air cleaner from the carburettor.

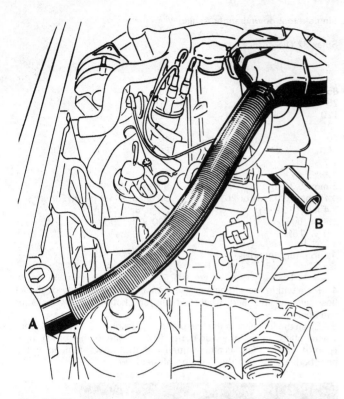

Fig. 3.1 Throw-away type air cleaner and inlet duct (Sec 3)

A Summer position   B Winter position

2 If a conventional air cleaner is fitted, unscrew the wing nut and where applicable release the clips securing the cover. Lift off the cover and remove the filter element (photos).
3 Clean the inside of the air cleaner body and fit a new filter if the old one is dirty or has exceeded its service life (see Routine maintenance). Refit the top cover and secure with the wing nut.
4 To remove the air cleaner body from the engine proceed as follows:

Zenith or Solex carburettor
5 Undo the two nuts securing the air cleaner to the rocker cover and the bolt securing the air cleaner to the left-hand rear support bracket (photos). Note the arrangement of rubber spacer, washers and sleeve under each front mounting nut.
6 Detach the hot air duct from the stove on the exhaust manifold and lift the air cleaner assembly off the engine (photo).

Weber carburettor
7 Remove the air cleaner top cover and filter element, as previously described.
8 Undo the nut securing the air cleaner body to the rocker cover, noting the arrangement of rubber spacer, washers and sleeve under the nut.
9 Undo the three nuts securing the air cleaner body to the top of the carburettor. Detach the hot air duct from the stove on the exhaust manifold, detach the peg on the side of the body from the support bracket and lift up the air cleaner. Disconnect the crankcase ventilation hose and remove the air cleaner from the car. Recover the gasket.

All models
10 If the air cleaner is equipped with an automatic air temperature control device, this may be tested as follows:
11 First remove the air filter element, if still in place, and the hot air duct.
12 Immerse the air cleaner body in water at 26°C (79°F) or less, ensuring that the wax capsule in the intake spout is completely submerged. After 5 minutes observe the position of the flap valve which should be blanking off the cold air intake.

3.2A Unscrew the wing nut ...

3.2B .. release the clips ...

3.2C ... then lift off the cover and remove the filter element

3.5A Air cleaner mounting on the rocker cover

3.5B Unscrew the bolt from the left-hand rear support bracket

3.6 Removing the air cleaner assembly

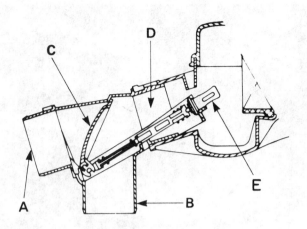

Fig. 3.2 Cross-section of the automatic air temperature control device (Sec 3)

A *Cold air inlet*   D *Mixed air flow*
B *Warm air inlet*   E *Wax thermostatic element*
C *Flap*

3.15 Manually-operated air temperature control on the air cleaner inlet

13 Now repeat the test in water at 36°C (97°F) and after 5 minutes check that the flap is blanking off the hot air intake. If the flap valve does not operate as described at the specified temperatures, the wax capsule control assembly is faulty and must be renewed.
14 After completing the tests, dry off the air cleaner body and refit the hot air duct.
15 Refitting the air cleaner and element is the reverse sequence of removal. On models with a manually-operated air temperature control, set the flap valve to the summer or winter setting (photo), as applicable, after refitting.

4 Fuel pump – testing and cleaning

1 To test the fuel pump on the engine temporarily disconnect the outlet pipe which leads to the carburettor, and hold a wad of rag over the pump outlet while an assistant spins the engine on the starter. *Keep the hands away from the electric cooling fan.* Regular spurts of fuel should be ejected as the engine turns.
2 The pump can also be tested by removing it, but leaving the inlet and return pipes connected. Hold the wad of rag by the pump outlet. Operate the pump lever by hand and if the pump is in a satisfactory condition a strong jet of fuel should be ejected from the pump outlet as the lever is released. If this is not the case, check that fuel will flow from the inlet pipe when it is held below tank level, if so the pump is faulty or the filter blocked.
3 To clean the pump filter, first disconnect the fuel return pipe from the cover.
4 Remove the screws, lift off the cover and withdraw the flat and dome filters (photos). Clean the filters and brush or wipe out any dirt and sediment from the pump interior.
5 Reassemble the components in the reverse order of dismantling, but make sure that the retaining screws are not overtightened. If crimp type retaining clips were used to secure the fuel pipes, these should be replaced by screw type clips when reassembling.

4.4A Removing the fuel pump cover ...

4.4B .. and dome filter

5 Fuel pump – removal and refitting

1 Disconnect the battery negative terminal.
2 Note the location of the fuel inlet, outlet and return pipes then disconnect them from the pump (photo).
3 Unscrew the nut and bolt together with washers and withdraw the fuel pump from the cylinder block (photos).
4 Unscrew the bottom bolt and withdraw the insulating block over the stud (photo).
5 Thoroughly clean the mating faces of the pump and cylinder block then fit a new insulating block and tighten the bottom bolt.
6 Refit the fuel pump and tighten the nut and bolt. Depending on the position of the camshaft some initial pressure may be required to depress the operating lever as the pump is being fitted.
7 Reconnect the fuel pipes to their original positions, as noted during removal. If crimp type retaining clips were used to secure the fuel pipes, these should be replaced by screw type clips.
8 Reconnect the battery negative terminal.

6 Fuel tank – removal, servicing and refitting

1 A drain plug is not provided on the fuel tank and it is therefore preferable to carry out the removal operation when the tank is nearly empty. Before proceeding, disconnect the battery negative terminal and then syphon or hand pump the remaining fuel from the tank.
2 Jack up the rear of the car and securely support it on axle stands. Chock the front wheels.
3 Lift the rear seat cushion and fold it forward then prise out the plastic cover for access to the fuel gauge sender unit.
4 Disconnect the electrical multi-plug and tape it to the rear seat floor.
5 Disconnect the fuel feed and return pipes leaving the vent pipe still attached.
6 Disconnect the handbrake cable from the primary rod adjusting yoke with reference to Chapter 8 and tie the cable to the rear of the car.
7 Unbolt the exhaust downpipe from the manifold with reference to Section 19 then tie it as far forward as it will go on its mountings without damaging them.
8 Disconnect the short length of hose connecting the filler neck to the rear of the fuel tank.
9 Disconnect the tank vent pipes.
10 Take the weight of the tank on a suitable jack with a block of wood interposed. The plastic tank is not heavy so alternatively an assistant could support it.

5.2 Pipe connections on the fuel pump showing flow direction arrows

5.3A Unscrewing the fuel pump mounting nut

5.3B Removing the fuel pump

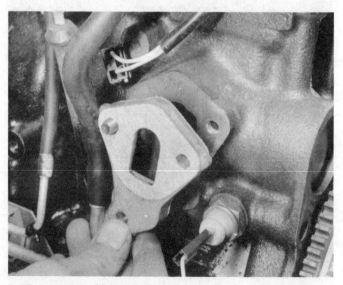

5.4 Removing the fuel pump insulating block

**Fig. 3.3 Fuel tank and filler neck components
(Secs 6 and 7)**

The vent pipe dimension E must be 5.0 mm (0.2 in)

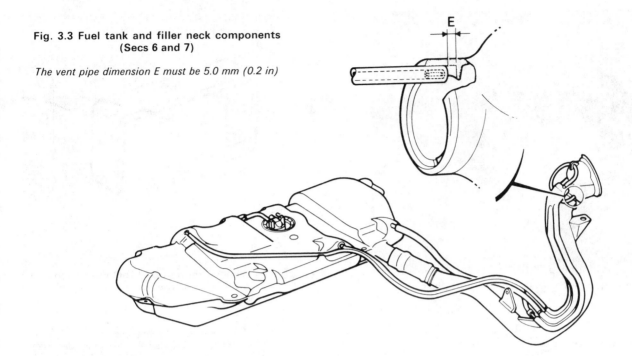

11 Unscrew the mounting bolts and lower the tank from the underbody (photo).

12 If the tank is contaminated with sediment or water, remove the sender unit, as described in Section 8, and swill the tank out with clean fuel. If the tank is damaged, or leaks, it should be repaired by a specialist or, alternatively, renewed.

13 Refitting the tank is the reverse sequence to removal.

7 Fuel tank filler neck – removal and refitting

1 Carry out the procedure described in Section 6 paragraphs 1 and 2. Remove the right-hand rear wheel, the spare wheel and the spare wheel carrier.

2 Disconnect the short length of hose connecting the filler neck to the rear of the fuel tank.

3 Disconnect the tank vent pipes.

4 Open the filler lid and remove the filler cap.

5 Undo the screws and remove the plastic filler head (photo). Disconnect the vent pipes.

6 Remove the mounting bolts and withdraw the filler neck from the car.

7 Refitting is a reversal of removal, but when fitting the vent pipe to the filler head ensure that there is a gap as shown in Fig. 3.3.

8 Fuel gauge sender unit – removal and refitting

1 Disconnect the battery negative terminal.

2 Lift the rear seat cushion and fold it forward then prise out the plastic cover for access to the sender unit (photo).

3 Disconnect the electrical multi-plug and tape it to the rear seat floor.

6.11 Fuel tank mounting bolt

7.5 Plastic filler head

8.2 Fuel gauge sender unit viewed through the access hole

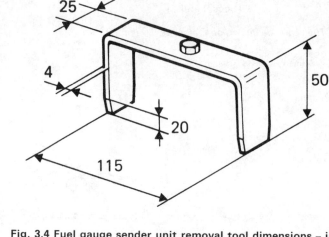

Fig. 3.4 Fuel gauge sender unit removal tool dimensions – in millimetres (Sec 8)

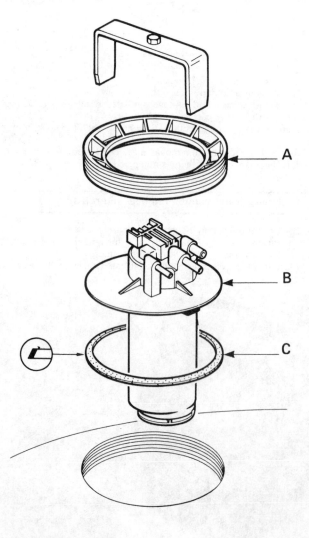

Fig. 3.5 Fuel gauge sender unit components (Sec 8)

A   Ring nut   C   Gasket
B   Sender unit

4   Disconnect the fuel feed, return and vent pipes.
5   Unscrew the plastic ring nut. To do this it is recommended that a removal tool is made to the dimensions shown in Fig. 3.4. Do not use a screwdriver and hammer to loosen the nut otherwise there is a risk of damage to both the nut and the fuel tank.
6   Withdraw the sender unit from the tank followed by the special gasket.
7   Refitting is a reversal of removal, but use a new gasket if the old one is damaged or shows signs of deterioration.

9   Accelerator cable – removal and refitting

1   Remove the air cleaner assembly, as described in Section 3, then disconnect the throttle/cable return spring (photo).
2   From inside the car release the cable end fitting, which is a push fit in the accelerator pedal rod.
3   At the carburettor, for Zenith and Solex types slacken the clamp bolt and remove the outer cable from the bracket then release the inner

9.1 Throttle/cable return spring

cable end fitting from the throttle lever. For the Weber type remove the spring clip from the ferrule (noting its location groove), remove the ferrule from the bracket then release the inner cable end fitting from the bellcrank.

4 According to model, the cable may be secured to a bracket attached to the brake master cylinder or engine compartment bulkhead, or it may be retained by a circlip adjacent to its bulkhead grommet. Disconnect the cable, depending on its method of retention and withdraw it from the car.

5 Refitting the cable is the reverse sequence to removal. Before finally securing the outer cable to the support bracket on the manifold, adjust its position so that there is a small amount of slack in the cable when the throttle is closed.

10 Accelerator pedal – removal and refitting

1 Working inside the car, release the accelerator cable end fitting, which is a push fit in the pedal rod (photo).
2 Undo the bolt securing the pedal assembly to the bulkhead and withdraw it from inside the car.
3 Refitting is the reverse sequence of removal.

11 Choke cable – removal and refitting

1 Disconnect the battery negative terminal.
2 Remove the air cleaner assembly as described in Section 3.
3 Prise out and remove the spring clip securing the outer cable to the bracket on the carburettor (photo).
4 Prise the inner cable spring loop from the choke operating linkage.
5 Remove the screw securing the choke control knob assembly to the facia and withdraw the assembly (photos).
6 Disconnect the warning lamp lead, the inner and outer cable and remove the assembly.
7 Prise out the bulkhead grommet then withdraw the cable into the engine compartment and remove it.
8 Refitting is a reversal of removal, but initially place the control knob in the position shown in Fig. 3.6 then adjust the outer cable at the carburettor end so that the choke valve is fully open. New choke knob assemblies in fact incorporate a temporary limit stop at this position, and, after the cable adjustment, the knob must be pushed right down to break the stop.

10.1 Accelerator pedal and cable end fitting (arrowed)

11.3 Choke cable attachment to the carburettor

11.5A Remove the screw ...

11.5B ... and withdraw the choke control knob assembly

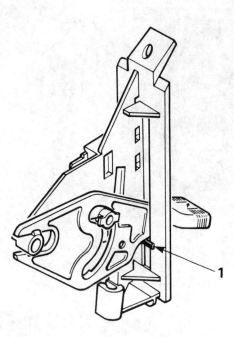

Fig. 3.6 Temporary limit stop (1) fitted to new choke knob assemblies (Sec 11)

12 Zenith carburettor – description and identification

The Zenith 32IF2 carburettor is a single throat downdraught type and is fitted to the C1C 956 cc engine, the C1E 1108 cc engine and the C1J 1397 cc engine (photos). The type identification number is stamped on the float chamber body and reference should be made to this number before consulting the Specifications for repair or adjustment data.

The carburettor functions as follows: Fuel, maintained at a constant level in the float chamber by the float and needle valve, passes through the main jet where it reaches the emulsion tube.

Air is drawn through the air calibration jet to mix with the fuel in the emulsion tube. The vacuum created in the main and secondary venturis, according to engine speed and load, causes this emulsified mixture to be discharged into the airstream through the carburettor.

The calibration of the main and air jets and the shape of the venturi ensures that this emulsified mixture is in the right proportions at all engine speeds.

Under conditions of high engine speed, high engine load or acceleration, additional enrichment is provided by a pneumatic enrichment device and by an accelerator pump. The pneumatic enrichment device senses high manifold vacuum below the throttle valve and opens an additional fuel circuit calibrated by a jet. A tube immersed in the float chamber and also fitted with a jet supplies fuel through the auxiliary jet tube when the vacuum rises above the throttle valve. Movement of the throttle linkage actuates the accelerator pump assembly thgough a series of levers. The pump, consisting of two pistons, springs and two valves, pumps fuel to the delivery tube where it is injected into the airstream.

When the engine is idling, the high manifold vacuum below the throttle valve draws fuel from the float chamber to the idling jet. The fuel is emulsified with air drawn through a calibrated jet and atomized as it is discharged into the airstream below the throttle valve. As the throttle is opened during the progression stage, the mixture is discharged through additional holes. The strength of the mixture is controlled by the mixture adjusting screw.

A manually-operated cold start (choke) control is used to provide the necessary rich mixture from starting. When the choke knob is pulled out the choke flap is closed by the action of the linkage. When the engine is cranking, high vacuum is created below the choke flap and a very rich mixture is discharged. The linkage also opens the throttle valve by a predetermined amount so that the engine will run at a fast idle speed.

13 Solex carburettor – description and identification

The solex 32BIS carburettor is a single throat downdraught type and is fitted to the C1E 1108 cc engine and the C1J 1397 cc engine. The carburettor type identification number is stamped to a plate attached to one of the float chamber retaining screws.

The function of the unit is as follows: Fuel, maintained at a constant level in the float chamber by the float and needle valve, passes through the main jet to the emulsion tube. The fuel is emulsified with air drawn in through the air compensating jet. The vacuum created in the carburettor venturi causes the emulsified mixture to be discharged and atomized by the air passing through the venturi. The calibration of the main and air jets and the shape of the venturi ensures that this emulsified mixture is in the right proportions at all engine speeds.

Under condition of high engine speed, high engine load or acceleration, additional enrichment is provided by a full throttle enrichment device and an accelerator pump. The diaphragm of the full throttle enrichment device moves under the influence of manifold

12.1 Left-hand side view of the Zenith 32 IF 2 carburettor

12.2 Front view of the Zenith 32 IF 2 carburettor

vacuum and spring pressure to open an additional fuel circuit calibrated by a jet. This provides an additional fuel mixture at high engine speed. The accelerator pump is operated by a cam and rod connected to the throttle valve spindle. The necessary rich mixture needed for acceleration is provided by the accelerator pump diaphragm which ejects a stream of neat fuel through the discharge nozzle whenever the throttle is operated.

When the engine is idling, the high manifold vacuum below the throttle valve draws fuel from the float chamber to the idling jet. The fuel is emulsified with air drawn through a calibrated orifice and atomized as it is discharged into the airstream below the throttle valve. The strength of this mixture is controlled by the mixture ajdusting screw. An additional idling circuit is also used, whereby an emulsified mixture of fuel from the auxiliary jet and air from a calibrated orifice are mixed with air from a drilling in the venturi wall. This mixture is regulated by the volume control screw before being discharged below the throttle plate. This circuit allows a fine degree of engine idling speed adjustment via the volume control screw without upsetting the mixture strength to any degree.

A slotted bypass machined in line with the higher edge of the throttle valve is supplied with an emulsified mixture in the same way as the main idling circuit. This provides the correct mixture strength during progression from the idling phase to the main jet phase.

A manually-operated cold start (choke) control is used to provide the necessary rich mixture from starting. When the choke knob is pulled out the choke flap is closed by the action of the linkage. When the engine is cranking, high vacuum is created below the choke flap and a very rich mixture is discharged. The linkage also opens the throttle valve by a predetermined amount so that the engine will run at a fast idle speed.

14 Weber carburettor – description and identification

The Weber 32 DRT carburettor is a dual throat downdraught type and is fitted to the C2J 1397 cc engine. The type identification number is stamped on the carburettor lower flange and reference should be made to this number before consulting the Specifications for repair or adjustment data.

The carburettor functions as follows: During normal running, fuel maintained at a constant level in the float chamber by the float and needle valve passes through the main jet to the emulsion tubes.

Air is drawn through the air calibration jets to mix with the fuel in the emulsion tubes. The vacuum created in the main and secondary venturis, according to engine speed and load causes this emulsified mixture to be discharged into the airstream through the carburettor. The calibration of the main and air jets and the shape of the venturi ensures that this emulsified mixture is in the right proportions at all engine speeds.

Under conditions of high engine speed, high engine load or acceleration, additional enrichment is provided by a pneumatic enrichment device and by an accelerator pump. Under the action of manifold vacuum and spring pressure a diaphragm in the pneumatic enrichment device opens a valve to allow fuel, calibrated by a jet, to enter the main jet circuit to the primary throat. Under full load and at high engine speed, the vacuum created in the venturi of the secondary throat draws an emulsified mixture of fuel and air from the secondary enrichment jets and discharges it into the airstream above the secondary venturi. The accelerator pump is actuated by movement of the throttle valve to inject fuel into the primary throat via a discharge nozzle.

When the engine is idling the high manifold vacuum below the throttle valve draws fuel from the float chamber to the idling jet. The fuel is emulsified with air drawn through a calibrated jet and atomized as it is discharged into the airstream below the throttle valve. As the throttle is opened during the progression stage, the mixture is discharged through additional holes. The strength of the mixture is controlled by the mixture adjusting screw.

A manually-operated cold start (choke) control is used, operating on the primary throat only, to provide the necessary rich mixture for starting. When the choke knob is pulled out, the choke flap is closed by the action of the linkage. With the engine cranking, high vacuum is created below the choke flap and a very rich mixture is discharged. The linkage also opens the primary throat throttle valve by a predetermined amount so that the engine will run at a fast idle, but holds the

secondary throat throttle valve closed while the choke is in operation. A pneumatically-controlled cold start device allows manifold vacuum to act on a diaphragm connected to the choke flap. Under certain conditions this 'override' device alters the position of the choke flap on demand, thus altering the strength of the cold start mixture.

15 Carburettor – idle speed and mixture adjustment

1 The procedure for idle speed and mixture adjustment is the same on each of the three carburettor types that may be fitted. Refer to the accompanying illustrations and identify the carburettor type fitted and the adjustment screw locations. Note that on the Weber carburettor, the mixture adjustment screw is contained in an extension housing attached to the side of the carburettor body and a 200 to 250 mm (7.87 to 9.84 in) long screwdriver will be required to adjust the idle speed screw.

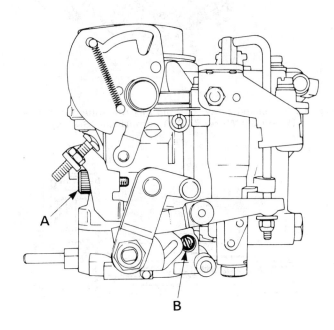

Fig. 3.7 Idle speed screw (A) and mixture adjustment screw (B) on the Zenith 32 IF 2 carburettor (Sec 15)

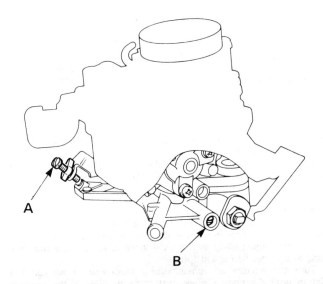

Fig. 3.8 Idle speed screw (A) and mixture adjustment screw (B) on the Solex 32 BIS carburettor (Sec 15)

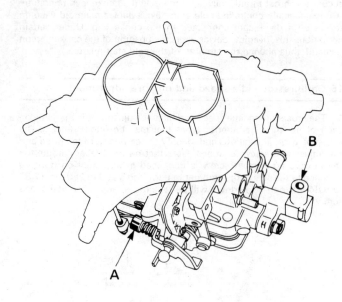

Fig. 3.9 Idle speed screw (A) and mixture adjustment screw (B) on the Weber 32 DRT carburettor (Sec 15)

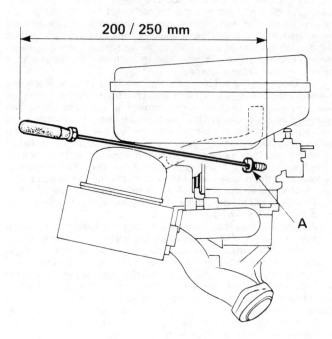

Fig. 3.10 A long screwdriver is required to reach the idle speed screw (A) on the Weber 32 DT carburettor (Sec 15)

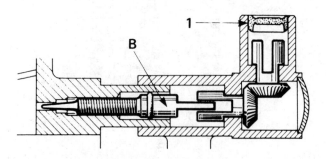

Fig. 3.11 Extension housing on the Weber 32 DRT carburettor for the mixture adjustment screw (B) (Sec 15)

1   Tamperproof cap

2   Before carrying out the following adjustments, ensure that the spark plugs are in good condition and correctly gapped and that, where applicable, the contact breaker points and ignition timing settings are correct.
3   Connect a tachometer to the engine in accordance with the manufacturer's instructions if one is not already fitted to the car. The use of an exhaust gas analyser (CO meter) is also preferable, although not essential. If a CO meter is available this should also be connected in accordance with the maker's recommendations.
4   Before proceeding with the adjustments, remove the tamperproof cap (if fitted) over the mixture adjustment screw by hooking it out with a scriber or small screwdriver.
5   Run the engine unitl it reaches normal operating temperature. Increase the engine speed to 2000 rpm for 30 seconds and repeat this at three minute intervals during the adjustment procedure. This will ensure that any excess fuel is cleared from the inlet manifold.
6   With the engine idling, turn the idle speed screw until the engine is idling at the specified speed (photo).
7   Turn the mixture adjustment screw clockwise to weaken the mixture until the engine screw just starts to drop or the tickover becomes lumpy. Now turn the screw slowly anti-clockwise to richen the mixture until the maximum engine speed is obtained consistent

15.6 Idle speed screw location on the Zenith 32 IF 2 carburettor

with even running. If a CO meter is being used, turn the mixture adjustment screw as necessary to obtain the specified CO content.
8   Return the engine idling speed to the specified setting by means of the idle speed screw.
9   Repeat the above procedure a second time and then switch off the engine and disconnect the instruments.

16 Carburettor – removal and refitting

1   Unscrew the filler cap on the cooling system expansion tank. If the engine is hot, place a rag over the cap and unscrew it slowly, allowing

all the pressure in the system to be released before completely removing the cap.

2   Place a suitable container beneath the radiator bottom hose outlet. Disconnect the hose and drain approximately 1 litre (1.76 pint) of the coolant. Refit the hose and tighten the clip.

3   Refer to Section 3, and remove the air cleaner assembly.

4   On Zenith and Solex carburettors disconnect the accelerator cable with reference to Section 9. On the Weber carburettor prise the accelerator bellcrank rod ball socket off the stud on the carburettor throttle linkage.

5   Disconnect the choke cable from the carburettor with reference to Section 11.

6   Disconnect the fuel inlet pipe from the carburettor and plug the pipe end after removal (photo).

7   Disconnect the crankcase ventilation hose(s) and vacuum pipe(s) (photo).

8   Slacken the clips and remove the coolant hoses from their outlets on the base of the carburettor.

9   Unscrew the mounting nuts, remove the washers and withdraw the carburettor from the inlet manifold. Recover the set of gaskets and where applicable the heat shield from the manifold studs (photos).

16.6 Disconnect the fuel inlet pipe

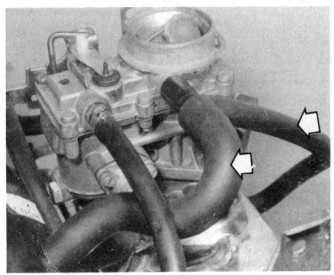

16.7 Crankcase ventilation hose attachment to the Zenith 32 IF 2 carburettor

16.9A Unscrew the mounting nuts and remove the carburettor ...

16.9B ... followed by the set of gaskets ...

16.9C ... and heat shield

10 Refitting is a reversal of removal, bearing in mind the following points:

(a) *Ensure that the mating faces of the carburettor and heat shield are clean and use a new gasket set*

(b) *If crimp type clips were used to secure the coolant or fuel hoses these should be replaced by the screw type clips*

(c) *Adjust the position of the choke and accelerator cables in their support bracket clips to give a small amount of free play at rest, consistent with full travel of the relevant linkage*

(d) *Refill the cooling system, with reference to Chapter 2*

17 Carburettor – overhaul

1 Under normal circumstances, overhaul means removing the fixing screws and separating the main bodies of the carburettor so that the float chamber can be cleaned out and the jets and other passages cleaned with compressed air.

2 If the carburettor has been in service for a high mileage or the throttle spindles and their bushes have become worn, it is recommended that a new carburettor is obtained. It is unlikely that the individual parts will be available to recondition the carburettor yourself, and the cost involved in purchasing a new unit will soon be offset by the increase in fuel economy.

3 When reassembling the carburettor, carry out the following adjustments as work proceeds and use all the new gaskets, seals and other items supplied in the special repair kit for each carburettor.

4 It is necessary to remove the carburettor from the engine to carry out the following adjustments.

Zenith carburettors
Initial throttle opening (fast idle) adjustment
5 Turn the choke operating cam on the side of the carburettor by hand as far as it will go, so that the choke flap is fully closed.
6 A twist drill or suitable rod having a diameter equal to the initial throttle opening setting given in the Specifications, should just slide between the throttle valve and the venturi wall (Fig. 3.13).
7 If adjustment is necessary, slacken the locknut and turn the fast idle adjusting screw to obtain the special setting. Tighten the locknut when adjustment is complete (photo).
Float height adjustment
8 Turn the carburettor top cover upside down.
9 Measure the distance between the upper face of the needle valve body washer and the end of the needle valve (Fig. 3.14). If the measured dimension is greater than specified, tighten the needle valve body to compress the washer until the dimension is correct. If the measured dimension is less than specified, renew the washer and tighten the needle valve body until the correct dimension is obtained.
Auxiliary jet tube (Econostat) setting
10 Measure the distance between the top of the carburettor venturi and the top of the tube (Fig. 3.15).
11 If necessary bend the tube up or down slightly to obtain the specified dimension.
Accelerator pump delivery tube setting
12 Measure the distance between the end of the tube and the bottom of the carburettor mounting flange. If necessary bend the tube slightly to achieve the specified setting.
13 Also make sure that the jet of fuel that flows from the tube strikes the diffuser in the position shown in Fig. 3.16. Again bend the tube slightly as required.

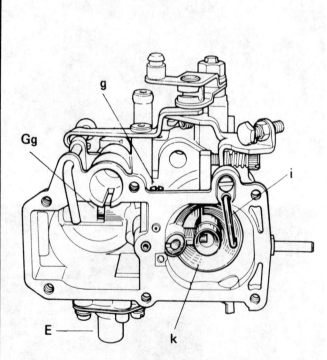

Fig. 3.12 Zenith carburettor overhaul (Sec 17)

E   Pneumatic enrichment device
Gg Main jet
g   Idling jet
i   Accelerator pump jet
k   Venturi

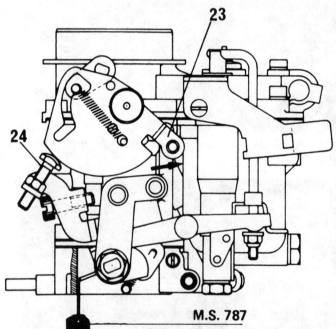

Fig. 3.13 Initial throttle opening adjustment – Zenith carburettor (Sec 17)

M.S. 787 Gauge rod equal to specified initial throttle opening setting

23 Choke operating cam
    fully open
24 Fast idle adjusting
    screw

17.7 Fast idle adjusting screw location on the Zenith 32 IF 2 carburettor

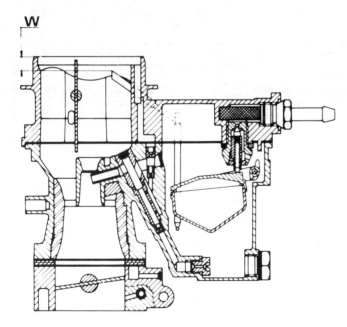

Fig. 3.15 Auxiliary jet tube setting – Zenith carburettor (Sec 17)

W Specified auxiliary jet tube setting dimension

Accelerator pump stroke
14 With the carburettor top cover removed, withdraw the fuel delivery valve.
15 With the choke flap open and the throttle valve fully closed, measure the depth between the delivery valve locating face and the bottom of the piston (Fig. 3.17).
16 Turn the nut on the pump operating rod as necessary to obtain the specified dimension.

Defuming valve adjustment
17 With the throttle valve open in the idling position the defuming valve on the float chamber should also be open by the amount shown in Fig. 3.18. With the choke flap closed, the valve should also be closed and a small amount of free play should exist between the spring blade and the lifting peg. Bend the spring blade as necessary to achieve these conditions.

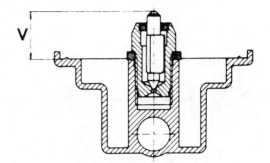

Fig. 3.14 Float height adjustment – Zenith carburettor (Sec 17)

V Specified float height dimension

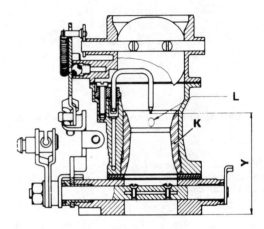

Fig. 3.16 Accelerator pump delivery tube setting – Zenith carburettor (Sec 17)

Y Specified delivery tube height setting
Fuel should strike diffuser (K) in the zone indicated (L)

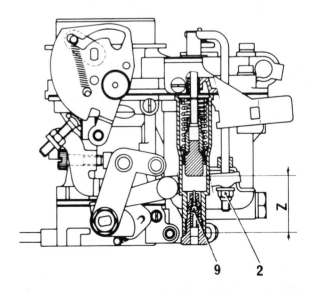

Fig. 3.17 Accelerator pump stroke – Zenith carburettor (Sec 17)

2 Pump operating rod adjusting nut
9 Fuel delivery valve
Z Specified accelerator pump stroke dimension

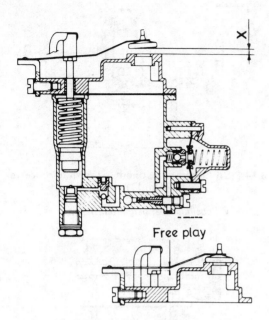

Fig. 3.18 Defuming valve adjustment – Zenith carburettor (Sec 17)

X   Specified defuming valve setting
Lower illustration indicates desired free play between blade and lifting peg with choke flap closed

Pneumatically-controlled cold start device adjustment

18 On certain Zenith carburettors a vacuum diaphragm is used to control the opening of the choke flap when the choke is in operation. Adjustment of the unit is as follows:

19 Move the choke linkage by hand to the fully closed position. A twist drill or suitable rod having a diameter equal to the specified choke flap opening dimension should just fit between the edge of the flap and the venturi wall (Fig. 3.19). Bend the vacuum diaphragm mounting bracket as necessary to achieve the specified dimension.

Solex carburettors
Initial throttle opening (fast idle) adjustment

20 Turn the carburettor upside down and turn the choke linkage by hand as far as it will go, so that the choke flap is fully closed.

21 A twist drill or suitable rod having a diameter equal to the specified initial throttle opening should just slide between the throttle valve and the venturi wall.

22 If adjustment is necessary, remove the tamperproof cap (where fitted) and turn the fast idle adjusting screw as necessary to obtain the specified setting.

Defuming valve adjustment

23 With the choke flap fully open and the throttle valve against the idling stop, the defuming valve should be open by an amount equal to the specified defuming valve stroke. If adjustment is required, bend the defuming valve lever as necessary (Fig. 3.21)

Weber carburettors
Float level adjustment

24 With the float chamber cover held vertically so that the float just closes the fuel needle valve without causing the valve ball to enter the housing, the dimension A in Fig. 3.23 should be as specified. Note that the cover gasket should be in position. Bend the tag of the float arm that contacts the needle valve if adjustment is necessary.

25 Allow the float to hang under its own weight and measure dimension B in Fig. 3.23. Bend the float stop tag as necessary to achieve the specified dimension.

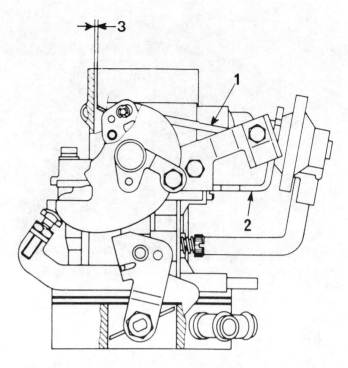

Fig. 3.19 Pneumatic cold start device choke flap opening – Zenith carburettor (Sec 17)

1   Operating rod   3   Specified choke flap
2   Mounting bracket   opening

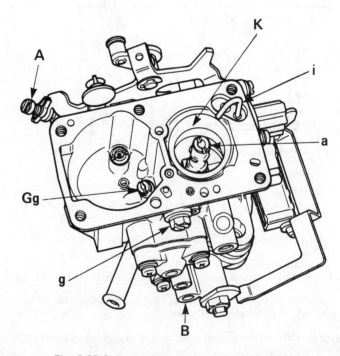

Fig. 3.20 Solex carburettor overhaul (Sec 17)

A   Idle speed screw   g   Idling jet
a   Air compensating jet   K   Venturi
B   Mixture adjustment screw   i   Accelerator pump jet
Gg Main jet

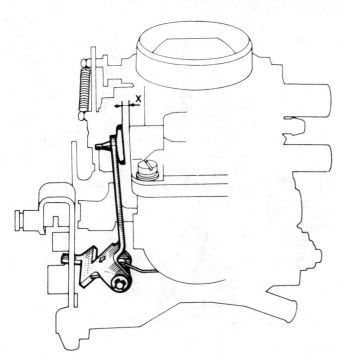

Fig. 3.21 Defuming valve adjustment – Solex carburettor (Sec 17)

X   Specified defuming valve setting

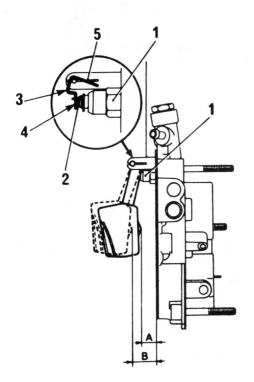

Fig. 3.23 Float level adjustment – Weber carburettor (Sec 17)

1   Needle valve
2   Needle valve ball
3   Float arm tag
4   Float arm tag end must remain at right-angles to the valve ball
5   Float stop tag
A   Specified float height dimension
B   Specified float travel dimension

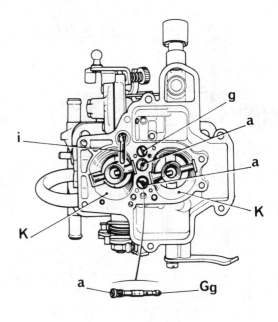

Fig. 3.22 Weber carburettor overhaul (Sec 17)

a   Air compensating jets
Gg Main jet
g   Idling jet
i   Accelerator pump jet
k   Venturis

Initial throttle opening (fast idle) adjustment

26 Turn the carburettor upside down and turn the choke linkage by hand as far as it will go, so that the choke flap is fully closed.

27 A twist drill or suitable rod having a diameter equal to the specified initial throttle opening should just slide between the throttle valve and the venturi wall (Fig. 3.24).

28 If adjustment is required, slacken the locknut and turn the fast idle adjusting screw on the linkage as necessary. Tighten the locknut after adjustment.

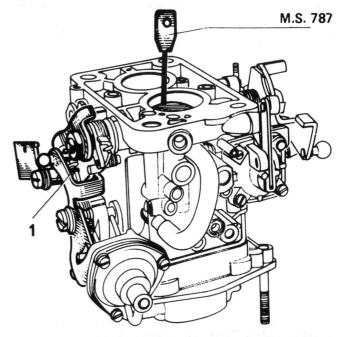

Fig. 3.24 Initial throttle opening adjustment – Weber carburettor (Sec 17)

M.S.787 Gauge rod equal to specified initial throttle opening
1   Fast idle adjusting screw

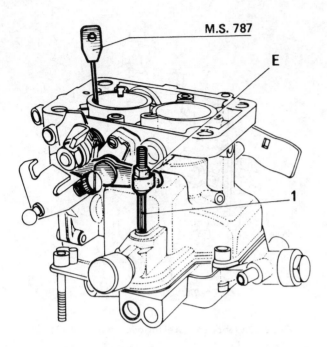

Fig. 3.25 Defuming valve adjustment – Weber carburettor (Sec 17)

M.S.787 Gauge rod equal to the specified defuming valve throttle opening dimension
1   Defuming valve rod
E   Defuming valve rod nut

Defuming valve adjustment

29 With the carburettor upside down and the choke flap open, press the defuming valve rod down as far as it will go (Fig. 3.25).
30 In this position a twist drill or suitable rod have a diameter equal to the specified defuming valve throttle opening should just fit between the throttle valve and venturi wall.
31 Alter the position of the nuts of the defuming valve rod as necessary to achieve the correct setting.

Choke flap pneumatic part open setting

32 Move the choke linkage by hand to the fully closed position and push the operating rod as far as it will go into the vacuum diaphragm unit (Fig. 3.26). In this position a twist drill or suitable rod having a diameter equal to the choke flap pneumatic part open setting should just fit between the choke flap and venturi wall.
33 If adjustment is necessary, turn the small screw in the vacuum unit cover as required.

18 Carburettor – cleaning

Note: *This Section describes dismantling the Zenith carburettor for cleaning of the float chamber and jets. The procedure is basically the same for Solex and Weber carburettors although different components are involved.*

1 Remove the carburettor as described in Section 16 then clean the exterior with paraffin.
2 Using a screwdriver depress the defuming valve rod and swivel the angled lever (from the choke control) away from the top cover. Turn the plastic cap through 90° and remove it from the tip of the defuming valve rod (photos).
3 Undo the top cover retaining screws then lift the cover from the main body (photos). Remove the gasket.
4 Extract the plastic spacer and lift out the float and pivot (photo).
5 Unscrew the plug from the bottom outside of the float chamber then insert a screwdriver and unscrew the main jet (photo).
6 Unscrew the idling jet from the throttle lever side of the carburettor (photo).

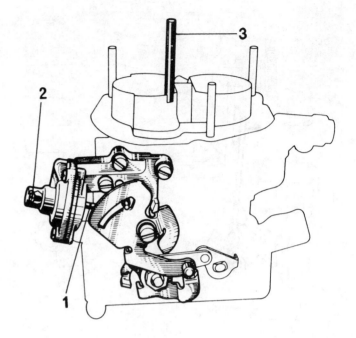

Fig. 3.26 Choke flap pneumatic part opening setting – Weber carburettor (Sec 17)

1   Operating rod
2   Adjuster screw
3   Twist drill equal to the specified choke flap pneumatic part opening setting dimension

7 Unscrew the needle valve from the top cover (photo).
8 Using paraffin or preferably clean fuel, clean all sediment from the float chamber. Clean the main body and top cover then use low air pressure from a tyre pump or air line to clear all internal passages (photo).
9 Reassembly is a reversal of the dismantling procedure using a new gasket, but make all the necessary adjustments as described in Section 17. Refit the carburettor with reference to Section 16.

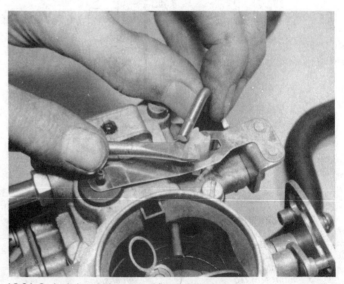

18.2A Swivel the choke control angled lever clear ...

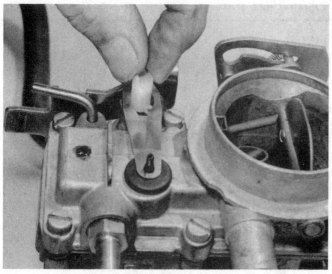

18.2B ... and remove the plastic cap

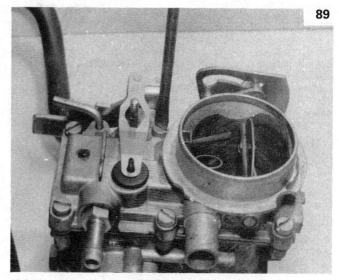

18.3A Undo the retaining screws ...

18.3B ... and lift off the cover

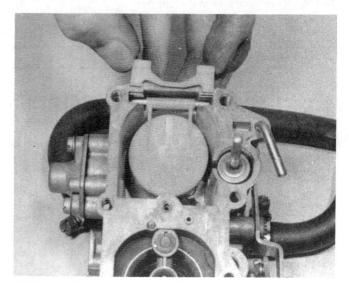

18.4 Extract the plastic spacer and float

18.5 Removing the main jet

18.6 Idling jet location

18.7 Needle valve location in the top cover

18.8 Top view of the main body with cover removed

19 Inlet and exhaust manifolds – removal and refitting

1   Remove the carburettor as described in Section 16.
2   Disconnect the brake servo vacuum hose and the crankcase ventilation hose from the inlet manifold (photos).
3   Remove the starter motor protective shield with reference to Chapter 11.
4   Remove the hot air ducting then unbolt the metal tube and air cleaner support bracket (photo).
5   Unscrew the nut and withdraw the heat shield from the exhaust manifold (photo).
6   Unscrew the two nuts, washers and tension springs securing the exhaust front pipe to the manifold (photo). Slide the flange plate off the manifold studs to separate the joint.
7   Progressively unscrew the nuts securing the manifold assembly to the cylinder head and remove the washers (photos).
8   Withdraw the manifold assembly from the studs on the cylinder head (photo). Remove the gasket.
9   Refitting the manifold assembly is the reverse sequence of removal. Ensure that the cylinder head and manifold mating faces are clean and use a new gasket. Tighten the manifold nuts to the specified torque and tighten the front pipe flange nuts so that the springs are

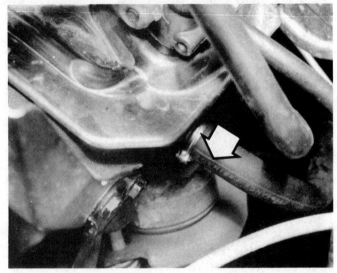

19.2A Brake servo vacuum hose connection to the inlet manifold

19.2B Crankcase ventilation hose connection to the inlet manifold

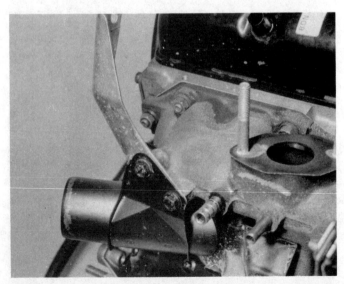

19.4 Hot air tube and air cleaner support bracket

19.5 Removing the heat shield

19.6 Exhaust front pipe to manifold flange plate and tension springs

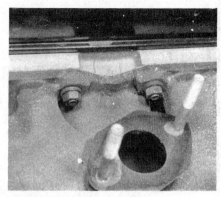

19.7A Manifold upper mounting nuts

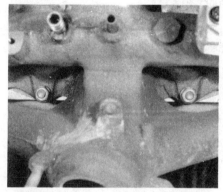

19.7B Manifold centre lower mounting nuts

19.8 Removing the manifold assembly

coil-bound then loosen them by 1$\frac{1}{2}$ turns. Refit the carburettor with reference to Section 16.

20 Exhaust system – checking, removal and refitting

1   The exhaust system should be examined for leaks, damage and security at regular intervals (see Routine Maintenance). To do this, apply the handbrake and allow the engine to idle. Lie down on each side of the car in turn and check the full length of the exhaust system for leaks while an assistant temporarily places a wad of cloth over the end of the tailpipe. If a leak is evident, stop the engine and use a proprietary repair kit, such as Holts Gun Gum or Holts Flexiwrap to

seal it. Holts Flexiwrap is an MOT approved permanent repair. If the leak is excessive, or damage is evident, renew the section. Check the rubber mountings for deterioration, and renew them if necessary.
2   To remove the system, jack up the front and/or the rear of the car and support it securely on axle stands. Alternatively drive the front or rear wheels up on ramps.
3   The system consists of three sections which can be individually removed. If the intermediate section is to be removed it will, however, be necessary to remove the front or rear section also.
4   To remove the rear or intermediate sections of the system, unscrew the retaining clamp nut and bolt and tap the clamp clear of the joint (photos).

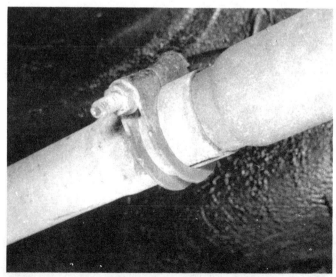

20.4A Exhaust intermediate section to front pipe joint

20.4B Exhaust intermediate section to rear pipe joint

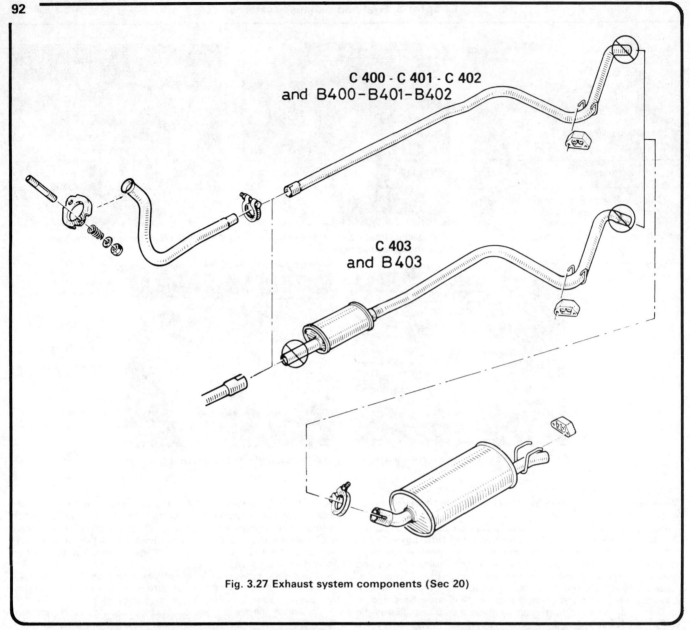

C 400 - C 401 - C 402
and B400 – B401 – B402

C 403
and B403

Fig. 3.27 Exhaust system components (Sec 20)

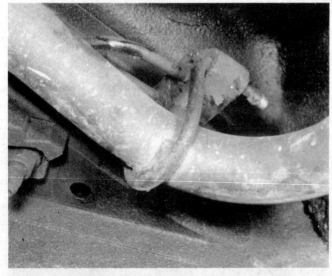

20.5A Exhaust intermediate section mounting

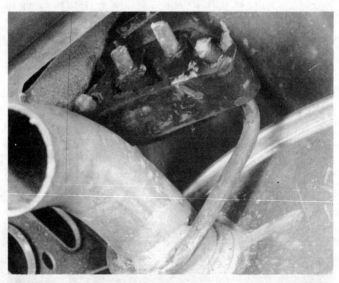

20.5B Exhaust rear section mounting

5   Release the mounting hooks from the rubber mounting blocks and twist the section clear (photos). If the joint is stubborn, liberally apply penetrating oil and leave it to soak. Tap the joint with a hammer and it should now be possible to twist it free. If necessary, carefully heat the joint with a blowlamp to assist removal, but shield the fuel tank, fuel pipes and underbody adequately from heat.

6   To remove the front section, undo the nuts and tension springs securing the front pipe flange to the exhaust manifold. Slide the flange off the manifold studs and separate the joint. Undo the retaining clamp nut and bolt and withdraw the front section forwards, as previously described.

7   Refitting is the reverse sequence to removal. Position the joints so that there is adequate clearance between all parts of the system and the underbody, and ensure that there is equal load on all mounting blocks. Holts Firegum is suitable for the assembly of all exhaust system joints. When refitting the front section tighten the front pipe flange retaining nuts so that the tension springs are coil-bound then loosen them by 1^1/$_2$ turns.

21 Fault diagnosis – fuel and exhaust systems (Part 1)

Unsatisfactory engine performance and excessive fuel consumption are not necessarily the fault of the fuel system or carburettor. In fact they more commonly occur as a result of ignition and timing faults, particularly on models equipped with conventional contact breaker point ignition systems. Before acting on the following it is necessary to check the ignition system first. Even though a fault may lie in the fuel system it will be difficult to trace unless the ignition system is correct. The faults below, therefore, assume that this has been attended to first (where appropriate).

Symptom	Reason(s)
Engine difficult to start when cold	Choke cable incorrectly adjusted Choke flap not closing Insufficient fuel in float chamber
Engine difficult to start when hot	Choke cable incorrectly adjusted Air cleaner element dirty or choked Insufficient fuel in float chamber Float chamber flooding
Engine will not idle or idles erratically	Air cleaner dirty or choked Choke cable incorrectly adjusted Carburettor idling adjustments incorrectly set Blocked carburettor jets or internal passages Disconnected, perished or leaking crankcase ventilation hoses Air leaks at carburettor or manifold joint faces Generally worn carburettor Engine internal defect
Engine performance poor accompanied by hesitation, missing or cutting out	Blocked carburettor jets or internal passages Accelerator pump faulty or diaphragm punctured Float level low Fuel filter choked Fuel pump faulty or delivery pressure low Fuel tank vent blocked Fuel pipes restricted Air leaks at carburettor or manifold joint faces Engine internal components worn or out of adjustment
Fuel consumption excessive	Choke cable incorrectly adjusted or linkage sticking Air cleaner dirty or choked Fuel leaking from carburettor, fuel pump, fuel tank or fuel pipes Float chamber flooding
Excessive noise or fumes from exhaust system	Leaking pipe or manifold joints Leaking, corroded or damaged silencers or pipe System in contact with body or suspension due to broken mounting

Part 2: Turbo models

22 General description and precautions

The fuel system consists of a main and auxiliary fuel tank mounted under the rear of the car, electric fuel pump and canister type fuel filter also mounted at the rear, fuel pressure regulator and sealed carburettor.

The inlet system consists of a thermostatically controlled air cleaner, turbocharger and an air-to-air intercooler.

The turbocharger consists of two turbines mounted on a single shaft. One turbine is driven by the flow of exhaust gases from the exhaust manifold and this turns the turbine in the inlet system forcing air into the engine under pressure. The system is controlled by a vacuum capsule operating a bypass (or wastegate) for the exhaust turbine.

The intake air is maintained at constant temperature by the intercooler which functions like a conventional radiator, but with the intake air passing through it instead of water.

Since the intake air pressure varies according to the speed of the turbocharger turbines, the fuel pressure within the carburettor must also be varied. This requirement is controlled by the pressure regulator located in the carburettor supply line. The unit incorporates a spring tensioned diaphragm subject to intake air pressure on one side and fuel pressure on the other. Under full load conditions the boost pressure forces the diaphragm valve against the fuel return outlet which effectively causes the fuel pressure to rise.

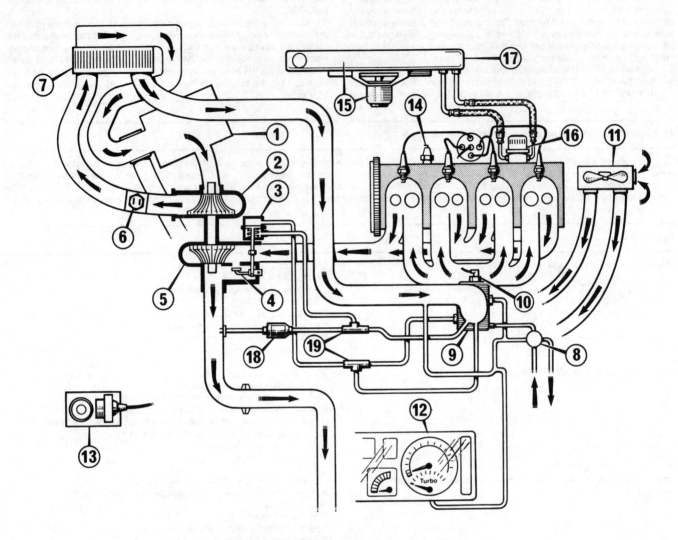

Fig. 3.28 Diagram of Turbocharging system (Sec 22)

1 Air filter with 26°-32°C
   thermostatic flap
2 Compressor
3 Pressure regulator capsule
4 Exhaust gas bypass valve
   (wastegate)

5 Turbine
6 Safety pressure switch
7 Air-cooler with 43°-47°C
   thermostatic flap
8 Fuel pressure regulator
9 Blown carburettor

10 Anti-percolation system
    temperature switch
11 Anti-percolation fan motor
12 Pressure gauge on
    instrument panel
13 Electronic ignition system
    module

14 Pinking detector
15 Radiator and cooling fan
16 Oil filter
17 Oil-water cooler
18 Non-return valve
19 T-piece unions

The turbocharger turbines rotate at very high speeds and, in order
to prevent damage to the bearings through lack of oil, the engine
should always be allowed to idle for approximately 30 seconds before
switching it off.

If a fault develops in the turbocharger wastegate control system it
should be checked by a Renault dealer since special calibration
equipment is required which is not normally available to the home
mechanic.

A four section exhaust system is fitted with rubber block type
mountings.

Observe the warning given in Part 1, Section 1.

23 Routine maintenance

*At the intervals specified in the Routine Maintenance section in the
front of the manual carry out the following procedures*
1 Check the condition and security of all intake hoses, turbocharger

control hoses, crankcase ventilation hoses, vacuum/pressure hoses
and fuel hoses.
2 Renew the fuel filter as described in Section 28.

24 Air cleaner and filter element – removal and refitting

1 Release the strap securing the air cleaner to the left-hand side of
the engine compartment and lift out leaving the hoses still connected.
2 Release the clips and separate the cover from the main body then
remove the filter element.
3 Clean the inside of the air cleaner body and fit a new filter element if
the old one is dirty or has exceeded its service life.
4 Refit the cover then secure the unit to the bracket with the strap,
making sure that the location peg on the bottom engages the grommet.
5 To remove the main body first remove the filter element as
previously described then disconnect the three ducts for the cold air
inlet, hot air shroud and turbocharger.

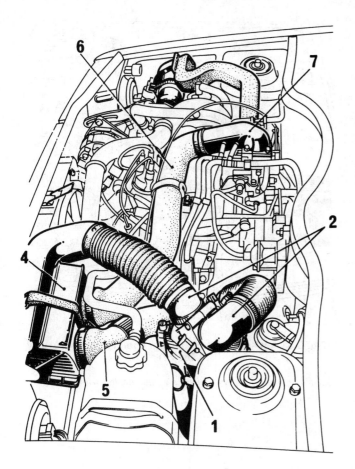

Fig. 3.29 Air intake system (Sec 22)

1 *Air cleaner*
2 *Cold and hot air supplies to air cleaner*
4 *Intercooler*

5 *Turbocharger-to-intercooler hose*
6 *Intercooler-to-carburettor hose*
7 *Carburettor inlet elbow*

6   The automatic air temperature control device within the air cleaner cover may be checked using the procedure given in Part 1, Section 3 paragraphs 12 and 13 however the operating temperatures are 26°C (79°F) and 32°C (90°F).
7   Refitting of the air cleaner main body is a reversal of removal.

25 Intercooler – removal, testing and refitting

1   Disconnect the inlet and outlet hoses from the intercooler, then release the strap and lift the unit from its location at the front left-hand side of the engine compartment.
2   Clean any debris from the matrix by hosing or using an air line.
3   A thermostatic capsule is fitted in the intercooler outlet its purpose being to prevent further cooling of incoming air which is less than 43 ± 2°C (109 ± 4°F). It does this by activating an internal flap between the unit inlet and outlet. To check the operation of the capsule immerse it in water at 43 ± 2°C (109 ± 4°F). After five minutes the internal flap should open the direct passage between the inlet and outlet.
4   Repeat the test in water at 47 ± 2°C (117 ± 2°F). After five minutes the flap should close the direct passage between the inlet and outlet so that the flow of air is through the intercooler matrix. If the flap does not operate correctly renew the intercooler complete.
5   Refitting is a reversal of removal, but make sure that the hoses are fitted correctly as they form part of the boost pressure circuit. The hoses must be clean and dry before refitting.

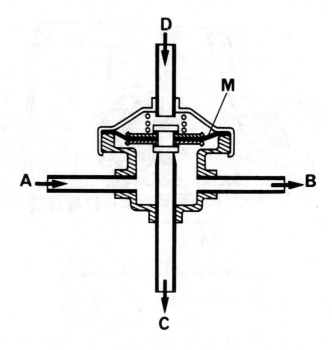

Fig. 3.30 Cross-section of the pressure regulator (Sec 22)

A *Fuel inlet from pump*
B *Fuel outlet to carburettor*
C *Fuel return to tank*

D *Air inlet pressure*
M *Diaphragm*

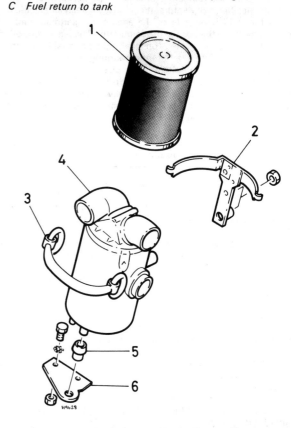

Fig. 3.31 Air cleaner components (Sec 24)

1 *Element*
2 *Bracket*
3 *Strap*

4 *Air cleaner body*
5 *Grommet*
6 *Bracket*

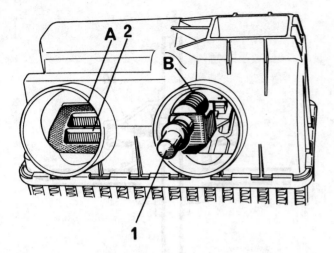

Fig. 3.32 Intercooler header tank (Sec 25)

1 *Thermostatic capsule*   A *Inlet*
2 *Flap*   B *Outlet*

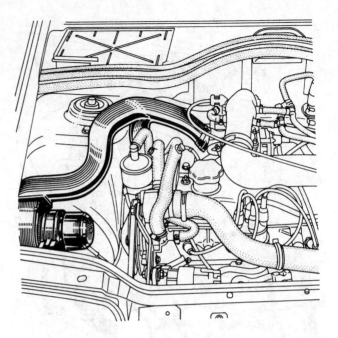

Fig. 3.33 Anti-percolation system cooling fan and hose (Sec 26)

Cut-away section shows fuel supply pipe located within the hose

26 Anti-percolation system – description

The anti-percolation system is provided to maintain the carburettor and fuel pressure regulator together with associated hoses at a constant specified temperature. It comprises a fresh air electric cooling fan on the right-hand side of the engine compartment and a hose directing the air to the base of the carburettor. The fan is controlled by a thermostatic switch located on the right-hand side of the inlet manifold just below the carburettor mounting flange.

The anti-percolation system is energised at all times regardless of whether the ignition is switched on or off, therefore it is important to disconnect the battery negative terminal when working on or near the components. The cooling fan will normally operate approximately 10 minutes after the engine is switched off.

27 Turbocharger – removal and refitting

1 Disconnect the battery negative terminal.
2 Remove the air cleaner as described in Section 24.
3 Disconnect the inlet and outlet hoses from the turbocharger and the air cleaner cold air supply from the intake at the front of the engine compartment.
4 Disconnect the wiring from the engine safety pressure switch located in the turbocharger outlet hose, then disconnect the hose from the intercooler and remove it.
5 Remove the electronic ignition computer module from the bulkhead as described in Chapter 4.
6 Remove the non-return valve and bracket and disconnect the hoses.
7 Unscrew the mounting bolts and withdraw the hot air shroud from the exhaust manifold. Recover the washers, spacer and mounting components.
8 Unscrew the two bolts from the flange securing the angled exhaust pipe to the turbocharger outlet.
9 Unscrew the union nut and disconnect the oil inlet pipe from the top of the turbocharger. Loosen the clip and disconnect the oil return pipe from the bottom of the unit. Plug the pipes and holes to prevent entry of dirt.
10 Identify the location of the pipes on the wastegate regulator capsule then disconnect them.
11 Unscrew the nuts securing the turbocharger to the end of the exhaust manifold then withdraw it from the car. Do not however lift it by the wastegate operating rod. As some of the mounting nuts are difficult to reach a thin spanner is required.

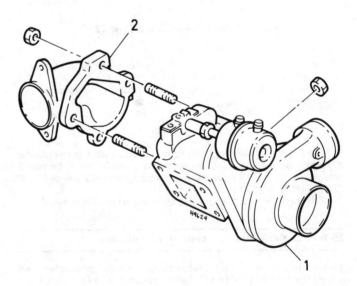

Fig. 3.34 Turbocharger (1) and exhaust outlet elbow (2) (Sec 27)

12 Clean the mating faces of the turbocharger and exhaust manifold before refitting the unit using a reversal of the removal procedure. However before starting the engine it is most important to prime the oil circuit, otherwise the turbine bearings may be damaged. To do this, temporarily disconnect the centre plug from the top of the electronic ignition computer module (Fig. 3.35) and spin the engine on the starter motor until the oil pressure light is extinguished. Reconnect the plug then start the engine and let it idle for several minutes.

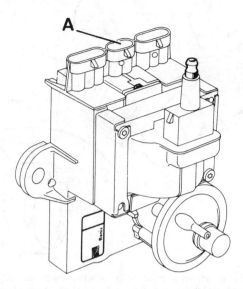

Fig. 3.35 Disconnect plug (A) on the electronic ignition computer module when priming the turbocharger (Sec 27)

28 Fuel filter – renewal

1 Chock the front wheels then jack up the rear of the car and support on axle stands.
2 The filter is located on the right-hand rear crossmember in front of the fuel pump. First clamp the inlet and outlet hoses.
3 Loosen the clips and disconnect the hoses then pull the filter from its spring clip mounting.
4 Fit the new filter using a reversal of the removal procedure, but make sure that the arrow on the unit faces the hose which leads to the fuel pressure regulator and carburettor.

29 Fuel pump – removal and refitting

1 Chock the front wheels then jack up the rear of the car and support on axle stands.
2 The fuel pump is located on the right-hand rear crossmember. First clamp the inlet and outlet hoses.

3 Disconnect the battery negative terminal.
4 Disconnect the wiring from the fuel pump.
5 Disconnect the hoses then unscrew the clamp bolt, lift and unhook the clamp, and withdraw the fuel pump.
6 Refitting is a reversal of removal.

30 Auxiliary fuel pump – removal and refitting

1 Chock the front wheels then jack up the rear of the car and support on axle stands.
2 The auxiliary fuel pump is located on the front of the auxiliary fuel tank. First clamp the inlet and outlet hoses.
3 Disconnect the battery negative terminal.
4 Disconnect the wiring from the fuel pump.
5 Disconnect the hoses then detach the pump from the mounting clip.
6 Refitting is a reversal of removal, but ensure that the pump is located correctly in the notch.

31 Fuel pressure regulator – removal and refitting

1 Apply the handbrake then jack up the front of the car and support on axle stands.
2 The fuel pressure regulator is located on the right-hand front sidemember above the steering gear. First clamp the fuel inlet, outlet and return hoses.
3 Disconnect the fuel hoses and the boost pressure hose then detach the regulator from the bracket by unscrewing the nut.
4 Refitting is a reversal of removal.

32 Fuel tanks – removal, servicing and refitting

Note: *The removal, servicing and refitting of the main and auxiliary fuel tanks follows closely the procedure for the fuel tank and filler neck given in Part 1, Sections 6 and 7. This Section therefore only outlines the additional work necessary.*

Fig. 3.37 Fuel pressure regulator location (Sec 31)

A   Fuel inlet from pump   C   Fuel outlet to carburettor
B   Fuel return to tank   D   Air inlet pressure

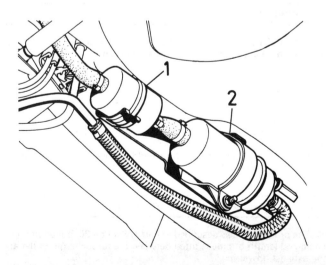

Fig. 3.36 Fuel filter (1) and fuel pump (2) (Sec 28)

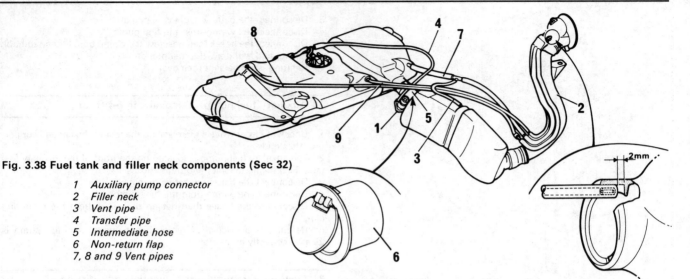

Fig. 3.38 Fuel tank and filler neck components (Sec 32)

    1   Auxiliary pump connector
    2   Filler neck
    3   Vent pipe
    4   Transfer pipe
    5   Intermediate hose
    6   Non-return flap
    7, 8 and 9 Vent pipes

Main fuel tank

1   Remove the fuel filter (Section 28) and the fuel pump (Section 29), then unbolt and remove the fuel pump mounting bracket.
2   Disconnect the fuel transfer pipe from the front of the tank.
3   Refitting is a reversal of removal with reference also to Sections 28 and 29.

Auxiliary tank and filler neck

4   Disconnect the wiring from the auxiliary fuel pump.
5   Disconnect the short length of hose connecting the filler neck to the fuel tank.
6   Disconnect the additional vent pipe and the fuel transfer pipe.
7   Unscrew the nut from the mounting strap then pull open the strap sufficiently to withdraw the auxiliary fuel tank.
8   Refitting is a reversal of removal, but if the non-return flap is removed from the front of the tank make sure it is refitted with the notch uppermost. When refitting the vent pipe to the filler head ensure that there is a gap as shown in Fig. 3.38.

33 Fuel gauge sender unit – removal and refitting

Refer to Part 1, Section 8.

34 Accelerator cable – removal and refitting

The procedure is similar to that described in Part 1, Section 9, however there is no need to remove the air cleaner. A ball and socket arrangement is used to connect the cable to the throttle lever on the carburettor.

35 Accelerator pedal – removal and refitting

Refer to Part 1, Section 10.

36 Choke cable – removal and refitting

The procedure is similar to that described in Part 1, Section 11, however there is no need to remove the air cleaner. The inner cable is attached to the linkage on the carburettor by a pivoting clamp bolt

37 Solex carburettor – description

The Solex 32 DIS carburettor is a single throat downdraught type. It is located downstream of the turbocharger and therefore all its internal circuits are subject to boost pressure when the turbocharger is in operation. As the carburettor operation depends on a fine balance of air pressure and fuel pressure the entire unit must be completely sealed at every joint. To this end the carburettor incorporates a magnesium cover and float chamber, a reinforced cover gasket, strengthened accelerator pump and enrichener diaphragms, and seals for the throttle shaft, idling jet and mixture screw.

Apart from the differences described the carburettor operates conventionally.

38 Carburettor – idle speed and mixture adjustment

The procedure is as described in Part 1, Section 15, but prior to commencing work check that all intake hoses, turbocharger central hoses, crankcase ventilation hoses, vacuum hoses and fuel hoses are secure and in good condition.

39 Carburettor – removal and refitting

The procedure is as described in Part 1, Section 16, but instead of removing the air filter unbolt the intake elbow from the top of the carburettor and remove the O-ring. Refer also to Sections 34 and 36. The anti-percolation duct must be removed when disconnecting the fuel inlet hose.

40 Carburettor – overhaul

1   Refer to Part 1, Section 17 and also Part 2 Specifications. Although there are differences, the procedures are the same.

41 Inlet and exhaust manifolds – removal and refitting

1   Refer to Part 1, Section 19, however the inlet and exhaust manifolds can be removed separately although a one-piece gasket is fitted.
2   Before removing the exhaust manifold remove the turbocharger as described in Section 27.

42 Exhaust system – checking, removal and refitting

1   The procedure is as described in Part 1, Section 20, but additionally an angled length of pipe is fitted between the turbocharger outlet and the exhaust downpipe.
2   When refitting the downpipe flange bolts and tension springs, maintain the dimension shown in Fig. 3.43.

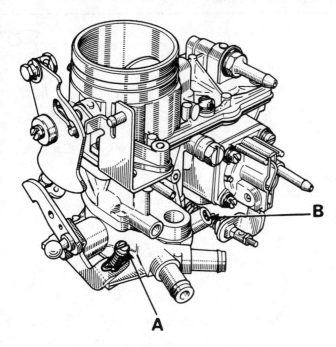

Fig. 3.39 Idle speed screw (A) and mixture adjustment
screw (B) on the Solex 32 DIS carburettor (Sec 38)

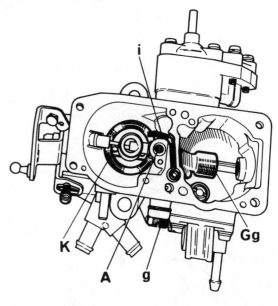

Fig. 3.40 Solex 32 DIS carburettor overhaul (Sec 40)

A   Air compensating jet   Gg Main jet
K   Venturi   i   Accelerator pump jet
g   Idling jet

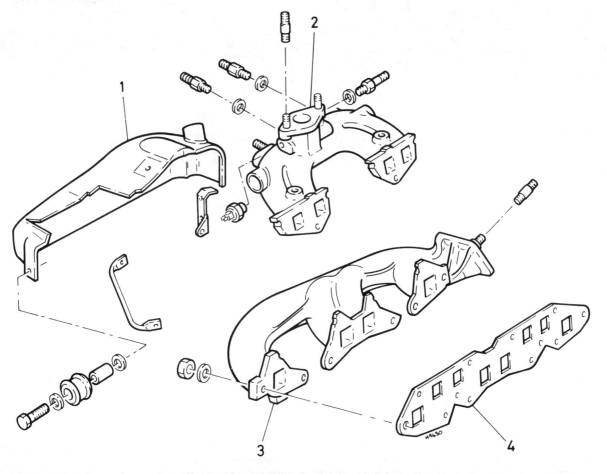

Fig. 3.41 Manifold components (Sec 41)

1   Hot air shroud   2   Inlet manifold   3   Exhaust manifold   4   Gasket

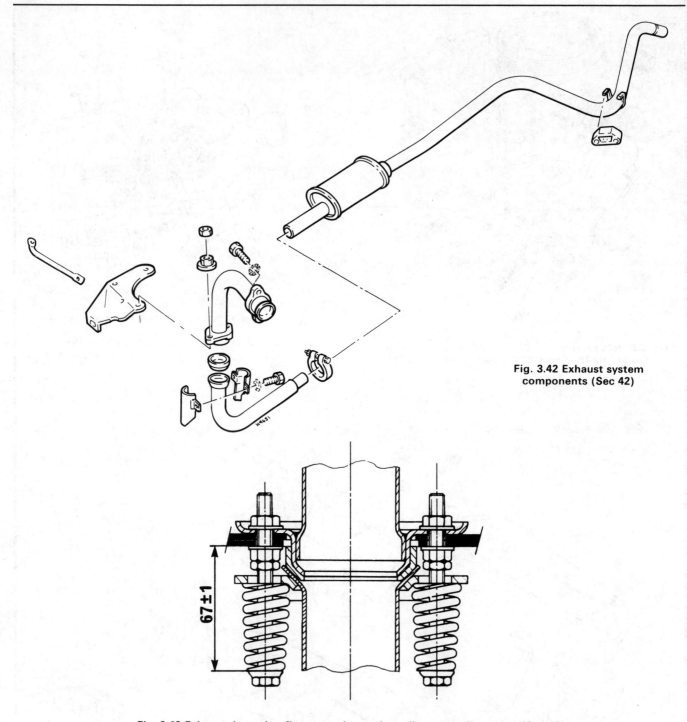

Fig. 3.42 Exhaust system components (Sec 42)

Fig. 3.43 Exhaust downpipe flange tension spring adjustment dimension (Sec 42)

43 Fault diagnosis – fuel and exhaust systems (Part 2)

Refer to Part 1, Section 21 and the following additional items.

Symptom	Reason(s)
Engine difficult to start when hot	Anti-percolation cooling fan not working or thermostatic switch faulty
Engine performance poor	Turbocharger wastegate system not functioning correctly
Excessive noise	Turbocharger bearings worn

Chapter 4 Ignition system

For modifications, and information applicable to later models, see Supplement at end of manual

Contents

Specifications

Part 1: Conventional ignition system

System type .... Coil, and distributor with contact breaker points and condenser

Application .... 956 cc (C1C) engine

Distributor
Rotor arm rotation .... Clockwise
Firing order .... 1 – 3 – 4 – 2 (No 1 cylinder nearest flywheel)
Contact breaker points gap .... 0.4 mm (0.016 in)
Dwell angle .... 57° ± 3°
Dwell percentage .... 63% ± 3%

Ignition timing
Static, or dynamic with vacuum pipe disconnected .... 10° ± 1° BTDC

Spark plugs
Type .... Champion N9YCC or N281YC
Electrode gap .... 0.8 mm (0.032 in)

HT leads .... Champion LS-07 (boxed set)

Torque wrench settings

	Nm	lbf ft
Spark plugs	15 to 20	11 to 15

Part 2: Transistorized ignition system

System type .... As conventional system but with transistor assistance unit in low tension circuit

Application .... 1108 cc (C1E) engine

Distributor .... As conventional system

Ignition timing
Static, or dynamic with vacuum pipe disconnected .... 8° ± 1° BTDC

Spark plugs .... As conventional system
HT leads .... As conventional system

Part 3: Full electronic ignition system
System type .... Computer module incorporating a coil and vacuum advance unit, basic distributor for HT circuit, and a flywheel angular position sensor

| Application | .... | 1397 cc (C1J and C2J) engine |

Distributor

| Rotor arm rotation | .... | Clockwise |
| Firing order | .... | 1 – 3 – 4 – 2 (No 1 cylinder nearest flywheel) |

Ignition timing (not adjustable)

At idle, with vacuum pipe disconnected:

Turbo models	....	8° BTDC
Non-Turbo mdoels (manual gearbox)	....	10° BTDC (C1J) or 8° BTDC (C2J)
Non-turbo models (automatic transmission)	....	6° BTDC

Spark plugs

Type:

| Turbo models | .... | Champion N3G or N6YCC |
| Non-Turbo models | .... | Champion N9YCC or N281YC |

Gap:

| Champion N3G | .... | 0.6 mm (0.024 in) |
| Champion N6YCC, N9YCC or N281YC | .... | 0.8 mm (0.032 in) |

| **HT leads** | .... | Champion LS-21 |

| **Torque wrench settings** | .... | As conventional system |

Part 1: Conventional ignition system

1 General description

In order that the engine may run correctly it is necessary for an electrical spark to ignite the fuel/air mixture in the combustion chamber at exactly the right moment in relation to engine speed and load.

Basically the ignition system functions as follows: Low tension voltage from the battery is fed to the ignition coil where it is converted into high tension voltage. The high tension voltage is powerful enough to jump the spark plug gap in the cylinder many times a second under high compression pressure, providing that the ignition system is in good working order and that all adjustments are correct.

The ignition system consists of two individual circuits known as the low tension (LT) circuit and high tension (HT) circuit.

The low tension circuit (sometimes known as the primary circuit) consists of the battery, lead to ignition switch, lead to the low tension or primary coil windings and the lead from the low tension coil windings to the contact breaker points and condenser in the distributor.

The high tension circuit (sometimes known as the secondary circuit) consists of the high tension or secondary coil winding, the heavily insulated ignition lead from the centre of the coil to the centrre of the distributor cap, the rotor arm, the spark plug leads and the spark plugs.

The complete ignition system operation is as follows: Low tension voltage from the battery is changed within the ignition coil to high tension voltage by the opening and closing of the contact breaker points in the low tension circuit. High tension voltage is then fed, via a contact in the centre of the distributor cap, to the rotor arm of the distributor. The rotor arm revolves inside the distributor cap, and each time it comes in line with one of the four metal segments in the cap, the opening and closing of the contact breaker points causes the high tension voltage to build up, jump the gap from the rotor arm to the appropriate metal segment and so, via the spark plug lead, to the spark plug where it finally jumps the gap between the two spark plug electrodes, one being earthed.

The ignition timing is advanced and retarded automatically to ensure the spark occurs at just the right instant for the particular load at the prevailing engine speed.

The ignition advance is controlled both mechanically and by a vacuum-operated system. The mechanical governor mechanism consists of two weights which move out under centrifugal force from the central distributor shaft as the engine speed rises. As they move outwards they rotate the cam relative to the distributor shaft, and so advance the spark. The weights are held in position by two light springs, and it is the tension of these springs which is largely responsible for correct spark advancement.

The vacuum control consists of a diaphragm, one side of which is

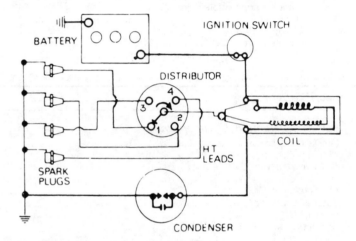

Fig. 4.1 Diagrammatic representation of the ignition circuit (Sec 1)

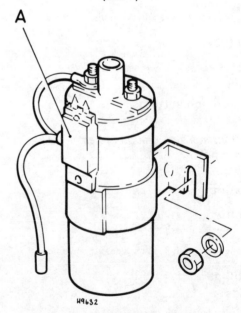

Fig. 4.2 Location of the ballast resistor (A) on the ignition coil (Sec 1)

connected, via a small bore tube, to the carburettor and the other side to the contact breaker plate. Depression in the induction manifold and carburettor, which varies with engine speed and throttle opening, causes the diaphragm to move so rotating the contact breaker plate and advancing or retarding the spark.

The LT circuit incorporates a ballast resistor located on the ignition coil bracket which is in circuit all the time that the engine is running. When the starter motor is operated, the resistance is bypassed to provide increased voltage at the spark plugs.

2 Routine maintenance

At the intervals specified in the Routine Maintenance section in the front of the manual carry out the following procedures.

1 Check the condition of the distributor cap and contact breaker points, as described in Section 3. Renew the points if necessary using the procedure contained in Section 4.

2 With the distributor cap removed, lift off the rotor arm and the plastic shield. Carefully apply two drops of engine oil to the felt pad in the centre of the cam spindle. Also lubricate the centrifugal advance mechanism by applying two or three drops of oil through one of the holes in the distributor baseplate. Wipe away any excess oil and refit the plastic shield, rotor arm and distributor cap.

3 Renew the spark plugs as described in Section 10. Preferably using a stroboscopic timing light, check and, if necessary, reset the ignition timing, as described in Section 8. Finally wipe off all traces of dirt, oil and grease from the HT and LT leads and all wiring and also check the security of all cables and connectors.

3 Contact breaker points – adjustment

1 Release the two spring clips and lift off the distributor cap. Pull the rotor arm off the shaft and remove the plastic shield (photo).

2 Clean the distributor cap on the inside and outside with a clean dry cloth and examine the four HT lead segments inside the cap. Scrape away any deposits that may have built up on the segments, using a knife or small screwdriver. If the segments appear badly burned or pitted, renew the cap.

3 Push in the carbon brush located in the centre of the cap, and ensure that it moves freely and stands proud by at least 3 mm (0.1 in). Renew the cap if the brush is worn or if there are signs of burning on the brush holder.

4 Gently prise the contact breaker points open to examine the condition of their faces. If they are rough and pitted, or dirty, they should be renewed, as described in Section 4.

5 Assuming that the points are in a satisfactory condition, or that they have been renewed, the gap between the two faces should be measured using feeler gauges. To do this turn the engine over using a socket or spanner on the crankshaft pulley bolt, until the heel of the contact breaker arm is on the peak of one of the four cam lobes.

6 With the points fully open, a feeler gauge equal to the contact breaker points gap, as given in the Specifications, should now just fit between the contact faces (photo).

7 If the gap is too large or too small turn the adjusting nut on the side of the distributor body using a small spanner until the specified gap is obtained.

8 With the points correctly adjusted, refit the plastic shield, rotor arm and distributor cap.

9 If a dwell meter is available, a far more accurate method of setting the contact breaker points is by measuring and setting the distributor dwell angle.

3.1 With the distributor cap removed, lift off the rotor arm and plastic shield to gain access to the contact breaker points

3.6 Measure the points gap with a feeler gauge and adjust if necessary by turning nut (A)

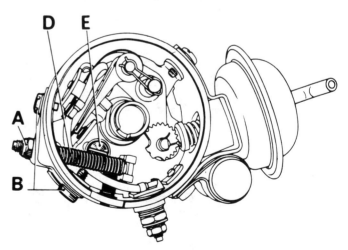

Fig. 4.3 Conventional ignition distributor components

(Secs 3 and 4)

A Contact breaker points adjusting nut
B Baseplate retaining screws
D Adjustment rod and spring
E Fixed contact retaining screw

10 The dwell angle is the number of degrees of distributor shaft rotation during which the contact breaker points are closed, ie the period from when the points close after being opened by one cam lobe until they are opened again by the next cam lobe. The advantages of setting the points by this method are that any wear of the distributor shaft or cam lobes is taken into account, and also the inaccuracies of using a feeler gauge are eliminated.

11 To check and adjust the dwell angle connect one lead of the meter to the ignition coil + terminal and the other lead to the coil − terminal, or in accordance with the maker's instructions.

12 Start the engine, allow it to idle and observe the reading on the dwell meter scale. If the dwell angle is not as specified, turn the adjusting nut on the side of the distributor body as necessary to obtain the correct setting. **Note:** Owing to machining tolerances, or wear in the distributor shaft or bushes, it is not uncommon for a contact breaker points gap correctly set with feeler gauges, to give a dwell angle outside the specified tolerances. If this is the case the dwell angle should be regarded as the preferred setting.

13 After completing the adjustment, switch off the engine and disconnect the dwell meter.

4   Contact breaker points – removal and refitting

1   Release the two spring clips and lift off the distributor cap. Pull the rotor arm off the shaft and remove the plastic shield.

2   Undo the contact breaker adjusting nut on the side of the distributor body and then unscrew the two baseplate retaining screws (photo). Lift off the support bracket.

3   Disengage the end of the adjustment rod from the fixed contact and slide the rod and spring out of the distributor body (photo).

4   Prise out the small plug and then remove the retaining clip, noting that the hole in the clip is uppermost (photos).

5   Slacken the LT terminal nut and detach the lead (photo).

6   Remove the spring retaining clip from the top of the moving contact pivot post and take off the fibre insulating washer (photo).

7   Ease the spring blade away from its nylon support and lift the moving contact upwards and off the pivot post (photo).

8   Undo the retaining screw and remove the fixed contact from the baseplate (photo).

9   Examine the faces of the breaker points and if they are rough, pitted or dirty they should be renewed.

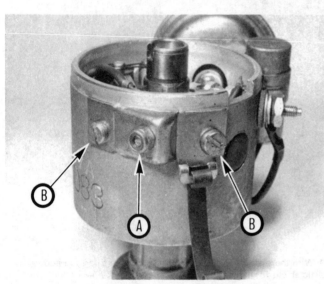

4.2 To remove the contact breaker points, undo the adjusting nut (A), the two screws (B) and lift off the support bracket

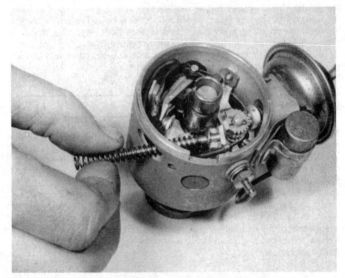

4.3 Disengage the adjustment rod from the fixed contact and withdraw the rod and spring

4.4A Prise out the small plastic plug ...

4.4B ... to gain access to the retaining clip (arrowed) ...

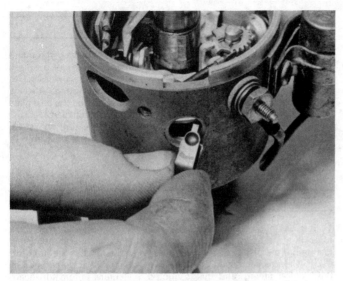

4.4C ... which can then be removed using pliers. Note the fitted position of the clip

4.5 Slacken the LT terminal nut (A) and detach the lead (B) from the connector

4.6 Remove the spring retaining clip and fibre washer from the pivot post

4.7 Ease the spring blade off its support and withdraw the moving contact from the pivot post

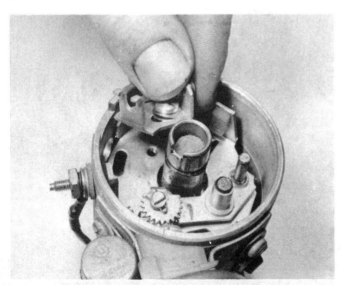

4.8 Undo the retaining screw and remove the fixed contact

10 Refitting the contact breaker points is the reverse sequence to removal, but clean the point faces with methylated spirit, to ensure complete freedom from greasy deposits.

11 After refitting adjust the contact breaker points gap, as described in Section 3.

5 Condenser – testing, removal and refitting

1 The purpose of the condenser, which is located externally on the side of the distributor body, is to ensure that, when the contact breaker points open, there is no sparking across them, which would cause wear of their faces and prevent the rapid collapse of the magnetic field in the coil. This would cause a reduction in coil HT voltage and ultimately lead to engine misfire.

2 If the engine becomes very difficult to start, or begins to miss after several miles of running, and the contact breaker points show signs of excessive burning, the condition of the condenser must be suspect. A further test can be made by separating the points by hand with the ignition switched on. If this is accompanied by a strong bright flash, it is indicative that the condenser has failed.

3 Without special test equipment, the only sure way to diagnose

condenser trouble is to substitute a suspect unit with a new one and note if there is any improvement.
4   To remove the condenser, unscrew the nut at the LT terminal post and slip off the lead. Undo the condenser retaining screw and remove the component from the side of the distributor body.
5   Refitting is the reverse sequence to removal.

6   Distributor – removal and refitting

1   Mark the spark plug HT leads to aid refitting and pull them off the ends of the plugs. Release the distributor cap retaining clips and place the cap and leads to one side.
2   Remove No 1 spark plug (nearest the flywheel end of the engine).
3   Place a finger over the plug hole and turn the engine in the normal direction of rotation (clockwise from the crankshaft pulley end) until pressure is felt in No 1 cylinder. This indicates that the piston is commencing its compression stroke. The engine can be turned with a socket or spanner on the crankshaft pulley bolt.
4   Continue turning the engine until the mark on the flywheel is aligned with the TDC notch on the clutch bellhousing (photo).
5   Using a dab of paint or a small file, make a reference mark between the distributor base and the cylinder block.
6   Detach the vacuum advance pipe and disconnect the LT lead at the wiring connector. Release the wiring loom from the support clip on the distributor body.
7   Unscrew the distributor clamp retaining nut and lift off the clamp. Withdraw the distributor from the engine and recover the seal.
8   To refit the distributor, first check that the engine is still at the TDC position with No 1 cylinder on compression. If the engine has been turned while the distributor was removed return it to the correct position, as previously described.
9   With the rotor arm pointing directly away from the engine and the vacuum unit at approximately the 5 o'clock position, slide the distributor into the cylinder block and turn the rotor arm slightly until the offset peg on the distributor drive dog positively engages with the drivegear.
10 Align the previously made reference marks, if a new distributor is being fitted, position the distributor body so that the rotor arm points toward the No 1 spark plug HT lead segment in the cap. Hold the distributor in this position, refit the clamp and secure with the retaining nut.
11 Reconnect the LT lead at the connector, refit the vacuum advance pipe and secure the wiring loom in the support clip.
12 Before refitting the distributor cap, leads and spark plug, refer to Section 8 and adjust the ignition timing as necessary.

7   Distributor – overhaul

1   Renewal of the contact breaker assembly, condenser, rotor and distributor cap should be regarded as the limit of overhaul on these units, as few other spares are available separately. It is possible to renew the vacuum unit, but this must then be set up to suit the advance curve of the engine, by adjustment of the serrated cam on the baseplate (photo), and is best left to a dealer or automotive electrician.
2   When the distributor has seen extended service and the shaft, bushes and centrifugal mechanism become worn it is advisable to purchase a new distributor.

8   Ignition timing – adjustment

1   In order that the engine can run efficiently, it is necessary for a spark to occur at the spark plug and ignite the fuel/air mixture at the instant just before the piston on the compression stroke reaches the top of its travel. The precise instant at which the spark occurs is determined by the ignition timing, and this is quoted in degrees before top-dead-centre (BTDC).
2   The timing may be checked and adjusted in one of two ways; either by using a test bulb to obtain a static setting with the engine stationary or by using a stroboscopic timing light to obtain a dynamic setting with the engine running.
3   Before checking or adjusting the ignition timing, make sure that the contact breaker points are in good condition and correctly adjusted, as described in Section 3.

Static setting
4   Refer to the Specifications at the beginning of this Chapter and note the specified setting for static ignition timing. This value will also be found stamped on a clip fastened to one of the HT leads (photo).
5   Pull off the HT lead and remove No 1 spark plug (nearest the flywheel end of the engine).
6   Place a finger over the plug hole and turn the engine in the normal direction of rotation (clockwise from the crankshaft pulley end) until pressure is felt in No 1 cylinder. This indicates that the piston is commencing its compression stroke. The engine can be turned using a socket or spanner on the crankshaft pulley bolt.
7   Continue turning the engine until the mark on the flywheel is aligned with the appropriate notch on the clutch bellhousing (Fig. 4.4).
8   Remove the distributor cap and check that the rotor arm is pointing towards the No 1 spark plug HT lead segment in the cap.

6.4 With Nos 1 and 4 cylinders at TDC the mark on the flywheel (A) will be aligned with the notch (B) in the bellhousing

7.1 Distributor vacuum unit serrated cam adjuster (arrowed)

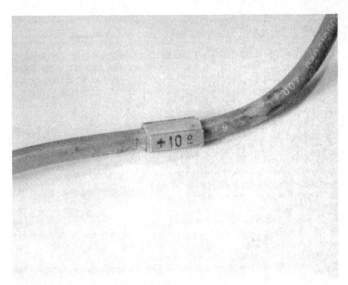

8.4 Ignition timing static setting is stamped on a clip fastened to one of the HT leads

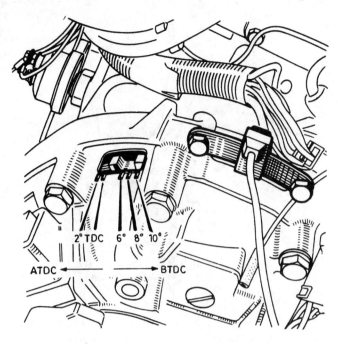

Fig. 4.4 Timing mark positions on clutch bellhousing (Sec 8)

9   Connect a 12 volt test lamp and leads between a good earth and the LT terminal nut on the side of the distributor body.
10 Slacken the distributor clamp retaining nut and then switch on the ignition.
11 If the test lamp is on, turn the distributor slightly clockwise until the lamp goes out.
12 Now turn the distributor anti-clockwise until the test lamp just lights up, hold the distributor in this position and tighten the clamp retaining nut.
13 Test the setting by turning the engine two complete revolutions and observing when the lamp lights up in relation to the timing marks.
14 Switch off the ignition and remove the test lamp. Refit No 1 spark plug, the distributor cap and HT lead.

Dynamic setting
15 Refer to the Specifications at the beginning of this Chapter and note the specified setting for dynamic ignition timing. This initial value will also be found stamped on a clip fastened to one of the HT leads. To make subsequent operations easier it is advisable to highlight the mark on the flywheel and the appropriate notch on the clutch bellhousing with white paint or chalk (Fig. 4.4).
16 Connect the timing light in accordance with the manufacturer's instructions (usually interposed between the end of No 1 spark plug HT lead and No 1 spark plug terminal).
17 Disconnect the vacuum advance pipe from the distributor vacuum unit and plug its end.
18 Start the engine and leave it idling at the specified idling speed (refer to Specifications, Chapter 3).
19 Point the timing light at the timing marks and they should appear to be stationary with the mark on the flywheel aligned with the appropriate notch on the clutch bellhousing.
20 If adjustment is necessary (ie the flywheel mark does not line up with the appropriate notch) slacken the distributor clamp retaining nut and turn the distributor body anti-clockwise to advance the timing, and clockwise to retard it. Tighten the clamp nut when the setting is correct.
21 Gradually increase the engine speed while still pointing the timing light at the marks. The mark on the flywheel should appear to advance further, indicating that the distributor centrifugal advance mechanism is functioning. If the mark remains stationary or moves in a jerky, erratic fashion, the advance mechanism must be suspect.
22 Reconnect the vacuum pipe to the distributor and check that the advance alters when the pipe is connected. If not, the vacuum unit on the distributor may be faulty.
23 After completing the checks and adjustments, switch off the engine and disconnect the timing light.

9   Diagnostic socket and TDC sensor – general

1   A diagnostic socket, used in conjunction with special test equipment to check the function of the complete ignition system, is mounted on the left-hand side of the engine, adjacent to the TDC sensor. Although the related test equipment is not normally available to the home mechanic it is useful to know of the existence and purpose of these components.

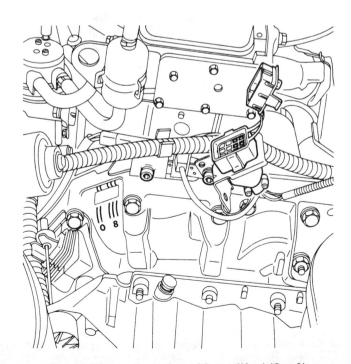

Fig. 4.5 Diagnostic socket with cap lifted (Sec 9)

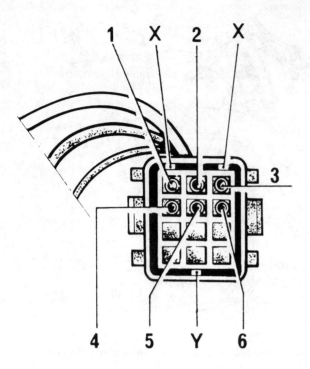

Fig. 4.6 Diagnostic socket terminals (Sec 9)

1	TDC sensor (supply)	4	TDC sensor (return)
2	Distributor earth	5	TDC sensor (screen)
3	Coil earth	6	Coil +

X and Y Location studs

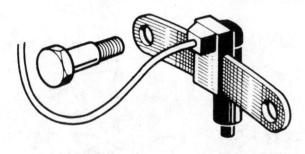

Fig. 4.7 TDC sensor and shouldered mounting bolt (Sec 9)

2   When connected to the appropriate equipment the socket enables the following checks to be carried out:

LT circuit voltage
Ignition timing
Centrifugal and vacuum advance curves
Dwell angle
Engine rpm

3   The six pins in the socket are connected to various engine earthing points, to the supply voltage terminal of the ignition coil and to the TDC sensor. The sensor itself is mounted on a bracket attached to the clutch bellhousing. The probe of the sensor is positioned directly in line with the periphery of the flywheel and is used to check the ignition timing and advance curves.

10 Spark plugs and HT leads – general

1   The correct functioning of the spark plugs is vital for the correct running and efficiency of the engine. It is essential that the plugs fitted are appropriate for the engine; the suitable type is specified at the beginning of this chapter. If this type is used and the engine is in good condition, the spark plugs should not need attention between scheduled replacement intervals. Spark plug cleaning is rarely necessary, and should not be attempted unless specialised equipment is available, as damage can easily be caused to the firing ends.
2   To remove the plugs, first mark the LT leads to ensure correct refitment, and then pull them off the plugs. Using a spark plug spanner, or suitable deep socket and extension bar, unscrew the plugs and remove them from the engine.
3   The condition of the spark plugs will also tell much about the overall condition of the engine.
4   If the insulator nose of the spark plug is clean and white, with no deposits, this is indicative of a weak mixture, or too hot a plug. (A hot plug transfers heat away from the electrode slowly – a cold plug transfers it away quickly).
5   If the tip and insulator nose are covered with hard black-looking deposits, then this is indicative that the mixture is too rich. Should the plug be black and oily, then it is likely that the engine is fairly worn, as well as the mixture being too rich.
6   If the insulator nose is covered with light tan to greyish brown deposits, then the mixture is correct and it is likely that the engine is in good condition.
7   The spark plugs should be renewed at the interval specified in Routine maintenance, regardless of their apparent condition. Note that the spark plugs should always be renewed as a complete set. Prior to installing the new plugs check their gaps as follows
8   The spark plug gap is of considerable importance as, if it is too large or too small, the size of spark and its efficiency will be seriously impaired. The spark plug gap should be set to the figure given in the Specifications at the beginning of this Chapter.
9   To set it, measure the gap with a feeler gauge, and then bend open, or close, the *outer* plug electrode until the correct gap is achieved. The centre electrode should **never** be bent as this may crack the insulation and cause plug failure, if nothing worse.
10   To refit the plugs, screw them in by hand initially and then fully tighten to the specified torque. If a torque wrench is not available, tighten the plugs until initial resistance is felt as the sealing washer contacts its seat and then tighten by a further eighth of a turn. Refit the HT leads in the correct order, ensuring that they are a tight fit over the plug ends. Periodically wipe the leads clean to reduce the risk of HT leakage by arcing.

11 Fault diagnosis – conventional ignition system

By far the majority of breakdown and running troubles are caused by faults in the ignition system, either in the low tension or high tension circuits.

There are two main symptoms indicating faults. Either the engine will not start or fire, or the engine is difficult to start and misfires. If it is a regular misfire, ie the engine is running on only two or three cylinders, the fault is almost sure to be in the secondary or high tension circuit. If the misfiring is intermittent, the fault could be in either the high or low tension circuits. If the car stops suddenly, or will not start at all, it is likely that the fault is in the low tension circuit. Loss of power and overheating, apart from faulty carburation settings, are normally due to faults in the distributor or to incorrect ignition timing.

Engine fails to start

1   If the engine fails to start and the car was running normally when it was last used, first check that there is fuel in the petrol tank. If the

engine turns over normally on the starter motor and the battery is evidently well charged, then the fault may be in either the high or low tension circuits. First check the HT circuit. If the battery is known to be fully charged, the ignition lights comes on, and the starter motor fails to turn the engine, check the tightness of the leads on the battery terminals and also the secureness of the earth lead to its connection to the body. It is quite common for the leads to have worked loose, even if they look and feel secure. If one of the battery terminal posts gets very hot when trying to work the starter motor this is a sure indication of a faulty connection to that terminal.

2 One of the most common reasons for bad starting is wet or damp spark plug leads and distributor. Remove the distributor cap. If condensation is visible a moisture dispersant such as Holts Wet Start can be very effective. Refit the cap. To prevent the problem recurring, Holts Damp start can be used to provide a sealing coat, so excluding any further moisture from the ignition system. In extreme difficulty, Holts Cold Start will help to start a car when only a very poor spark occurs.

3 If the engine still fails to start, check that the current is reaching the plugs, by disconnecting each plug lead in turn at the spark plug end, and holding the end of the cable about 5 mm (0.2 in) away from the cylinder block. Spin the engine on the starter motor.

4 Sparking between the end of the cable and the block should be fairly strong with a good, regular blue spark. (Hold the lead with rubber to avoid electric shocks). If current is reaching the spark plugs, then they are confirmed faulty. Renew or re-gap the plugs as described in Section 10; the engine should now start.

5 If there is no spark at the plug leads, take off the HT lead from the centre of the distributor cap and hold it to the block as before. Spin the engine on the starter once more. A rapid succession of blue sparks between the end of the lead and the block indicates that the coil is in order and that the distributor cap is cracked, the rotor arm faulty, or the carbon brush in the top of the distributor cap is not making good contact with the rotor arm.

6 If there are no sparks from the end of the lead from the coil check the connections at the coil end of the lead. If it is in order start checking the low tension circuit.

7 Use a 12V voltmeter or a 12V bulb and two lengths of wire. With the ignition switched on and the points open, test between the low tension wire to the coil positive (+) terminal and earth. No reading indicates a break in the supply from the ignition switch. Check the connections at the switch to see if any are loose. Refit them and the engine should run. A reading shows a faulty coil or condenser, or broken lead between the coil and the distributor.

8 Take the condenser wire off the points assembly, and with the points open test between the moving point and earth. If there is now a reading then the fault is in the condenser. Fit a new one, as described in this Chapter, Section 5, and the fault should clear.

9 With no reading from the moving point to earth, take a reading between earth and the coil negative (−) terminal. A reading here shows a broken wire which will need to be renewed between the coil and distributor. No reading confirms that the coil has failed and must be renewed, after which the engine will run once more. Remember to refit the condenser wire to the points assembly. For these tests it is sufficient to separate the points with a piece of paper while testing with the points open.

Engine misfires
10 If the engine misfires regularly, run it at a fast idling speed. Pull off each of the plug caps in turn and listen to the note of the engine. Hold the plug cap in a dry cloth or with a rubber glove as additional protection against a shock from the HT supply.

11 No difference in engine running will be noticed when the lead from the defective circuit is removed. Removing the lead from one of the good cylinders will accentuate the misfire.

12 Remove the plug lead from the end of the defective plug and hold it about 5 mm (0.2 in) away from the block. Restart the engine. If the sparking is fairly strong and regular the fault must lie in the spark plug.

13 The plug may be loose, the insulation may be cracked, or the electrodes may have burnt away, giving too wide a gap for the spark to jump. Worse still, one of the electrodes may have broken off.

14 If there is no spark at the end of the plug lead, or if it is too weak and intermittent, check the ignition lead from the distributor to the plug. If the insulation is cracked or perished, renew the lead. Check the connections at the distributor cap.

15 If there is still no spark, examine the distributor cap carefully for tracking. This can be recognised by a very thin black line running betweeen two or more electrodes, or between an electrode and some other part of the distributor. These lines are paths which now conduct electricity across the cap, thus letting it run to earth. The only answer is a new distributor cap.

16 Apart from the ignition timing being incorrect, other causes of misfiring have already been dealt with under the section dealing with the failure of the engine to start. To recap – these are that:

(a) The coil may be faulty giving an intermittent misfire
(b) There may be a damaged wire or loose connection in the low tension circuit
(c) The condenser may be short circuiting
(d) There may be a mechanical fault in the distributor (broken driving spindle or contact breaker spring)

17 If the ignition timing is too far retarded, it should be noted that the engine will tend to overheat, and there will be quite a noticeable drop in power. If the engine is overheating and the power is down, and the ignition timing is correct, then the carburettor should be checked, as it is likely that this is where the fault lies.

Part 2: Transistorized ignition system

12 General description

This type of ignition system is fitted to some 1108 cc engines. It consists of the basic conventional ignition system as described in Part 1, but with the addition of a transistor assistance unit (see Fig. 4.8).

Fig. 4.8 Transistor assistance unit showing normal plug locations (1) and emergency socket (2) (Sec 12)

The system functions as described in Section 1, but the action of the contact breaker points is used to switch a transistor on and off thus relieving the points carrying the full primary current.

The transistor operates as follows. With the points open the base (B) and emitter (E) are of the same potential and therefore no current flows. When the points close, the base (B) becomes negative due to the voltage drop at point (A) (Fig. 4.9) and current then flows through the transistor collector (C). The resistances R1 and R2 are fitted in the circuit to provide a low control voltage, and this also greatly increases the life of the contact points as they only carry a small current. When the points open again the voltage increases at point (A) and the base (B), and the transistor is switched off.

The transistorized ignition system does not incorporate a ballast resistor.

Fig. 4.9 Diagram of the transistorized ignition system (Sec 12)

A   *Battery*
B   *Ignition coil*
C   *Distributor body and contact*
       points
D   *Distributor cap*
E   *Spark plugs*
F   *Transistor and resistances*

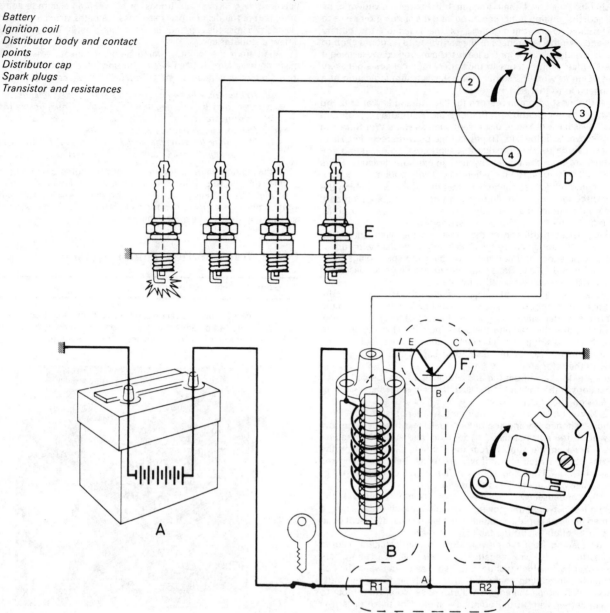

13 Transistorized ignition system – servicing

1   The transistorized ignition system is serviced using the same procedures described in Part 1, however before checking the dwell angle, checking the condenser, or setting the ignition timing *statically*, the transistorized circuit should be bypassed by pulling the connector from the top of the transistor assistance unit (Fig. 4.10) then fitting it in the lower socket. Refit the connector in the upper socket after completing the work.
2   If a fault occurs in the ignition system first transfer the connector as described in paragraph 1. If the fault then disappears the transistor assistance unit is proved unserviceable and it should be checked for damage such as broken or corroded terminals. If the fault persists check the system as for the conventional type in Section 11. Where the transistor assistance unit is faulty the engine can be run smoothly with the connector in the lower socket, but if it is left in this position the contact points will deteriorate quicker and there may be a slight loss of performance.

Part 3: Full electronic ignition system

14 General description

The electronic ignition system operates on an advanced principle whereby the main functions of the distributor are replaced by a computer module.

The system consists of three main components, namely the computer module which incorporates an ignition coil and a vacuum advance unit, the distributor which directs the HT voltage received from the coil to the appropriate spark plug, and an angular position sensor which determines the position and speed of the crankshaft by sensing special segments in the flywheel.

The computer module receives information on crankshaft position relative to TDC and BDC and also engine speed from the angular position sensor, and receives information on engine load from the vacuum advance unit. From these constantly changing variables, the computer calculates the precise instant at which HT voltage should be

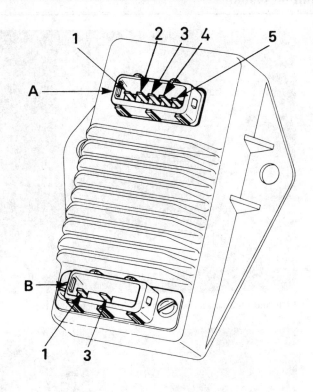

Fig. 4.10 Transistor assistance unit socket terminals (Sec 13)

A Normal socket using transistor assistance
B Socket by-passing transistor assistance
1 Coil –
2 Transistor circuit + supply
3 Contact breaker points
4 Earth
5 Transistor circuit to contact breaker points

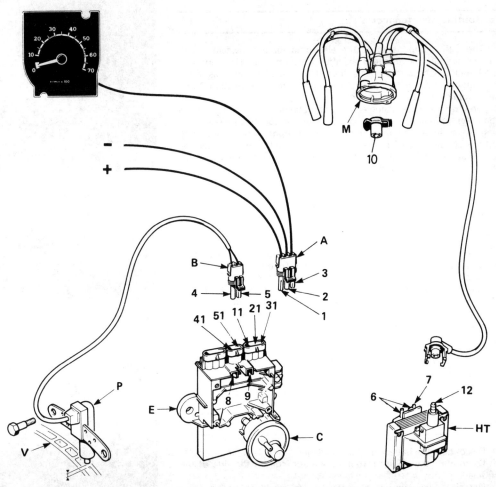

Fig. 4.11 Full Electronic ignition system components (Sec 14)

1 Positive (+) supply
2 Earth (–)
3 Tachometer
4 and 5 TDC sensor
6 Coil positive (+) terminal and interference suppression capacitor terminal
7 Coil negative (–) terminal
8 Coil positive (+) contact (joined internally to 11)
9 Coil negative (–) contact
10 Rotor arm
11 Positive (+) supply (joined internally to 8)
12 Coil HT terminal
21 Earth (–)
31 Tachometer
41 and 51 TDC sensor
A Supply connector
B TDC sensor connector
C Vacuum capsule
E Computer module
HT Ignition coil
M Distributor cap
P Angular position sensor
V Flywheel

supplied and triggers the coil accordingly. The voltage then passes from the coil to the appropriate spark plug, via the distributor in the conventional way. The function of the centrifugal and vacuum advance mechanisms as well as the contact breaker points normally associated with a distributor, are all catered for by the computer module, so that the sole purpose of the distributor is to direct the HT voltage from the coil to the appropriate spark plug.

On Turbo models a 'pinking' detector is fitted to the cylinder head in order to retard the ignition by 6° in the event of 'pinking' (detonation in the combustion chambers).

15 Electronic ignition system – precautions

Due to the sophisticated nature of the electronic ignition system the following precautions must be observed to prevent damage to the components and reduce the risk of personal injury.

1 Ensure that the ignition is switched off before disconnecting any of the ignition wiring.
2 Ensure that the ignition is switched off before connecting or disconnecting any ignition test equipment such as a timing light.
3 Do not connect a suppression condenser or test lamp to the ignition coil negative terminal.
4 Do not connect any test appliance or stroboscopic timing light requiring a 12 volt supply to the ignition coil positive terminal.
5 Do not allow an HT lead to short out or spark against the computer module body.
6 Do not earth the coil primary or secondary circuits.

16 Routine maintenance

1 The only components of the electronic ignition system which require periodic maintenance are the distributor cap, HT leads and spark plugs. These should be treated in the same way as on a conventional system and reference should be made to Section 2 and other applicable Sections of Part 1.
2 On this system dwell angle and ignition timing are a function of the computer module and there is no provision for adjustment. It is possible to check the ignition timing using a stroboscopic timing light, but this should only be necessary as part of a fault finding procedure, as any deviation from the specified setting would indicate a possible fault in the computer module.

17 Distributor – removal and refitting

1 Undo the two screws securing the distributor cap to the distributor body, lift off the cap and move it to one side (photo).
2 Undo the bolt securing the distributor to the cylinder block, withdraw the distributor from its location and recover the seal (photo).
3 To refit the distributor, place it in position in the cylinder block and turn the rotor arm until the drive dog at the base of the distributor shaft positively engages with the driveshaft.
4 Align the hole at the base of the distributor with that in the block and refit the retaining bolt.
5 Refit the distributor cap and tighten the two screws.

18 Computer module – removal and refitting

1 Disconnect the battery negative terminal.
2 Disconnect the HT lead from the ignition coil on the side of the module.
3 Detach the vacuum pipe from the vacuum advance unit (photo).
4 Disconnect the two multi-plug wiring connectors from the module (photo).

17.1 Undo the two screws and lift off the distributor cap

18.3 Vacuum pipe location on the computer module (arrowed)

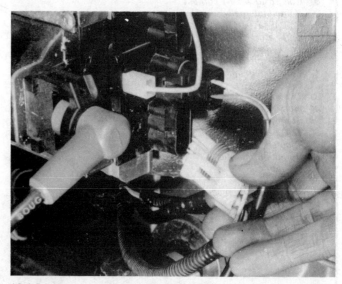
18.4 Pull the multi-plugs from the computer module

18.5 The interference suppression capacitor is located beneath the upper mounting nut

5 Unscrew the two nuts securing the unit to the bulkhead and withdraw it from the car. Note the location of the interference suppression capacitor beneath the upper nut (photo).
6 If required, the ignition coil may be removed after disconnecting the wires and undoing the four retaining screws. Do not, however, attempt to remove the vacuum unit, as it is attached internally by a very fine wire which will break if the unit is removed.
7 Refitting the ignition coil to the module, and the module to the car is the reverse sequence of removal.

19 Angular position sensor – removal and refitting

1 Disconnect the battery negative terminal.

2 Disconnect the smaller of the two wiring multi-plugs from the computer module.
3 Undo and remove the two bolts securing the sensor to the top of the clutch bellhousing and lift off the unit (photo). Note that the two retaining bolts are of the shouldered type and must not be replaced with ordinary bolts.
4 Refitting is the reverse sequence to removal.

20 Spark plugs and HT leads

Refer to Section 10.

19.3 The angular position sensor

21 Fault diagnosis – electronic ignition system

Problems associated with the electronic ignition system can usually be grouped into one of two areas, those caused by the more conventional HT side of the system, such as the spark plugs, HT leads, rotor arm and distributor cap, and those caused by the LT circuitry including the computer module and its related components.

It is recommended that the checks described in Section 11 paragraphs 1 to 6 under the heading 'Engine fails to start' or paragraphs 10 to 15 under the heading 'Engine misfires' should be carried out first, according to the symptoms, paying careful attention to Section 15. If the fault still exists, the following step by step test procedure should be used. For these tests a good quality 0 to 12 volt voltmeter and an ohmmeter will be required.

Engine fails to start
Note: *The figures and numbers shown in brackets refer to the multi-plug connectors and terminal locations shown in Fig. 4.11*

	Test conditions	Test	Remedy
1	Connector (A) disconnected, ignition switched on, starter cranking	Is the voltage between pin (1) in connector (A) and earth at least 9.5 volts?	Yes: Proceed to next test No: Check battery condition, check feed wire to connector (A)
2	Connector (A) disconnected, ignition switched off	Is the resistance between pin (2) in connector (A) and earth 0 ohms?	Yes: Proceed to next test No: Check module earth wire to connector (A)
3	Connector (A) disconnected, ignition switched off	Is the resistance between module pin (11) and coil terminal (6) 0 ohms?	Yes: Proceed to next test No: Renew the computer module
4	Connector (A) plugged in, ignition switched on	Is the voltage between coil terminal (6) and earth at least 9.5 volts?	Yes: Proceed to next test No: Move connector (A) in and out, and check coil terminal connections. Renew connector (A) if necessary

Test conditions	Test	Remedy
5 Connector (B) disconnected, ignition switched off	Is the resistance between pins (4) and (5) in connector (B) 200 ± 50 ohms?	Yes: Proceed to next test No: Renew the angular position sensor
6 Connector (B) disconnected, ignition switched off	Is the distance between the angular position sensor and the flywheel 1.0 ± 0.5 mm (0.04 ± 0.02 in)?	Yes: Proceed to next test No: Renew the angular position sensor
7 Connectors (A) and (B) plugged in, coil removed, starter cranking	Does a test bulb connected between terminal (8) and (9) flash at starter motor speed?	Yes: Proceed to next test No: Renew the computer module
8 Coil removed, ignition switched off	Is the resistance between coil terminals (7) and (12) 2000 to 12000 ohms?	Yes: Proceed to next test No: Renew the ignition coil
9 Coil removed, ignition switched off	Is the resistance between coil terminals (6) and (7) 0.4 to 0.8 ohms?	Yes: Proceed to next test No: Renew the ignition coil
10 Connector (A) disconnected, ignition switched off	Is the resistance between pins (2) and (3) of connector (A) greater than 20 000 ohms?	Yes: Renew computer module if no HT No: Repair wiring or renew tachometer

Engine is difficult to start, but performs satisfactorily once running

Test conditions	Test	Remedy
1 Disconnect HT lead from centre of distributor cap, hold lead 5 to 20 mm away from the cylinder block	Is there a rapid succession of blue sparks between the end of the lead and the cylinder block with the engine cranking?	Yes: Proceed to next test No: Carry out the test procedure under 'Engine fails to start' earlier in this Section
2 Stroboscopic timing light connected to No 1 cylinder, engine idling, vacuum pipe disconnected	Is the ignition timing in accordance with the specified setting?	Yes: Check carburation and engine mechanical condition No: Renew the computer module

Engine performance unsatisfactory

Test conditions	Test	Remedy
1 Run engine at a steady 3000 rpm, disconnect vacuum pipe at computer module	Does the engine speed drop as the vacuum pipe is disconnected?	Yes: Carry out the previous tests under 'Engine difficult to start' No: Renew the computer module after checking that the vacuum pipe is in good condition and correctly fitted

Engine 'pinking' (pinging noise under load)

Test conditions	Test	Remedy
1 Stroboscopic timing light connected to No. 1 cylinder, engine idling	Does the ignition timing retard by 6° when the cylinder head is tapped gently with a bronze drift near the 'pinking' detector?	Yes: Check ignition timing, carburettor settings and carbon build-up in engine No: Renew the 'pinking' detector

Chapter 5 Clutch

For modifications, and information applicable to later models, see Supplement at end of manual

Contents

Specifications

Type .... Single dry plate, self-adjusting cable operation

Clutch disc diameter
Non-Turbo models .... 181.5 mm (7.146 in)
Turbo models .... 200.0 mm (7.874 in)

Disc lining thickness (total) .... 7.7 mm (0.303 in)

Torque wrench settings

	Nm	lbf ft
Clutch cover bolts	25	18

1 General description

All manual transmission models are equipped with a cable-operated, single dry plate diaphragm spring clutch assembly. The unit consists of a steel cover which is dowelled and bolted to the rear face of the flywheel, and contains the pressure plate and diaphragm spring.

The clutch disc is free to slide along the splined gearbox input shaft and is held in position between the flywheel and the pressure plate by the pressure of the diaphragm spring. Friction lining material is riveted to the clutch disc which has a spring cushioned hub to absorb transmission shocks and help ensure a smooth take-up of the drive.

The clutch is actuated by a cable controlled by the clutch pedal. The clutch release mechanism consists of a release arm and bearing which are in permanent contact with the fingers of the diaphragm spring.

Depressing the clutch pedal actuates the release arm by means of the cable. The arm pushes the release bearing against the diaphragm fingers, so moving the centre of the diaphragm spring inwards. As the centre of the spring is pushed in, the outside of the spring pivots out, so moving the pressure plate backwards and disengaging its grip on the clutch disc.

When the pedal is released, the diaphragm spring forces the pressure plate into contact with the friction linings on the clutch disc. The disc is now firmly sandwiched between the pressure plate and the flywheel, thus transmitting engine power to the gearbox.

Wear of the friction material on the clutch disc is automatically compensated by a self-adjusting mechanism attached to the clutch pedal. The mechanism consists of a serrated quadrant, a notched cam and a tension spring. One end of the clutch cable is attached to the quadrant which is free to pivot on the pedal, but is kept in tension by the spring (photo). As the pedal is depressed the notched cam contacts the quadrant thus locking it and allowing the pedal to pull the cable and operate the clutch. As the pedal is released the tension spring causes the quadrant to move free of the notched cam and rotate slightly, thus taking up any free play that may exist in the cable.

There are no Routine Maintenance procedures for the clutch components as attention is only necessary when a component is worn out.

1.1 Self-adjusting quadrant (1) and tension spring (2) on the clutch pedal

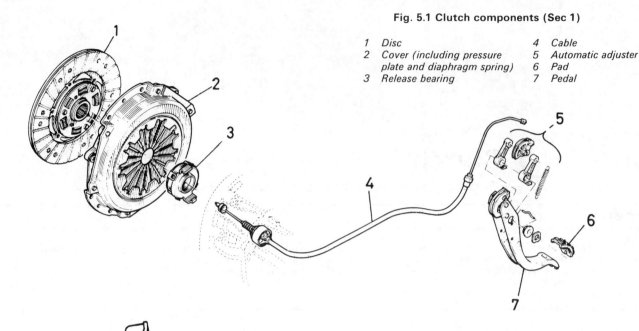

Fig. 5.1 Clutch components (Sec 1)

1   Disc
2   Cover (including pressure
    plate and diaphragm spring)
3   Release bearing

4   Cable
5   Automatic adjuster
6   Pad
7   Pedal

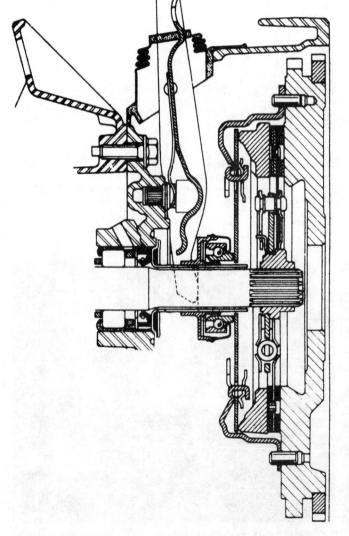

Fig. 5.2 Cross-section of clutch components (Sec 1)

2   Clutch assembly – removal and refitting

Note: *For Turbo and 1721 cc models, see Chapter 12.*

1   Access to the clutch is gained by separating the gearbox from the engine, and there is a choice of three ways to achieve this. The engine and gearbox can be removed as one unit then separated on the bench, the engine can be removed leaving the gearbox in situ, or the gearbox can be removed leaving the engine in situ. If no other work is necessary it is suggested that the latter method is used as described in Chapter 6.
2   Having separated the gearbox from the engine, undo and remove the clutch cover retaining bolts, working in a diagonal sequence and slackening the bolts only a few turns at a time (photo).
3   Ease the clutch cover off its locating dowels and be prepared to catch the clutch disc which will drop out as the cover is removed. Note which way round the disc is fitted.
4   It is important that no oil or grease is allowed to come into contact with the friction material of the clutch disc or the pressure plate and

2.2 Removing the clutch cover retaining bolts

flywheel faces. It is advisable to refit the clutch assembly with clean hands and to wipe down the pressure plate and flywheel faces with a clean dry rag before assembly begins.

5   Begin reassembly by placing the clutch disc against the flywheel with the side having the larger offset facing away from the flywheel.

6   Place the clutch cover over the dowels, refit the retaining bolts and tighten them finger tight so that the clutch disc is gripped, but can still be moved.

7   The clutch disc must now be centralised so that, when the engine and gearbox are mated, the splines of the gearbox input shaft will pass through the splines in the centre of the clutch disc hub.

8   Centralisation can be carried out quite easily by inserting a round bar or long screwdriver through the hole in the centre of the clutch disc so that the end of the bar rests in the hole in the end of the crankshaft containing the input shaft support bearing.

9   Using the support bearing as a fulcrum, moving the bar sideways or up and down will move the clutch disc in whichever direction is necessary to achieve centralisation.

10   Centralisation is easily judged by removing the bar and viewing the clutch disc hub in relation to the support bearing. When the support bearing appears exactly in the centre of the clutch disc hub, all is correct.

11   An alternative and more accurate method of centralisation is to use a commercially available clutch aligning tool obtainable from most accessory shops (photo).

12   Once the clutch is centralised, progressively tighten the cover bolts in a diagonal sequence to the torque setting given in the Specifications. If necessary prevent the flywheel from turning by inserting a screwdriver in the teeth of the starter ring gear by one of the gearbox location studs.

13   Assemble the gearbox to the engine in reverse order. Check that the self-adjusting mechanism on the clutch pedal is correctly positioned with the quadrant teeth opposite the notched cam. The mechanism will automatically set itself to the correct position.

3   Clutch assembly – inspection

1   With the clutch assembly removed, clean off all traces of asbestos dust using a dry cloth. This is best done outside or in a well-ventilated area; *asbestos dust is harmful, and must not be inhaled.*

2   Examine the linings of the clutch disc for wear and loose rivets, and the disc rim for distortion, cracks, broken torsion springs and worn splines. The surface of the friction linings may be highly glazed, but, as long as the friction material pattern can be clearly seen, this is satisfactory. If there is any sign of oil contamination, indicated by a continuous, or patchy, shiny black discolouration, the disc must be renewed and the source of the contamination traced and rectified. This will be either a leaking crankshaft oil seal or gearbox input shaft oil seal – or both. Renewal procedures are given in Chapter 1 and Chapter 6 respectively. The disc must also be renewed if the lining thickness has worn down to, or just above, the level of the rivet heads.

3   Check the machined faces of the flywheel and pressure plate. If either is grooved, or heavily scored, renewal is necessary. The pressure plate must also be renewed if any cracks are apparent, or if the diaphragm spring is damaged or its pressure suspect.

4   With the gearbox removed it is advisable to check the condition of the release bearing, as described in the following Section.

4   Clutch release bearing – removal, inspection and refitting

1   To gain access to the release bearing it is necessary to separate the engine and gearbox either by removing the engine or gearbox individually, or by removing both units as an assembly and separating them after removal. Depending on the method chosen, the appropriate procedures will be found in Chapter 1 or Chapter 6.

2   With the gearbox removed from the engine, tilt the release fork and slide the bearing assembly off the gearbox input shaft guide tube (photo).

3   To remove the bearing from its holder (where applicable), release the four tags of the spring retainer, lift off the retainer and remove the bearing.

4   Check the bearing for smoothness of operation and renew it if there is any roughness or harshness as the bearing is spun.

5   To remove the release fork, disengage the rubber cover and then pull the fork upwards to release it from its ball pivot stud (photos).

6   Refitting the release fork and release bearing is the reverse sequence to removal, but note the following points:

(a)   *Lubricate the release fork pivot ball stud and the release bearing-to-diaphragm spring contact areas sparingly with molybdenum disulphide grease.*

(b)   *Ensure that the release fork spring retainer locates behind the flat shoulder of the ball pivot stud.*

2.11 Centralising the clutch disc with a special tool

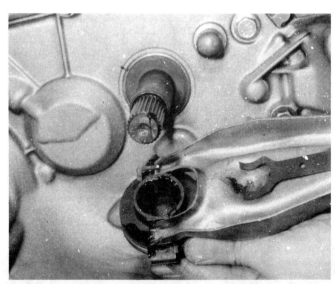

4.2 Showing attachment of release bearing to release fork

4.5A Release fork rubber cover

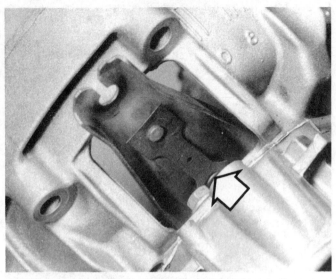

4.5B Pull the release fork from the ball pivot stub (arrowed)

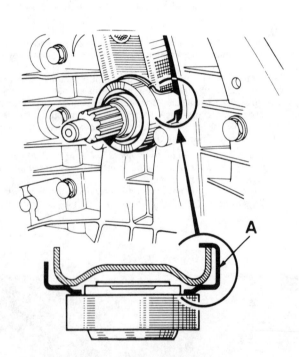

Fig. 5.3 Showing correct location of the release fork in the release bearing (Sec 4)

A   Retaining shoulder

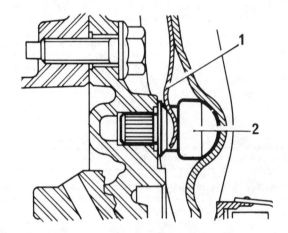

Fig. 5.4 Cross-section of ball pivot stud showing correct location of release fork spring (1) on pivot stud (2) (Sec 4)

5.1 Detach the inner cable from the release fork

5 Clutch cable – removal and refitting

1   Working in the engine compartment pull the inner cable and remove it from the end of the release fork (photo), then disengage the outer cable from the bracket on the bellhousing.
2   Working inside the car release the inner cable from the quadrant and cam on the pedal.
3   Using a screwdriver push the outer cable from its location in the bulkhead.
4   Pull the cable through into the engine compartment, detach it from the support clips and remove it from the car.

5   Refitting is a reversal of removal. When the inner cable is attached to the end of the release fork, the quadrant on the pedal will be repositioned in relation to the cam automatically. Depress the pedal several times to settle the cable ends so that the self-adjusting mechanism obtains its final working position which provides 2.0 mm (0.079 in) free play on the inner cable.

6   Clutch pedal – removal and refitting

1   Working in the engine compartment pull the inner cable and remove it from the end of the release fork.

2   Working inside the car release the inner cable from the quadrant and cam on the pedal self-adjusting mechanism. Remove the steering column lower shroud if necessary.
3   Prise the spring clip from the clutch pedal end of the pivot shaft and remove the washer.
4   Slide the pivot shaft to the right until the clutch pedal and quadrant arms can be withdrawn.
5   With the pedal removed inspect the two bushes and the self-adjusting mechanism for wear and damage. Renew the components as necessary.
6   Refitting is a reversal of removal, but lubricate the pivot shaft and self-adjusting mechanism components with molybdenum disulphide grease. After re-connecting the cable depress the pedal several times.

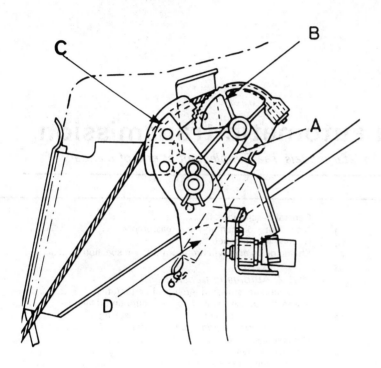

Fig. 5.5 Diagram of cable self-adjusting mechanism on the pedal (Sec 6)

A   *Quadrant arms (free to pivot on shaft)*
B   *Quadrant (free to pivot on arms)*
C   *Toothed cam (fixed to pedal)*
D   *Tension spring*

7 Fault diagnosis – clutch

Symptom	Reason(s)
Judder when taking up drive	Loose or worn engine mountings Clutch disc contaminated with oil, or linings worn Clutch cable sticking or frayed Faulty pressure plate assembly
Clutch fails to disengage	Clutch self-adjusting mechanism faulty or inoperative Clutch disc sticking on input shaft splines Faulty pressure plate assembly Cable broken
Clutch slips	Clutch self-adjusting mechanism faulty or inoperative Clutch disc contaminated with oil or linings worn Faulty pressure plate assembly Diaphragm spring broken
Noise when depressing clutch pedal	Worn release bearing Faulty pressure plate assembly Diaphragm spring broken Worn or dry cable or pedal bushes
Noise when releasing clutch pedal	Faulty pressure plate assembly Broken clutch disc cushioning springs Gearbox internal wear (see Chapter 6)

Chapter 6
Manual gearbox and automatic transmission

For modifications, and information applicable to later models, see Supplement at end of manual

Contents

Specifications

Part 1: Manual gearbox
Type .... Four or five forward speeds (all synchromesh) and reverse. Final drive differential integral with main gearbox

Designation:
Four-speed units .... JB 4
Five-speed units .... JB3 or JB5

Ratios
JB 4:
   1st .... 3.727 : 1
   2nd .... 2.053 : 1
   3rd .... 1.320 : 1
   4th .... 0.903 : 1
   Reverse .... 3.545 : 1
   Final drive .... 3.867 : 1 (58/15) or 3.294 : 1 (56/17)
JB3 .... See Chapter 12
JB5:
   1st .... 3.727 : 1 or 3.091 : 1
   2nd .... 2.053 : 1 or 1.842 : 1
   3rd .... 1.320 : 1
   4th .... 0.967 : 1
   5th .... 0.794 : 1 or 0.758 : 1
   Reverse .... 3.545 : 1
   Final drive .... 4.067 : 1 (61/15), 3.428 : 1 (55/16), or 3.294 : 1 (56/17)

Lubricant
Type/specification:
    Non-Turbo models .... Gear oil, viscosity SAE 80W (Duckhams Hypoid 80S)
    Turbo models .... Gear oil, viscosity SAE 75W/90S (Duckhams Hypoid 75W/90S)

	Steel filler plug	Plastic filler plug
Capacity:		
JB4	3.25 litre (5.72 Imp pt)	2.75 litre (4.34 Imp pt)
JB3 and JB5	3.40 litre (5.98 Imp pt)	2.90 litre (5.10 Imp pt)

Torque wrench settings

	Nm	lbf ft
Gearbox mounting nuts	40	30
Bellhousing-to-engine nuts and bolts	25	18
Mechanism casing to clutch and differential housing	25	18
Input shaft nut (five-speed)	135	100
Mainshaft bolt (five-speed)	80	59

Part 2: Automatic transmission

Type .... Three forward speeds and reverse, final drive differential integral with transmission

Designation MB1

Ratios
1st .... 2.50 : 1
2nd .... 1.50 : 1
3rd .... 1.00 : 1
Reverse .... 2.00 : 1
Final drive .... 3.294 : 1 (56/17)

Lubricant
Type/specification .... Dexron type ATF (Duckhams Uni-Matic or D-Matic)
Capacity:
    Total – dry unit .... 4.5 litre (7.92 Imp pt)
    Refill after fluid change – approximate .... 2.0 litre (3.52 Imp pt)

Torque wrench settings

	Nm	lbf ft
Transmission mounting nuts	40	30
Bellhousing-to-engine nuts and bolts	25	18
Torque converter to driveplate:		
Bolts	30	22
Nuts	19	14
Fluid cooler union nuts	20	15
Fluid cooler mounting bolts	40	30

Part 1: Manual gearbox

1 General description

The gearbox is equipped with either four forward and one reverse gear or five forward and one reverse gear, according to model. Baulk ring synchromesh gear engagement is used on all forward gears.

The final drive (differential) unit is integral with the main gearbox and is located between the mechanism casing and clutch and differential housing. The gearbox and differential both share the same lubricating oil.

Gearshift is by means of a floor-mounted lever connected by a remote control housing and gearchange rod to the gearbox fork control shaft.

If gearbox overhaul is necessary, due consideration should be given to the costs involved, since it is often more economical to obtain a service exchange or good secondhand gearbox rather than fit new parts to the existing unit.

2 Routine maintenance

At the intervals specified in the Routine Maintenance section in the front of the manual carry out the following procedures.
1 Unscrew the filler plug from the front-facing side of the gearbox with the car positioned on a level surface. Check and if necessary top up the level with reference to Section 3.
2 Drain and refill the gearbox with fresh oil as described in Section 3.
3 Visually inspect the gearbox joint faces and oil seals for signs of oil leakage or damage.

3 Gearbox – draining and refilling

1 Position the car over an inspection pit, on car ramps, or jack it up but make sure that it is level.
2 Place a suitable container beneath the gearbox.

3.3 Disconnecting the gearbox breather tube (shown with gearbox removed)

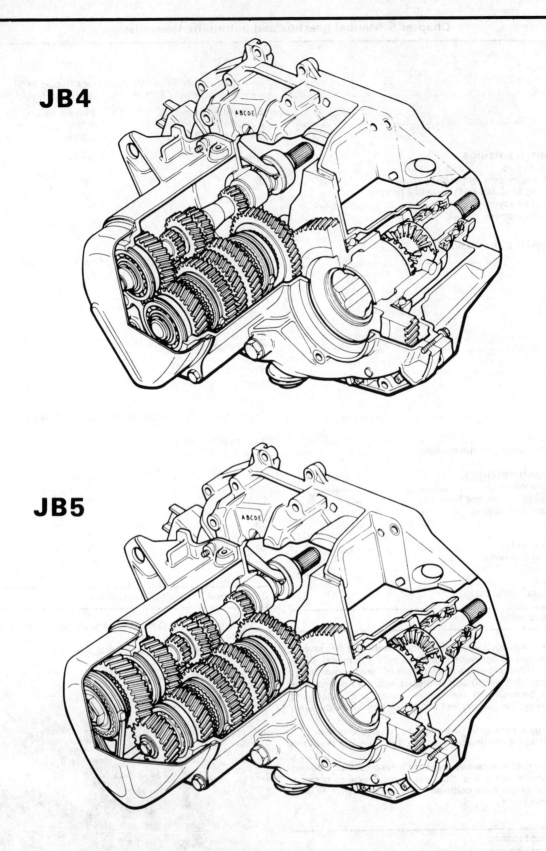

JB4

JB5

Fig. 6.1 Cut-away view of the four-speed (JB4) and five-speed (JB5) manual gearboxes (Sec 1)

Note: *JB3 five-speed gearbox similar to JB5*

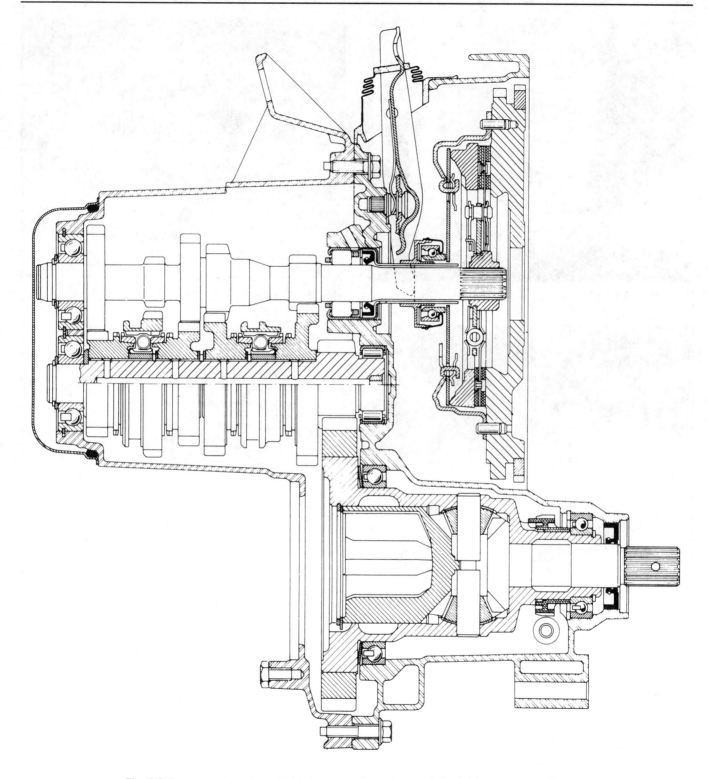

Fig. 6.2 Cross-section view of the four-speed gearbox and final drive assembly (Sec 1)

3   Where applicable remove the splash shield from the underbody. Disconnect the gearbox breather tube (photo).

4   Unscrew the drain plug and allow the oil to drain into the container (photo).

5   With all the oil drained wipe clean the drain plug then refit and tighten it.

6   Unscrew the filler plug from the side of the gearbox then pour in the specified grade and quantity of oil (photos).

7   Where a steel filler plug is fitted the oil level should be up to the lower edge of the filler hole. Insert a finger to check the level.

8   Where a plastic filler plug is fitted check the level by inserting the shouldered end of the plug through the hole without engaging the threads, then positioning the plug so that the outer arrow is pointing upwards. On removal of the plug the level should be at the top of the black section (Fig.6.3). The bottom of the black indicates the minimum level (photo).

9   After filling refit and tighten the filler plug and re-connect the breather tube.

3.4 Drain plug location

3.6A Filler plug location (plastic plug shown)

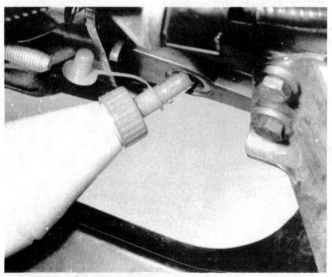

3.6B Filling the gearbox with oil

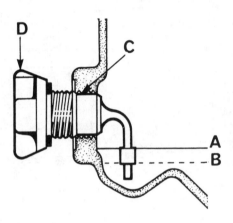

**Fig. 6.3 Method of using plastic filler plug
to check the gearbox oil level (Sec 3)**

A   Maximum level   C   Locating shoulder
B   Minimum level   D   Point of arrow

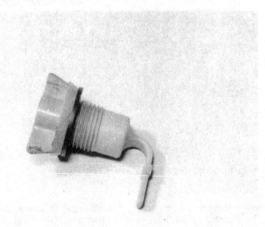

3.8 Showing the plastic filler plug and level extension

---

4   Gearbox – removal and refitting

Note: *For Turbo and 1721 cc models, see Chapter 12.*

1   Apply the handbrake then jack up the front of the car and support on axle stands.
2   Remove the bonnet as described in Chapter 10.
3   Drain the gearbox as described in Section 3.
4   Remove both driveshafts as described in Chapter 7.
5   Disconnect the gearchange rod from the gearbox with reference to Section 15 (photos).
6   Unbolt the tie-rod from the clutch bellhousing and engine cylinder block.
7   Unbolt the cover plate from the clutch bellhousing.
8   Disconnect the battery negative lead, then disconnect the wiring from the reversing switch (photo).
9   Unbolt the starter cover plate.
10 Remove the splash shield from under the left-hand wheel arch.
11 Unscrew the nuts from the gearbox front and rear mountings and loosen only the engine mountings. Using a socket and universal joint bar unscrew the bolt from the gearbox rear mounting.
12 Remove the air cleaner as described in Chapter 3.

4.5A Slide back the gearchange rod rubber cover ...

4.5B ... undo the retaining nut and bolt ...

4.5C ... then slide off the rod and recover the distance sleeve (arrowed)

4.8 Reverse lamp switch location

13 Place a piece of thick cardboard on the engine large enough to take the radiator. Unclip the expansion bottle/tank and disconnect the wiring from the electric cooling fan and thermostatic switch. Lift the radiator from its mountings and place it on the cardboard together with the expansion tank. Do not disconnect the top and bottom hoses.

14 Remove the ignition transistor assistance unit or computer module and the angular position sensor (photo) as described in Chapter 4.

15 Disconnect the clutch cable (Chapter 5) and the speedometer cable (Chapter 11).

16 Unbolt the earthing braid from the body.

17 Disconnect the exhaust downpipe from the exhaust manifold with reference to Chapter 3.

18 Using a trolley jack and block of wood raise the engine until the gearbox mountings are free.

19 Unscrew the starter mounting bolts leaving the starter attached to the bracket on the cylinder block.

20 Support the weight of the gearbox using a suitable hoist. Alternatively a trolley jack can be used, but in this case an assistant will be required to help lift out the gearbox by hand.

21 Unscrew and remove the nuts and bolts securing the gearbox to

4.14 Angular position sensor location

the engine. On models where there is limited working room it will also be necessary to unscrew the two location studs from the engine using two nuts tightened together then turning the innermost nut.

22 Unbolt the front mounting bracket from the gearbox (photo).

23 Lower the engine a little then pull away the gearbox keeping it level with the engine and guiding it between the left-hand side members. Now raise the engine again and lift the gearbox from the engine compartment taking care not to damage the surrounding bodywork.

24 Refitting is a reversal of removal, but tighten all nuts and bolts to the specified torque. Refill the gearbox with oil as described in Section 3. Refer to Chapter 3 for the special method of tightening the exhaust downpipe nuts.

5 Gearbox overhaul – general

Complete dismantling and overhaul of the gearbox, particularly with respect to the differential and the bearings in the clutch and differential housing, entails the use of a hydraulic press and a number of special tools. For this reason it is not recommended that a complete overhaul be attempted by the home mechanic unless he has access to the tools required and feels reasonably confident after studying the procedure. However, the gearbox can at least be dismantled into its major assemblies without too much difficulty, and the following Sections described this and the overhaul procedure.

Before starting any repair work on the gearbox, thoroughly clean the exterior of the casings using paraffin or a suitable solvent. Dry the unit with a lint-free rag. Make sure that an uncluttered working area is available with some small containers and trays handy to store the various parts. Label everything as it is removed.

Before starting reassembly all the components must be spotlessly clean and should be liberally lubricated with the recommended grade of gear oil during assembly.

Apart from the additional 5th gear and slight differences in the selector mechanism, the four-and five-speed gearboxes are virtually identical and the following Sections are applicable to both types. Where any significant differences occur, these will be described in the text.

After dismantling, all roll pins, circlips and snap-rings must be renewed, regardless of their condition, before reassembling.

6 Gearbox – separating the housings

1 With the gearbox on the bench, begin by removing the clutch release bearing and release fork, referring to Chapter 5 if necessary.

4.22 Front mounting bracket

2 Undo the bolts securing the rear gearbox mounting bracket to the clutch and differential housing and remove the bracket (photo).

3 Remove the rubber O-ring from the splines of the differential stub shaft.

4 Undo the retaining bolts and lift off the mechanism casing rear cover. Recover the rubber O-ring seal (photos).

5 If working on the four-speed gearbox, proceed to paragraph 11, if working on the five-speed gearbox, proceed as follows:

6 Support the 5th speed selector shaft using a block of wood between the shaft and gears, then drive out the selector fork roll pin using a parallel pin punch (photo).

7 Engage 1st gear by moving the gear linkage fork control shaft and engage 5th gear by moving the 5th speed selector fork. With the geartrain now locked, undo the 5th gear retaining nut on the end of the input shaft and the bolt on the end of the mainshaft. Also remove the collar and washers (where fitted) from the mainshaft (photos).

8 Return the geartrain to neutral.

6.2 Rear mounting bracket

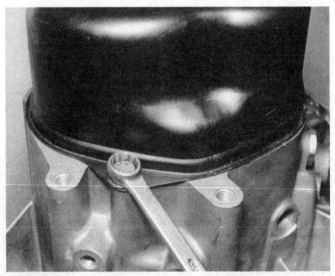

6.4A Remove the bolts ...

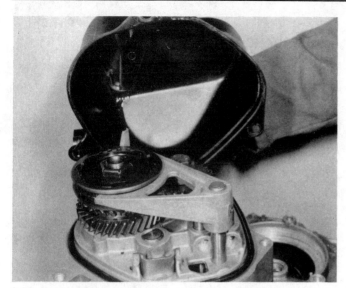

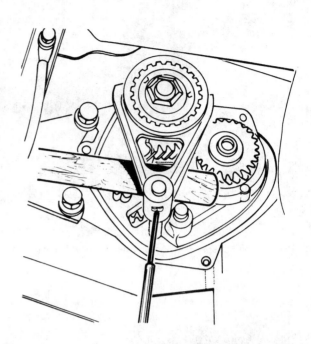

6.4B ... and lift off the mechanism casing rear cover

6.6 5th speed selector fork roll pin (arrowed)

Fig. 6.4 Using a block of wood to support the 5th speed selector shaft when driving out the selector fork roll pin (Sec 6)

9 Withdraw the 5th speed driving gear, synchroniser unit, and selector fork as an assembly using a suitable puller. Engage the puller legs over flat strips of metal slid under the teeth of the driven gear. Alternatively it is possible to tap off the synchroniser unit carefully with a soft metal drift, then lever off the gear, noting the shoulder is towards the bearing. Recover the needle roller bearing, bearing bush and the washer from the input shaft (photos).
10 Remove the driven gear from the mainshaft, if necessary using the puller (photo).
11 On the four-speed gearbox only, extract the circlip and dished washer over the end of the input shaft and mainshaft (photos).
12 Lift out the reverse shaft detent retaining plate then remove the spring and ball (photo). If the ball won't come out, leave it in place, but don't forget to retrieve it once the casing has been separated.

6.7A Unscrew the 5th gear retaining nut on the input shaft ...

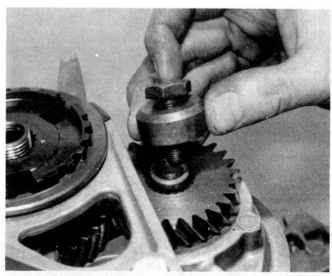

6.7B ... and the bolt on the mainshaft

6.9A Remove the 5th speed driving gear needle roller bearing ...

6.9B ... the bush, and the washer from the input shaft

6.10 Remove the 5th speed driven gear from the mainshaft

6.11A Extract the circlip ...

6.11B ... and dished washer from the input shaft and mainshaft

6.12 Lift out the reverse shaft detent retaining plate

13 Unscrew the limit stop threaded plug on four-speed units, or the 5th speed detent plug on five-speed units (photos).
14 Unscrew the reversing lamp switch (photo).
15 Undo and remove the bolts securing the mechanism casing to the clutch and differential housing, noting their different lengths and locations (photo).
16 Pull the fork control shaft on the side of the gearbox out as far as it will go and then lift the mechanism casing, complete with 5th speed selector shaft on five-speed units, up and off the geartrain and housing. It may be necessary to tap the input shaft down using a plastic mallet to free the casing and bearings from the shaft. As soon as the casing comes free, insert two bolts or suitable rods into the selector shaft holes and push them down firmly. These will retain the detent balls and springs and prevent them being ejected as the casing is lifted off (photos). On five-speed units if the 5th speed selector shaft remains in the clutch housing remove it separately after lifting off the casing, and recover the detent ball and spring from the mechanism casing.

6.13A Removing the limit stop threaded plug (four-speed unit)

6.13B Removing the 5th speed detent plug (five-speed unit)

6.14 Reverse lamp switch location in the mechanism casing

6.15 Mechanism casing bolts within the clutch bellhousing

6.16A Lift the mechanism casing from the clutch and differential housing

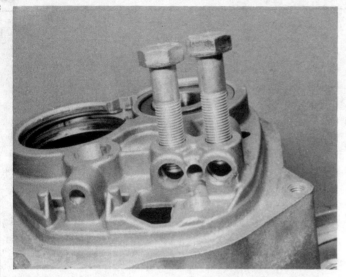

6.16B Two bolts in position to retain the selector shaft detent balls and springs

Fig. 6.5 Selector mechanism components (Secs 6, 7 and 8)

29 1st/2nd selector shaft
30 3rd/4th selector shaft
31 3rd/4th selector fork
32 Reverse shaft
33 Detent plunger
34 Selector fork roll pin
35 Detent plunger
36 Detent plunger
37 Detent plunger (five-speed only)
53 Circlip
54 Pivot arm bushes
55 Pivot arm
56 Fork finger
57 Fork control shaft
58 Bush
59 5th speed selector shaft
60 5th speed selector fork
61 Reverse shaft detent retaining plate
62 5th speed detent assembly

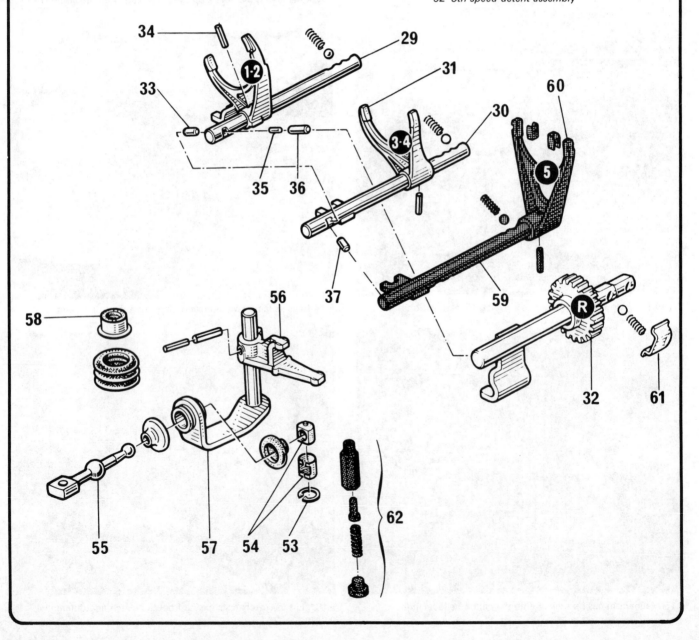

7 Gearbox mainshaft, input shaft and differential – removal

1 Having separated the casings, the geartrain components can now be dismantled as follows:
2 On the five-speed gearbox, recover the dentent plunger from the location in the clutch and differential housing vacated by the 5th speed selector shaft.
3 Remove the magnet from the clutch and differential housing (photo).
4 The geartrain assembly can be removed using one of two alternative methods.

Method 1

5 Using a parallel pin punch, drive out the roll pin securing the 3rd/4th selector fork to the shaft (photo). Slip a tube of suitable diameter down over the shaft and support it while the roll pin is being driven out.
6 Ensure that all the gears are in neutral, and then withdraw the 3rd/4th selector shaft, leaving the fork behind. It will be necessary to move the reverse shaft around slightly until the exact neutral position is found, otherwise the detent plungers will not locate properly in their grooves and it will be impossible to remove the 3rd/4th shaft (photo). With the shaft removed, lift off the selector fork.
7 Recover the detent plunger from the shaft location in the housing (photo).
8 Using the same procedure as for the 3rd/4th shaft, remove the 1st/2nd selector shaft and fork. As the shaft is withdrawn, recover the small detent plunger from the hole in the centre of the shaft (photos).
9 Withdraw the long detent plunger from its location at the base of the housing (photo).
10 Take hold of the mainshaft, input shaft and reverse shaft geartrains and lift them as an assembly out of their locations in the clutch and differential housing (photo).

Method 2

11 Using an old valve spring or metal tube (together with the end bolt and collar on five-speed units), hold the gears and synchroniser units together on the mainshaft (photo). If this precaution is not taken the synchroniser units are likely to fall apart in subsequent procedures.
12 Lift the reverse shaft and withdraw it by slightly lifting the input shaft so that the reverse idler gear clears the 4th gear on the shaft.
13 Lift the input shaft and mainshaft together with the two selector shafts from the clutch and differential housing, moving the selector shafts as necessary (photo).
14 Recover the detent plungers from their locations in the housing.

7.3 Magnet location in the clutch and differential housing

7.5 3rd/4th selector fork roll pin location (arrowed)

7.6 Withdraw the 3rd/4th selector shaft, followed by the fork

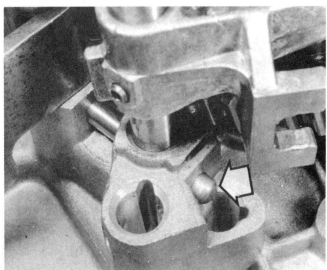

7.7 Recover the detent plunger (arrowed) after removing the 3rd/4th shaft

7.8A As the 1st/2nd selector shaft is withdrawn, recover the small detent plunger from the hole (arrowed) ...

7.8B ... then remove the fork

7.9 Remove the long detent plunger (arrowed) after removing the 1st/2nd shaft

7.10 Remove the mainshaft, input shaft and reverse shaft together from the housing

7.11 An old valve spring fitted to the mainshaft to retain the gears

7.13 Input shaft and mainshaft ready to be removed from the clutch and differential housing

After either method

15 The differential can now be removed if necessary, however the use of a large puller or press is required.

16 Using a parallel pin punch tap the edge of the oil seal in the housing so that it tilts then use a pair of pliers to extract the seal (photos).

17 The differential crownwheel face must now be pressed against the dished spring washer so that the circlip can be removed from the opposite end. To do this either position the crownwheel on a block of wood and use a press to push the casing down, or use a puller together with a flat bar to push on the crownwheel (photos).

18 With the circlip removed the differential can be drawn from the bearings, if necessary using a press or mallet. Recover the dished and plain washers noting which way round they are fitted (photos).

8 Gearbox mechanism casing – overhaul

1   To renew the bearings in the mechanism casing, spread the retaining circlip with a pair of outward opening circlip pliers, and drive the bearings out towards the inside of the casing. Use a hammer and tube of suitable diameter to do this.

2   To fit the new bearings, first locate the circlips in their grooves in the casing so that their ends are together (photo).

7.16A Tilt the oil seal with a punch ...

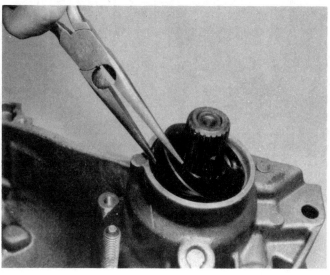

7.16B ... then extract it with pliers

7.17A Using a puller and flat bar to compress the differential dished spring washer ...

7.17B ... when removing the circlip

7.18A Removing the differential

7.18B Showing the differential dished and plain washers

8.2 Circlip located in the mechanism casing

3   Fit the bearings to the casing, ensuring that force is applied to the bearing outer race only. As the bearings are being fitted spread the circlips to allow the bearings to enter (photo).

4   With the bearings in place, locate the circlips into the bearing grooves and ensure that the clip ends are together (photo).

5   If it is necessary to renew the selector shaft detent balls and springs, remove the bolts or rods used to hold them in place during removal of the casing and withdraw the balls and springs as required.

6   Examine the condition of the fork control shaft and its mechanism for wear, particularly at the fork fingers, and renew these components if necessary as follows:

7   Extract the circlip then slide out the pivot arm bush and the arm (photos).

8   Using a parallel pin punch, tap out the double roll pin, securing the fork finger assembly to the fork control shaft. Withdraw the shaft and recover the fork and oil seal (photo).

9   With the new components at hand, reassemble the fork control assembly using the reverse of the removal procedure. The longer fork finger must be towards the casing. Apply grease to the pivot arm bush halves (photos).

8.3 Expand the circlip when fitting the bearing

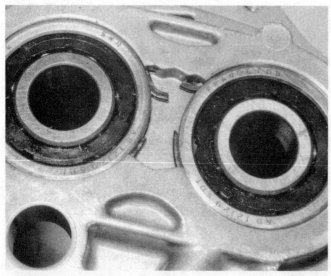

8.4 Bearings fitted in the mechanism casing

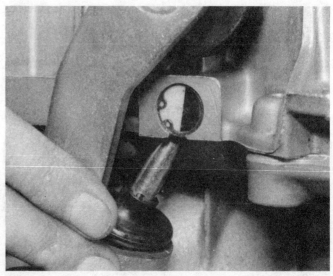

8.7A Extract the circlip ...

8.7B .. and slide out the fork control shaft pivot

8.8A Withdrawing the fork control shaft from the fork finger ...

8.8B ... and mechanism casing

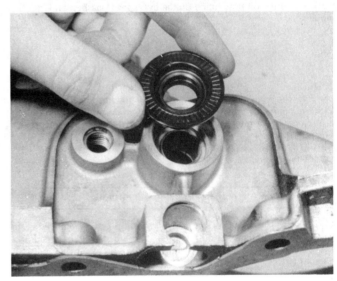

8.8C Fork control shaft oil seal

8.9A Fitting the roll pin in the fork finger and fork control shaft

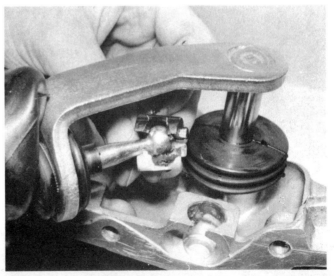

8.9B Assembling the pivot arm bush halves

8.10 Fitting the oil flow guide on the five-speed gearbox on later models

8.11 Inner breather tube on the mechanism casing

10 If the oil flow guide on the five-speed gearbox is to be renewed, bend flat the retaining lip edge on the guide and push it into the casing. Push the new guide up into position and bend over the lip edge to lock it in place. Some later models have a modified guide which clips into position (photo).

11 Check that the breather inner tube is correctly located and undamaged (photo).

9 Clutch and differential housing – overhaul

1 If a press is available the differential bearings can be removed quite easily. After removing the differential, as described previously, support the housing, bellhousing face downwards, and press the relevant bearing out. If the smaller bearing is to be removed, extract the circlip first. Fit the new bearings in the same way and use a new circlip to

secure the smaller bearing (photo).

2 If it is necessary to renew the mainshaft support bearing, take the housing to a Renault dealer and have him renew the bearing for you using the Renault removal and refitting tools (photo).

3 The gearbox input shaft oil seal is part of a complete assembly containing the input shaft roller bearing, and is located within a tubular housing. The complete assembly must be renewed if either the oil seal or the bearing require attention.

4 To remove the assembly, extract it using tubes of suitable diameter with washers, a long bolt or threaded rod and nuts (photos). Tighten the nuts and draw the assembly out of its location and into the tube. Alternatively a press, metal tube, or a socket can be used (photo).

5 Refit the new oil seal and bearing assembly in the same way, but position it so that the bearing lubrication holes in the bearing assembly and clutch and differential housing will be directly in line after fitting. To ensure correct alignment mark the bearing and casing before refitting, then check that the marks are adjacent after refitting (photos).

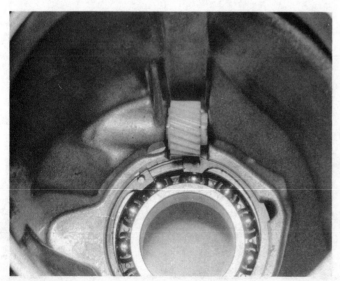

9.1 Showing a differential bearing and speedometer drive pinion gear

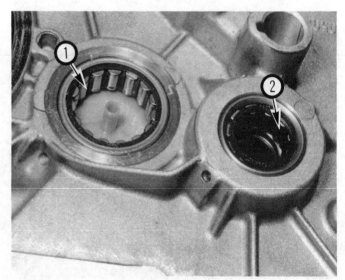

9.2 Mainshaft (1) and input shaft (2) bearings in the clutch and differential housing

9.4A Home made tool consisting of a tube, threaded rod, nut and washers on one side of the housing ...

9.4B ... and a socket, nut and washer on the other side for removing and refitting the input shaft oil seal and bearing

9.4C Using a socket to drive out the ...

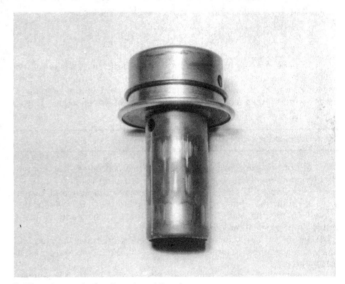

9.4D ... input shaft oil seal and bearing

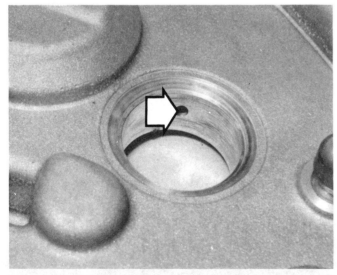

9.5A Input shaft bearing lubrication hole viewed from the clutch bellhousing side

9.5B Input shaft bearing lubrication hole viewed from inside the gearbox

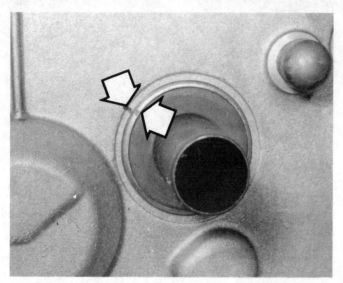

9.5C Mark the bearing and casing before fitting the bearing

CORRECT   INCORRECT

Fig. 6.6 Showing correct alignment of speedometer drive pinion gear and driveshaft (Sec 9)

6   If the speedometer drive pinion gear requires removal, the plastic driveshaft must be broken. When fitting the new gear make sure that the driveshaft is positioned as shown in Fig. 6.6 before tapping it smartly into the gear so that the locking notches are engaged.

10 Differential – overhaul

1   It is not advisable to dismantle the differential unless it is known that its components are suspect or require attention (photos).
2   If dismantling is to be undertaken, remove the sun and planet wheels from the differential by referring to Fig. 6.7. Keep the sunwheels together with their respective thrust washers and lay them out in strict order of removal.
3   If any of the sun wheels, planet wheels or thrust washers require renewal, it will be necessary to renew all the components as a matching set.
4   Reassemble the differential using the reverse of the dismantling sequence.

10.1A Differential unit

10.1B Showing the location recess in the differential for the left-hand driveshaft

10.1C Speedometer drive gear and right-hand differential stub

Fig. 6.7 Exploded view of the differential assembly (Sec 10)

38 O-ring
39 Oil seal
40 Circlip
41 Speedometer drivegear
42 Differential inner bearing
43 Plain thrust washer
44 Dished thrust washer
45 Differential crownwheel
   assembly

46 Snap-ring
47 Shim
48 Spider sun wheel
49 Planet wheel shaft
50 Planet wheels
51 Planet wheel thrust washers
52 Planet wheel and stub shaft

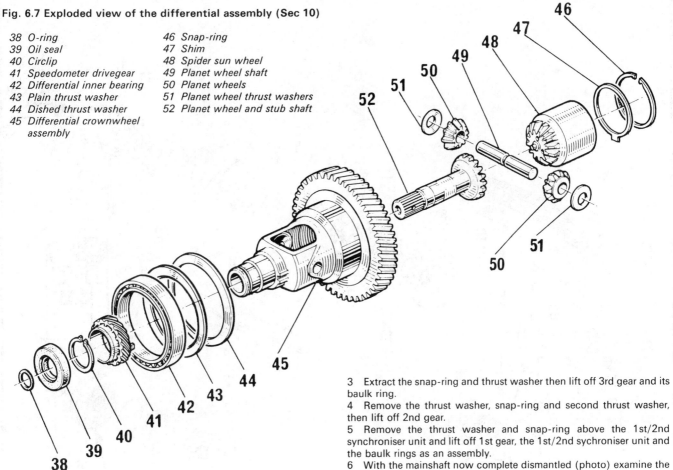

---

11 Mainshaft – dismantling and reassembly

1   Support the mainshaft in a vice with protected jaws and commence dismantling at the 4th gear end as follows:
2   Lift off the 3rd/4th and reverse synchroniser unit, completely with the 4th gear baulk ring, 4th gear and the upper thrust washer as a complete assembly.

3   Extract the snap-ring and thrust washer then lift off 3rd gear and its baulk ring.
4   Remove the thrust washer, snap-ring and second thrust washer, then lift off 2nd gear.
5   Remove the thrust washer and snap-ring above the 1st/2nd synchroniser unit and lift off 1st gear, the 1st/2nd sychroniser unit and the baulk rings as an assembly.
6   With the mainshaft now complete dismantled (photo) examine the gears and synchroniser units, as described in Section 12, then proceed with the reassembly as follows:
7   Place 1st gear on the mainshaft with the flat face of the gear towards the pinion (photo).
8   Place the baulk ring over 1st gear and then position the 1st/2nd synchroniser unit over it making sure that the sleeve and hub are positioned correctly as shown in Fig. 6.8 and that the lugs on the baulk ring engage with the roller grooves in the hub. Place the 2nd gear baulk ring on the 1st/2nd synchroniser unit then refit the snap-ring. If

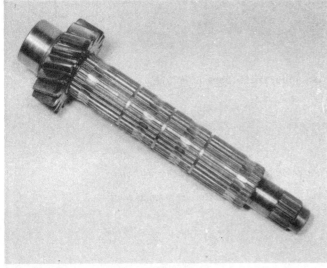

11.6 Mainshaft completely dismantled

11.7 Fit 1st gear followed by ...

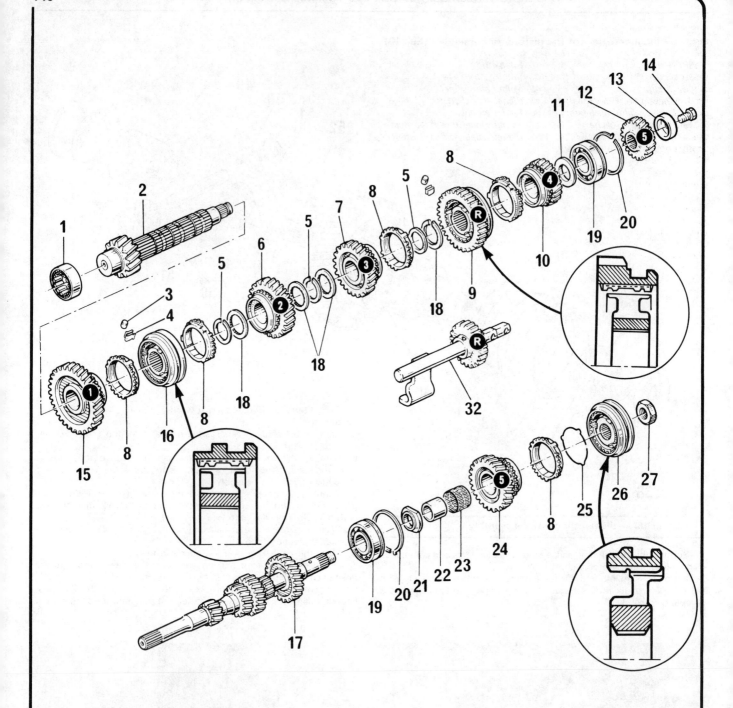

Fig. 6.8 Exploded view of the mainshaft and input shaft (Secs 11 and 12)

1 Roller bearing	11 Thrust washer	21 Thrust washer
2 Mainshaft	12 5th speed driven gear	22 Bush
3 Roller	13 Collar	23 Needle roller bearing
4 Spring plate	14 Bolt	24 5th speed driving gear
5 Snap-ring	15 1st speed gear	25 Spring
6 2nd speed gear	16 1st/2nd synchroniser unit	26 5th synchroniser unit
7 3rd speed gear	17 Input shaft	27 Nut
8 Baulk ring	18 Thrust washers	32 Reverse selector shaft
9 3rd/4th synchroniser unit	19 Ball bearing	and gear
10 4th speed gear	20 Circlip	

difficulty is experienced locating the snap ring in its groove, owing to insufficient room between the expanded snap-ring and synchroniser spring plates, proceed as follows. Remove the synchroniser unit then mark the sleeve and hub in relation to each other and slide them apart under some cloth to catch the rollers and spring plates. Place the hub alone on the mainshaft and fit the snap-ring. Locate the spring plates on the hub, fit the sleeve, then press each roller individually into position. Fit the 2nd gear baulk ring (photos).

9   Lay the thrust washer over the snap-ring, then slide 2nd gear onto the mainshaft with its flat side facing away from the pinion end of the shaft (photo).

10 Fit the assembly of thrust washer, snap-ring and thrust washer to the mainshaft, then slide on 3rd gear with its flat face towards the pinion end of the mainshaft (photos).

11 Place a thrust washer over 3rd gear and secure it with the remaining snap-ring (photos).

12 Fit the 2nd gear baulk ring to 3rd gear followed by the 3rd/4th and reverse synchroniser unit making sure that the sleeve and hub are positioned correctly as shown in Fig. 6.8 and that the lugs on the baulk ring engage with the roller grooves in the hub (photos).

13 Fit the 4th gear baulk ring to the 3rd/4th synchroniser unit, then slide on the 4th gear followed by the final thrust washer (photos).

11.8A ... the 1st gear baulk ring ...

11.8B ... the 1st/2nd synchroniser unit ...

11.8C ... the 2nd gear baulk ring ...

11.8D ... and the snap ring

11.8E Alternatively dismantle the synchroniser and fit the hub and snap ring followed by ...

11.8F ... the spring plates ...

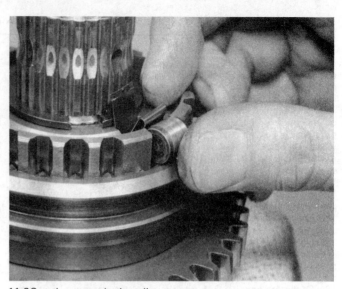

11.8G ... then press in the rollers ...

11.8H ... and fit the 2nd gear baulk ring

11.9 Fit the thrust washer and 2nd gear followed by ...

11.10A ... the thrust washer ...

11.10B ... snap-ring and further thrust washer ...

11.10C ... 3rd gear ...

11.11A ... thrust washer ...

11.11B ... the snap-ring ...

11.12A ... the 3rd gear baulk ring ...

11.12B ... the 3rd/4th synchroniser unit ...

11.13A ... the 4th gear baulk ring ...

11.13B ... the 4th gear ...

11.13C ... and finally the thrust washer

12 Shafts, gears and synchroniser units – inspection

1   With the gearbox completely dismantled, inspect the mainshaft, input shaft and reverse shaft for signs of damage, wear or chipping of the teeth, or wear or scoring of the shafts where they engage with their bearings (photo). If any of these conditions are apparent, the relevant shaft must be renewed.

2   If necessary, the synchroniser units can be dismantled for inspection by covering the assembly with a rag and then pushing the hub out of the sliding sleeve. Collect the spring plates and rollers which will have been ejected into the rag (photo). Note that each synchroniser unit hub and sliding sleeve is a matched set and they must not be interchanged.

3   Check that the hub and sleeve slide over each other easily and that there is a minimum of backlash or axial rock. Examine the dog teeth of the sliding sleeve for excessive wear and renew the assembly if wear is obvious.

4   To reassemble the synchroniser units slide the hub into the sliding sleeve, noting that for the 1st/2nd unit the selector fork groove in the sleeve and the offset boss of the hub are on opposite sides. On the 3rd/4th unit, the selector fork groove and the hub offset boss are on the same side. On the 5th speed unit the chamfered outer edge of the sleeve is on the same side as the hub offset boss.

5   Place the synchroniser on the bench with the offset side of the hub facing downwards. Locate the end of the spring plate, having the two tangs, against the hub and position the roller between the loop of the spring plate and the side of the sleeve.

6   Push down on the roller and spring plate until they locate correctly with the roller located in the internal groove of the sliding sleeve (photo). Repeat this for the remaining rollers and spring plates.

7   Check the condition of the baulk rings by sliding them onto the land of the relevant gears and note whether they lock on the tapered land before reaching the gear shoulder. Also inspect the baulk rings for cracks or wear of the dog teeth and renew as necessary. It is recommended, having dismantled the gearbox this far, that all the baulk rings are renewed as a matter of course. The improvement in the gear changing action, particularly if the car has covered a considerable

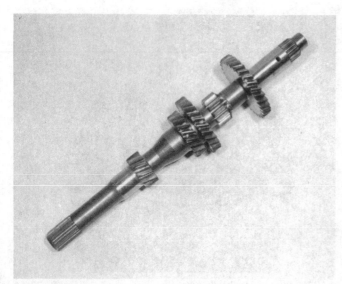

12.1 The input shaft and gears

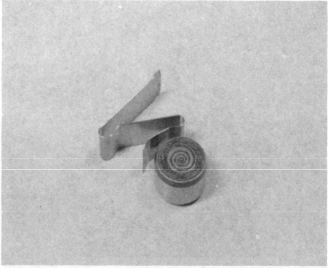

12.2 A synchroniser unit spring plate and roller

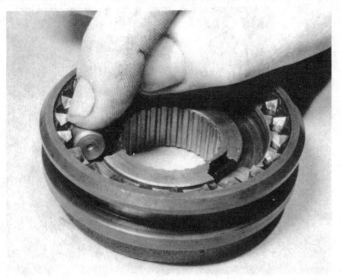

12.6 Fitting the synchroniser unit rollers

13.3A Locate the oil seal over the tape when fitting

mileage, will be well worth the expense. Note that the friction surface of all new baulk rings has a molybdenum disulphide coating and it is recommended that molybdenum disulphide grease is applied to this surface on assembly.

8   Finally check the selector fork clearance in the synchro-hub sliding sleeve groove, this should be minimal. If in doubt about the clearance, compare the forks with new ones and renew as necessary.

13 Gearbox mainshaft, input shaft and differential – refitting

1   If removed, first refit the differential in the clutch and differential housing. Locate the dished and plain washers against the crownwheel face as previously noted (i.e. plain washer first then concave side of dished washer against it).

2   Insert the differential into the bearings and use the puller or press to compress the dished washer. Fit the circlip then release the crownwheel. The dished washer will automatically provide the correct amount of preload on the bearings.

3   Wrap a little adhesive tape over the splines of the differential sunwheel stub in particular over the sealing face shoulder. Lubricate the lips of the new oil seal then slide it over the splines and tap it fully into the housing using a metal tube. Remove the adhesive tape (photo).

4   Refit the geartrain assembly using one of the following two alternative methods.

Method 1

5   Hold the assembled mainshaft, input shaft and reverse shaft together and locate all three shafts as an assembly into the housing.

6   Insert the long detent plunger into its location and push it through into contact with the reverse shaft detent grooves using a screwdriver (photo).

7   Locate the 1st/2nd selector fork in its groove in the synchro sleeve and engage the 1st/2nd selector shaft into it. Turn the shaft so that the detent grooves at the top are towards the mainshaft, insert the small detent plunger into the hole in the shaft and push the shaft down through the fork (photo). Manipulate the reverse shaft as necessary in the neutral position so that the 1st/2nd shaft can be pushed fully home.

8   Place the 3rd/4th selector fork into the groove in the synchro sleeve with its thicker side towards the differential.

9   Locate the detent plunger in its groove in the housing then slide the 3rd/4th selector shaft through the fork. Ensure that all the shafts are in

13.3B Using a metal tube to drive the oil seal in the housing

13.3C The oil seal in its final position

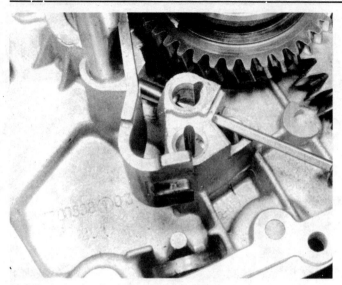

13.6 Push the detent plunger into its location with a screwdriver

13.7 Insert the small detent plunger (arrowed) into the 1st/2nd selector shaft

neutral and push the 3rd/4th shaft fully home. It may take a few attempts to get all the shafts, particularly reverse, in just the right position so that the detent plungers all locate fully into their grooves enabling the 3rd/4th shaft to be fitted.

10 Support the selector shafts using a tube of suitable diameter and refit the 1st/2nd and 3rd/4th selector fork roll pins. Tap in the pins until they are flush with the side of the forks (photos).

Method 2

11 Insert the small detent plunger in the hole in the 1st/2nd selector shaft (photo).

12 Locate the long detent plunger and the short detent plunger(s) in the clutch and differential housing between the selector shaft holes (photos).

13 Mesh the input shaft with the mainshaft gears and engage the 1st/2nd and 3rd/4th selector forks and shafts with their respective synchro sleeves. Move the selector forks to engage 2nd and 3rd gears.

14 Lift the geartrain assembly and lower it into the clutch and differential housing until the 3rd/4th selector shaft detent cut-out is in line with the short detent plunger in the housing then slide down the 1st/2nd selector shaft by moving it into neutral (photo).

13.10A Refit the 1st/2nd selector fork roll pin ...

13.10B ... and the 3rd/4th selector fork roll pin

13.11 Insert the detent plunger in the 1st/2nd selector shaft

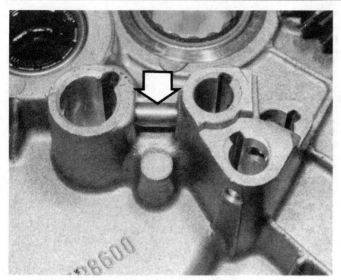

13.12A Long detent plunger location

13.12B Short detent plunger locations

15   Fit the valve spring or metal tube to the mainshaft as described in Section 7, paragraph 11.
16   Slightly lift the input shaft then lower the reverse idler gear and shaft into the clutch and differential housing (photo).

After either method
17   Refit the magnet in its location in the housing.

14 Gearbox – reassembling the housings

1   Make sure that the thrust washer is in position on top of the mainshaft (where applicable) and that the 5th speed selector shaft, detent ball and spring are in place in the mechanism casing on five-speed units. Alternatively the 5th speed selector shaft can be inserted in the clutch and differential housing, and the detent ball and spring fitted later (photo).
2   Wipe clean the mating faces of the two housings then apply a bead of CAF 4/60 THIXO jointing compound, available from Renault dealers, to both mating faces. *Note that no gasket is used (photo).*
3   Make sure that all the shafts are in neutral and that the engagement slots on the 1st/2nd and 3rd/4th shafts are exactly in line.

13.14 Lower the input shaft, mainshaft and selector shafts as an assembly into the clutch and differential housing

13.16 Reverse idler gear and shaft location

14.1 Fitting the 5th speed selector shaft

14.2 Apply jointing compound to the mating faces of the housings

4   Pull the fork control shaft on the mechanism casing outwards as far as it will go then lower the mechanism casing over the geartrains. Align the selector shafts with the holes in the casing and, as the shafts protrude, remove the two bolts or rods used to retain the detent balls and springs. Alternatively the detent springs and balls can be inserted as the casing is being fitted, starting with those for the 5th speed selector shaft (where applicable) then the 1st/2nd and 3rd/4th shafts (photos).

5   As the input shaft and mainshaft enter their bearings, tap the casing with a plastic mallet to assist entry.

6   Pass a hooked piece of wire through the aperture in the top of the casing. Lift up the reverse shaft and gear then retain the shaft with the detent ball, spring and retaining plate (photo).

7   Fit two of the retaining bolts to secure the housings, then check that it is possible to engage all the gears. On the five-speed gearbox turn the selector shaft anti-clockwise when checking the gears otherwise the selector gate will not be correctly aligned and it will be impossible to select the gears.

8   If satisfactory so far, refit the limit stop threaded plug on four-speed units, or the 5th speed detent assembly on five-speed units.

9   Insert and tighten the reverse lamp switch.

14.4A 5th speed selector shaft protruding through the mechanism casing

14.4B Inserting the 5th speed detent spring and ball

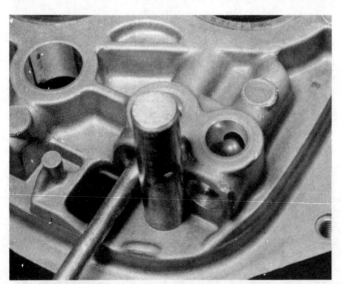

14.4C Depressing the detent ball for the 1st/2nd selector shaft

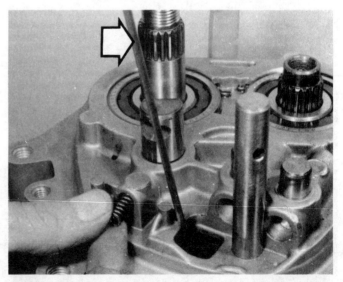

14.6 Inserting the reverse selector shaft detent ball and spring while lifting the gear and shaft with a hooked piece of wire (arrowed)

10 On the four-speed gearbox refit the dished washer and circlip to the end of the input shaft, then compress the washer by striking the circlip with a hammer and suitable socket or tube. As the washer compresses, the circlip will locate into its groove (photos). Repeat this procedure for the mainshaft dished washer and circlip, but on this shaft compress the washer using a socket and bolt screwed into the end of the mainshaft (photos).

11 Refit all the remaining housing retaining bolts tightened to the specified torque.

12 On the four-speed gearbox proceed to paragraph 17, on the five-speed gearbox proceed as follows:

13 Locate the 5th speed driven gear on the mainshaft splines (previously coated with a little locking fluid) and use a metal tube to tap it fully down.

14 Fit the washer, bearing bush and needle roller bearing to the input shaft then refit the driving gear, synchroniser unit and selector fork as an assembly. Make sure that the shoulder on the synchroniser unit sleeve is towards the driving gear (photo) and apply a little locking fluid to the splines of the unit.

15 Engage 1st gear by moving the gear linkage fork control shaft, and engage 5th gear by moving the 5th speed selector fork. With the geartrain now locked, refit and tighten the bolt and collar (with

14.10A Refit the dished washer and circlip to the input shaft ...

14.10B ... then tap the circlip using a hammer and tube to compress the washer

14.10C Refit the dished washer ...

14.10D ... and circlip to the mainshaft

14.10E Compress the dished washer using a socket, bolt and washer ...

14.10F ... in contact with the circlip

14.14 Fitting the 5th synchroniser unit and selector fork

washers where fitted) to the mainshaft, and the retaining nut to the input shaft using a little locking fluid on the threads.

16 Return the gears to neutral and refit the 5th gear selector fork roll pin.

17 On all types, place a new rubber 0-ring seal on the mechanism casing and refit the rear cover. Secure the cover with the retaining bolts.

18 Refit the 0-ring to the splines of the differential stub shaft.

19 Refit the gearbox mounting bracket then refer to Chapter 5 and refit the clutch release bearing and fork assembly.

15 Gear lever and remote control housing – removal, refitting and adjustment

1   To remove the gear lever and remote control housing first jack up the front of the car and support it on axle stands.

2   From underneath, unhook the tension spring fitted between the gearchange rod and the stud on the vehicle floor (photo).

3   Slacken the clamp bolt securing the gearchange rod to the gear lever yoke and withdraw the yoke from the rod.

4   Refer to Chapter 10 and remove the centre console where fitted, or on models without a centre console remove the rubber gaiter and slide it up the gear lever (photo).

5   Undo the four bolts securing the remote control housing to the floor and withdraw the assembly from the car. Recover the sealing gasket.

6   If necessary the gear lever assembly may be dismantled by referring to the component locations shown in Fig. 6.9. Note that the gear lever knob is bonded with adhesive to the lever.

7   Reassembly and refitting are the reverse of the above procedures. Adjust the gear lever as follows before tightening the yoke clamp bolt.

8   Select 2nd gear at the gearbox by moving the fork control shaft.

9   Move the gear lever so that the 0-ring on the gear lever rests against the rear left face of the housing (Fig. 6.10) and at the same time insert the yoke in the gearchange rod. There should be a space of 5.0 mm (0.2 in) between the end of the rod and the yoke end nearest the lever. Hold the components in this position and tighten the clamp bolt. Refit the tension spring.

10 Check that all the gears can be selected then refit the rubber gaiter or centre console as applicable. Lower the car to the ground.

15.2 Gearchange tension spring on the underbody

15.4 Gear lever with rubber gaiter removed

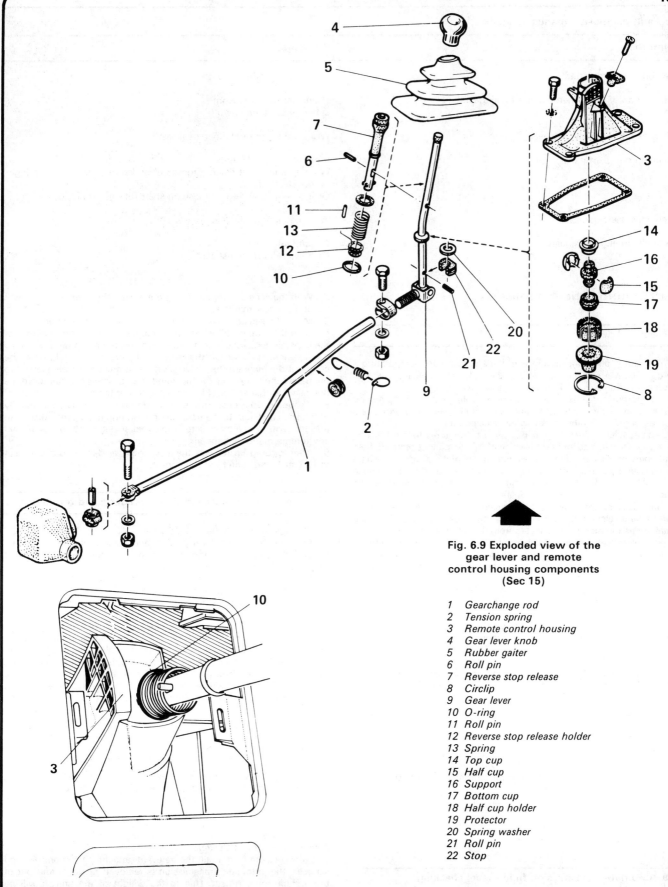

Fig. 6.9 Exploded view of the
gear lever and remote
control housing components
(Sec 15)

1   Gearchange rod
2   Tension spring
3   Remote control housing
4   Gear lever knob
5   Rubber gaiter
6   Roll pin
7   Reverse stop release
8   Circlip
9   Gear lever
10 O-ring
11 Roll pin
12 Reverse stop release holder
13 Spring
14 Top cup
15 Half cup
16 Support
17 Bottom cup
18 Half cup holder
19 Protector
20 Spring washer
21 Roll pin
22 Stop

Fig. 6.10 Gear lever O-ring (10) and remote control housing
(3) (Sec 15)

16 Fault diagnosis – manual gearbox

Symptom	Reason(s)
Gearbox noisy in neutral	Input shaft bearings worn
Gearbox noisy only when moving (in all gears)	Mainshaft bearings worn Differential bearings worn
Gearbox noisy in only one gear	Worn, damaged or chipped gear teeth
Jumping out of gear	Worn synchroniser units Worn selector shaft detent grooves or broken plunger or ball spring Worn selector forks Gear or synchroniser unit loose on shaft (5th gear only)
Ineffective synchromesh	Worn baulk rings or synchroniser units
Difficulty in engaging gears	Clutch fault Gear lever out of adjustment

Part 2: Automatic transmission

17 General description

The automatic transmission is of three-speed type incorporating a torque converter, an epicyclic geartrain, hydraulically-operated clutches and brakes, and an electronic control unit.

The torque converter provides a fluid coupling between engine and transmission which acts as an automatic clutch, and also provides a degree of torque multiplication when accelerating.

The epicyclic geartrain provides either of the three forward or one reverse gear ratios according to which of its component parts are held stationary or allowed to turn. The components of the geartrain are held or released by brakes and clutches which are activated by a hydraulic control unit. An oil pump within the transmission provides the necessary hydraulic pressure to operate the brakes and clutches.

Impulses from switches and sensors connected to the transmission, throttle and selector linkage are directed to a computer module which determines the ratio to be selected from the information received. The computer activates solenoid valves which in turn open or close ducts within the hydraulic control unit. This causes the clutches and brakes to hold or release the various components of the geartrain and provide the correct ratio for the particular engine speed or load. The information from the computer module can be overriden by use of the selector lever and a particular gear can be held if required, regardless of engine speed.

Due to the complexity of the automatic transmission any repair or overhaul work must be left to a Renault dealer with the necessary special equipment for fault diagnosis and repair. The contents of the following Sections are therefore confined to supplying general information and any service information and instruction that can be used by the owner.

18 Routine maintenance

At the intervals specified in the Routine Maintenance section in the front of the manual carry out the following procedures.

1   Check and if necessary top up the automatic transmission fluid level as described in Section 19.

2   Drain and refill the automatic transmission with fresh fluid as described in Section 20.

3   Visually inspect the automatic transmission joint faces and oil seals for signs of fluid leakage or damage.

19 Automatic transmission fluid – level checking

1   Check the fluid level when the car has been standing for some time and the fluid is cold.

2   With the car standing on level ground, start the engine and allow it to run for a few minutes.

3   Move the selector lever to P if not already in this position.

4   With the engine still idling withdraw the dipstick from the front of the transmission, wipe it on a clean cloth, insert it again then withdraw it once more and read off the level. Ideally the level should be in the centre of the mark on the dipstick. The fluid must never be allowed to fall below the bottom of the mark and the transmission must never be overfilled so that the level is above the top of the mark.

5   If topping-up is necessary, switch off the engine and add a quantity of the specified fluid to the transmission through the dipstick tube. Use a funnel with a fine mesh screen to avoid spillage and to ensure that any foreign matter is trapped.

6   After topping-up recheck the level again, as described above, refit the dipstick and switch off the engine.

20 Automatic transmission fluid – draining and refilling

1   The fluid must only be drained when cold.

2   Position the car on level ground and place a suitable container beneath the drain plug on the transmission fluid pan and at the base of the transmission housing (Fig. 6.15).

3   Remove the dipstick to speed up the draining operation, undo the two drain plugs and allow the fluid to drain.

4   When all the fluid has drained (this may take quite some time) refit the drain plugs.

5   Place a funnel with fine mesh screen in the dipstick tube and fill the transmission with the specified type of fluid. Depending on the extent to which the fluid was allowed to drain, refilling will only require approximately 2 litre (3.5 Imp pint). Add about half this amount and then check the level on the dipstick. When the level approaches the mark, place the selector lever in P, start the engine and allow it to run for approximately 2 minutes. Now check the level and complete the final topping up, as described in Section 19.

21 Automatic transmission – removal and refitting

Note: *This Section describes removal of the automatic transmission leaving the engine in the car, however as from 1986 models the transmission must be removed together with the engine as described in Chapter 1 then separated using the procedure described in paragraphs 6,10,14,16 to 18,20,23 and 25 of this Section. This is because a larger torque converter is fitted to these models. Refit with reference to paragraph 28 of this Section.*

1   After disconnecting all the relevant attachments, controls and services, the automatic transmission is removed upwards and out of the engine compartment. Due to the weight of the unit, it will be necessary to have some form of lifting equipment available, such as an engine crane or suitable hoist to enable the unit to be removed in this way.

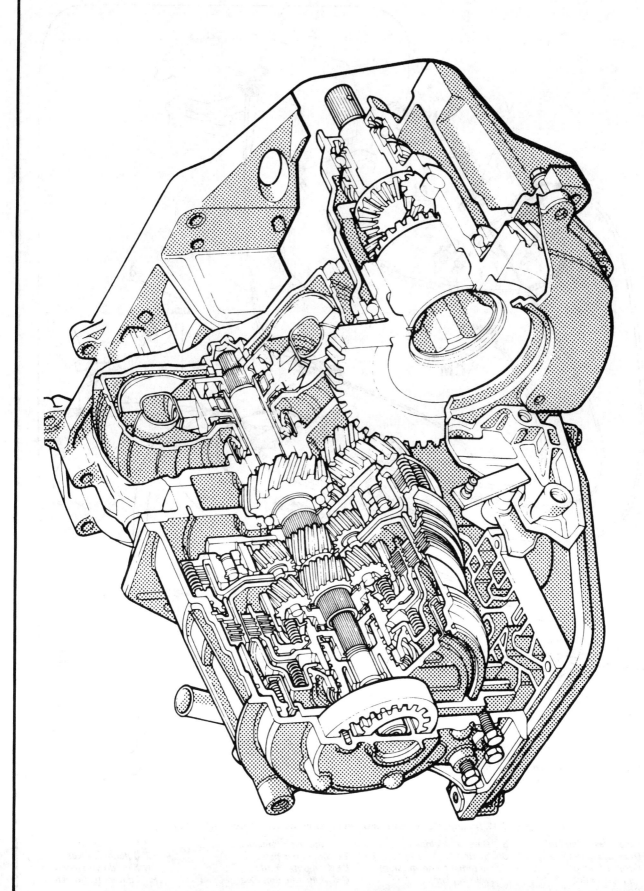

Fig. 6.11 Cut-away view of the automatic transmission (Sec 17)

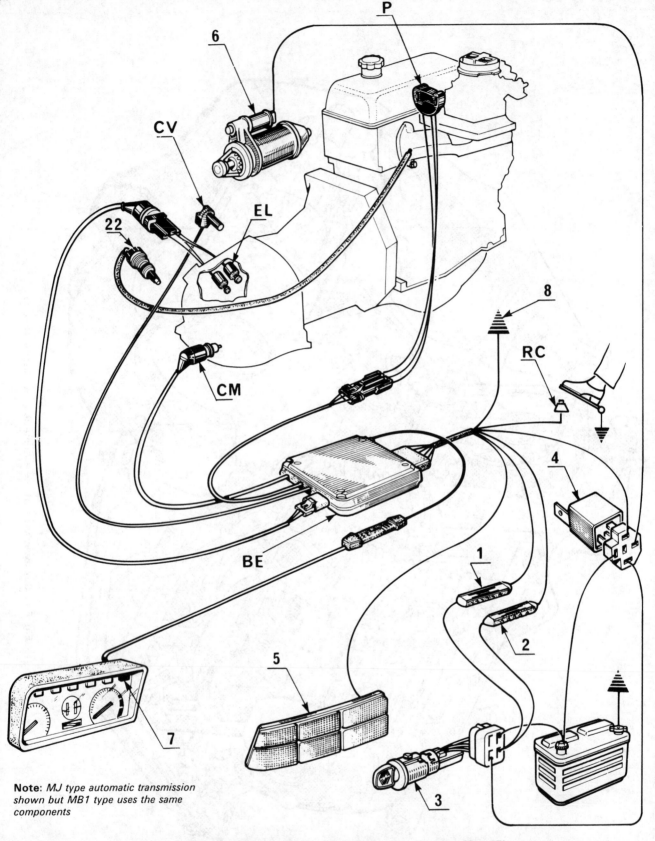

Fig. 6.12 Automatic transmission electronic control layout (Sec 17)

Note: *MJ type automatic transmission shown but MB1 type uses the same components*

1	Fuse – reversing lamp (5 amp)	5	Reversing lamps	8	Automatic transmission earth	CV	Speed sensor
2	Fuse (1.5 amp)	6	Starter	22	Vacuum capsule	EL	Solenoid valves
3	Ignition switch	7	Automatic transmission warning lamp	BE	Computer module	RC	Kick-down switch
4	Starter relay			CM	Multi-function switch	P	Load potentiometer

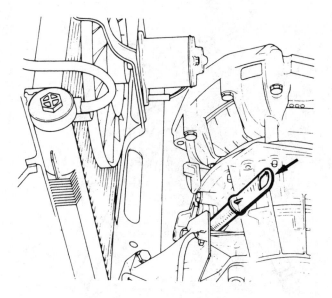

**Fig. 6.13 Transmission fluid dipstick location (arrowed)
(Sec 19)**

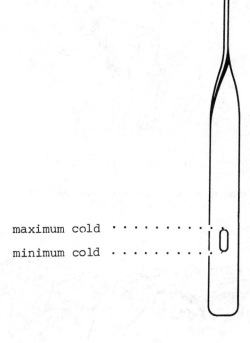

maximum cold · · · · · · · ·

minimum cold · · · · · · · · ·

Fig. 6.15 Dipstick fluid level markings (Sec 19)

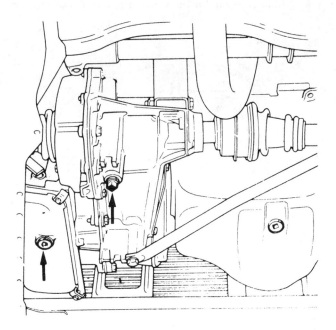

**Fig. 6.14 Transmission drain plug locations (arrowed)
(Sec 20)**

2   Begin by disconnecting the battery negative terminal and then refer to Section 20 and drain the transmission fluid.

3   Jack up the front of the car and support it on axle stands. Remove both front roadwheels.

4   Refer to Chapter 7 and remove the left-hand driveshaft completely, then disconnect the right-hand driveshaft inner joint yoke.

5   Working in the engine compartment, remove the air cleaner, as described in Chapter 3.

6   Undo the two shouldered bolts and remove the angular position sensor from the bellhousing.

7   Extract the speedometer cable wire retaining clip from its locating holes in the rear engine mounting bracket and transmission housing. Note the fitted direction of the clip. Withdraw the speedometer cable from the transmission.

8   Undo the two bolts and remove the tension springs securing the exhaust front section flange to the exhaust manifold.

9   Note the locations of the wires at the starter solenoid and disconnect them.

10 Undo the starter motor support bracket bolt and the three bolts securing the starter to the bellhousing, then remove the starter. Note the locating dowel in the upper rear bolt location.

11 Disconnect the wiring to the radiator fan motor and thermostatic switch on the right-hand side of the radiator. Release the radiator upper spring retaining clamp, lift the radiator up and lay it over the engine with the hoses still attached. Protect the matrix with a sheet of card.

12 Disconnect the transmission selector control rod from the bracket and bellcrank, as shown in Fig. 6.16.

13 Disconnect the vacuum hose from the vacuum capsule on the front of the transmission.

14 Remove the multi-function switch from the left-hand side of the transmission.

15 Detach any clips and remaining cables as necessary and position all the disconnected wiring, harness and cables to one side so that there is clear access to the transmission from above.

16 From under the car, undo the bolts securing the lower cover plate to the bellhousing and remove the plate.

17 Mark the driveplate in relation to the torque converter then turn the driveplate as necessary and undo the bolts or nuts securing it to the torque converter.

18 Undo the bolts securing the steady rod to the engine and transmission, then remove the rod.

19 Undo the fluid cooler union nuts and remove the pipes from the transmission. Plug the unions to prevent dirt entry.

20 Bolt a suitable strip of metal, using one of the coverplate bolt holes, so that the torque converter will remain in place on the transmission as it is removed.

21 Position a jack under the engine sump with an interposed block of

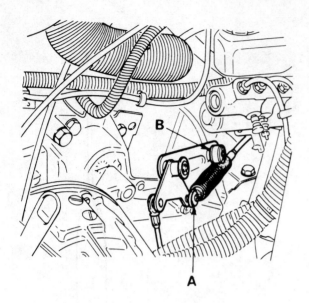

Fig. 6.16 Transmission selector control rod disconnection
points (A and B) (Sec 21)

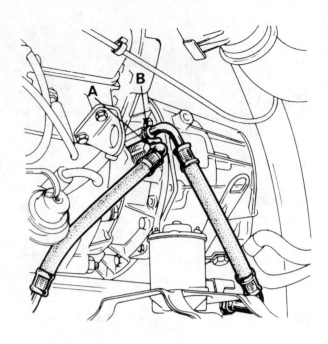

Fig. 6.17 Fluid cooler union nuts (A and B) at the transmission
(Sec 21)

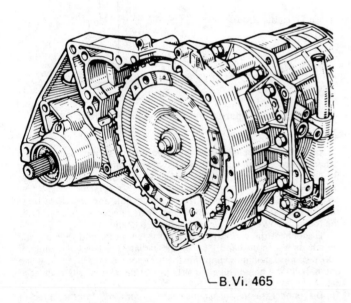

Fig. 6.18 The Renault tool shown or a suitable strip of metal
may be used to retain the torque converter (Sec 21)

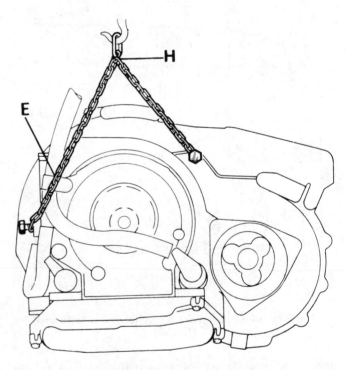

Fig. 6.19 After separating the transmission from the engine,
attach the lifting chains as shown and position the crane (H)
at point (E) on the chain (Sec 21)

wood, and attach a crane or hoist to the transmission using chain
slings. Depending on the type of lifting equipment being used, it may
be beneficial to remove the bonnet, as described in Chapter 10.
22 Raise the jack and crane and just take the weight of the engine and
transmission.
23 Undo all the bolts around the periphery of the bellhousing securing
the transmission to the engine. In addition to the bolts there are two
nuts or studs, one each side of the bellhousing. After undoing the nuts,
the studs must be removed and this can be done by locking two nuts
tightly together on the stud then unscrewing it using the innermost
nut.
24 Undo the bolts and nuts securing the transmission mounting
brackets to the rubber mountings. Raise the engine and transmission
slightly to free the mountings then remove the transmission mounting
brackets. Also slacken the engine mountings.

25 Move the engine and transmission as necessary and withdraw the
transmission sideways off the engine.
26 Temporarily lower the transmission onto blocks and reposition the
chain, as shown in Fig. 6.19. The transmission must be tipped up
vertically to provide clearance for removal.
27 Lift the transmission using the crane, move the engine within its

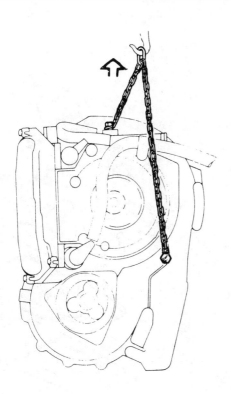

Fig. 6.20 The transmission must be tipped up vertically to allow removal from the engine compartment (Sec 21)

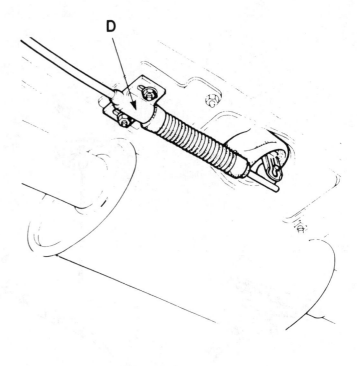

Fig. 6.21 Selector rod clamp plate location under the car (D) (Sec 22)

limits and allow the transmission to adopt the position shown in Fig. 6.20. Continue carefully lifting the transmission until it can swing over the wing or front panel, then lower the unit to the ground.

28 Refitting the automatic transmission is the reverse sequence to removal, but bear in mind the following points:

(a) *Lubricate the torque converter location in the crankshaft with molybdenum grease*
(b) *Fit the two studs to either side of the bellhousing before refitting the remainder of the transmission-to-engine retaining bolts.*
(c) *Refer to Chapter 3 for the special method of tightening the exhaust downpipe nuts*
(d) *Refit the driveshafts, as described in Chapter 7.*
(e) *Refill the transmission with fluid, as described in Section 20 of this Chapter.*

22 Selector mechanism – adjustment

1 Jack up the front of the car and support it on axle stands.
2 Move the selector lever inside the car to the P position.
3 Slacken the selector rod clamp plate nuts under the car so that the rod is free to move within the clamp plate.
4 Check that the selector lever on the transmission is also in the P position by turning it anti-clockwise as far as it will go if not already in this position.
5 Now tighten the selector rod clamp plate nuts.
6 Lower the car to the ground and check that all the selector positions can be engaged and that the starter only operates in the P and neutral positions.

23 Selector mechanism – removal and refitting

1 Jack up the front of the car and support it on axle stands.
2 Remove the centre console, as described in Chapter 11.
3 From under the car, extract the retaining clip, washer and clevis pin securing the gear selector lever to the selector rod.

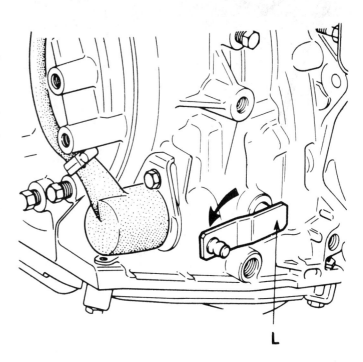

Fig. 6.22 Move the transmission selector lever (L) as shown to select P (Sec 22)

4 Undo the nuts and bolts securing the gear selector housing to the floor, disconnect the illumination bulb wiring and remove the housing from the car.
5 If necessary the housing can be dismantled by referring to the component locations shown in Fig. 6.23.
6 Reassembling and refitting are the reverse of the above procedures. Adjust the mechanism, as described in Section 22, after refitting.

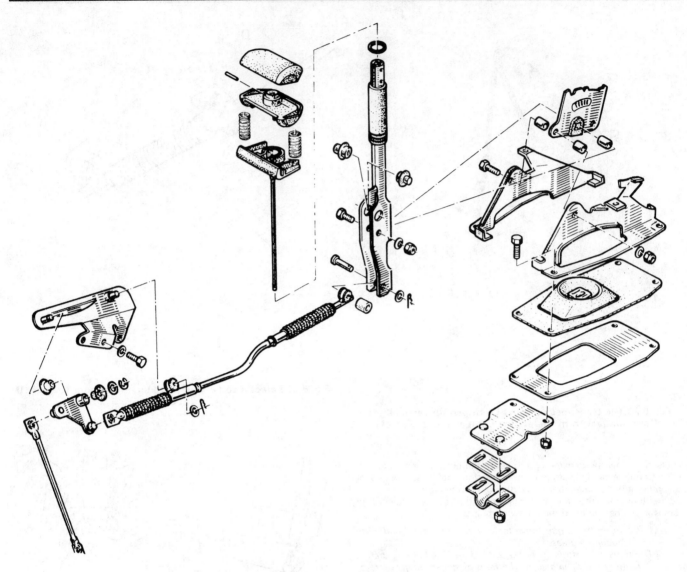

**Fig. 6.23 Exploded view of the selector mechanism
components (Sec 23)**

24 Fault diagnosis – automatic transmission

In the event of a fault occurring on the transmission, it is first necessary to determine whether it is of an electrical, mechanical or hydraulic nature and to do this special test equipment is required. It is therefore essential to have this work carried out by a Renault dealer if a transmission fault is suspected or if the transmission warning lamp on the instrument panel illuminates.

Do not remove the transmission from the car for possible repair before professional fault diagnosis has been carried out, since most tests require the transmission to be in the vehicle.

Chapter 7 Driveshafts

For modifications, and information applicable to later models, see Supplement at end of manual

Contents

Specifications

Type .... Unequal length tubular driveshafts with sliding tripod constant velocity joints

Lubrication

Outer CV joints and right-hand inner CV joint	Elf S747 (Duckhams LBM10)
Left-hand inner CV joint	Lubricated by gearbox oil or automatic transmission fluid

Grease quantities

Outer CV joints	196 g (6.91 oz)
Left-hand inner CV joint	140 g (4.94 oz)

Torque wrench settings

	Nm	lbf ft
Driveshaft retaining nut	250	184
Left-hand inner bellows retaining plate	25	18
Stub axle carrier to strut bolts	80	59
Steering tie-rod end	40	30

1 General description

Drive is transmitted from the differential to the front wheels by means of two, unequal length, tubular steel driveshafts.

Both driveshafts are fitted with a constant velocity joint of the sliding tripod type at their outer ends. The constant velocity joint consists of the stub axle member which is splined to engage with the front wheel hub, and a spider containing needle bearings and rollers which engage with the driveshaft yoke. The complete assembly is protected by a rubber bellows secured to the driveshaft and stub axle member.

At the driveshaft inner ends a different arrangement is used each side. On the right-hand side the driveshaft is splined to engage with a spider also containing needle bearings and rollers. The spider is free to slide within the joint yoke which is splined and retained by a roll pin to the differential sun wheel stub shaft. As on the outer joints a rubber bellows secured to the driveshaft and yoke protects the complete assembly.

On the left-hand side the driveshaft also engages with a spider, but the yoke in which the spider is free to slide is an integral part of the differential sun wheel. On this side the rubber bellows is secured to the transmission casing with a retaining plate and to a ball-bearing on the driveshaft with a retaining clip. The bearing allows the driveshaft to turn within the bellows which does not revolve.

The design and construction of the driveshaft components is such that the only repairs possible are renewal of the rubber bellows and renewal of the inner joint spiders. Wear or damage to the outer constant velocity joints or the driveshaft splines can only be rectified by fitting a complete new driveshaft assembly.

2 Routine maintenance

1 A thorough inspection of the driveshafts and driveshaft joints should be carried out at the intervals given in Routine Maintenance, using the following procedure:

2 Jack up the front of the car and support it securely on axle stands.

3 Slowly rotate the roadwheel and inspect the condition of the outer constant velocity joint rubber bellows. Check for signs of cracking, splits or deterioration of the rubber which may allow the grease to escape and lead to water and grit entry into the joint. Also check the security and condition of the retaining clips and then repeat these checks on the inner joint bellows. If any damage or deterioration is evident, renew the bellows.

4 Continue rotating the roadwheel and check for any distortion or damage to the driveshaft. Check for any free play in the outer joints by holding the driveshaft firmly and attempting to turn the wheel. Any noticeable movement indicates wear in the joints, wear in the constant velocity joint or wheel hub splines, a loose driveshaft retaining nut or loose wheel bolts.

3 Driveshaft – removal and refitting

1 Jack up the front of the car and support securely on axle stands. Apply the handbrake and remove the appropriate roadwheel.

2 Remove the front brake caliper with reference to Chapter 8, but leaving the hydraulic hose connected. Tie the caliper to one side with wire or string taking care not to damage the hose.

3 Hold the front hub stationary by using two roadwheel bolts to attach a length of metal bar, then unscrew the driveshaft nut (photo).

4 Disconnect the steering tie-rod end from the stub axle carrier with reference to Chapter 9.

5 Unscrew the two nuts and withdraw the bolts securing the stub axle carrier to the suspension strut. Note that the nuts are on the brake caliper side.

Left-hand driveshaft

6 Drain the gearbox oil or automatic transmission fluid with reference to Chapter 6.

7 Unscrew the three bolts securing the rubber bellows retaining plate to the side of the gearbox/transmission (photos).

Right-hand driveshaft

8 Using a parallel pin punch drive out the roll pin securing the inner

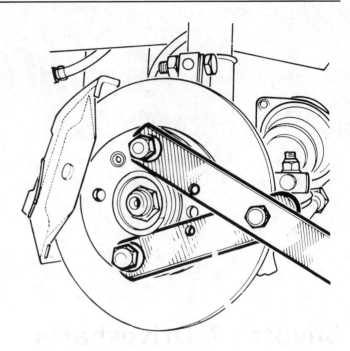

Fig. 7.1 Tool made from metal bar for holding the front hub stationary (Sec 3)

joint yoke to the differential stub shaft. The roll pin is in fact two roll pins, one inside the other.

Both driveshafts

9 Pull the top of the stub axle carrier outwards until the inner end of the driveshaft is released from the yoke (left-hand) (photo) or shaft (right-hand).

10 Withdraw the outer joint stub axle from the hub, if necessary using a soft metal drift or suitable extractor to release the stub axle from the splines.

11 When refitting, insert the driveshaft in the gearbox/transmission first then locate the outer joint stub axle in the hub splines. Lubricate the splines with molybdenum disulphide grease and make sure that the roll pin holes on the right-hand side inner joint yoke are correctly

3.3 Driveshaft nut

3.7A Rubber bellows and retaining plate on the left-hand driveshaft inner joint

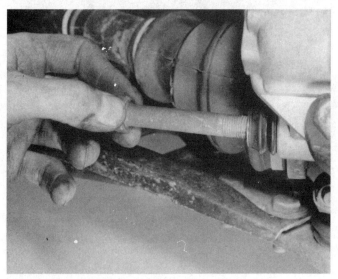

3.7B Removing the left-hand driveshaft retaining plate bolts

3.9 Withdraw the left-hand driveshaft spider from the differential yoke

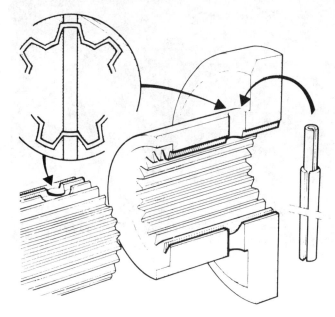

Fig. 7.2 Double roll pin location on the right-hand driveshaft inner joint yoke (Sec 3)

Fig. 7.3 Removing the left-hand driveshaft (Sec 3)

aligned. Drive in the roll pins with their slots 90° apart (Fig. 7.2) then seal the holes with sealing compound (photos).

12 Insert the stub axle carrier bolts and reconnect the steering tie-rod end. Tighten the nuts to the specified torque.

13 Fit the driveshaft nut and tighten it to the specified torque using the metal bar (paragraph 3).

14 Before locating the left-hand side inner joint bellows clean the contact area of the gearbox/transmission. Position the bellows evenly before fitting the retaining plate and tightening the bolts (photo). Fill the gearbox/transmission with oil/fluid with reference to Chapter 6.

15 Refit the front brake caliper (Chapter 8) and roadwheel, then lower the car to the ground. Depress the brake pedal several times to re-set the disc pads.

4 Outer constant velocity joint rubber bellows – renewal

1 Remove the driveshaft as described in Section 3.

2 Cut through the metal bands with snips without damaging the groove in the stub axle casing or the driveshaft itself.

3.11A The roll pin holes must be aligned when refitting the right-hand driveshaft

3.11B Secure the right-hand driveshaft to the differential stub shaft by driving in the large roll pin ...

3.11C ... followed by the small roll pin ...

3.11D ... then seal the holes with sealing compound

3.14 Showing the left-hand driveshaft spider located in the differential yoke prior to fitting the rubber bellows and retaining plate

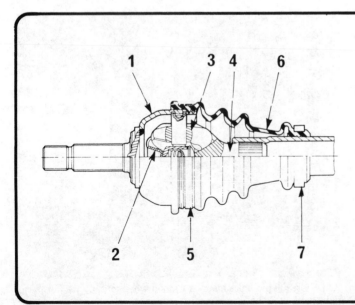

Fig. 7.4 Cut-away view of the outer constant velocity joint (Sec 4)

1 Stub axle member
2 Starplate
3 Spider and rollers
4 Driveshaft yoke
5 Metal band clip
6 Rubber bellows
7 Metal band clip

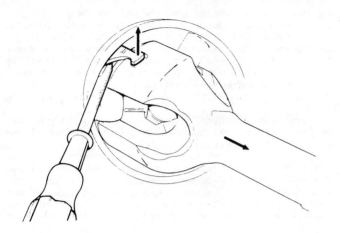

Fig. 7.5 Using a screwdriver to prise up the starplate retainer arms (Sec 4)

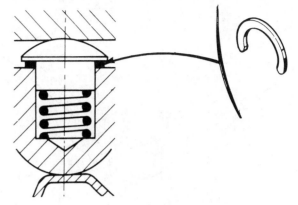

Fig. 7.6 Showing shim location beneath the thrust plunger (Sec 4)

3   Slide the bellows away from the constant velocity joint and scoop out as much grease as possible from the joint.

4   Mount the stub axle in a soft jawed vice then pull the driveshaft from it while prising up the starplate retainer arms with a screwdriver. Prising up one arm should be sufficient to release the driveshaft. Do not twist the arms.

5   Recover the thrust plunger, shim and spring from the stub axle. The original shim must be refitted to maintain the correct end play.

6   Cut the old bellows from the driveshaft. Clean the driveshaft yoke and remove as much of the remaining grease as possible from the spider and stub axle member. Do this using a wooden spatula or old rags; *do not use any cleaning solvent, petrol or paraffin.*

7   Obtain a new rubber bellows, retaining clips and a small quantity of the special lubricating grease. All these parts are available in the form of a repair kit obtainable through Renault parts stockists.

8   In order to fit the new bellows a special tool is required to expand the small end of the bellows and allow it to slide over the driveshaft yoke. The manufacturer's tool is shown in the accompanying illustrations, but a suitable alternative can be made by bending a sheet of tin in conical fashion and then bonding the seams using superglue or pop rivets. An old 5 litre oil container is quite useful for this purpose. Make sure that the seam is well protected with tape to prevent it cutting the new bellows.

9   Before fitting the new bellows generously lubricate the expander tool and the inside of the bellows with clean engine oil.

10 Position the small end of the bellows over the small end of the tool and move it up and down the expander two or three times to make the rubber more pliable.

11 Mount the driveshaft in a soft jawed vice with the yoke angled upwards.

12 Position the large end of the expander against the driveshaft yoke and pull the bellows up the expander and onto the yoke. Make sure that the end of the bellows does not tuck under as it is being fitted, and use plenty of lubricant.

13 When the small end of the bellows is in place over the yoke, remove the tool and slide the bellows up the driveshaft.

14 Insert the spring and thrust plunger in the stub axle and make sure that the spider rollers are fully on the trunnions.

15 Fit the starplate retainer with the arms between the rollers.

16 With the stub axle mounted in the vice offer the driveshaft and yoke to it. Move the driveshaft from side to side until one of the retainer arms can be engaged in its cut-out, then press the driveshaft firmly over the spider and insert the remaining arms. A slotted screwdriver will facilitate lifting the arms in position (Fig. 7.9).

17 Move the driveshaft in the direction of one of the spider trunnions. This will cause the thrust plunger to lift, and the shim can then be inserted beneath the plunger head.

18 Remove the driveshaft from the vice then articulate the joint through all angles and check that it moves freely.

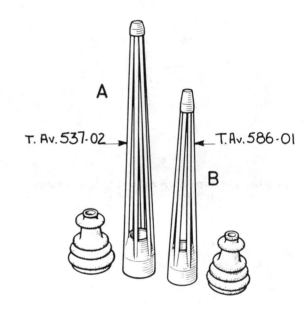

Fig. 7.7 Tools for fitting the outer joint bellows (Sec 4)

A   For 1397 cc models   *B   For 956 cc and 1108 cc models*

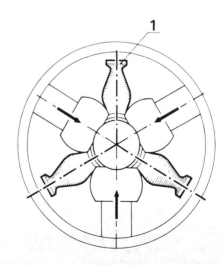

Fig. 7.8 Fit the starplate retainer (1) with the spider rollers pressed inwards (Sec 4)

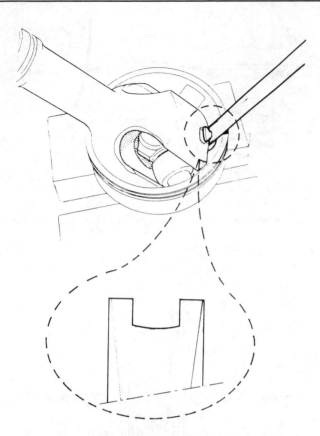

Fig 7.9 Using a slotted screwdriver to fit the starplate retainer arms (Sec 4)

support the spider under the rollers and press out the driveshaft. If a press is not available support the spider under its central boss, using suitable half-round packing pieces, and drive the shaft out using a hammer and brass drift. It is important, if this method is used, that only the central boss of the spider is supported and not the rollers. The shock loads imposed could easily damage the inner faces of the rollers and spider and also the small needle roller bearings.

7   With the spider removed the rubber bellows can now be slid off the driveshaft.

8   Clean the driveshaft and remove as much of the grease as possible from the spider and yoke using a wooden spatula or old rags. *Do not use any cleaning solvent, petrol or paraffin.*

9   Examine the spider, rollers and yoke for any signs of scoring or wear and for smoothness of movement of the rollers on the spider trunnions. If wear is evident the spider and rollers can be renewed, but it is not possible to obtain a replacement yoke. Obtain a new rubber bellows, retaining clips and a quantity of the special lubricating grease. These parts are available in the form of a repair kit available from Renault parts stockists.

10   Begin reassembly by lubricating the driveshaft and the inside of the bellows generously with engine oil.

11   Place the rubber retaining collar over the driveshaft and then fit the bellows.

12   Place the spider on the driveshaft splines in the same position as noted prior to removal.

13   Drive the spider fully onto the driveshaft using a hammer and tubular drift, then refit the retaining circlip.

14   Evenly distribute the special grease contained in the repair kit around the spider and inside the yoke.

15   Slide the yoke into position over the spider.

16   Using a piece of 2.5 mm (0.1 in) thick steel or similar material, make up a form plate to the dimensions shown in Fig. 7.11.

17   Position the form plate under each anti-separation plate tag in the yoke in turn, and tap the tag down onto the form plate. Remove the plate when all the tags have been returned to their original shape.

18   Slide the bellows up the driveshaft and locate the bellows in its respective grooves in the driveshaft and in the yoke.

19   Slip the rubber retaining collar into place over the bellows.

20   Insert a thin blunt instrument, such as a knitting needle, under the lip of the bellows to allow all trapped air to escape. With the instrument in position, compress the joint until the dimension from the small end of the bellows to the flat end face of the yoke is as shown in Fig. 7.13. Hold the yoke in this position and withdraw the instrument.

21   Slip a new retaining spring into place to secure the bellows and then refit the driveshaft, as described in Section 3.

19   Distribute the grease supplied in the repair kit evenly around the spider and the grooves in the driveshaft yoke.

20   Position the large end of the bellows on the stub axle casing making sure that the two lips are correctly located in the two grooves. Position the small end so that the bellows convolutions are neither stretched nor compressed.

21   With the stub axle and driveshaft aligned, lift the small end of the bellows temporarily to equalise the air pressure.

22   Fit the metal band clips on the ends of the bellows and secure by squeezing the raised portion. Ideally a crimping tool should be used, but alternatively pincers or pliers may be used.

23   Wipe away any external grease then refit the driveshaft as described in Section 3.

---

5   Right-hand driveshaft inner rubber bellows – renewal

1   Remove the driveshaft from the car, as described in Section 3.

2   Using a screwdriver, slip off the retaining spring securing the bellows to the yoke (photo).

3   Release the rubber retaining collar securing the bellows to the driveshaft and slide the bellows down the shaft.

4   Using pliers, carefully bend back the anti-separation plate tags and then slide the yoke off the spider. Be prepared to hold the rollers in place otherwise they will fall off the spider trunnions as the yoke is withdrawn. Secure the rollers in place using tape after removal of the yoke. The rollers are matched to their trunnions and it is most important that they are not interchanged.

5   Extract the circlip securing the spider to the driveshaft using circlip pliers. Using a dab of paint or a small file mark, identify the position of the spider in relation to the driveshaft, as a guide to refitting.

6   The spider can now be removed in one of the following ways. Preferably using a press or by improvisation with a hydraulic puller,

5.2 Right-hand driveshaft inner joint and rubber bellows

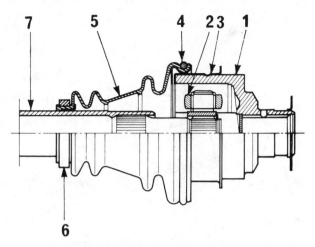

Fig. 7.10 Cut-away view of the right-hand constant velocity joint (Sec 5)

1 Yoke
2 Spider and rollers
3 Metal casing
4 Retaining spring
5 Rubber bellows
6 Retaining collar
7 Driveshaft

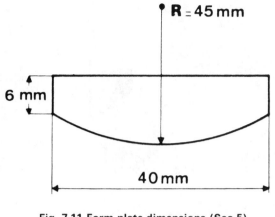

Fig. 7.11 Form plate dimensions (Sec 5)

Thickness = 2.5 mm (0.1 in)

Fig. 7.12 Using the form plate (1) to reshape the anti-separation plate tags (Sec 5)

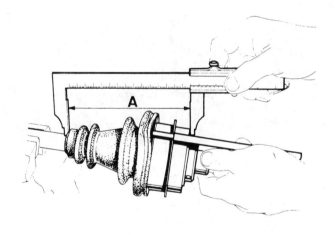

Fig. 7.13 Bellows setting dimension (Sec 5)

A = 153.5 ± 1.0 mm (6.043 ± 0.04 in)

6 Left-hand driveshaft inner rubber bellows – renewal

1   Remove the driveshaft, as described in Section 3.
2   Using circlip pliers, extract the circlip securing the spider to the driveshaft. Using a dab of paint or a small file mark, identify the position of the spider in relation to the driveshaft, as a guide to refitting (photo).
3   The spider can now be removed in one of the following ways. Preferably using a press or by improvisation with a hydraulic puller, support the spider under the rollers and press out the driveshaft. Alternatively support the spider under its central boss, using suitable half-round packing pieces, and drive the shaft out using a hammer and brass drift. It is important, if this method is used, that only the central boss of the spider is supported and not the rollers. The shock loads imposed could easily damage the inner faces of the rollers and spider and also the small needle roller bearings.
4   Now support the bearing at the small end of the bellows and press or drive the shaft out of the bellows and bearing assembly.
5   Carefully inspect the spider and rollers for signs of wear or deterioration. The rollers should be free from any signs of scoring and they should turn smoothly on the spider trunnions. Renew the spider assembly if necessary. Obtain a new bellows which is supplied complete with the small bearing.

6.2 Left-hand driveshaft inner joint spider, rubber bellows and retaining plate

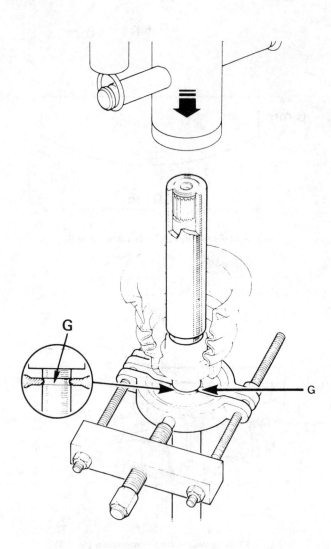

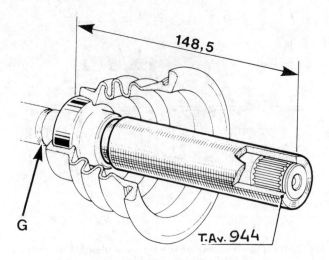

Fig. 7.15 Bellows bearing setting dimension (Sec 6)

G   Machined groove in driveshaft
Manufacturer's tool shown on driveshaft

6   Owing to the lip type seal used in the bearing, the bearing and bellows must be refitted using a press or by improvising using a hydraulic puller. There is a very great risk of damaging the seal by distortion if a hammer and tubular drift are used to drive the assembly onto the driveshaft.
7   Fig. 7.14 shows the arrangement for fitting the bellows and bearing if a press is being used. The bellows and bearing must be positioned so that the distance from the end of the driveshaft to the flat face at the small diameter end of the bellows is 148.5 mm (5.85 in) – see Fig. 7.15.
8   Now place the spider on the driveshaft in the same position as noted during removal. Drive or press the spider onto the shaft and refit the circlip.
9   Refit the driveshaft to the car, as described in Section 3.

7   Driveshaft inner joint spiders – removal and refitting

Removal and refitting of the spiders is an integral part of the rubber bellows renewal procedure and reference should be made to Section 5 or Section 6, as appropriate.

Fig. 7.14 Arrangement of hydraulic press and manufacturer's tool for refitting bellows bearing (Sec 6)

G   Machined groove in driveshaft

8   Fault diagnosis – driveshafts

Symptom	Reason(s)
Vibration	Worn joints
	Worn wheel or differential bearings
Noise on taking up drive	Worn driveshaft splines
	Worn joints
	Loose driveshaft nut

Chapter 8 Braking system

For modifications, and information applicable to later models, see Supplement at end of manual

Contents

Specifications

System type	Dual hydraulic circuit split diagonally with pressure regulating valve to rear brakes. Disc front brakes, and drum rear brakes on non-Turbo models, disc rear brakes on Turbo models. Servo assistance on some models. Cable-operated handbrake on rear brakes
Brake fluid type/specification	Hydraulic fluid to SAE J1073F, DOT 3, or DOT 4 (Duckhams Universal Brake and Clutch Fluid)

Front brakes

Type	Disc with Bendix or Girling single piston sliding calipers
Disc diameter	238.0 mm (9.37 in)
Disc thickness (new):	
Except 1397 cc models	8.0 mm (0.315 in)
1397 cc models (except Turbo)	12.0 mm (0.472 in)
Turbo models	20.0 mm (0.787 in)
Minimum disc thickness:	
Except 1397 cc models	7.0 mm (0.276 in)
1397 cc models (except Turbo)	10.5 mm (0.413 in)
Turbo models	18.0 mm (0.709 in)
Maximum disc run-out	0.07 mm (0.003 in)
Minimum disc pad thickness (including backplate)	6.0 mm (0.236 in)

Rear brakes (drum)

Type	Self-adjusting Bendix or Girling type
Drum diameter (new)	180.25 mm (7.097 in)
Maximum drum diameter	181.25 mm (7.136 in)
Minimum lining thickness (including shoe)	2.5 mm (0.098 in)

Rear brakes (disc)

Type	Bendix single piston sliding calipers incorporating self-adjusting handbrake mechanism
Disc diameter	238.0 mm (9.37 in)
Disc thickness (new)	8.0 mm (0.315 in)
Minimum disc thickness	7.0 mm (0.276 in)
Maximum disc run-out	0.07 mm (0.003 in)
Minimum disc pad thickness (including backplate)	5.0 mm (0.197 in)

Servo unit
Diameter .... 178.0 mm (7.0 in)

Handbrake
Lever minimum travel .... 12 notches

Torque wrench settings

	Nm	lbf ft
Bleed screws	6 to 8	4 to 6
Hose or pipe unions	13	10
Master cylinder	13	10
Servo unit	20	15
Brake caliper	100	74
Brake caliper reaction frame (Bendix)	60	44
Brake caliper guide bolts (Girling)	35	26
Rear hub nut	160	118

---

1 General description

The braking system is of dual hydraulic circuit type employing a tandem master cylinder. The circuit is split diagonally with the primary and secondary circuits each supplying one front brake and one diagonally opposite rear brake. Under normal conditions both circuits operate in unison, however in the event of failure of one circuit the remaining circuit will provide adequate braking to stop the car in an emergency. A dual circuit pressure regulating valve controls the braking pressure to the rear wheels in order to prevent rear wheel locking; on some models the valve is load sensitive.

Disc brakes are fitted to the front wheels. On non-Turbo models the rear brakes are drum type and on Turbo models disc type.

The cable operated handbrake operates independently on the rear wheels. A vacuum servo is fitted to some models to provide additional braking effort when the brake pedal is depressed.

---

2 Routine maintenance

At the intervals specified in the Routine Maintenance section in the front of the manual carry out the following procedures

1 Check that the brake fluid level in the reservoir is at or near the maximum mark (photo). The reservoir is located on the master cylinder on the right-hand side of the bulkhead in the engine compartment. Slight variations of level will occur according to the wear of the brake linings, however if the level drops towards the minimum mark the complete hydraulic system should be checked for leaks.

2 With the car raised on a hoist, over an inspection pit or supported on ramps or axle stands, carefully inspect all the hydraulic pipes, hoses and unions for chafing, cracks, leaks and corrosion. Details will be found in Section 17.

3 Remove the plugs over the inspection holes in the rear brake

2.1 Topping-up brake fluid level

backplates and check the thickness of the brake linings. Renew the brake shoes if the linings have worn to the specified minimum thickness. Note that it is only possible to check the thickness of the brake shoe linings in one position when viewing through the inspection holes. To check the lining condition and the operation of the wheel cylinders, it is recommended that the rear brake drums be removed so that a thorough inspection can be carried out, as described in Section 6.

4 Check the operation of the handbrake on each rear wheel and lubricate the exposed cables and linkages under the car.

5 Remove the front wheels and check the thickness of the front brake pads. Renew the pads, as described in Section 3, if they are worn to the specified minimum thickness.

6 At less frequent intervals (see Routine maintenance) the brake servo air filter and non-return valve should also be renewed, using the procedure described in Section 25. Also renew the brake fluid by bleeding it completely as described in Section 18 and allowing for all old fluid to be removed.

---

3 Front disc pads – inspection and renewal

1 Jack up the front of the car and support it on axle stands. Remove the front roadwheels.

2 View the brake pads end on and measure their thickness. If any of the pads is less than the specified minimum thickness, all four pads must be renewed as follows, according to brake caliper type.

Bendix calipers

3 Remove the brake fluid reservoir cap. Disconnect the brake pad wear warning light wire at the connector.

4 Extract the small spring clip and then withdraw the retaining key (photos).

5 Using a screwdriver, carefully lever between the disc and caliper so that the piston is pushed back sufficiently to allow removal of the pads.

6 Using pliers, if necessary, withdraw the pads from the caliper, and remove the anti-rattle spring from each pad (photos).

7 With the pads removed, check that the caliper is free to slide on the guide sleeves and that the rubber dust excluders around the piston and guide sleeves are undamaged. If attention to these components is necessary refer to Section 4.

8 To refit the pads, move the caliper sideways as far as possible towards the centre of the car. Fit the anti-rattle spring to the innermost pad making sure that this pad is the one with the wear warning light wire, then locate the pad in position, with the backing plate against the piston.

9 Note that the pads are symmetrical for non-1397 cc models or offset for 1397 cc models (photo). The offset type must be fitted as shown in Fig. 8.2.

10 Move the caliper outwards then fit the anti-rattle spring to the outer pad and locate the pad in the caliper.

11 Slide the retaining key into place and refit the small spring clip at the inner end (photo). It may be necessary to file an entry chamfer on the edge of the retaining key to enable it to be fitted without difficulty.

12 Reconnect the brake pad wear warning light wire, refit the roadwheel and repeat the renewal procedures on the other front brake. On completion check the hydraulic fluid level in the reservoir then depress the footbrake two or three times to bring the pads into contact with the disc, refit the roadwheels and lower the car to the ground.

3.4A Extract the small spring ...

3.4B ... and withdraw the retaining key

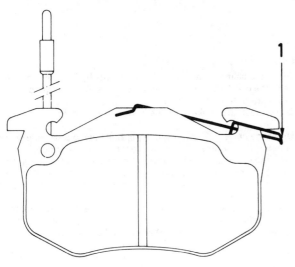

Fig. 8.1 Correct fitting of the anti-rattle spring (1) to the
Bendix disc pad (Sec 3)

3.6A Removing the outer disc pad ...

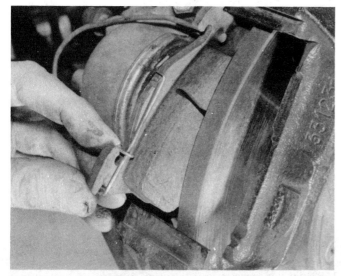

3.6B ... and inner disc pad

3.9 Showing offset disc pads fitted to 1397 cc models

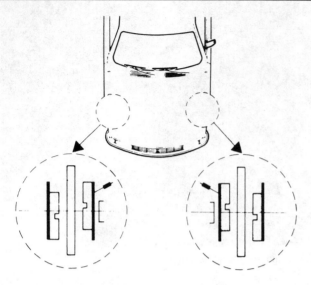

Fig. 8.2 Correct fitting of Bendix off-set disc pads viewed
from the front (Sec 3)

3.11 Showing retaining key correctly fitted

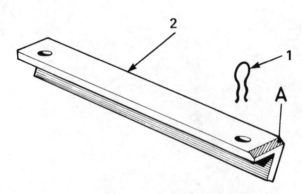

Fig. 8.3 Bendix disc pad retaining key (2) and spring (1)
showing filed chamfer (A) (Sec 3)

Girling calipers

13 Grasp the caliper body and pull it outwards by hand away from the
centre of the car. This will push the piston back into its bore to facilitate
removal and refitting of the pads.

14 Disconnect the brake pad wear warning light at the connector
(photo).

15 Undo the upper and lower guide pin bolts using a suitable spanner
while holding the guide pins with a second spanner (photo).

16 With the guide pin bolts removed, lift the caliper off the brake pads
and carrier bracket (photo), and tie it up in a convenient place under
the wheel arch. Do not allow the caliper to hang unsupported on the
flexible brake hose.

17 Withdraw the two brake pads from the carrier bracket (photo).

18 Before refitting the pads, check that the guide pins are free to slide
in the carrier bracket and check that the rubber dust excluders around
the guide pins are undamaged. Brush the dust and dirt from the caliper
and piston but **do not** *inhale as it is injurious to health.* Inspect the
dust excluder around the piston for damage and the piston for

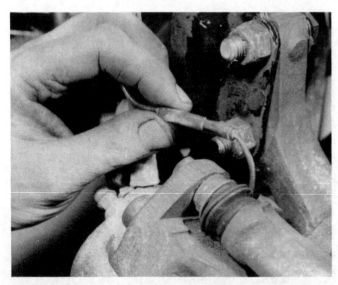

3.14 Disconnect the brake pad wear warning light wire

3.15 Using two spanners, undo the guide pin bolts

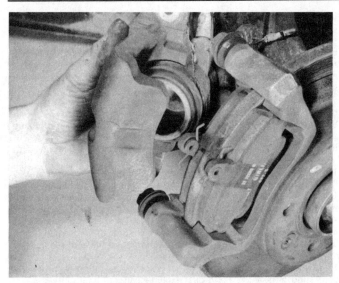

3.16 Lift the caliper off the carrier bracket ...

3.17 ... and withdraw the brake pads

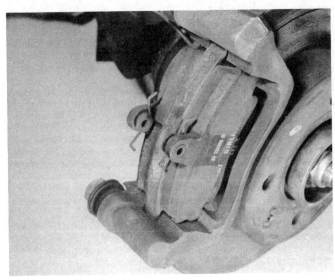

3.19 Refit the pads as shown so that the pad with the warning light is on the inside

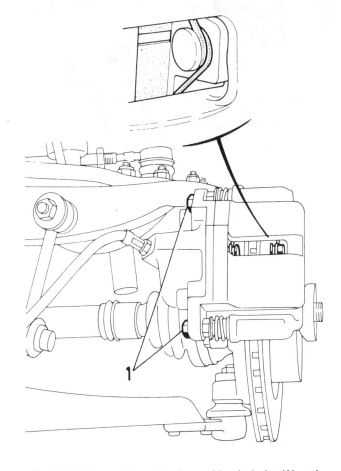

Fig. 8.4 Girling caliper showing guide pin bolts (1) and anti-rattle spring location on the disc pads (Sec 3)

evidence of fluid leaks, corrosion or damage. If attention to any of these components is necessary, refer to Section 4.

19 To refit the pads, place them in position on the carrier bracket noting that the pad with the warning light must be nearest to the centre of the car (photo). The anti-rattle springs must be located as shown in Fig. 8.4.

20 Make sure that the caliper piston is fully retracted in its bore. If not, carefully push it in using a flat bar or screwdriver as a lever or preferably use a G-clamp.

21 Position the caliper over the pads then fit the lower guide pin bolt having first coated its threads with locking fluid. Apply the fluid to the upper guide pin bolt, press the caliper into position, and fit the bolt. Tighten the bolts to the specified torque starting with the lower bolt.

22 Reconnect the brake pad wear warning light wire and repeat the renewal procedures on the other front brake. On completion check the hydraulic fluid level in the reservoir, depress the footbrake two or three times to bring the pads into contact with the disc, then refit the roadwheels and lower the car to the ground.

4 Front brake caliper – removal, overhaul and refitting

Bendix calipers

1 Jack up the front of the car and support it on axle stands. Remove the appropriate front roadwheel.

2 Remove the brake pads, as described in the previous Section.
3 Undo the two bolts securing the caliper assembly to the stub axle carrier and withdraw the caliper.
4 With the flexible brake hose still attached to the caliper, have an assistant very slowly depress the brake pedal until the piston has been ejected just over halfway out of its bore.

5 Using a brake hose clamp, or self-locking wrench with protected jaws, clamp the brake hose. This will minimise brake fluid loss during subsequent operations.
6 Slacken the brake hose-to-caliper body union, and then, while holding the hose, rotate the caliper to unscrew it from the hose. Lift away the caliper and plug or tape over the end of the hose to prevent dirt entry.
7 With the caliper on the bench wipe away all traces of dust and dirt, but *avoid inhaling the dust as it is injurious to health.*
8 Undo the two bolts securing the caliper body to the reaction frame and lift off the body.
9 Withdraw the partially ejected piston from the caliper body and remove the dust cover.
10 Using a suitable blunt instrument such as a knitting needle or a thick feeler blade, carefully extract the piston seal from the caliper bore.
11 Clean all the parts in methylated spirit or clean brake fluid, and wipe dry using a lint-free cloth. Inspect the piston and caliper bore for signs of damage, scuffing or corrosion, and if these conditions are evident renew the caliper body assembly. Inspect the condition of the dust excluders over the guide sleeves and renew these too if there is any sign of damage or deterioration.
12 If the components are in a satisfactory condition, a repair kit consisting of new seals and dust excluders should be obtained.
13 Thoroughly lubricate the components and piston seal with clean brake fluid and carefully fit the seal to the caliper bore.
14 Insert the piston into its bore, fit the new dust cover and then push the piston fully into its bore.
15 Place the caliper in position on the reaction frame and secure with the two bolts, tightened to the specified torque.
16 Where necessary fit the new seals and dust excluders to the caliper guide sleeves.
17 Hold the flexible brake hose and screw the caliper body back onto the hose.
18 Refit the two bolts securing the caliper assembly to the stub axle carrier and tighten the bolts to the specified torque (photo).
19 Fully tighten the brake hose-to-caliper body union and remove the brake hose clamp.
20 Refit the brake pads, as described in Section 3, and bleed the hydraulic system, as described in Section 18. Note that providing the precautions described were taken to minimise brake fluid loss, it should only be necessary to bleed the relevant front brake.
21 Refit the roadwheel and lower the car to the ground.

Girling calipers

22 Jack up the front of the car and support it on axle stands. Remove the appropriate front roadwheel.
23 Using a suitable spanner, unscrew the guide pin bolts while holding the guide pins with a second spanner.

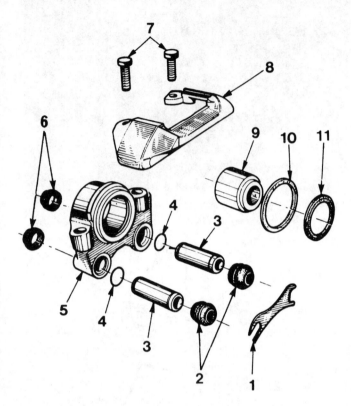

Fig. 8.5 Bendix type brake caliper components (Sec 4)

1   Retaining strip
2   Guide sleeve inner dust
    excluders
3   Guide sleeves
4   Guide sleeve seals
5   Caliper body
6   Guide sleeve outer dust
    excluders
7   Reaction frame retaining bolts
8   Reaction frame
9   Piston
10 Piston seal
11 Piston dust excluder

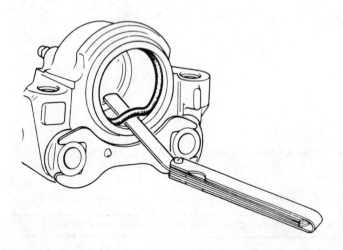

Fig. 8.6 Using a feeler blade to remove the piston seal from the Bendix type caliper (Sec 4)

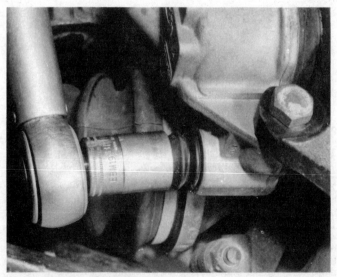

4.18 Tightening the caliper guide bolts

24 Disconnect the pad wear indicator wiring and lift away the caliper body, leaving the disc pads and carrier bracket still in position. It is not necessary to remove the carrier bracket unless it requires renewal because of accident damage or severe corrosion.
25 With the flexible brake hose still attached to the caliper body, very slowly depress the brake pedal until the piston has been ejected just over halfway out of its bore.
26 Using a brake hose clamp or self-locking wrench with protected jaws, clamp the flexible brake hose. This will minimise brake fluid loss during subsequent operations.
27 Slacken the brake hose-to-caliper body union, and then, while holding the hose, rotate the caliper to unscrew it from the hose. Lift away the caliper and plug or tape over the end of the hose to prevent dirt entry.
28 With the caliper on the bench wipe away all traces of dust and dirt, but *avoid inhaling the dust as it is injurious to health.*
29 Withdraw the partially ejected piston from the caliper body and remove the dust cover and clip.
30 Using a suitable blunt instrument, such as a knitting needle, carefully extract the piston seal from the caliper bore.
31 Clean all the parts in methylated spirit, or clean brake fluid, and wipe dry using a lint-free cloth. Inspect the piston and caliper bore for signs of damage, scuffing or corrosion and if these conditions are evident renew the caliper body assembly. Also renew the guide pins if bent or damaged.
32 If the components are in a satisfactory condition, a repair kit consisting of new seals and dust cover should be obtained.
33 Thoroughly lubricate the components and new seals with clean brake fluid and carefully fit the seal to the caliper bore.
34 Position the dust cover over the innermost end of the piston so that the caliper bore sealing lip protrudes beyond the base of the piston. Using a blunt instrument, if necessary, engage the sealing lip of the dust cover with the groove in the caliper. Now push the piston into the bore until the other sealing lip of the dust cover can be engaged with the groove in the piston. Having done this, push the piston fully into its bore. Ease the piston out again slightly, and make sure that the cover lip is correctly seating in the piston groove. Fit the clip.
35 Remove the guide pins from the carrier bracket and smear them with high melting-point brake grease. Fit new dust covers to the guide pins and refit them to the carrier bracket.
36 Hold the flexible brake hose and screw the caliper body back onto the hose.
37 With the piston pushed fully into its bore, refit the caliper and secure it with the guide pin bolts. Tighten the bolts to the specified torque.
38 Fully tighten the brake hose union and remove the clamp. Reconnect the pad warning light wiring.
39 Refer to Section 18 and bleed the brake hydraulic system, noting

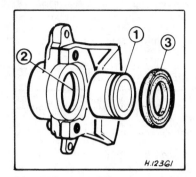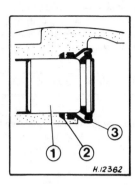

Fig. 8.7 Girling type brake caliper components (Sec 4)

1 Piston
2 Piston seal
3 Dust cover

that if precautions were taken to minimise fluid loss, it should only be necessary to bleed the relevant front brake.
40 Refit the roadwheel and lower the car to the ground.

5 Front brake disc – inspection, removal and refitting

1 Jack up the front of the car and support it on axle stands. Remove the appropriate front roadwheel.
2 Rotate the disc by hand and examine it for deep scoring, grooving or cracks. Light scoring is normal, but, if excessive, the disc must be renewed. Any loose rust and scale around the outer edge of the disc can be removed by lightly tapping it with a small hammer while rotating the disc. Measure the disc thickness with a micrometer if available (photo).
3 To remove the disc, undo the two bolts securing the brake caliper assembly to the stub axle carrier. Withdraw the caliper, complete with pads, off the disc and support it to one side. Avoid straining the flexible brake hose. An alternative method on models with Bendix brakes is to unbolt the reaction frame from the caliper body.
4 Using a Torx type socket bit or driver, undo the two screws securing the disc to the hub and withdraw the disc (photo). If it is tight, lightly tap its rear face with a hide or plastic mallet.

5.2 Checking the disc thickness with a micrometer

5.4 Torx type disc securing screw

5   Refitting the disc is the reverse sequence to removal. Ensure complete cleanliness of the hub and disc mating faces and tighten all bolts to the specified torque. Coat the threads of the caliper or reaction frame bolts with locking fluid before fitting and tightening them.

6   Rear brake shoes – inspection and renewal

1   Jack up the rear of the car and support it on axle stands. Remove the rear roadwheels. Release the handbrake.
2   By judicious tapping and levering, remove the hub cap from the centre of the brake drum.
3   Using a socket and long bar, undo the hub nut and remove the thrust washer.
4   It should now be possible to withdraw the brake drum and hub bearing assembly from the stub axle by hand. It may be difficult to remove the drum due to the tightness of the hub bearing on the stub axle, or due to the brake shoes binding on the inner circumference of the drum. If the bearing is tight, tap the periphery of the drum using a hide or plastic mallet, or use a universal puller, secured to the drum with the wheel bolts, to pull it off. If the brake shoes are binding, proceed as follows.
5   First ensure that the handbrake is fully off. From under the car slacken the locknut then back off the knurled adjuster on the primary rod.
6   Refer to Fig. 8.9 and insert a screwdriver through one of the wheel bolt holes in the brake drum so that it contacts the handbrake operating lever on the trailing brake shoe. Push the lever until the peg slips behind the brake shoe web allowing the brake shoes to retract. The brake drum can now be withdrawn.
7   With the brake drum assembly removed, brush or wipe the dust from the drum, brake shoes, wheel cylinder and backplate. *Take great care not to inhale the dust as it is injurious to health.*
8   Measure the thickness of the friction material, including the shoe. If any of the brake shoes have worn down to the specified minimum thickness, all four brake shoes must be renewed. The shoes must also be renewed if any are contaminated with brake fluid or grease, or show signs of cracking or scoring. If contamination is evident, the cause must be traced and rectified before fitting new brake shoes. Contamination will be caused either by leaking fluid seals in the wheel

cylinder or by a faulty hub bearing oil seal in the brake drum assembly.
9   Examine the internal surface of the brake drum for signs of scoring or cracks. If any deterioration of the surface finish is evident the drum may be skimmed to a maximum of 1.0 mm (0.04 in) on the internal diameter, otherwise renewal is necessary. If the drum is to be skimmed it will be necessary to have the work carried out on both drums to maintain a consistent internal diameter on both sides.
10 If the brake shoes and drum are in a satisfactory condition, proceed to paragraph 26. If the brake shoes are to be removed proceed as follows, according to type:

Bendix brake assemblies

11 Before proceeding, make a note of the position and fitted direction of the brake shoe return springs and components as a guide to reassembly (photo).
12 Using pliers, detach the upper shoe return spring from both brake shoes.

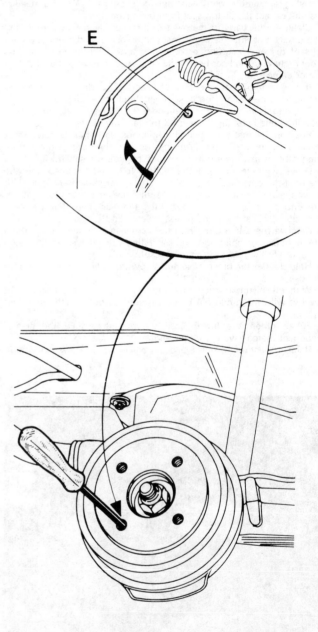

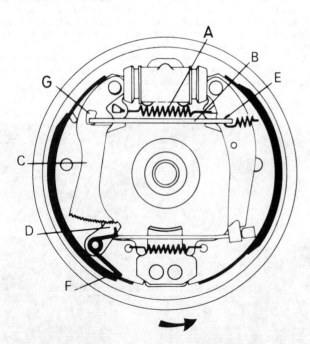

Fig. 8.8 Bendix type rear brake components (Sec 6)

A *Return spring*	E *Spring for link*
B *Link*	F *Spring for quadrant*
C *Adjusting arm*	G *Clearance slot*
D *Quadrant*	

Fig. 8.9 Using a screwdriver inserted through the brake drum to release the handbrake operating lever (Sec 6)

E   *Handbrake operating lever peg (Bendix type brake shown)*

6.11 Bendix rear brake layout

6.13 Removing the brake shoe steady springs and cups

13 Again using pliers, depress the brake shoe steady spring cups while supporting the steady spring pin from the rear of the backplate with your finger. Turn each spring cup through 90° and withdraw it, together with the spring, from the pin (photo). Withdraw the trailing shoe steady spring pin from the backplate, but note that it is not possible to withdraw the leading shoe pin due to the close proximity of the suspension trailing arm. Note also that there is a hole in the hollow suspension arm directly in line with the steady pin, and, if care is not taken, the pin will drop into the arm. Place a wooden wedge or other suitable packing between the backplate and suspension arm to stop this happening.

14 Move the serrated adjusting arms on the leading shoe as far as possible towards the stub axle then release the shoe and arm from the operating link while twisting the shoe outwards.

15 Return the serrated adjusting arm beneath the shoe web then pull the lower end of the leading shoe from the anchor and disconnect the return spring. Remove the shoe.

16 Disconnect the handbrake cable from the operating lever on the trailing brake shoe and lift off the shoe complete with operating link (photo).

17 Extract the spring clips and pivot pins and transfer the self-

adjusting mechanism and handbrake lever to the new brake shoes (photos). Also fit the operating link and spring to the new trailing shoe.

18 Before refitting the new brake shoes, clean off the backplate with a rag and apply a trace of silicone grease to the shoe contact areas and pivots on the backplate.

19 Engage the handbrake cable with the operating lever on the trailing shoe and position the shoe complete with operating link on the backplate.

20 Hook one end of the lower return spring into the hole in the trailing shoe and attach the other end to the leading shoe (photo). Place the leading shoe in position on the backplate.

21 Move the leading shoe adjusting arm in towards the stub axle as far as possible and engage the notch on the operating link with the slot on the adjusting arm (photo).

22 Move the serrated quadrant towards the stub axle and allow the adjusting arm to move back to the fully retracted position.

23 Refit the upper return spring.

24 Refit the steady pins, springs and cups to both brake shoes.

25 Ensure that the adjusting arm is fully retracted and that the brake shoes are centrally positioned on the backplate.

26 Slide the brake drum onto the stub axle and refit the thrust washer

6.16 Disconnecting the handbrake cable from the trailing shoe lever

6.17A Fit the spring ...

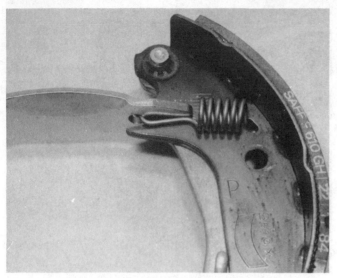

6.17B ... and operating link to the trailing shoe

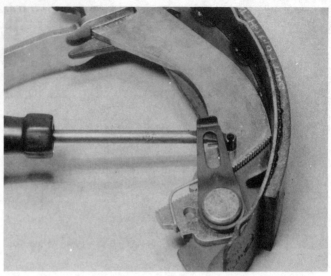

6.17C Fit the serrated adjusting arm mechanism to the leading shoe

6.20 Lower return spring position

6.21 Showing operating link attachment to the adjusting arm on the leading shoe

and hub nut. Tighten the hub nut to the specified torque and then tap the hub cap into place.

27 Depress the footbrake several times to operate the self-adjusting mechanism.

28 The handbrake should now be adjusted, as described in Section 16, or after attending to the brake shoes on the other rear brake if this is being done.

29 On completion, refit the roadwheels and lower the car to the ground.

Girling brake assemblies

30 Before proceeding, make a note of the position and fitted direction of the brake shoe return springs and components as a guide to reassembly (photo).

31 Using pliers, detach the upper and lower brake shoe return springs from both brake shoes.

32 Again using pliers, depress the brake shoe steady spring cups while supporting the steady spring from the rear of the backplate with your finger. Turn each spring cup through 90° and withdraw it, together with the spring, from the pin. Withdraw the trailing shoe steady spring pin from the backplate, but note that it is not possible to withdraw the leading shoe pin due to the close proximity of the suspension trailing

6.30 Girling rear brake layout

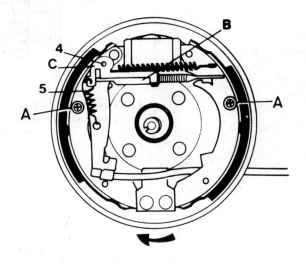

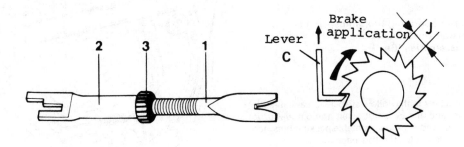

Fig. 8.10 Girling type rear brake components (Sec 6)

1	Threaded rod	4	Pivot	A	Shoe steady springs	J	Ideal clearance between
2	Link	5	Adjusting lever tension	B	Link		linings and drum
3	Serrated nut		spring	C	Adjusting lever		

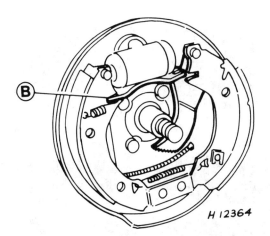

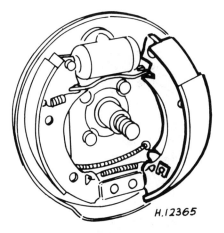

Fig. 8.11 Detach the operating link (B) from the adjusting arm after moving the arm toward the stub axle – Bendix brake assemblies (Sec 6)

Fig. 8.12 Turn the brake shoe at right-angles to the backplate. Detach the handbrake cable and remove both shoes – Bendix brake assemblies (Sec 6)

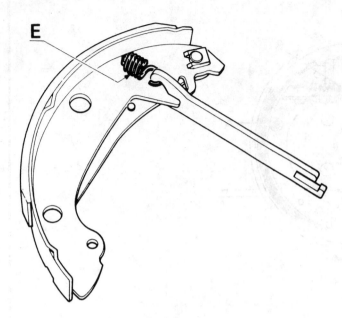

Fig. 8.13 Position the operating link and spring (E) as shown before refitting the brake shoes – Bendix brake assemblies (Sec 6)

Fig. 8.14 Adjusting link notch (A) must locate against the adjusting lever on the leading brake shoe – Girling brake assemblies (Sec 6)

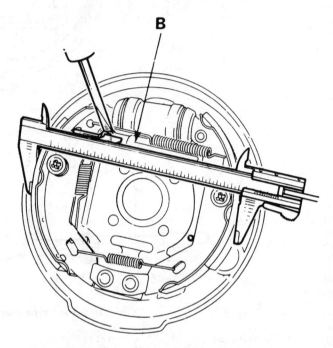

Fig. 8.15 Before refitting the brake drum, turn the toothed wheel on the adjusting link (B) to give a brake shoe diameter of between 178.7 and 179.2 mm (7.04 and 7.06 in) – Girling brake assemblies (Sec 6)

arm. Note also that there is a hole in the hollow suspension arm directly in line with the steady pin, and, if care is not taken, the pin will drop into the arm. Place a wooden wedge or other suitable packing between the backplate and suspension arm to stop this happening.

33 Lift off the leading shoe and the adjusting link, detach the handbrake cable from the trailing shoe operating lever and lift off the trailing shoe.

34 Detach the return spring and adjusting lever from the leading shoe and fit these components to the new leading shoe. Make sure that the spring is fitted correctly (photo).

35 Before fitting the new brake shoes, clean off the backplate with a rag and apply a trace of silicone grease to the shoe contact areas and pivots on the backplate (photo).

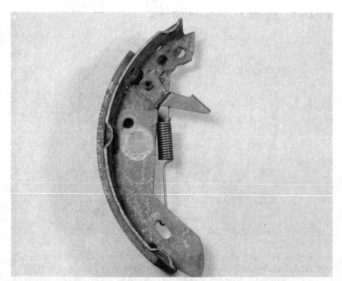

6.34 Correct fitting of the leading brake shoe adjusting lever and return spring

6.35 Apply a trace of silicone grease to the areas arrowed before refitting the brake shoes

6.36A Engage the handbrake cable with the trailing shoe operating lever ...

6.36B ... then secure the shoe in place with the steady pin, spring and cup (arrowed)

36 Engage the handbrake cable with the operating lever on the trailing shoe, position the shoe on the backplate and retain it in place with the steady pin, spring and cup (photos).

37 Lubricate the threads in the adjusting link and make sure it is free to turn. Note that the links are not interchangeable from side to side and are colour coded for identification. The link fitted to the left-hand side of the car has a silver coloured end, while the link fitted to the right-hand side has a gold coloured end.

38 Engage the adjusting link ends with both brake shoes (photo) ensuring that the notch on the threaded end locates against the adjusting lever on the leading shoe (photo).

39 Position the leading shoe on the backplate and retain it in place with the steady pin, spring and cup (photo).

40 Refit the upper and lower brake shoe return springs (photos).

41 Hold the adjusting lever clear and turn the toothed wheel on the adjusting link as necessary so that the overall diameter of the brake shoes is between 178.7 and 179.2 mm (7.04 to 7.06 in).

42 Refit the brake drum and complete the remainder of the reassembly, as described in paragraphs 26 to 29 inclusive.

6.38A Engage the adjusting link ends with both brake shoes ...

6.38B ... ensuring that the notch on the adjusting link locates against the adjusting lever (arrowed)

6.39 Secure the leading shoe in place with the steady pin, spring and cup (arrowed)

6.40A Refit the upper return spring in the holes (arrowed) ...

6.40B ... followed by the lower return spring in the elongated slots (arrowed)

7 Rear wheel cylinder – removal and refitting

1 Begin by removing the brake drum assembly, as described in Section 6, paragraphs 1 to 6 inclusive.
2 Using pliers, detach the brake shoe upper return spring from both brake shoes.
3 Using a brake hose clamp or self-locking wrench with protected jaws, clamp the flexible brake hose just in front of the rear suspension transverse member. This will minimise brake fluid loss during subsequent operations.
4 Wipe away all traces of dirt around the brake pipe union at the rear of the wheel cylinder (photo).
5 Unscrew the union nut securing the brake pipe to the wheel cylinder. Carefully ease out the pipe and plug or tape over its end to prevent dirt entry.
6 Undo the two bolts securing the wheel cylinder to the backplate. Move the brake shoes apart at the top and withdraw the cylinder from between the two shoes.

7 To refit the wheel cylinder, spread the brake shoes and place the cylinder in position on the backplate.
8 Engage the brake pipe and screw in the union nut two or three turns to ensure that the thread has started.
9 Refit the two retaining bolts and tighten them to the specified torque. Now fully tighten the brake pipe union nut.
10 On models equipped with Bendix brakes, move the serrated quadrant of the self-adjusting mechanism towards the stub axle so that the adjusting arm moves back to the fully retracted position. Refit the upper brake shoe return spring. On models equipped with Girling brakes, refit the upper brake shoe return spring and turn the toothed wheel on the adjusting link as necessary so that the overall diameter of the brake shoes is between 178.7 and 179.2 mm (7.04 and 7.06 in).
11 Slide the brake drum over the stub axle, refit the thrust washer and hub nut then tighten the hub nut to the specified torque. Tap the hub cap into place.
12 Remove the clamp from the brake hose and bleed the brake hydraulic system, as described in Section 18. Providing suitable precautions were taken to minimise loss of fluid, it should only be necessary to bleed the relevant rear brake.
13 After bleeding the system, depress the brake pedal several times to operate the self-adjusting mechanism. If it was necessary to slacken the handbrake linkage to remove the brake drum, adjust the handbrake, as described in Section 19.
14 Refit the roadwheel and lower the car to the ground.

8 Rear wheel cylinder – overhaul

1 Remove the wheel cylinder from the car, as described in the previous Section.
2 With the wheel cylinder on the bench, remove the dust covers, the two pistons, cup seals and spring. If necessary tap the end of the cylinder on a block of wood to eject the pistons. Unscrew the bleed screw from the cylinder body.
3 Thoroughly clean all the components in methylated spirits or clean brake fluid, and dry with a lint-free rag.
4 Carefully examine the surfaces of the pistons and cylinder bore for wear, score marks or corrosion and, if evident, renew the complete wheel cylinder. If the components are in a satisfactory condition, obtain a repair kit consisting of new seals and dust covers.
5 Dip the new seals and pistons in clean brake fluid and assemble them wet, as follows:
6 Insert one of the seals into one end of the cylinder with the flat face of the seal facing outwards. Insert the piston and fit the new dust cover.

7.4 Rear wheel cylinder viewed from behind the backplate

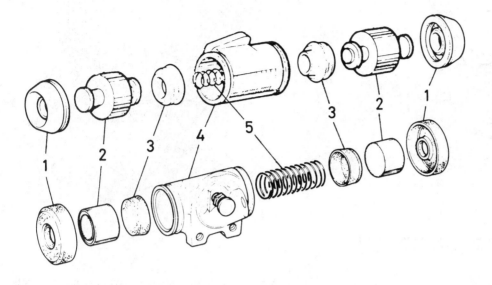

**Fig. 8.16 Exploded view of
the two types of rear wheel
cylinder (Sec 8)**

1   Dust covers
2   Pistons
3   Seals
4   Body
5   Spring

7   From the other end of the cylinder, slide in the spring followed by the second seal, flat face outwards, then the piston and finally the dust cover.
8   Screw the bleed screw into the cylinder body and then refit the wheel cylinder to the car, as described in Section 7.

9   Rear brake backplate – removal and refitting

1   Begin by removing the rear brake shoes, as described in Section 6, and the wheel cylinder, as described in Section 7.
2   Slide the hub bearing inner spacer off the stub axle, undo the four retaining bolts and withdraw the backplate (photo).
3   To refit the backplate, place it in position over the stub axle and refit the four bolts. Tighten the bolts to the specified torque.
4   Place the spacer over the stub axle and refit the wheel cylinder and brake shoes, as described in Sections 7 and 6 respectively.
5   Bleed the hydraulic system after the brake shoes and brake drum have been refitted using the procedure described in Section 18.

9.2 Rear brake backplate retaining bolts (arrowed)

1   Hub bearing inner spacer

10   Rear disc pads – inspection and renewal

1   Chock the front wheels then jack up the rear of the car and support on axle stands. Remove the rear roadwheels and release the handbrake.
2   View the disc pads end on and measure their thickness including the backplates. If any of the pads is less than the specified minimum thickness, all four pads must be renewed as follows.
3   Extract the small spring clip then withdraw the retaining key.
4   Using pliers if necessary, withdraw the pads from the caliper and remove the anti-rattle springs from each pad.
5   Brush away the accumulated dust and dirt *taking care not to inhale it as it is injurious to health*. Check the condition of the piston and guide sleeve dust covers and if necessary renew them with reference to Section 11.
6   Using a suitable tool, turn the piston until it is screwed in as far as possible and further rotation will not make it enter any deeper. Align the piston so that the two lines on the rim point to the bleed screw.
7   Fit the anti-rattle springs to the new pads (see Fig. 8.1).
8   Insert the pads in the caliper with the anti-rattle springs toward the bottom, then tap in the retaining key and fit the spring clip at the inner end of the key next to the frame bolt.
9   Depress the brake pedal several times to reset the disc pads.
10 Repeat the procedure on the remaining side then refit the roadwheels and lower the car to the ground.

11   Rear brake caliper – removal, overhaul and refitting

1   Remove the disc pads as described in Section 10.
2   Remove the brake fluid reservoir filler cap and retighten it onto a piece of polythene in order to reduce the loss of fluid when the caliper is removed. Alternatively, use a hose clamp on the relevant rear flexible hose.
3   Unscrew the union nut securing the hydraulic pipe to the caliper.
4   Disconnect the handbrake cable from the lever on the caliper.
5   Unbolt the caliper from the trailing arm. If necessary unbolt the frame from the caliper.
6   Clean away external dirt then grip the caliper in a soft-jawed vice.
7   Prise off the piston dust cover.
8   Using a suitable tool unscrew the piston and at the same time apply air pressure from a tyre pump to the part of the caliper to eject the piston.
9   Examine the piston and cylinder bore for scoring and excessive wear. If evident renew the caliper complete, however if they are in good condition remove the seal from the bore using a blunt instrument and obtain a repair kit including a new seal and dust covers.

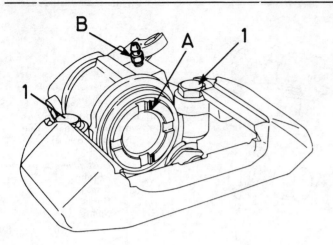

Fig. 8.17 Showing correct alignment of piston marks (A)
with bleed screw (B) (Sec 10)

1   *Frame retaining bolts*

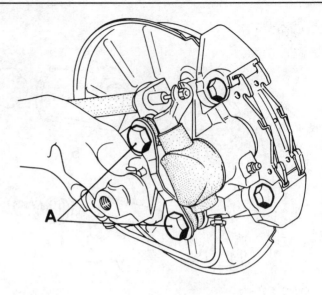

Fig. 8.18 Rear disc brake caliper showing mounting bolts
(A) (Sec 11)

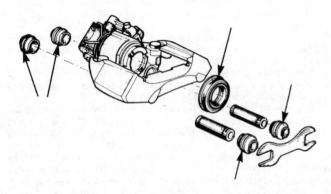

Fig. 8.19 Rear disc brake caliper dust covers (arrowed)
(Sec 11)

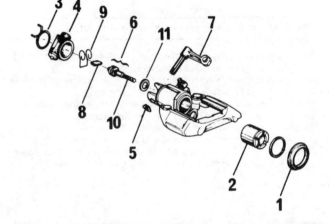

Fig. 8.20 Exploded view of the rear disc brake caliper
(Sec 11)

1	*Dust cover*	7 *Lever and spindle*
2	*Piston*	8 *Control cam*
3	*Clip*	9 *Return spring*
4	*Dust cover*	10 *Threaded adjustment screw*
5	*Circlip*	11 *Plain washer*
6	*Belleville spring washers*	

10 If required the handbrake operating lever components can be
dismantled. To do this first remove the clip and release the dust seal
cover from the caliper.
11 Extract the circlip from the end of the spindle.
12 The spring washers on the adjustment screw must now be
compressed. The Renault tools for this operation are shown in Fig.
8.21 however it should be possible to use a universal puller and a
locally made adaptor.
13 Remove the lever and spindle together with the dust cover,
followed by the plunger cam and spring clip.
14 Remove the tool and pull out the adjustment screw together with
the spring and plain washers.
15 Using a soft metal drift, drive the guide sleeve from the caliper and
extract the O-ring seal.
16 Clean all the components using only hydraulic fluid or methylated
spirit.
17 Commence reassembly by locating the O-ring seal in the caliper,
then drive in the guide sleeve until flush with the face of the caliper as
shown in Fig. 8.22.
18 Fit the spring washers on the adjacent screw as shown in Fig. 8.22,
then locate the plain washer in its recess and insert the adjustment
screw in the caliper.
19 Fit the dust cover to the lever and spindle.

20 Compress the adjustment screw spring washers and fit the plunger
cam, spring clip, lever and spindle. Retain the spindle with the circlip.
21 Position the dust cover on the caliper and fit the clip.
22 Fit the new piston seal, manipulating it into its groove using the
fingers only.
23 Apply clean hydraulic fluid to the piston and cylinder bore and
insert the piston squarely using hand pressure.
24 Using a suitable tool turn the piston until it is screwed in as far as
possible and further rotation will not make it enter any deeper. Align
the piston so that the two lines on the rim point to the bleed screw.
25 Apply a little brake grease to the outer surface of the piston which
contacts the bore, then fit the new dust cover.

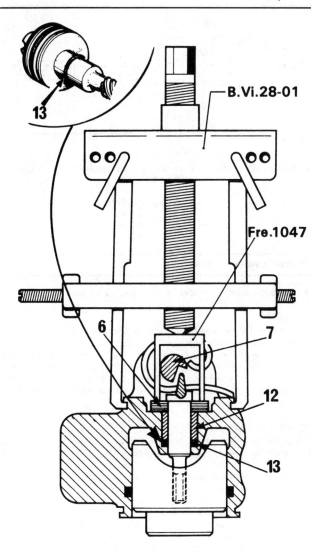

Fig. 8.21 Using the Renault tools to compress the Belleville spring washers (Sec 11)

6   Belleville spring washers   12 Sleeve
7   Lever and spindle   13 O-ring

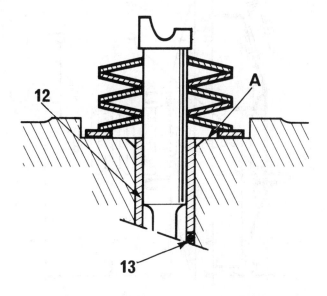

Fig. 8.22 The sleeve must be flush with face A (Sec 11)

12 Sleeve   13 O-ring

13.1 Master cylinder on a model fitted with a vacuum servo unit (1)

12 Rear brake disc – inspection, removal and refitting

1   Remove the rear disc pads as described in Section 10.
2   Inspect the disc with reference to Section 5.
3   To remove the disc unbolt the caliper frame then remove the disc and hub assembly as described in Chapter 9.
4   Refitting is as described in Chapter 9. Apply locking fluid to the caliper frame bolt threads before inserting and tightening them. Refit the rear disc pads with reference to Section 10.

13 Master cylinder – removal and refitting

1   The master cylinder is located on the bulkhead behind the right-hand side of the engine (photo). For better access on non-Turbo models remove the air cleaner as described in Chapter 3.
2   Syphon the brake fluid from the reservoir or alternatively place a container beneath the master cylinder and cover the surrounding components with rags.

3   Pull the reservoir direct from the top of the master cylinder.
4   Identify the brake pipes for position then unscrew the union nuts and disconnect them. Tape over the pipe ends to prevent entry of dust and dirt.
5   Unscrew the mounting nuts and withdraw the master cylinder from the servo unit or bulkhead (as applicable). On servo-equipped models, recover the sealing ring. Use a new seal on reassembly.
6   Before refitting the master cylinder, clean the mounting faces. On models with a servo unit, check that the thrust rod protrusion is as shown in Fig. 8.23. Adjust the thrust rod extension if necessary.
7   Refitting is a reversal of removal, but tighten the nuts to the specified torque. Working inside the car check the length of the pedal pushrod with reference to Fig. 8.23 or 8.24 and adjust it if necessary. Finally bleed the hydraulic system as described in Section 18.

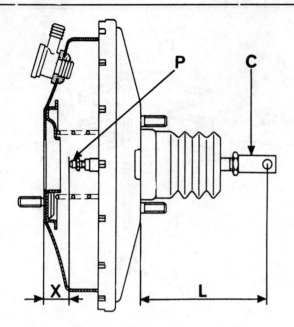

Fig. 8.23 Thrust/pushrod dimensions on models with a servo unit (Sec 13)

P   Adjustable extension
E   Clip
C   Clevis
X   = 22.3 mm (0.878 in)
L   = 137.5 mm (5.413 in) for RHD models
     or 121.0 mm (4.764 in) for LHD models

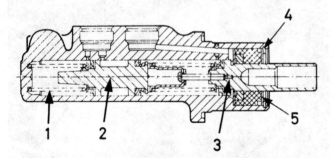

Fig. 8.25 Cross-section of the Teves master cylinder (Sec 14)

1 Spring	4 Circlip
2 Secondary piston	5 Stop washer
3 Primary piston	

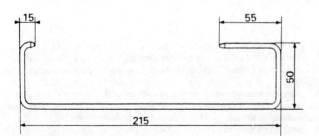

Fig. 8.26 Piston retaining tool for early Bendix master cylinder (Sec 14)

Note: *all dimensions are in mm*

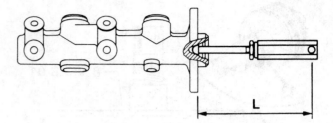

Fig. 8.24 Pushrod dimension on models without a servo unit (Sec 13)

L   = 110.0 mm (4.331 in)

14 Master cylinder – overhaul

1   Remove the master cylinder as described in Section 13.

Teves type

2   Mount the master cylinder in a soft-jawed vice.
3   Prise out the reservoir seals.
4   Depress the primary piston extension then extract the circlip from the mouth of the cylinder using circlip pliers. Remove the stop washer.
5   Extract the primary piston and spring followed by the secondary piston and spring. If the latter is tight remove the master cylinder from the vice and tap it on a block of wood.

Early Bendix type

6   To dismantle the master cylinder it will be necessary to make up a piston retaining tool from 6 mm diameter steel rod, as shown in Fig. 8.26.
7   Locate the retaining tool over the cylinder so that it holds the primary piston in place.
8   Place a 3.5 mm diameter twist drill in a vice and place the master cylinder over it so that the drill engages with the secondary piston retaining roll pin through the reservoir port. Turn the master cylinder round the drill and then pull it to extract the roll pin.
9   Extract the primary piston roll pin in the same way.
10   Release the retaining tool and withdraw the two piston assemblies by tapping the cylinder on a block of wood. Prise out the reservoir seals.

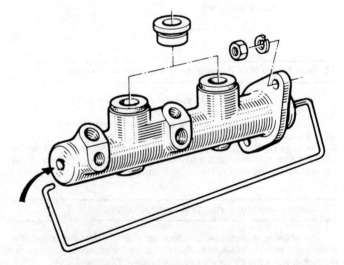

Fig. 8.27 Using the retaining tool to compress the pistons on the early Bendix master cylinder (Sec 14)

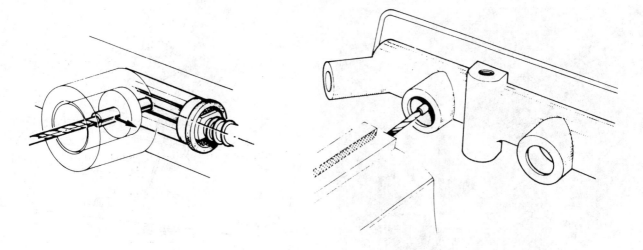

Fig. 8.28 Using a twist drill to extract the piston roll pins on the early Bendix master cylinder (Sec 14)

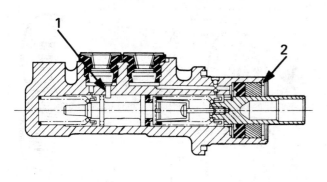

Fig. 8.29 Cross-section of the later Bendix master cylinder (Sec 14)

1   Secondary piston stop pin *2   Circlip*

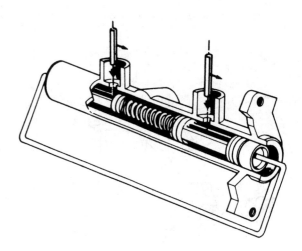

Fig. 8.30 On the early Bendix master cylinder fit the roll pins with their slots facing the flange (Sec 14)

Late Bendix type

11 Mount the master cylinder in a soft-jawed vice.
12 Prise out the reservoir seals.
13 Depress the primary piston extension then extract the secondary piston stop pin from the secondary port.
14 Using circlip pliers extract the circlip from the mouth of the cylinder.
15 Extract the primary piston and spring followed by the secondary piston and spring. If necessary tap the cylinder on a block of wood to remove the components.

All types

16 Clean the two piston assemblies and the cylinder body in methylated spirit or clean brake fluid and dry with a lint-free cloth.
17 Carefully examine the cylinder bore and the two piston assemblies for signs of wear ridges, scoring or corrosion. If these conditions are evident on the cylinder bore, a new master cylinder must be obtained. If the cylinder bore is serviceable it will be necessary to obtain a new primary and secondary piston assembly, as the rubber seals and piston components are not available separately. The assembly includes new reservoir seals.

18 Before reassembling, liberally lubricate all the parts in clean brake fluid and assemble them wet.
19 Reassembly is a reversal of dismantling, but on the early Bendix type fit the pistons with their slots aligned with the reservoir ports, and fit the roll pins with their slots facing the master cylinder mounting flange. Refit the master cylinder with reference to Section 13.

15 Pressure regulating valve – description and testing

1 The pressure regulating valve is located beneath the rear of the car (photo) and it effectively limits the braking force available at the rear wheels in order to prevent locking especially during heavy braking. On some models the unit is load sensitive to vary the pressure according to the load being carried, and this unit is identified by having a spring connection to the rear axle.
2 In the event of continual rear wheel locking the rear brake shoes should first be checked for correct operation before checking the pressure regulating valve.
3 To check the unit, pressure gauges must be fitted to the front and rear hydraulic circuits and this work is therefore best left to a Renault dealer. On the load sensitive type one person must be sitting in the

15.1 Pressure regulating valve

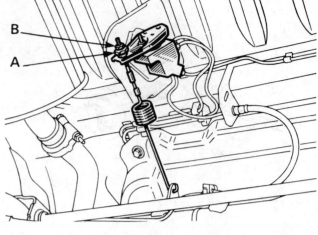

Fig. 8.31 Load sensitive pressure regulating valve fitted to
non-Turbo models (Sec 15)

A   Adjusting nut   B   Locknut

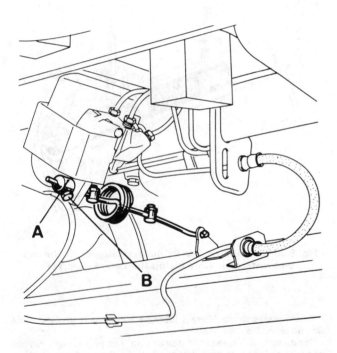

Fig. 8.32 Load sensitive pressure regulating valve fitted to
Turbo models (Sec 15)

A   Adjusting sleeve   B   Locking screw

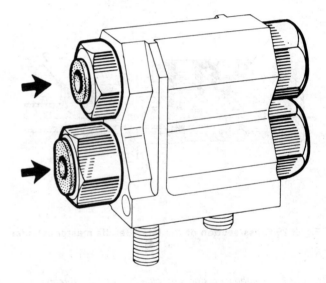

Fig. 8.33 Inlet pipe locations on the non-load sensitive type
pressure regulating valve (Sec 15)

reservoir cap then tighten it down onto a piece of polythene sheeting.
This will minimise brake fluid loss during subsequent operations.
3   Clean the regulating valve then identify the hydraulic pipes for
position.
4   Unscrew the union nuts and disconnect the pipes. Plug the pipe
ends to prevent loss of fluid.
5   Unscrew the mounting bolts or nuts and withdraw the unit from
the underbody. On the load sensitive type unhook the spring from the
rear axle.
6   Refitting is a reversal of removal. On completion bleed the
hydraulic system as described in Section 18 and where applicable have
the unit adjusted by a Renault dealer. On the non-load sensitive type
the inlet hydraulic pipes must be fitted to the end with unequal height
unions (Fig. 8.33).

driver's seat and a load according to model placed in the rear luggage
compartment, then the spring tension adjusted as required. No
adjustment is possible on the non-load sensitive type.

16 Pressure regulating valve – removal and refitting

1   Check the front wheels then jack up the rear of the car and support
it on axle stands.
2   Working in the engine compartment unscrew the brake fluid

17 Hydraulic pipes and hoses – inspection, removal and refitting

1   At the specified service intervals, carefully examine all brake pipes,
hoses, hose connections and pipe unions.

2   First check for signs of leakage at the pipe unions. Then examine the flexible hoses for signs of cracking, chafing and fraying.
3   The brake pipes must be examined carefully and methodically. They must be cleaned off and checked for signs of dents, corrosion or other damage. Corrosion should be scraped off, and, if the depth of pitting is significant, the pipes renewed. This is particularly likely in those areas underneath the vehicle body where the pipes are exposed and unprotected.
4   If any section of the pipe or hose is to be removed, first unscrew the master cylinder reservoir filler cap and place a piece of polythene over the filler neck. Refit and tighten the cap. This will minimise brake fluid loss when the pipe or hose is removed.
5   Brake pipe removal is usually quite straightforward. The union nuts at each end are undone, the pipe and union pulled out and the centre section of the pipe removed from the body clips. Where the union nuts are exposed to the full force of the weather they can sometimes be quite tight. As only an open-ended spanner can be used, burring of the flats on the nuts is not uncommon when attempting to undo them. For this reason a self-locking wrench is often the only way to separate a stubborn union.
6   To remove a flexible hose, wipe the unions and bracket free of dirt and undo the union nut from the brake hose end(s) (photos).

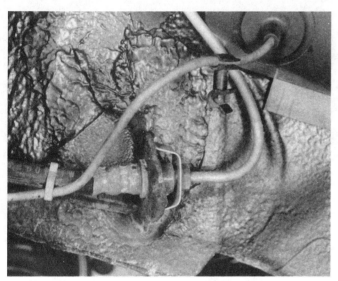

17.6A Front brake flexible hose to rigid pipe connection

17.6B Rear brake flexible hose to rigid pipe connection

7   Next lift off the hose retaining spring clip and withdraw the end of the hose out of its serrated mounting. If a front brake hose is being removed, it can now be unscrewed from the brake caliper.
8   Brake pipes with flared ends and union nuts in place can be obtained individually or in sets from Renault dealers or accessory shops. The pipe is then bent to shape, using the old pipe as a guide, and is ready for fitting to the car.
9   Refitting the pipes and hoses is a reversal of the removal sequence. Make sure that the brake pipes are securely supported in their clips and ensure that the hoses are not kinked. Check also that the hoses are clear of all suspension components and underbody fittings and will remain clear during movement of the suspension or steering. Reposition one of the hose ends in its serrated mounting if necessary. After refitting, remove the polythene from the reservoir and bleed the brake hydraulic system, as described in Section 18.

18 Hydraulic system – bleeding

1   The correct functioning of the brake hydraulic system is only possible after removal of all air from the components and circuit; this is achieved by bleeding the system. Note that only clean unused brake fluid, which has remained unshaken for at least 24 hours, must be used.
2   If there is any possibility of incorrect fluid being used in the system, the brake lines and components must be completely flushed with uncontaminated fluid and new seals fitted to the components.
3   **Never** reuse brake fluid which has been bled from the system.
4   During the procedure, do not allow the level of brake fluid to drop more than halfway down the reservoir.
5   Before starting work, check that all pipes and hoses are secure, unions tight and bleed screws closed. Take great care not to allow brake fluid to come into contact with the car paintwork, otherwise the finish will be seriously damaged. Wash off any spilled fluid immediately with cold water.
6   If the brake fluid has been lost from the master cylinder due to a leak in the system, ensure that the cause is traced and rectified before proceeding further.
7   If the hydraulic system has only been partially disconnected and suitable precautions were taken to prevent further loss of fluid, then it should only be necessary to bleed the brake concerned, or that part of the circuit 'downstream' from where the work took place.
8   If possible, one of the DIY brake bleeding kits available from accessory shops should be used, particularly the type which pressurise the system, as they greatly simplify the task and reduce the risk of expelled air and fluid being drawn back into the system. Where one of these kits is being used, follow the manufacturer's instructions concerning their operation.
9   If a brake bleeding kit is not being used, the system may be bled in the conventional way as follows:
10   Obtain a clean glass jar, a suitable length of plastic or rubber tubing which is a tight fit over the bleed screws, a tin of the specified brake fluid and the help of an assistant.
11   On models fitted with a servo unit depress the footbrake pedal several times so that the vacuum is dissipated.
12   Clean the area around the bleed screw and remove the rubber dust cap. If the complete system is to be bled, start at the left-hand rear brake first.
13   Fit the tube to the bleed screw (photo), immerse the free end of the tube in the jar and pour in sufficient brake fluid to keep the end of the tube submerged. Open the bleed screw half a turn and have your assistant depress the brake pedal to the floor and then release it. Tighten the bleed screw at the end of each downstroke to prevent the expelled air and fluid from being drawn back into the system. Repeat the procedure until clean brake fluid, free from air bubbles, can be seen emerging from the tube then finally tighten the bleedscrew, remove the tube and refit the dust cap. Remember to check the brake fluid level in the reservoir periodically and keep it topped up.
14   Repeat the procedure on the right-hand front brake (photo) followed by the right-hand rear brake and left-hand front brake. When completed, recheck the fluid level in the reservoir, top up if necessary and refit the cap. Depress the brake pedal several times; it should feel firm and free from 'sponginess' which would indicate air is still present in the system.

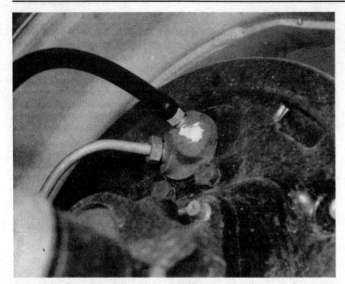

18.13 Bleed tube fitted to a rear wheel cylinder

18.14 Bleed tube fitted to a front brake caliper

19.2 Handbrake primary rod and adjusting yoke

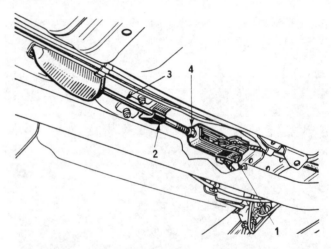

Fig. 8.34 Handbrake primary rod components (Sec 19)

1	Clevis pin	3	Primary rod
2	Support/guide block	4	Adjustment locknut

19 Handbrake – adjustment

1   Jack up the rear of the car and support on axle stands. Chock the front wheels and fully release the handbrake.

2   Working under the car loosen the locknut on the handbrake primary rod in front of the adjusting yoke and unscrew the locknut several turns (photo).

Non-Turbo models (rear drum brakes)

3   Make sure that the rear brake self-adjusting mechanism is set correctly by depressing the footbrake pedal several times.

4   Tighten the nut inside the adjusting yoke until the rear wheels begin to bind, then loosen it until the wheels just turn freely.

5   Tighten the locknut then check that from fully released, the handbrake lever moves a minimum of 12 notches to the fully applied position. If necessary make final adjustments to the adjusting yoke.

6   Lower the car to the ground.

Turbo models (rear disc brakes)

7   Loosen the nut inside the adjusting yoke until the cable ends can be pulled approximately 5.0 mm (0.2 in) clear of the levers on the rear calipers (Fig. 8.35).

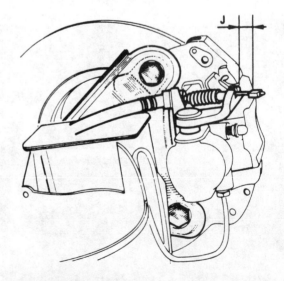

Fig. 8.35 On Turbo models loosen the cable adjustment until dimension J is 5.0 mm (0.2 in) (Sec 19)

8   Depress the footbrake pedal several times.
9   Operate the levers on the calipers several times and check that they return fully by themselves. If not, the caliper(s) will need to be overhauled or renewed as described in Section 11.
10 Tighten the nut inside the adjusting yoke until the cable end stops just touch the levers, then tighten the locknut.
11 Check that from fully released, the handbrake lever moves at least 11 or 12 notches to the fully applied position. If necessary make final adjustments to the adjusting yoke.
12 Lower the car to the ground.

20 Handbrake lever – removal and refitting

1   Chock the front wheels then jack up the rear of the car and support on axle stands. Fully release the handbrake lever.
2   Working under the car remove the split pin, washer and clevis pin securing the primary rod adjusting yoke to the cable compensator.
3   Release the primary rod from the support/guide block.
4   Undo the retaining bolts and remove the two seat belt flexible stalk anchorages.
5   Make a slit in the carpet just to the rear of the lever assembly to provide access to the lever mountings.
6   Spread the carpet and disconnect the warning light switch wires.
7   Undo the two bolts securing the lever to the floor and remove the assembly from inside the car.
8   Refitting is the reverse sequence to removal, but finally adjust the handbrake as described in Section 19.

21 Handbrake cable – removal and refitting

1   Chock the front wheels then jack up the rear of the car and support on axle stands. Fully release the handbrake lever and remove the rear wheels.
2   Remove the rear brake shoes on all models except the GT Turbo (fitted with rear disc brakes). Refer to Section 6.
3   Working under the car remove the split pin, washer and clevis pin securing the primary rod adjusting yoke to the cable compensator.
4   Release the cables from the rear suspension trailing arms by unscrewing the rear bolt and opening up the bracket (photo).
5   Tap the outer cables from the brake backplates (photo) or disconnect the inner cables from the handbrake levers on the rear calipers as applicable, then withdraw the cable assembly from under the car.
6   Refitting is a reversal of removal. On completion adjust the handbrake as described in Section 19.

22 Footbrake pedal – removal and refitting

1   Remove the steering column lower shroud with reference to Chapter 9.
2   Extract the split pin, washer and clevis pin securing the master cylinder or servo pushrod to the pedal (photo).
3   Prise the spring clip from the brake pedal end of the pivot shaft and remove the washer.
4   Slide the pivot shaft to the left until the footbrake pedal can be withdrawn.
5   Inspect the bushes for wear and damage. Also inspect the return spring where fitted. Renew the components as necessary.
6   Refitting is a reversal of removal, but lubricate the bushes and pivot shaft with molybdenum disulphide grease.

23 Stoplamp switch – removal, refitting and adjustment

1   The stoplamp switch is located on the pedal bracket beneath the facia.

21.4 Handbrake cable support bracket on the rear suspension trailing arm

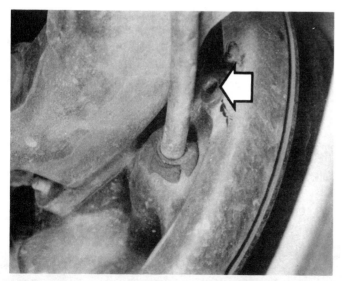

21.5 Handbrake outer cable entry in rear brake backplate, also showing brake lining inspection hole plug (arrowed)

22.2 Footbrake pedal and bracket

23.2 Disconnecting the stoplamp switch wiring plug

2 To remove the switch, pull off the wiring plug then unscrew it from the bracket (photo).
3 Refitting is a reversal of removal, but adjust the position of the switch so that the stop lights operate after approximately 6.0 mm (0.24 in) of pedal travel.

24 Vacuum servo unit – description

On some models a vacuum servo unit is fitted into the brake hydraulic circuit in series with the master cylinder, to provide assistance to the driver when the brake pedal is depressed. This reduces the effort required by the driver to operate the brakes under all braking conditions.

The unit operates by vacuum obtained from the inlet manifold and comprises basically a booster diaphragm, control valve and a non-return valve.

The servo unit and hydraulic master cylinder are connected together so that the servo unit piston rod acts as the master cylinder pushrod. The driver's braking effort is transmitted through another pushrod to the servo unit piston and its built-in control system. The servo unit piston does not fit tightly into the cylinder, but has a strong diaphragm to keep its edges in constant contact with the cylinder wall, so assuring an airtight seal between the two parts. The forward chamber is held under vacuum conditions created in the inlet manifold of the engine and, during periods when the brake pedal is not in use, the controls open a passage to the rear chamber so placing it under vacuum conditions as well. When the brake pedal is depressed, the vacuum passage to the rear chamber is cut off and the chamber opened to atmospheric pressure. The consequent rush of air pushes the servo piston forward in the vacuum chamber and operates the main pushrod to the master cylinder.

The controls are designed so that assistance is given under all conditions and, when the brakes are not required, vacuum in the rear chamber is established when the brake pedal is released. All air from the atmosphere entering the rear chamber is passed through a small air filter.

25 Vacuum servo unit – servicing and testing

1 At the specified service intervals the servo unit air filter and non-return valve should be renewed, as follows:

Air filter
2 Working inside the car remove the steering column lower shroud with reference to Chapter 9.

3 Ease the convoluted rubber cover off the servo end and move it up the pushrod.
4 Using a screwdriver or scriber, hook out the old air filter and remove it from the servo.
5 Make a cut in the new filter, as shown in Fig. 8.36 and place it over the pushrod and into position in the servo end.
6 Refit the rubber cover and moulded plastic cover.

Non-return valve
7 Slacken the clip and disconnect the vacuum pipe from the non-return valve on the front face of the servo.
8 Withdraw the valve from its rubber sealing grommet by pulling and twisting.
9 Refit the new valve using the reverse of the removal sequence.

Testing
10 If the operation of the servo is suspect, the following test can be carried out to determine whether the unit is functioning correctly.

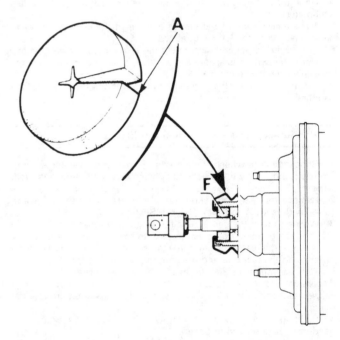

Fig. 8.36 Servo unit air filter renewal (Sec 25)

A   Cut in filter to facilitate fitting
F   Filter location in servo end

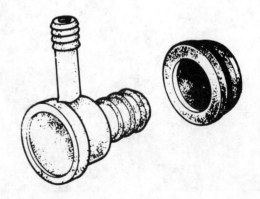

Fig. 8.37 Servo unit non-return valve and grommet (Sec 25)

11 Depress the footbrake several times then hold it down and start the engine. As the engine starts there should be a noticeable 'give' in the brake pedal. Allow the engine to run for at least two minutes and then switch it off. If the brake pedal is now depressed again it should be possible to detect a hiss from the unit as the pedal is depressed. After about four or five applications no further hissing will be heard and the pedal will feel noticeably firmer.

12 If the servo does not work as described, check the vacuum pipe condition and ensure that it is not kinked. Run the engine with the pipe disconnected at the servo and check that there is vacuum at the pipe end. If the servo air filter and non-return valve are in a satisfactory condition then the servo is faulty and renewal will be necessary.

26 Vacuum servo unit – removal and refitting

1   Disconnect the battery negative terminal.
2   Refer to Section 13 and remove the master cylinder.
3   Slacken the clip and disconnect the vacuum pipe at the servo non-return valve.
4   Working inside the car remove the steering column lower shroud with reference to Chapter 9.
5   Extract the split pin, washer and clevis pin securing the servo unit pushrod to the brake pedal.
6   Undo the four nuts and remove the washers securing the servo to the bulkhead and withdraw the unit into the engine compartment (photo).
7   Note that the servo cannot be dismantled for repair or overhaul and, if faulty, must be renewed.
8   Before refitting the servo, measure the length of the servo pushrod and output rod, ensuring that they are set to the specified length, as

shown in Fig. 8.23. If necessary, slacken the locknuts and adjust the rod lengths. Tighten the locknuts after adjustment.
9   Refitting the servo unit is the reverse sequence to removal. Bleed the brake hydraulic system, as described in Section 18 after refitting the master cylinder.

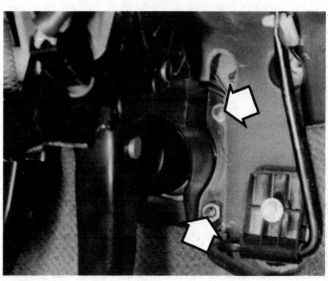

26.6 Vacuum servo unit mounting nuts

27 Fault diagnosis – braking system

Symptom	Reason(s)
Excessive pedal travel	Rear brake self-adjusting mechanism faulty (except GT Turbo) Air in hydraulic system
Brakes pull to one side	Worn or contaminated linings Seized caliper or wheel cylinder Incorrect tyre pressures
Brake judder	Excessive run-out or distortion of discs or drums Worn or contaminated linings Brake backplate or disc caliper loose Worn suspension balljoints
Excessive effort to stop car	Servo unit faulty Worn or contaminated linings
Rear wheels locking under normal braking	Faulty pressure regulating valve

Chapter 9 Suspension and steering

For modifications, and information applicable to later models, see Supplement at end of manual

Contents

Specifications

Front suspension
Type .... Independent by MacPherson struts with inclined coil springs, integral telescopic shock absorbers and anti-roll bar (except C and TC models)

Anti-roll bar diameter
Except Turbo models .... 22.0 mm (0.866 in)
Turbo models .... 21.0 mm (0.827 in)

Front underbody height
H1 – H2 (see Section 18):
    956 cc models .... 79 mm (3.11 in)
    1108 cc models .... 66 mm (2.60 in)
    1237 cc, 1397 cc (except Turbo) and 1721 cc models .... 72 mm (2.84 in)
    Turbo models up to 1988 .... 97 mm (3.82 in)
    Turbo models from 1988 .... 101 mm (3.98 in)
    Tolerance .... +10 −5 mm (+0.39 −0.20 in)

Rear suspension
Type .... Independent by trailing arms with transverse torsion bars (enclosed on non-Turbo models, open on Turbo models), inclined telescopic shock absorbers and anti-roll bar

Anti-roll bar diameter
TC models .... 13.5 mm (0.532 in)
Other non-Turbo models .... 15.5 mm (0.610 in)
Turbo models .... 23.4 mm (0.921 in)

Torsion bar diameter
Except Turbo models .... 18.0 mm (0.709 in)
Turbo models .... 20.8 mm (0.819 in)

Rear underbody height
H4 – H5 (see Section 18):
    All except Turbo models .... −10 mm (−0.39 in)
    Turbo models up to 1988 .... +20 mm (+0.79 in)
    Turbo models from 1988 .... +23 mm (+0.91 in)
    Tolerance:
        Except Turbo models .... −10 +5 mm (−0.39 +0.20 in)
        Turbo models .... +10 −5 mm (+0.39 −0.30 in)

Rear wheel camber angle (unladen) .... − 0° 50′ ± 30′

Rear wheel toe setting
Except Turbo models .... 0° to 30′ toe-in (equivalent to 0 to 3.0 mm/0.118 in toe-in)
Turbo models .... 20′ to 50′ toe-in (equivalent to 2.0 to 5.0 mm/0.079 to 0.197 in toe-in)

Steering
Type .... Rack and pinion

Camber angle
Except Turbo models .... 30′ ± 30′
Turbo models .... − 1° ± 30′

Maximum camber angle difference side-to-side .... 1°

Castor angle at specified underbody heights
H5 – H2 (see Section 18):   Castor angle
    50.0 mm (1.969 in) .... 3° 30′
    70.0 mm (2.756 in) .... 3° 0′
    90.0 mm (3.543 in) .... 2° 30′
    110.0 mm (4.331 in) .... 2° 0′
    130.0 mm (5.118 in) .... 1° 30′

Maximum castor angle difference side-to-side .... 1°

Steering axis inclination
Except Turbo models .... 12° 10′ ± 30′
Turbo models .... 13° 10′ ± 30′

Front wheel toe setting .... 0° 10′ ± 10′ toe-out (equivalent to 1.0 ± 1.0 mm/0.039 ± 0.039 in toe-out)

Roadwheels
Type .... Pressed steel or aluminium alloy according to model

Size .... 4.5 B 13, 5J 13, 5.5 J 13 or 5B 13 according to model

Maximum wheel run-out (measured at rim) .... 1.2 mm (0.047 in)

Tyres
Tyre size .... 145/70 R 13, 155/70 R 13, 165/65 SR 13, 175/60 HR 13 or 195/55 HR 13 according to model

Tyre pressures (cold) – bar/lbf/in²

	Front	Rear
Except Turbo models	2.0/29	2.2/32
Turbo models	1.8/26	1.8/26

Suspension and steering
Torque wrench settings

	Nm	lbf ft
Front suspension		
Driveshaft nut	250	184
Lower balljoint to stub axle carrier	60	44
Lower balljoint to arm	75	55
Lower suspension arm pivot	80	59
Strut to stub axle carrier	80	59

	Nm	lbf ft
Strut upper mounting	25	18
Shock absorber piston rod nut	60	44
Anti-roll bar mountings	30	22
Rear suspension		
Bearing bracket	85	63
Hub bearing	160	118
Anti-roll bar (enclosed bar rear axle)	50	37
Shock absorber mountings	60	44
Steering		
Steering gear mounting	60	44
Track rod to stub axle carrier	40	30
Track rod locknut	40	30
Track rod inner balljoint	50	37
Steering wheel	40	30
Column intermediate shaft joints	25	18
Damper plunger adjusting nut	10	8
Roadwheels		
Wheel bolts	80	59

1 General description

The independent front suspension is of the MacPherson strut type incorporating inclined coil springs, integral telescopic shock absorbers and on some models an anti-roll bar. The struts are attached to stub axle carriers at their lower ends, and the carriers are in turn attached to the lower suspension arm by balljoints. Where an anti-roll bar is fitted it is attached to the subframe and lower suspension arms by rubber bushes.

The independent rear suspension is of the trailing arm type incorporating torsion bars. On non-Turbo models the torsion bars are enclosed within tubes which are themselves part of the trailing arms, and the one-piece anti-roll bar is mounted externally between the arms. On Turbo models the trailing arms are connected by a length of flexible metal section with open torsion bars and anti-roll bars mounted beneath.

Rack and pinion steering is fitted together with a conventional column and 'safety' intermediate shaft.

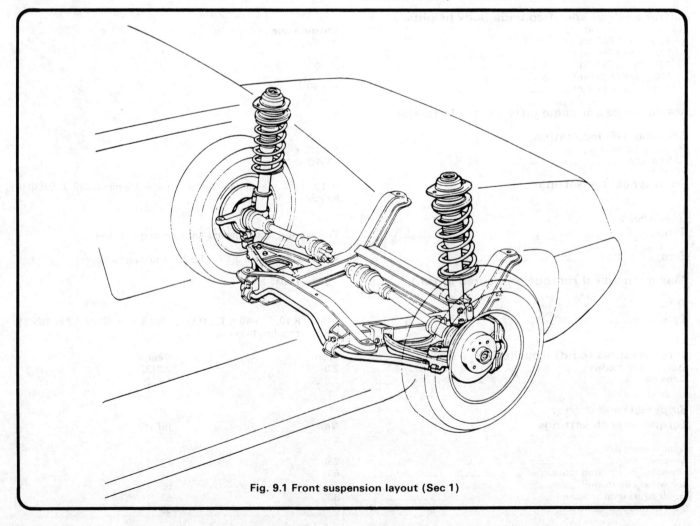

Fig. 9.1 Front suspension layout (Sec 1)

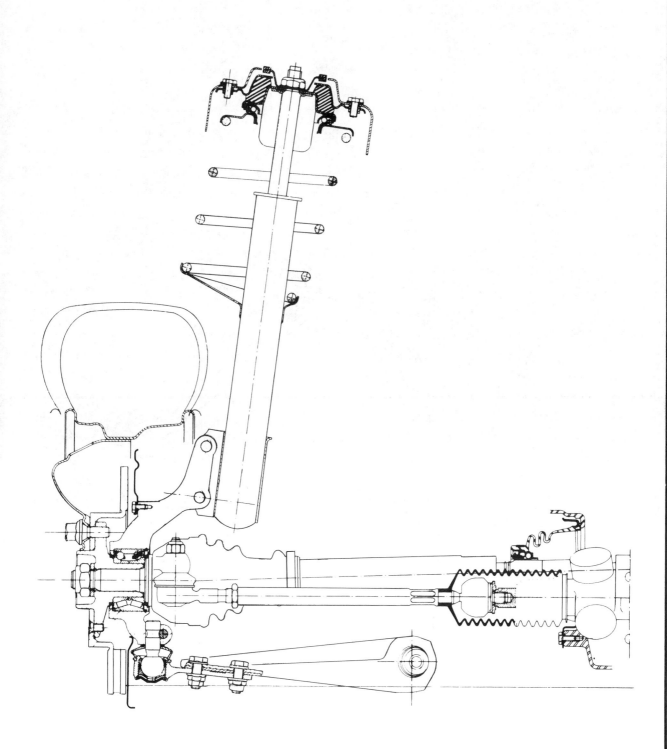

Fig. 9.2 Cross-section of the front suspension and steering components (Sec 1)

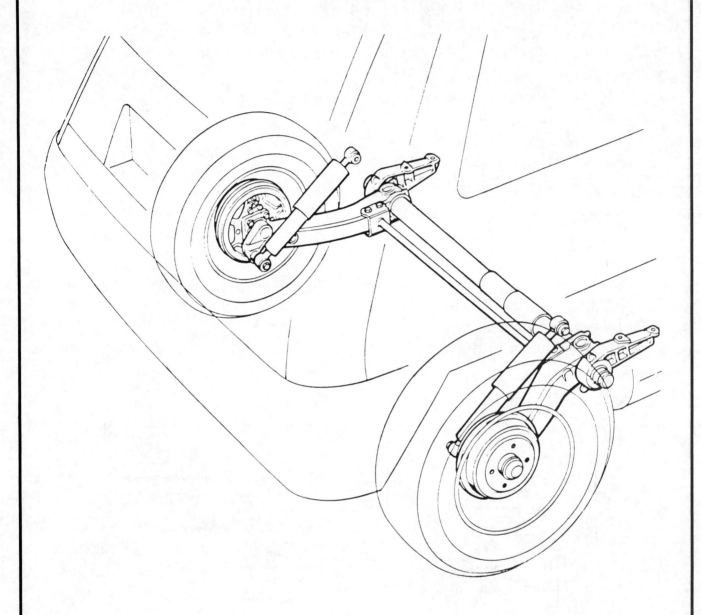

Fig. 9.3 Rear suspension layout (enclosed bar rear axle) (Sec 1)

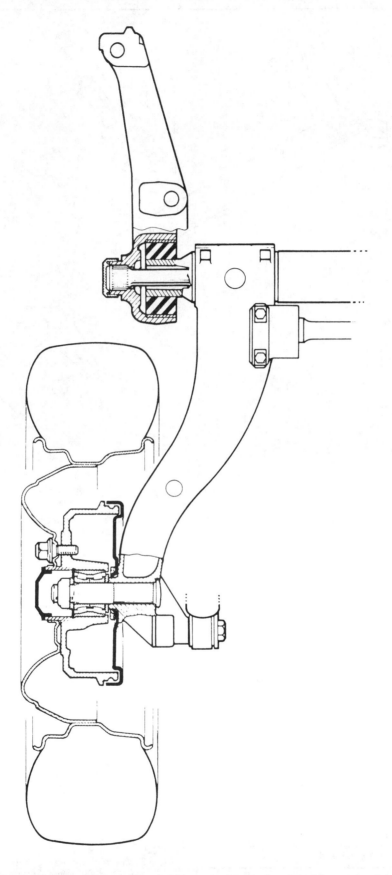

Fig. 9.4 Cross-section of the rear suspension components (enclosed bar rear axle) (Sec 1)

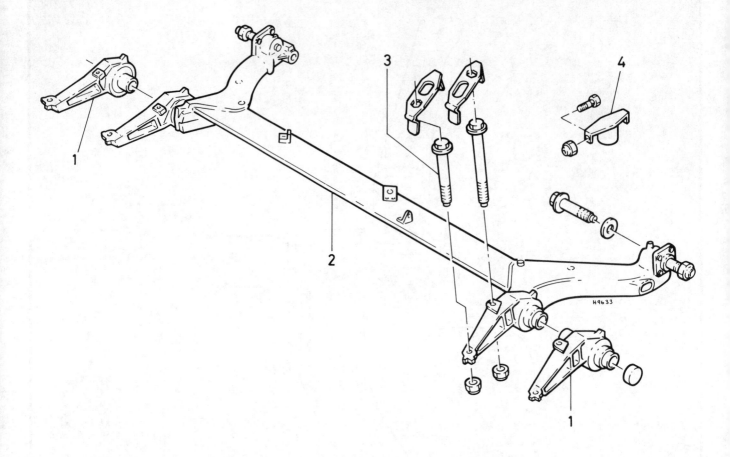

Fig. 9.5 Rear suspension components (open bar rear axle) (Sec 1)

1   Bearing brackets
2   Rear axle complete with trailing arms
3   Bearing bracket mounting bolts
4   Bump stop

2   Routine maintenance

At the intervals specified in the Routine Maintenance section in the front of the manual carry out the following procedures.

1   Check each tyre for excessive or uneven wear and for damage or tread separation. For better access to the inner sides of the tyres use car ramps or jack up the car.

2   Jack up the front of the car and support on axle stands. Grip the top and bottom of the roadwheel and attempt to rock it. If excessive play is evident check if this is in the lower suspension balljoint or hub bearing and repair as necessary.

3   Check the track rod ends for wear by pushing the socket against the ball. Excessive movement will require renewal of the track rod end.

4   Although not specified by Renault it is worthwhile checking the operation of the shock absorbers annually. To do this press down on one corner of the car and release it quickly. The body should rise then find its level on the next downward movement. If it oscillates a number of times the relevant shock absorber should be renewed. Repeat the check at the three remaining corners of the car.

3   Front stub axle carrier – removal and refitting

1   Jack up the front of the car and support on axle stands. Apply the handbrake and remove the appropriate roadwheel.

2   Remove the front brake caliper with reference to Chapter 8, but leaving the hydraulic hose connected. Tie the caliper to one side with

wire or string taking care not to damage the hose.

3   Hold the front hub stationary by using two roadwheel bolts to attach a length of metal bar, then unscrew the driveshaft nut. Remove the washer.

4   Disconnect the steering track rod end from the stub axle carrier with reference to Section 22.

5   Unscrew the two nuts and withdraw the bolts securing the stub axle carrier to the suspension strut (photo). Note that the nuts are on the side of the brake caliper.

6   Unscrew the nut and withdraw the clamp bolt securing the lower suspension arm balljoint to the base of the stub axle carrier (photo).

7   Release the stub axle carrier from the strut and then lift it, while pushing down on the suspension arm, to disengage the lower balljoint. Withdraw the stub axle carrier from the driveshaft and remove it from the car (photo). If the driveshaft is a tight fit in the hub bearings, tap it out using a plastic mallet, or use a suitable puller.

8   If the stub axle carrier is being removed for attention to the hub bearings, undo the two Torx type screws securing the disc to the hub flange using a splined key (photo). The disc can now be withdrawn from the hub. If it is tight, lay the disc over two blocks of wood and tap the hub out (photos).

9   Refitting is the reverse sequence to removal, bearing in mind the following points:

(a)   Ensure that the mating faces of the disc and hub flange are clean and flat before refitting the disc

(b)   Lubricate the hub splines with molybdenum disulphide grease

(c)   Tighten all nuts and bolts to the specified torque (photo)

(d)   Depress the brake pedal several times to reset the disc pads

3.5 Removing the bolts securing the stub axle carrier to the suspension strut

3.6 Clamp bolt securing the balljoint to the stub axle carrier

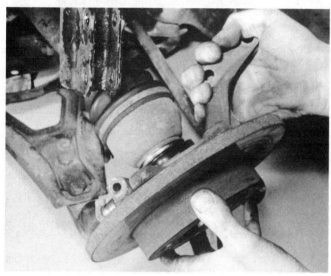

3.7 Disengage the stub axle carrier from the balljoint then withdraw the assembly from the driveshaft

3.8A Undo the two Torx type screws securing the disc to the hub flange using a splined key ...

3.8B ... then lift off the disc

3.8C If the disc is tight, support it on blocks and drive out the hub

3.9 Tightening the stub axle carrier-to-strut bolts

4 Front hub bearings – renewal

Note: *The front hub bearings should only be removed from the stub axle carrier if they are to be renewed. The removal procedure renders the bearings unserviceable and they must not be reused.*

1   Remove the stub axle carrier from the car, as described in the previous Section.
2   Support the stub axle carrier securely on blocks or in a vice. Using a tube of suitable diameter in contact with the inner end of the hub flange (photo), drive the hub flange out of the bearing.
3   The bearing will come apart as the hub flange is removed and one

of the bearing inner races will remain on the hub flange. To remove it, support the flange in a vice and lever off the inner race using two tyre levers with packing pieces, or preferably use a two- or three-legged puller. Recover the thrust washer from the hub flange after removal of the inner race.
4   Extract the bearing retaining circlip from the inner end of the stub axle carrier.
5   Support the stub axle carrier on blocks or in a vice so that the side nearest the roadwheel is uppermost.
6   Place the previously removed inner race back in position over the ball cage. Using a tube of suitable diameter in contact with the inner race, drive the complete bearing assembly out of the stub axle carrier.
7   Before fitting the new bearing, remove the plastic covers protecting the seals at each end, but leave the inner plastic sleeve in position to hold the inner races together.
8   Support the stub axle carrier so that the side away from the roadwheel is uppermost, and place the new bearing squarely in position.
9   Using a tube of suitable diameter in contact with the bearing outer race, drive the bearing into the stub axle carrier. Ensure that the bearing does not tip slightly and bind as it is being fitted. If this happens the outer race may be damaged so take great care to keep it square.
10 With the bearing in position, lubricate the lips of the two seals with multi-purpose grease. Remove the plastic retaining sleeve.
11 Place the thrust washer over the hub flange and lay it on the bench, flat face down.
12 Locate the stub axle carrier and bearing inner race over the hub flange and drive the bearing onto the flange using a tube in contact with the bearing inner race.
13 Fit a new bearing retaining circlip to the stub axle carrier and then refit the assembly to the car, as described in the previous Section.

5 Front suspension strut – removal and refitting

1   Jack up the front of the car and support it on axle stands. Remove the appropriate front roadwheel.
2   Undo the nuts and remove the two bolts and washers securing the suspension strut to the upper part of the stub axle carrier.
3   From within the engine compartment undo the two bolts securing the strut upper mounting to the turret (photos).
4   Release the strut from the stub axle carrier and withdraw it from under the wheel arch while pressing on the lower suspension arm to prevent damage to the driveshaft bellows (photo).
5   Refitting the strut is the reverse sequence to removal. Ensure that the strut-to-stub axle carrier bolts are fitted with the nuts facing the rear of the car and tighten all the retaining bolts to the specified torque.

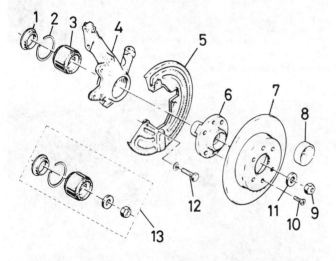

Fig. 9.6 Exploded view of front stub axle carrier showing hub bearings (Sec 4)

1	Spacer/thrust washer	8	Cup
2	Circlip	9	Driveshaft nut
3	Bearing	10	Screw
4	Stub axle carrier	11	Washer
5	Splash guard	12	Bolt
6	Hub flange	13	Bearing kit
7	Disc		

4.2 Hub flange inner end (A) and bearing retaining circlip (B) in the stub axle carrier

5.3A Unscrew the strut upper mounting bolts ...

5.3B ... and remove them

5.4 Front suspension strut removed from the car

6 Front suspension strut – dismantling and reassembly

Note: *Before attempting to dismantle the front suspension strut, a tool to hold the coil spring in compression must be obtained. The Renault tool is shown in Fig. 9.7 and consists of upper and lower plates, four through-bolts, locating studs and two bolts to hold the upper mounting, however, careful use of conventional coil spring compressors should prove satisfactory*

1 With the strut removed from the car clean away all external dirt then mount it upright in a vice.

2 Fit the spring compressor tool and compress the coil spring until all tension is relieved on the upper mounting (photo).

3 Withdraw the plastic cap over the strut upper mounting nut, hold the strut piston with an Allen key and undo the nut with a ring spanner (photo).

4 Lift off the washer and cup, the mounting and rubber, and the bearing assembly followed by the spring and compressor tool. Leave the tool or the spring unless the latter is to be renewed. Finally remove the bump stop.

5 With the strut assembly now completely dismantled, examine all the components for wear, damage or deformation and check the bearing for smoothness of operation. Renew any of the components as necessary.

6 Examine the strut for signs of fluid leakage. Check the strut piston for signs of wear or pitting along its entire length and check the strut body for signs of damage or elongation of the mounting bolt holes. Test the operation of the strut, while holding it in an upright position, by moving the piston through a full stroke and then through short strokes of 50 to 100 mm (2 to 4 in). In both cases the resistance felt should be smooth and continuous. If the resistance is jerky, or uneven, or if there is any visible sign of wear or damage to the strut, renewal is necessary.

7 Reassembly is a reversal of dismantling. The spring must be

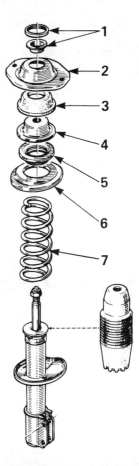

Fig. 9.8 Front suspension strut components (Sec 6)

1	Washer and cup	5	Collar
2	Mounting plate	6	Spring seat
3	Rubber	7	Coil spring
4	Bearing		

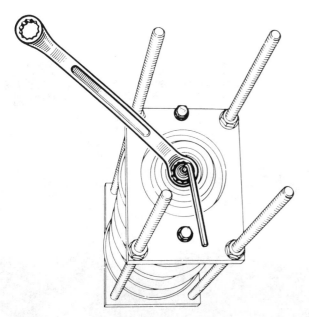

Fig. 9.7 Removing the nut from the front shock absorber piston rod (Sec 6)

6.2 Spring compressor tool fitted to the front suspension coil spring

6.3 Strut upper mounting showing nut on piston rod

compressed to less than 300.0 mm (11.8 in) to allow the mounting nut to be fitted to the piston rod. Tighten the nut to the specified torque. Make sure that the spring ends are correctly located in the upper and lower seats when releasing the compressor tool.

7 Front anti-roll bar – removal and refitting

1   Apply the handbrake then jack up the front of the car and support on axle stands.
2   Remove the exhaust downpipe with reference to Chapter 3.
3   Disconnect the gearchange linkage from the gearbox with reference to Chapter 6.
4   Unscrew the nuts and remove the clamp bolts holding the ends of the anti-roll bar to the lower suspension arms. Pull down the clamps.
5   Unscrew the nuts and remove the clamp bolts from the mountings on the subframe (photo). Pull down the clamps and remove them.
6   Lower the anti-roll bar from the rear of the subframe.

7   Check the bar for damage and the rubber bushes for wear and deterioration. If the bushes are in need of renewal slide them off the bar and fit new ones after lubricating them with rubber grease.
8   Refitting is a reversal of removal, but delay tightening the clamp bolts until the unladen weight of the car is on the suspension.

8 Front lower suspension arm – removal and refitting

1   Remove the front anti-roll bar as described in Section 7. Remove the roadwheel.
2   Unscrew the nut and remove the clamp bolt securing the lower suspension balljoint to the stub axle carrier.
3   Unscrew the nuts and remove the spacers and pivot bolts from the inner end of the suspension arm then withdraw the arm from the subframe and stub axle carrier (photo). If the balljoint stub is seized in the stub axle carrier, lever or drive it out with a mallet. Recover the protector from the balljoint boot.

7.5 Front anti-roll bar mounting on the subframe

8.3 Front lower suspension arm inner mounting

4   If the inner pivot bushes are to be renewed this can be done using suitable lengths of tube and a press or wide-opening vice. Renew the bushes one at a time so that the distance between the bush inner edges is maintained at 146.5 to 147.5 mm (5.77 to 5.81 in).

5   Refitting is a reversal of removal. Make sure that the plastic protector is positioned over the balljoint boot. Tighten the pivot and clamp bolts to the specified torque, and refit the anti-roll bar with reference to Section 7.

9   Front lower suspension balljoint – renewal

1   Apply the handbrake then jack up the front of the car and support on axle stands. Remove the roadwheel.

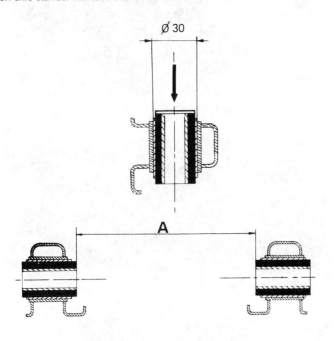

Fig. 9.9 Front lower suspension arm pivot bush renewal (Sec 8)

Use a 30.0 mm (1.18 in) diameter tube to remove and refit the bushes. Dimension A must be 146.5 to 147.5 mm (5.77 to 5.81 in)

2   Unscrew the nut and remove the clamp bolt securing the lower suspension balljoint to the stub axle carrier.

3   Unscrew the two nuts and bolts securing the balljoint to the lower suspension arm and withdraw the balljoint (photo). Recover the plastic protector from the balljoint boot.

4   Fit the new balljoint using a reversal of the removal procedure, but tighten the nuts to the specified torque.

10   Rear hub bearings – renewal

1   Jack up the rear of the car and support on axle stands. Remove the appropriate rear roadwheel.

2   On models with rear disc brakes remove the disc pads and caliper frame with reference to Chapter 8.

3   Lever or tap off the grease cap from the centre of the brake drum or disc (photo).

4   Using a socket unscrew the hub nut then remove the thrust washer (photo).

5   Pull the brake drum or disc assembly from the stub axle, if necessary using a soft-head mallet to help release the bearing inner race from the stub axle. On rear brake drum models make sure that the handbrake is fully released, however if the shoes still bind on the drum use the procedures described in Chapter 8, Section 6 to further release the shoes.

6   With the brake drum or disc assembly removed extract the circlip and drive out the bearing using a tube of suitable diameter inserted through the inside of the hub and in contact with the bearing outer race (photo).

7   Place the new bearing in the hub and drive it fully home, again using a tube in contact with the bearing outer race. Take great care to keep the bearing square as it is installed, otherwise it may jam in the hub bore.

8   With the bearing in position, refit the retaining circlip.

9   Check that the bearing inner spacer/thrust washer is located on the stub axle. On rear brake drum models set the handbrake lever on the shoe to its normal position if moved and shorten the automatic adjuster as required.

10 Refit the brake drum or disc followed by the thrust washer and a new hub nut.

11 Tighten the hub nut to the specified torque then tap the grease cap back into place (photo).

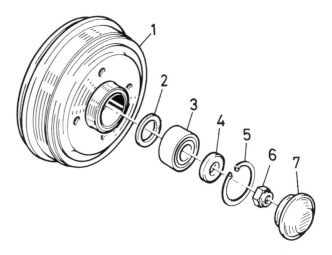

Fig. 9.10 Exploded view of the rear hub (Sec 10)

1 Hub/drum (disc on some models)	4 Thrust washer
2 Spacer/thrust washer	5 Circlip
3 Bearing	6 Hub nut
	7 Grease cap

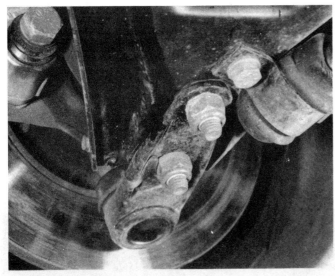

9.3 Front lower suspension balljoint

10.3 Removing the rear hub grease cap

10.4 Removing the rear hub nut and washer

10.6 Extracting the rear hub bearing circlip

10.11 Tightening the rear hub nut

12 On rear disc brake models refit the disc pads and caliper frame with reference to Chapter 8.

13 Refit the roadwheel then depress the footbrake pedal several times to reset the shoes or disc pads.

14 On rear brake drum models adjust the handbrake cable if necessary as described in Chapter 8.

15 Lower the car to the ground.

11 Rear shock absorber – removal and refitting

1 Jack up the rear of the car and support on axle stands. Chock the front wheels. Remove the appropriate rear wheel.

2 Using a trolley jack lift the trailing arm until the shock absorber is compressed slightly then unscrew and remove the lower mounting bolt (photo).

3 Unscrew and remove the upper mounting nut and bolt and withdraw the shock absorber from the underframe (photo).

4 Mount the shock absorber upright in a vice and test it as described in Section 6 for the front suspension strut. Also check the mounting

11.2 Rear shock absorber lower mounting

11.3 Rear shock absorber upper mounting

the torsion bar and placing the jaws of a spanner against the washer. Striking the spanner sharply with a hammer should free the torsion bar.
8 Once the splines of the torsion bar are free, the bar can be withdrawn completely from its location. Note that the torsion bars are not interchangeable from side to side and are marked with symbols on their ends for identification as shown in Fig. 9.12.
9 If the original torsion bar is being refitted insert it so that the marks made in paragraph 6 are aligned. However if a new bar is being fitted, the trailing arm must be positioned to provide the dimension shown in Fig. 9.13. A tool similar to that shown will hold the trailing arm in position, or the arm can be positioned with the trolley jack.
10 With the trailing arm supported in this position lubricate the torsion bar splines with molybdenum disulphide grease and insert the bar into the bracket. The number of splines at each end of the bar is different so it will be necessary to turn it to find the point where both sets of splines enter freely. Having found this, tap the bar fully home using a hammer and soft metal drift.
11 Refit the cap to the bearing bracket.
12 Refit the rear shock absorber (Section 11), if applicable the anti-roll bar (Section 12), and the rear roadwheel. Lower the car to the ground.
13 It is now necessary to check the rear underbody height. The fuel tank should be full or an equivalent weight placed in the luggage compartment and the tyres correctly inflated. Refer to Section 18 for further information.

rubbers for damage and deterioration. Renew the complete unit if any damage or excessive wear is apparent.
5 Before fitting the shock absorber mount it upright in the vice and operate it fully through several strokes in order to prime it.
6 Coat the threads of the mounting bolts with locking fluid then position the shock absorber, insert the bolts and screw on the upper nut finger tight.
7 Raise the trolley jack until the full weight of the car is on the suspension then tighten the mounting bolts to the specified torque.
8 Refit the roadwheel and lower the car to the ground.

12 Rear anti-roll bar (enclosed bar rear axle) – removal and refitting

Note: *The procedure for the open bar rear axle is given in Section 17.*
1 Chock the front wheels then jack up the rear of the car and support it on axle stands.
2 From each end of the anti-roll bar unscrew the through-bolts securing the brackets to the rear suspension trailing arms. Note the location of the handbrake cable brackets. Recover the plates with the trapped nuts.
3 Withdraw the anti-roll bar from under the car. If the bar is to be refitted identify it for position to ensure correct positioning when refitting.
4 Refitting is a reversal of removal, but tighten the through-bolts to the specified torque. Note that the cut-away sides of the brackets must be towards the front of the car.

13 Rear torsion bar – removal and refitting

1 Chock the front wheels then jack up the rear of the car and support on axle stands. Remove the appropriate rear roadwheel.
2 On models with the enclosed-bar rear axle remove the anti-roll bar as described in Section 12.
3 Remove the rear shock absorber as described in Section 11.
4 Lower the trailing arm until all the tension in the torsion bar is released.
5 Prise the cap from the trailing arm bearing bracket.
6 Mark the position of the torsion bar in relation to the bearing bracket, and on the open-bar rear axle in relation to the centre link block.
7 The torsion bar can now be withdrawn outwards using a slide hammer such as Renault tool Emb.880 or a suitable alternative. It is possible to improvise by screwing a long bolt with a flat washer into

Fig. 9.11 Using the Renault slide hammer to remove a rear torsion bar (Sec 13)

14 Rear suspension trailing arm (enclosed bar rear axle) – removal and refitting

1 Jack up the rear of the car and support it on axle stands. Remove the appropriate rear roadwheel.
2 Remove the anti-roll bar and the shock absorber, as decribed in Sections 12 and 11 respectively. Remove the torsion bar on the side concerned, as described in Section 13.
3 Refer to Chapter 8 and remove the brake drum and hub assembly.
4 With the drum removed, detach the handbrake cable from the operating lever on the trailing brake shoe and withdraw the cable from the brake backplate.
5 Using a brake hose clamp or self-locking wrench with protected jaws, clamp the appropriate flexible brake hose just in front of the rear axle. This will minimise brake fluid loss during subsequent operations.

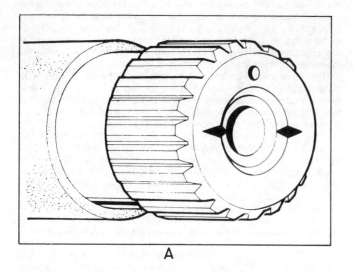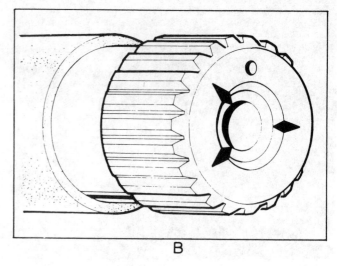

Fig. 9.12 Rear torsion bar identification (Sec 13)

A Left-hand bar – 2 marks   *B Right-hand bar – 3 marks*

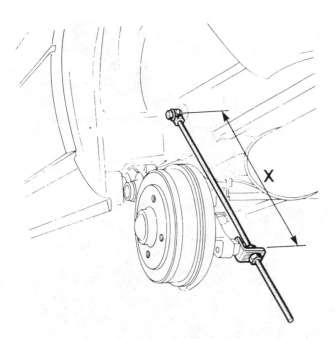

14.9 Rear suspension bearing bracket

Fig. 9.13 Rear trailing arm setting for fitting torsion bar (Sec 13)

X = 405.0 mm (15.945 in) for non-Turbo models
X = 385.0 mm (15.158 in) for Turbo models

Clean the union on the trailing arm then unscrew the union nut and withdraw the hose from the bracket. Recover the clip then tape over the ends of the hose and pipe to prevent entry of dirt.

6   Where applicable disconnect the brake pressure regulating control valve spring with reference to Chapter 8.

7   Support the weight of the trailing arm with a trolley jack.

8   Working inside the rear of the car remove the rear seat cushion and cut away the plastic to reveal the plates and bolt heads of the bearing bracket mounting bolts.

9   Unscrew the nuts from beneath the car then tap the bolts through the bearing bracket with a suitable drift (photo).

10 Lower the jack as necessary to allow the trailing arm to clear the sill.

11 Pull the trailing arm from the remaining arm. If it is tight Renault recommend using a hydraulic ram between the two arms, however a similar arrangement is possible using a length of wood and a screw or bottle jack.

12 With the arm removed the brake backplate can be unbolted if required and the spacer removed from the stub axle.

13 To refit the arm push it onto the other arm having first lubricated the inner bushes with grease. If it is tight use a rope as a tourniquet between the two arms. Temporarily position the anti-roll bar over the mounting holes to determine how far the bars should be interlocked.

14 Raise the trolley jack to lift the arm, and insert the mounting bolts, tightening the nuts to the specified torque.

15 Refit the rear seat cushion.

16 Refit the brake backplate and stub axle spacer.

17 Where applicable reconnect the brake pressure regulating control valve spring.

18 Refit the flexible brake hose and rigid pipe together with the clip and tighten the union nut.

19 Refit the handbrake cable and drum with reference to Chapter 8.

20 Refit the torsion bar (Section 13), shock absorber (Section 11), and anti-roll bar (Section 12).
21 Bleed the brake hydraulic system as described in Chapter 8, noting that it should only be necessary to bleed the relevant rear brake providing the hose was clamped as described.
22 Finally refit the roadwheel and lower the car to the gound.

15 Rear suspension trailing arm bushes (enclosed bar rear axle) – renewal

Note: *The rear suspension trailing arm bushes are located in the left-hand trailing arm.*
1 Remove the left-hand trailing arm as described in Section 14 and mount it in a vice. Prise out the oil seal.
2 To remove the bushes it will be necessary to obtain the Renault tool shown in Fig. 9.14 or make up a similar tool using the Renault tool as a pattern, as follows:
3 Obtain a threaded rod long enough to reach the inner bush, a tube of suitable diameter as shown, one thick washer of diameter equal to

that of the bush, a washer of diameter greater than the tube and two nuts. Cut two sides off the smaller washer so that just a flat strip with a hole in the centre remains. This will form the swivelling end part shown on the Renault tool. Pass the threaded rod through the hole in the strip and screw on a nut. Feed the strip and rod through the bush so that the strip locates behind the bush. Place the tube over the rod and in contact with the edge of the arm. Place the large washer over the end of the tube and then screw on the remaining nut. Hold the rod with grips and tighten the nut to draw out the bush, then repeat this operation to remove the remaining bush.
4 Clean the inside of the arm then drive in the new bushes using suitable tubing. Position the bushes to the dimensions shown in Fig. 9.15.
5 Press in a new seal and smear a little grease on its lip.
6 Refit the left-hand trailing arm with reference to Section 14.

16 Rear suspension bearing bracket bushes (enclosed bar rear axle) – renewal

1 Remove the trailing arm as described in Section 14.
2 Apply brake fluid to the bush to soften the rubber.
3 Using a two- or three-legged puller draw the bearing bracket from the trailing arm. The rubber will tear during this process leaving the inner part of the bush on the arm.
4 Remove the remaining part of the bush by cutting with a hacksaw taking care not to damage the trailing arm tube. Also remove the outer remains of the bush from the bearing bracket. Clean the tube and bracket.
5 The fitted position of the new bush must be flush with the end of the trailing arm tube so mark the inner part of the tube to indicate the final position of the bush.
6 Press or drive the new bush fully into the bearing bracket.
7 Position the bracket as shown in Fig. 9.17 in relation to the trailing arm then press or drive the bracket on the tube until the bush reaches the mark made in paragraph 5.
8 Refit the trailing arm with reference to Section 14.

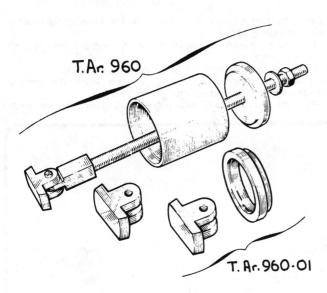

Fig. 9.14 Renault tool for removing the rear suspension trailing arm bushes (Sec 15)

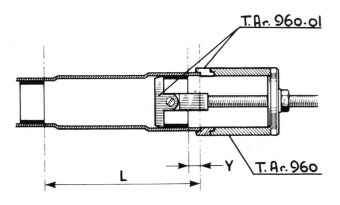

Fig. 9.15 Showing trailing arm bush removal and bush fitting dimensions (Sec 15)

$$L = 140.0 + 2 (5.512 + 0.079$$
$$- 0 mm \quad - 0 in)$$
$$Y = 15.0 + 2 (0.591 + 0.079$$
$$- 0 mm \quad - 0 in)$$

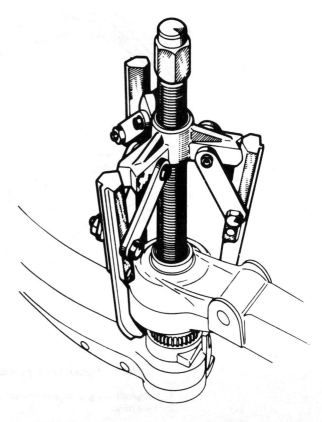

Fig. 9.16 Using a puller to remove the rear suspension bearing bracket (Sec 16)

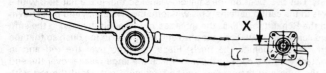

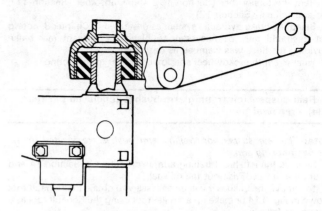

Fig. 9.17 Trailing arm and bearing bracket positioning for assembly (Sec 16)

$$X = 80.0 \pm 2.0 \text{ mm } (3.150 \pm 0.079 \text{ in})$$

17 Rear axle (open bar type) – removal and refitting

1   Remove the rear shock absorbers as described in Section 11.
2   Remove both rear torsion bars with reference to Section 13.
3   Remove the brake components from the trailing arms with reference to Chapter 8.
4   Using a brake hose clamp compress both rear flexible hoses then disconnect them by unscrewing the union nuts. Recover the clips and tape over the ends of the hoses and pipes to prevent entry of dirt.
5   Disconnect the brake pressure regulating control valve spring with reference to Chapter 8.
6   Support the weight of the rear axle with a trolley jack.
7   Working inside the rear of the car remove the rear seat cushion and

Fig. 9.18 Showing correct fitted positions of rear bearing bracket bush (Sec 16)

cut away the mastic to reveal the plates and bolt heads of the bearing bracket mounting bolts.
8   Unscrew the nuts from beneath the car then tap the bolts through the bearing brackets.
9   Lower the rear axle from the underbody and remove it.
10   If required, remove the bearing brackets using the method described for the enclosed bar rear axle in Section 6.
11   Mark the anti-roll bars in relation to the trailing arms and link block,

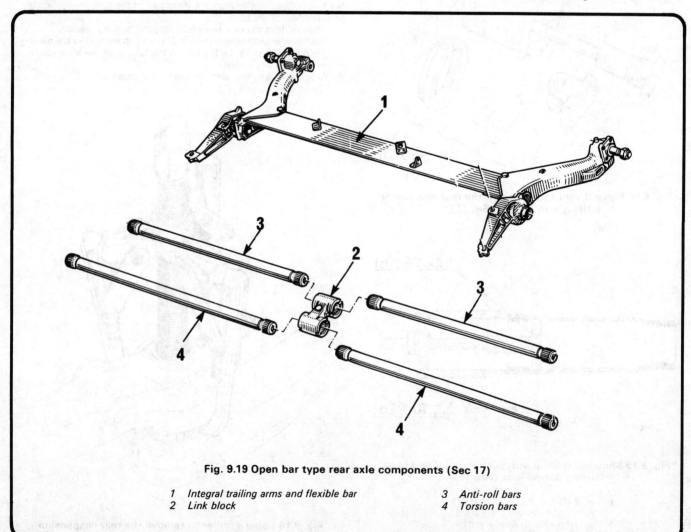

Fig. 9.19 Open bar type rear axle components (Sec 17)

1   Integral trailing arms and flexible bar
2   Link block

3   Anti-roll bars
4   Torsion bars

then extract them using a slide hammer such as Renault tool Emb.880 or a suitable alternative.

12 Examine all the components for damage and wear. Check the splines on the torsion bars, anti-roll bars, link block and trailing arms. If the trailing arms or L-shaped section is damaged it will be necessary to obtain a new rear axle which is supplied with the bearing brackets already fitted, but requiring the torsion bars and anti-roll bars to be fitted. If the bearing bracket bushes require renewal use the procedure described in Section 16.

13 Commence re-assembly by placing the rear axle upside-down on blocks of wood positioned under the L-shaped section so that the bearing brackets are free.

Anti-roll bars with no marks

14 Make up a small block of wood 8.0 mm (0.315 in) thick and position it on the middle of the L-shaped section with the link block on top (Fig. 9.20).

15 Clean the anti-roll bar splines and grease them well.

16 Insert one anti-roll bar through the trailing arm and engage the splines with the link block. It will be necessary to try the bar in different positions to find the point where both sets of splines enter freely.

17 Fit the remaining anti-roll bar using the same procedure then mark each bar in relation to the trailing arms and link block. Remove the wooden block.

Anti-roll bars with special marks

18 Using a ruler as shown in Fig. 9.21 mark each trailing arm between the centres of the torsion bar and anti-roll bar holes.

19 Clean the anti-roll bar splines and grease them well.

20 Insert one anti-roll bar with the marked spline aligned with the mark made in paragraph 18.

21 Fit the link block with the centre section parallel to the L-shaped section.

22 Insert the remaining anti-roll bar from the opposite side with the marked spline aligned with the mark made in paragraph 18.

All types

23 The clearance between the centre of the link block and the L-shaped section must now be measured. If it is more than 2.0 mm (0.08 in) the block must be re-positioned bearing in mind that one spline is equal to 2.0 mm (0.08 in) clearance. If the clearance is incorrect the link block may touch the L-shaped section during movement of the suspension.

24 Clean the torsion bar splines and grease them well.

25 Insert the torsion bars on their correct sides until fully entered in the link block. Try them in different positions to find the point where both sets of splines enter freely.

26 Place the rear axle on the trolley jack and lift it into positon.

27 Tap the bolts through the bearing brackets then fit the nuts and tighten them to the specified torque. Refit the rear seat cushion.

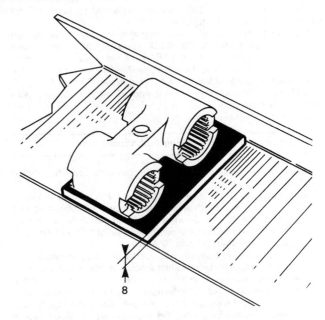

Fig. 9.20 Place the link block and block of wood on the L-shaped sections (Sec 17)

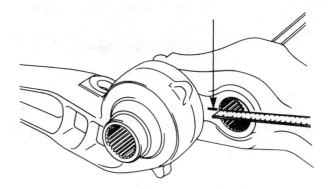

Fig. 9.21 Using a ruler to mark the trailing arms (Sec 17)

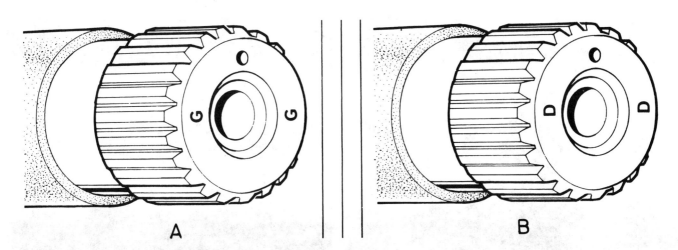

Fig. 9.22 Rear torsion bar identification on some Turbo models (Sec 17)

A Left-hand bar   B Right-hand bar

28 Refit the brake components, flexible hoses and pressure control valve spring with reference to Chapter 8.
29 Check that with the weight of the trailing arms taken off the torsion bars the distance between the shock absorber upper and lower mounting centres is 385.0 mm (15.16 in). If not, remove the torsion bars and re-position them in the splines with reference to Section 13.
30 Refit the rear shock absorbers with reference to Section 11.
31 Check the rear underbody height and adjust if necessary with reference to Section 18.

18 Underbody height – checking and adjustment

1 Position the car on a level surface with the tyres correctly inflated and the fuel tank full.
2 Measure and record the dimensions H1, H2, H4, and H5 shown in Fig. 9.23. The results should be within the specified tolerances and should not vary side-to-side by more than 10.0 mm (0.40 in) except on Turbo models where the *rear* suspension height should not vary side-to-side by more than 5.0 mm (0.20 in).
3 It is not possible to adjust the front underbody height, however, if the rear height is outside the specified amount proceed as follows.
4 *If the side-to-side height difference is excessive* on the open bar type rear axle, the anti-roll bar on the lower side must be re-positioned to raise that side. On the enclosed type rear axle, excessive side-to-side difference may be due to a distorted anti-roll bar in which case it should be removed and checked. To adjust the open bar type first remove both rear torsion bars and the anti-roll bar on the lower side after marking their positions. Determine the position of the trailing arm where the anti-roll bar can be refitted in its original location freely, then lower the arm by the side-to-side difference previously noted and insert the anti-roll bar again, this time turning it as required to find the position where both sets of splines enter freely. Finally refit the torsion bars.

5 *If the height is incorrect* remove the torsion bar from the appropriate side after marking its position. Determine the position of the trailing arm where the torsion bar can be refitted in its original location freely, then adjust the arm up or down as necessary by the difference of height required, and insert the torsion bar again this time turning it as required to find the position where both sets of splines enter freely.
6 After adjusting the underbody height the load sensitive type brake pressure regulator spring tension should be checked and adjusted (Chapter 8) and the headlight beam alignment adjusted (Chapter 11).

19 Steering wheel – removal and refitting

1 Set the front wheels in the straight-ahead position.
2 Ease off the steering wheel pad to provide access to the retaining nut.
3 Using a socket and knuckle bar undo and remove the retaining nut (photo).
4 Mark the steering wheel and steering column shaft in relation to each other and withdraw the wheel from the shaft splines (photo). If it

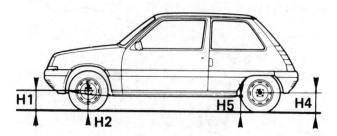

Fig. 9.23 Underbody height checking points (Sec 18)

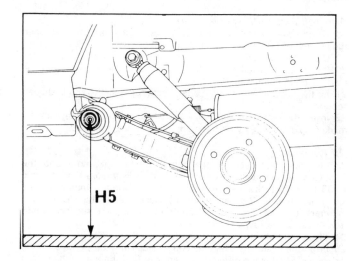

Fig. 9.24 The underbody height H5 is measured from the centre of the torsion bar (Sec 18)

19.3 Unscrew the retaining nut ...

19.4 ... and remove the steering wheel

is tight, tap it upwards near the centre, using the palm of your hand. Refit the steering wheel retaining nut two turns before doing this, for obvious reasons.

5   Refitting is the reverse of removal, but align the previously made marks and tighten the retaining nut to the specified torque.

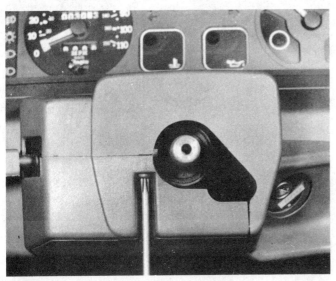

20.3A Remove the screws ...

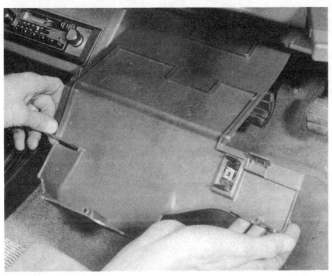

20.3B ... and withdraw the steering column lower shroud

20 Steering column assembly – removal, overhaul and refitting

1   Disconnect the battery negative lead.
2   Remove the steering wheel as described in Section 19.
3   Remove the screws and withdraw the lower shroud from the column (photos).
4   Unscrew the direction indicator switch mounting screws.
5   Extract the circlip from the top of the column.
6   At the base of the column unscrew and remove the clamp bolt securing the intermediate shaft to the inner column. Mark both components in relation to each other.
7   Check that the ignition switch is in the 'Garage' position with the steering unlocked, then temporarily refit the steering wheel with the nut finger tight. Pull on the steering wheel to release the inner column from the intermediate shaft and also to release the upper bush.
8   Unscrew the facia-to-column bolts and also the steering column mounting bolts/nuts (photo).
9   Where applicable separate the centre console from the facia then release the facia panel lower mountings with reference to Chapter 10.
10 Disconnect the ignition switch wiring multi-plug.
11 Lift the facia panel as necessary and withdraw the steering column from the car.
12 Using a long metal tube of 35.0 mm (1.378 in) outside diameter drive the lower bush from the outer column. Also pull the upper bush from the inner column.
13 Clean the inner and outer columns. Renew the inner column if it is worn excessively. Obtain two new bushes.

20.8 Steering column mounting bolts and nuts

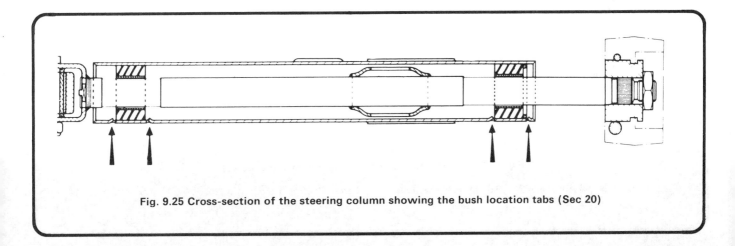

Fig. 9.25 Cross-section of the steering column showing the bush location tabs (Sec 20)

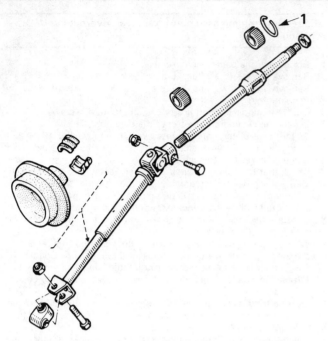

Fig. 9.26 Inner steering column and intermediate shaft components (Sec 20)

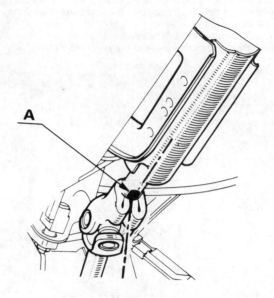

Fig. 9.27 The flat (A) on the inner column must be aligned with the clamp opening (Sec 20)

14 Lubricate the bushes with grease then drive the lower bush into the outer column between the location tabs. Tap in the tabs using a punch in order to lock the bush.
15 Insert the inner column through the top of the outer column and through the lower bush.
16 Drive in the upper bush and refit the circlip. Tap in the location tabs to lock the bush.
17 Refitting is a reversal of removal, but when re-connecting the intermediate shaft to the inner column, the flat on the column must be aligned with the clamp opening as shown in Fig. 9.27. Tighten all nuts and bolts to the specified torque. Refit the steering wheel with reference to Section 19.

21 Steering column intermediate shaft – removal and refitting

1 Jack up the front of the car and support on axle stands. Apply the handbrake.

2 Remove the screws and withdraw the lower shroud from the column.
3 At the base of the column unscrew and remove the clamp bolt securing the intermediate shaft to the inner column. Mark both components in relation to each other.
4 Working in the engine compartment or from beneath the car unscrew and remove the lower bolt from the flexible coupling, but leave the clamp and clamp bolt on the steering gear. Mark the coupling and clamp in relation to each other.
5 Prise the rubber boot from the bulkhead, pull the intermediate shaft down to release it from the inner column then withdraw the shaft from inside the car.
6 Release the rubber boot from the bearing halves and pull it from the shaft.
7 Check the intermediate shaft for wear and damage. There should be no noticeable play between the yokes of the universal joint. The shaft incorporates a safety feature whereby the two tubes slide into each other in the event of accident impact, however the shaft must not be used after accidental damage and it is therefore important to check that its length is as given in Fig. 9.28 before refitting it. Check and if necessary renew the rubber boot and bearing halves.

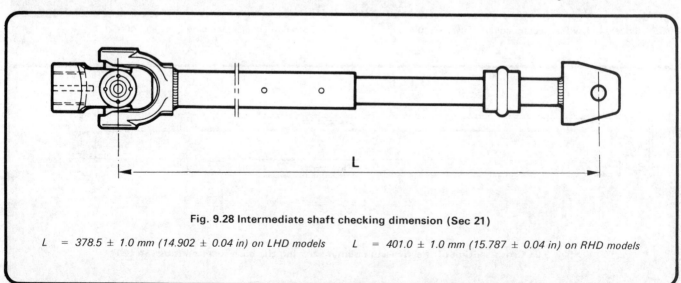

Fig. 9.28 Intermediate shaft checking dimension (Sec 21)

L = 378.5 ± 1.0 mm (14.902 ± 0.04 in) on LHD models L = 401.0 ± 1.0 mm (15.787 ± 0.04 in) on RHD models

8   To refit the shaft first locate the rubber boot and bearing halves on the small diameter end.
9   Insert the shaft through the bulkhead and connect it to the lower flexible coupling and inner column making sure that the flat on the column is aligned with the clamp opening (Fig. 9.27). Do not tighten the bolts at this stage.
10   Tighten each of the lower flexible coupling bolts only when the bolt head is facing vertically upwards. This will ensure the centre rubber block flexes equally in both directions.
11   Tighten the upper clamp bolt.
12   Refit the rubber boot and lower shroud then lower the car to the ground.

22 Track rod end balljoint – renewal

1   Jack up the front of the car and support it on axle stands. Remove the appropriate front roadwheel.
2   Using a suitable spanner, slacken the balljoint locknut on the track rod by a quarter of a turn. Hold the track rod with a second spanner engaged with the flats at its inner end to prevent it from turning.
3   Undo and remove the locknut securing the balljoint to the stub axle carrier and then release the tapered shank using a balljoint separator tool (photos).
4   Count the number of exposed threads between the end of the balljoint and the locknut and record this figure.
5   Unscrew the balljoint from the track rod and unscrew the locknut from the balljoint.
6   Screw the locknut onto the new balljoint and position it so that the same number of exposed threads are visible as was noted during removal.
7   Screw the balljoint onto the track rod until the locknut just contacts the arm. Now tighten the locknut while holding the track rod as before.
8   Engage the shank of the balljoint with the stub axle carrier and refit the locknut. Tighten the locknut to the specified torque. If the balljoint shank turns while the locknut is being tightened, place a jack under the balljoint and raise it sufficiently to push the tapered shank fully into the stub axle carrier. The tapered fit of the shank will lock it and prevent rotation as the nut is tightened.
9   On completion, remove the jack, refit the roadwheel and lower the car to the ground.
10   Check the front wheel alignment, as described in Section 28.

23 Steering gear rubber bellows – renewal

1   Remove the track rod end balljoint as described in Section 22.
2   Release the retaining wire or unscrew the retaining clip screws and slide the bellows off the rack and pinion housing and track rod.
3   Lubricate the inner ends of the new bellows with rubber grease and position it over the housing and track rod.
4   Using new clips, or two or three turns of soft iron wire, secure the bellows in position.
5   Refit the outer balljoint, as described in the previous Section.

24 Track rod and inner balljoint – removal and refitting

1   Remove the outer balljoint and rubber bellows, as described in Sections 22 and 23 respectively.
2   Hold the thrust washer with grips to prevent the rack turning and unscrew the inner balljoint housing with a small stilson wrench. Remove the balljoint housing and track rod assembly from under the wheel arch.
3   Clean the components and inspect them for damage. Always renew the lockplate and thrust washer. Check the balljoint for excessive play and damage to the lockplate serrations, and renew it if necessary.
4   Fit the thrust washer and lockplate to the rack ensuring that the two tabs on the lockplate are in line with the two flats on the end of the rack.
5   Apply a drop of locking compound to the threads of the balljoint and screw the balljoint housing and track rod assembly into position. Tighten the housing securely.

22.3A Unscrew the nut ...

22.3B ... and use a separator tool to remove the track rod end balljoint

6   Refit the rubber bellows and outer balljoint, as described in Sections 23 and 22 respectively.

25 Steering rack support bearing – removal and refitting

Note: *The support bearing is located in the left-hand end of the steering gear on RHD models, and in the right-hand end on LHD models.*
1   Remove the appropriate track rod and inner balljoint as described in Section 24.
2   Turn the steering onto full lock so that the rack is clear of the bearing.
3   Working under the wheel arch, extract the bearing from the rack and pinion housing by prising it out with a screwdriver.
4   Clean the rack, and rack and pinion housing, and then lubricate both with molybdenum disulphide grease. Liberally lubricate the new bearing also.
5   Carefully insert the new bearing into the housing and position it so that each of the three bearing tags enter their slots in the housing.

Fig. 9.29 Steering rack support bearing (Sec 25)

6   Move the steering on the opposite lock to settle the bearing and distribute the grease.
7   Refit the track rod and inner balljoint with reference to Section 24.

26 Steering gear – removal and refitting

1   Jack up the front of the car and support on axle stands. Apply the handbrake. Remove both front roadwheels.
2   On each side unscrew the nuts securing the track rod end balljoints to the stub axle carrier and use a separator tool to release the balljoints.
3   Working in the engine compartment unscrew and remove the lower bolt from the flexible coupling on the intermediate shaft, but leave the clamp and clamp bolt on the steering gear (photo). Mark the coupling and clamp in relation to each other.
4   Unscrew and remove the mounting nuts and bolts, spacers and clamp, then withdraw the steering gear sideways at the same time releasing the clamp from the flexible coupling (photo).
5   If necessary remove the track rod end balljoints as described in Section 22.

6   Refitting is a reversal of removal, but tighten all nuts and bolts to the specified torque. The flexible coupling bolt should be tightened with the bolt head facing upwards to ensure correct flexing of the centre rubber block. When fitting a new steering gear it will be necessary to place both the steering wheel and steering rack in their central straight-ahead positions before connecting the flexible coupling clamp to the steering gear pinion. Finally check and adjust the front wheel alignment as described in Section 28.

27 Steering gear – overhaul

Note: *Overhaul of the steering gear is limited as only certain parts are available separately. Renewal of the track rod end balljoints, track rods, rack support bearing and the rubber bellows may be carried out with the steering gear either in or out of the car, and these operations are covered in previous Sections of this Chapter. The only other repair possible is renewal and/or adjustment of the rack damper plunger. To carry out this work the steering gear must be removed from the car and the procedure is then as follows:*
1   With the steering gear on the bench, unlock the damper adjusting nut by straightening the tabs around the periphery of the nut (photo).

26.3 Intermediate shaft to steering gear coupling

26.4 View of the steering gear, shown with engine and gearbox removed

27.1 Steering gear rack damper adjusting nut, shown in position in the car

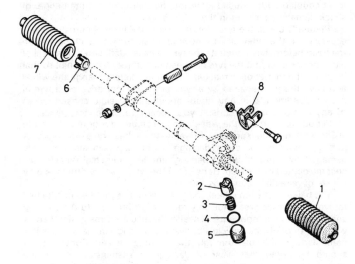

Fig. 9.30 Steering gear components (Sec 27)

1	Rubber bellows	5	Adjusting nut
2	Rack damper plunger	6	Rack support bearing
3	Spring	7	Rubber bellows
4	Washer	8	Yoke

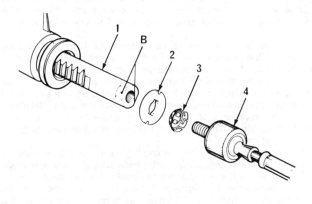

Fig. 9.31 Track rod inner balljoint components (Sec 27)

1	Rack	4	Inner balljoint
2	Thrust washer	B	Flats
3	Lockplate		

2   Using a suitable Allen key or hexagon socket bit, unscrew the adjusting nut and remove it from the rack and pinion housing.
3   Lift out the washer, spring and damper plunger.
4   Inspect the damper plunger and renew it if there is any sign of excessive scoring or wear of its contact face.
5   Lubricate the plunger and housing with molybdenum disulphide grease, then refit the plunger, spring, washer and adjusting nut.
6   To adjust the plunger, tighten the adjusting nut using a hexagon socket bit and torque wrench to the specified torque. Now back off the nut by a quarter of a turn.
7   Move the rack from lock to lock by turning the pinion yoke and check for any tight spots. If any are felt, slacken the adjusting nut further by a small amount until the rack will turn smoothly from lock to lock. Note that the rack will feel tight, but as long as the tightnesss is uniform over the entire length of travel, all is well.
8   After adjustment, secure the adjusting nut by punching the tabs down into the recesses in the housing.

28 Front wheel alignment and steering angles

1   Accurate front wheel alignment is essential to provide positive steering and prevent excessive tyre wear. Before considering the steering/suspension geometry, check that the tyres are correctly inflated, the front wheels are not buckled and the steering linkage and suspension joints are in good order, without slackness or wear.
2   Wheel alignment consists of four factors: **Camber** is the angle at which the front wheels are set from the vertical when viewed from the front of the car. 'Positive camber' is the amount (in degrees) that the wheels are tilted outward at the top of the vertical. **Castor** is the angle between the steering axis and a vertical line when viewed from each side of the car. 'Positive castor' is when the steering axis is inclined rearward at the top. **Steering axis inclination** is the angle (when viewed from the front of the car) between the vertical and an imaginary line drawn between the suspension strut upper mounting and the lower suspension arm balljoint. **Toe setting** is the amount by which the distance between the front inside edges of the roadwheels (measured at hub height) differs from the diametrically opposite distance measured between the rear inside edges of the front roadwheels.
3   With the exception of the toe setting all other steering angles are set during manufacture and no adjustment is possible. It can be assumed, therefore, that unless the car has suffered accident damage

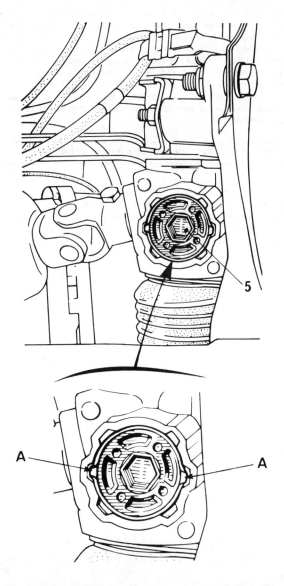

Fig.9.32 Rack damper adjustment/renewal (Sec 27)

A   Adjusting nut retaining tabs   *5   Adjusting nut* all the preset steering angles will be correct. Should there be some doubt about their accuracy it will be necessary to seek the help of a Renault dealer, as special gauges are needed to check the steering angles.

4   Two methods are available to the home mechanic for checking the toe setting. One method is to use a gauge to measure the distance between the front and rear inside edges of the roadwheels. The other method is to use a scuff plate in which each front wheel is rolled across a movable plate which records any deviation, or scuff, of the tyre from the straight-ahead position as it moves across the plate. Relatively inexpensive equipment of both types is available from accessory outlets to enable these checks, and subsequent adjustments to be carried out at home.

5   If, after checking the toe setting using whichever method is preferable, it is found that adjustment is necessary, proceed as follows.

6   Turn the steering wheel onto full left lock and record the number of exposed threads on the right-hand track rod end. Now turn the steering onto full right lock and record the number of threads on the left-hand side. If there are the same number of threads visible on both sides then subsequent adjustments can be made equally on both sides. If there are more threads visible on one side than the other it will be necessary to compensate for this during adjustment. *After adjustment there must be the same number of threads visible on each track rod end. This is most important.*

7   To alter the toe-setting slacken the locknut on the track rod end and turn the track rod using a self-grip wrench to achieve the desired setting. When viewed from the side of the car, turning the rod clockwise will increase the toe-in, turning it anti-clockwise will increase the toe-out. Only turn the track rods by a quarter of a turn each time and then recheck the setting using the gauges, or scuff plate. Note that turning the track rod by one complete turn will alter the toe-in or toe-out by 30' or 3 mm (0.12 in).

8   After adjustment tighten the locknuts and reposition the steering gear rubber bellows, if necessary, to remove any twist caused by turning the track rods.

29 Wheels and tyres – general care and maintenance

Wheels and tyres should give no real problems in use provided that a close eye is kept on them with regard to excessive wear or damage. To this end, the following points should be noted.

Ensure that tyre pressures are checked regularly and maintained correctly. Checking should be carried out with the tyres cold and not immediately after the vehicle has been in use. If the pressures are checked with the tyres hot, an apparently high reading will be obtained owing to heat expansion. Under no circumstances should an attempt be made to reduce the pressures to the quoted cold reading in this instance, or effective underinflation will result.

Underinflation will cause overheating of the tyre owing to excessive flexing of the casing, and the tread will not sit correctly on the road surface. This will cause a consequent loss of adhesion and excessive wear, not to mention the danger of sudden tyre failure due to heat build-up.

Overinflation will cause rapid wear of the centre part of the tyre tread coupled with reduced adhesion, harsher ride, and the danger of shock damage occurring in the tyre casing.

Regularly check the tyres for damage in the form of cuts or bulges, especially in the sidewalls. Remove any nails or stones embedded in the tread before they penetrate the tyre to cause deflation. If removal of a nail *does* reveal that the tyre has been punctured, refit the nail so that its point of penetration is marked. Then immediately change the wheel and have the tyre repaired by a tyre dealer. Do *not* drive on a tyre in such a condition. If in any doubt about the possible consequences of any damage found, consult your local tyre dealer for advice.

Periodically remove the wheels and clean any dirt or mud from the inside and outside surfaces. Examine the wheel rims for signs of rusting, corrosion or other damage. Light alloy wheels are easily damaged by 'kerbing' whilst parking, and similarly steel wheels may become dented or buckled. Renewal of the wheel is very often the only course of remedial action possible.

The balance of each wheel and tyre assembly should be maintained to avoid excessive wear, not only to the tyres but also to the steering and suspension components. Wheel imbalance is normally signified by vibration through the vehicle's bodyshell, although in many cases it is particularly noticeable through the steering wheel. Conversely, it should be noted that wear or damage in suspension or steering components may cause excessive tyre wear. Out-of-round or out-of-true tyres, damaged wheels and wheel bearing wear/maladjustment also fall into this category. Balancing will not usually cure vibration caused by such wear.

Wheel balancing may be carried out with the wheel either on or off the vehicle. If balanced on the vehicle, ensure that the wheel-to-hub relationship is marked in some way prior to subsequent wheel removal so that it may be refitted in its original position.

General tyre wear is influenced to a large degree by driving style – harsh braking and acceleration or fast cornering will all produce more rapid tyre wear. Interchanging of tyres may result in more even wear, but this should only be carried out where there is no mix of tyre types on the vehicle. However, it is worth bearing in mind that if this is completely effective, the added expense of replacing a complete set of tyres simultaneously is incurred, which may prove financially restrictive for many owners.

Front tyres may wear unevenly as a result of wheel misalignment. The front wheels should always be correctly aligned according to the settings specified by the vehicle manufacturer.

Legal restrictions apply to the mixing of tyre types on a vehicle. Basically this means that a vehicle must not have tyres of differing construction on the same axle. Although it is not recommended to mix tyre types between front axle and rear axle, the only legally permissible combination is crossply at the front and radial at the rear. When mixing radial ply tyres, textile braced radials must always go on the front axle, with steel braced radials at the rear. An obvious disadvantage of such mixing is the necessity to carry two spare tyres to avoid contravening the law in the event of a puncture.

In the UK, the Motor Vehicles Construction and Use Regulations apply to many aspects of tyre fitting and usage. It is suggested that a copy of these regulations is obtained from your local police if in doubt as to the current legal requirements with regard to tyre condition, minimum tread depth, etc.

30 Fault diagnosis – suspension and steering

Note: *Before diagnosing steering or suspension faults, be sure that the trouble is not due to incorrect tyre pressures, a mixture of tyre types or binding brakes*

Symptom	Reasons(s)
Vehicle pulls to one side	Incorrect wheel alignment Wear in suspension or steering components Faulty tyre Accident damage to steering or suspension components
Steering stiff or heavy	Lack of steering gear lubricant Seized balljoint Wheel alignment incorrect Steering rack or column bent or damaged
Excessive play in steering	Worn steering or suspension joints Wear in intermediate shaft universal joints Worn rack and pinion assembly Worn or incorrectly adjusted rack damper
Wheel wobble and vibration	Roadwheels out of balance Roadwheels buckled or distorted Faulty or damaged tyre Worn steering or suspension joints Wheel bolts loose Worn rack and pinion assembly
Tyre wear uneven	Wheel alignment incorrect Worn steering or suspension components Wheels out of balance Accident damage

Chapter 10 Bodywork and fittings

For modifications, and information applicable to later models, see Supplement at end of manual

Contents

Specifications

Torque wrench settings

	Nm	lbf ft
Seat belt anchorage and mounting bolts	20	15

1 General description

The bodyshell and underframe is of all-steel welded construction, incorporating progressive crumple zones at the front and rear and a rigid centre safety cell. The assembly and welding of the main body unit is completed by computer-controlled robots, and is checked for dimensional accuracy using computer and laser technology.

The front and rear bumpers are of collapsible cellular construction to minimise minor accident damage and the front wings are bolted in position to facilitate accident damage repair. The plastic side panels below the waistline are also designed to absorb light impact without damage.

2 Maintenance – bodywork and underframe

1 The general condition of a vehicle's bodywork is the one thing that significantly affects its value. Maintenance is easy but needs to be regular. Neglect, particularly after minor damage, can lead quickly to further deterioration and costly repair bills. It is important also to keep watch on those parts of the vehicle not immediately visible, for instance the underside, inside all the wheel arches and the lower part of the engine compartment.

2 The basic maintenance routine for the bodywork is washing – preferably with a lot of water, from a hose. This will remove all the loose solids which may have stuck to the vehicle. It is important to flush these off in such a way as to prevent grit from scratching the finish. The wheel arches and underframe need washing in the same way to remove any accumulated mud which will retain moisture and tend to encourage rust. Paradoxically enough, the best time to clean the underframe and wheel arches is in wet weather when the mud is thoroughly wet and soft. In very wet weather the underframe is usually cleaned of large accumulations automatically and this is a good time for inspection.

3 Periodically, except on vehicles with a wax-based underbody protective coating, it is a good idea to have the whole of the underframe of the vehicle steam cleaned, engine compartment included, so that a thorough inspection can be carried out to see what minor repairs and renovations are necessary. Steam cleaning is available at many garages and is necessary for removal of the accumulation of oily grime which sometimes is allowed to become thick in certain areas. If steam cleaning facilities are not available, there are one or two excellent grease solvents available, such as Holts Engine Cleaner or Holts Foambrite, which can be brush applied. The dirt can then be simply hosed off. Note that these methods should not be used on vehicles with wax-based underbody protective coating or the coating will be removed. Such vehicles should be inspected annually, preferably just prior to winter, when the underbody should be washed down and any damage to the wax coating repaired using Holts Undershield. Ideally, a completely fresh coat should be applied. It would also be worth considering the use of such wax-based protection for injection into door panels, sills, box sections, etc, as an additional safeguard against rust damage where such protection is not provided by the vehicle manufacturer.

4 After washing paintwork, wipe off with a chamois leather to give an unspotted clear finish. A coat of clear protective wax polish, like the many excellent Turtle Wax polishes, will give added protection against chemical pollutants in the air. If the paintwork sheen has dulled or oxidised, use a cleaner/polisher combination such as Turtle Extra to restore the brilliance of the shine. This requires a little effort, but such dulling is usually caused because regular washing has been neglected. Care needs to be taken with metallic paintwork, as special non-abrasive cleaner/polisher is required to avoid damage to the finish. Always check that the door and ventilator opening drain holes and pipes are completely clear so that water can be drained out (photo). Bright work should be treated in the same way as paint work. Windscreens and windows can be kept clear of the smeary film which often appears by the use of a proprietary glass cleaner like Holts Mixra. Never use any form of wax or other body or chromium polish on glass.

2.4 Checking a door drain hole for obstruction

3 Maintenance – upholstery and carpets

Mats and carpets should be brushed or vacuum cleaned regularly to keep them free of grit. If they are badly stained remove them from the vehicle for scrubbing or sponging and make quite sure they are dry before refitting. Seats and interior trim panels can be kept clean by wiping with a damp cloth and Turtle Wax Carisma. If they do become stained (which can be more apparent on light coloured upholstery) use a little liquid detergent and a soft nail brush to scour the grime out of the grain of the material. Do. not forget to keep the headlining clean in the same way as the upholstery. When using liquid cleaners inside the vehicle do not over-wet the surfaces being cleaned. Excessive damp could get into the seams and padded interior causing stains, offensive odours or even rot. If the inside of the vehicle gets wet accidentally it is worthwhile taking some trouble to dry it out properly, particularly where carpets are involved. *Do not leave oil or electric heaters inside the vehicle for this purpose.*

4 Minor body damage – repair

The colour bodywork repair photographic sequences between pages 32 and 33 illustrate the operations detailed in the following sub-sections.

Note: *For more detailed information about bodywork repair, the Haynes Publishing Group publish a book by Lindsey Porter called The Car Bodywork Repair Manual. This incorporates information on such aspects as rust treatment, painting and glass fibre repairs, as well as details on more ambitious repairs involving welding and panel beating.*

Repair of minor scratches in bodywork

If the scratch is very superficial, and does not penetrate to the metal of the bodywork, repair is very simple. Lightly rub the area of the scratch with a paintwork renovator like Turtle Wax New Color Back, or a very fine cutting paste like Holts Body + Plus Rubbing Compound to remove loose paint from the scratch and to clear the surrounding bodywork of wax polish. Rinse the area with clean water.

Apply touch-up paint, such as Holts Dupli-Color Color Touch or a paint film like Holts Autofilm, to the scratch using a fine paint brush; continue to apply fine layers of paint until the surface of the paint in the scratch is level with the surrounding paintwork. Allow the new paint at least two weeks to harden: then blend it into the surrounding paintwork by rubbing the scratch area with a paintwork renovator or a very fine cutting paste, such as Holts Body + Plus Rubbing Compound or Turtle Wax New Color Back. Finally, apply wax polish from one of the Turtle Wax range of wax polishes.

Where the scratch has penetrated right through to the metal of the bodywork, causing the metal to rust, a different repair technique is required. Remove any loose rust from the bottom of the scratch with a penknife, then apply rust inhibiting paint, such as Turtle Wax Rust Master, to prevent the formation of rust in the future. Using a rubber or nylon applicator fill the scratch with bodystopper paste like Holts Body + Plus Knifing Putty. If required, this paste can be mixed with cellulose thinners, such as Holts Body + Plus Cellulose Thinners, to provide a very thin paste which is ideal for filling narrow scratches. Before the stopper-paste in the scratch hardens, wrap a piece of smooth cotton rag around the top of a finger. Dip the finger in cellulose thinners, such as Holts Body + Plus Cellulose Thinners, and then quickly sweep it across the surface of the stopper-paste in the scratch; this will ensure that the surface of the stopper-paste is slightly hollowed. The scratch can now be painted over as described earlier in this Section.

Repair of dents in bodywork

When deep denting of the vehicle's bodywork has taken place, the first task is to pull the dent out, until the affected bodywork almost attains its original shape. There is little point in trying to restore the original shape completely, as the metal in the damaged area will have stretched on impact and cannot be reshaped fully to its original contour. It is better to bring the level of the dent up to a point which is about ⅛ in (3 mm) below the level of the surrounding bodywork. In cases where the dent is very shallow anyway, it is not worth trying

to pull it out at all. If the underside of the dent is accessible, it can be hammered out gently from behind, using a mallet with a wooden or plastic head. Whilst doing this, hold a suitable block of wood firmly against the outside of the panel to absorb the impact from the hammer blows and thus prevent a large area of the bodywork from being 'belled-out'.

Should the dent be in a section of the bodywork which has a double skin or some other factor making it inaccessible from behind, a different technique is called for. Drill several small holes through the metal inside the area – particulary in the deeper section. Then screw long self-tapping screws into the holes just sufficiently for them to gain a good purchase in the metal. Now the dent can be pulled out by pulling on the protruding heads of the screws with a pair of pliers.

The next stage of the repair is the removal of the paint from the damaged area, and from an inch or so of the surrounding 'sound' bodywork. This is accomplished most easily by using a wire brush or abrasive pad on a power drill, although it can be done just as effectively by hand using sheets of abrasive paper. To complete the preparation for filling, score the surface of the bare metal with a screwdriver or the tang of a file, or alternatively, drill small holes in the affected area. This will provide a really good 'key' for the filler paste.

To complete the repair see the Section on filling and re-spraying.

Repair of rust holes or gashes in bodywork

Remove all paint from the affected area and from an inch or so of the surrounding 'sound' bodywork, using an abrasive pad or a wire brush on a power drill. If these are not available a few sheets of abrasive paper will do the job just as effectively. With the paint removed you will be able to gauge the severity of the corrosion and therefore decide whether to renew the whole panel (if this is possible) or to repair the affected area. New body panels are not as expensive as most people think and it is often quicker and more satisfactory to fit a new panel than to attempt to repair large areas of corrosion.

Remove all fittings from the affected area except those which will act as a guide to the original shape of the damaged bodywork (eg headlamp shells etc). Then, using tin snips or a hacksaw blade, remove all loose metal and any other metal badly affected by corrosion. Hammer the edges of the hole inwards in order to create a slight depression for the filler paste.

Wire brush the affected area to remove the powdery rust from the surface of the remaining metal. Paint the affected area with rust inhibiting paint like Turtle Wax Rust Master; if the back of the rusted area is accessible treat this also.

Before filling can take place it will be necessary to block the hole in some way. This can be achieved by the use of aluminium or plastic mesh, or aluminium tape.

Aluminium or plastic mesh or glass fibre matting, such as the Holts Body + Plus Glass Fibre Matting, is probably the best material to use for a large hole. Cut a piece to the approximate size and shape of the hole to be filled, then position it in the hole so that its edges are below the level of the surrounding bodywork. It can be retained in position by several blobs of filler paste around its periphery.

Aluminium tape should be used for small or very narrow holes. Pull a piece off the roll and trim it to the approximate size and shape required, then pull off the backing paper (if used) and stick the tape over the hole; it can be overlapped if the thickness of one piece is insufficient. Burnish down the edges of the tape with the handle of a screwdriver or similar, to ensure that the tape is securely attached to the metal underneath.

Bodywork repairs – filling and re-spraying

Before using this Section, see the Sections on dent, deep scratch, rust holes and gash repairs.

Many types of bodyfiller are available, but generally speaking those proprietary kits which contain a tin of filler paste and a tube of resin hardener are best for this type of repair, like Holts Body + Plus or Holts No Mix which can be used directly from the tube. A wide, flexible plastic or nylon applicator will be found invaluable for imparting a smooth and well contoured finish to the surface of the filler.

Mix up a little filler on a clean piece of card or board – measure the hardener carefully (follow the maker's instructions on the pack) otherwise the filler will set too rapidly or too slowly. Alternatively,

Holts No Mix can be used straight from the tube without mixing, but daylight is required to cure it. Using the applicator apply the filler paste to the prepared area; draw the applicator across the surface of the filler to achieve the correct contour and to level the filler surface. As soon as a contour that approximates to the correct one is achieved, stop working the paste – if you carry on too long the paste will become sticky and begin to 'pick up' on the applicator. Continue to add thin layers of filler paste at twenty-minute intervals until the level of the filler is just proud of the surrounding bodywork.

Once the filler has hardened, excess can be removed using a metal plane or file. From then on, progressively finer grades of abrasive paper should be used, starting with a 40 grade production paper and finishing with 400 grade wet-and-dry paper. Always wrap the abrasive paper around a flat rubber, cork, or wooden block – otherwise the surface of the filler will not be completely flat. During the smoothing of the filler surface the wet-and-dry paper should be periodically rinsed in water. This will ensure that a very smooth finish is imparted to the filler at the final stage.

At this stage the 'dent' should be surrounded by a ring of bare metal, which in turn should be encircled by the finely 'feathered' edge of the good paintwork. Rinse the repair area with clean water, until all of the dust produced by the rubbing-down operation has gone.

Spray the whole repair area with a light coat of primer, either Holts Body + Plus Grey or Red Oxide Primer – this will show up any imperfections in the surface of the filler. Repair these imperfections with fresh filler paste or bodystopper, and once more smooth the surface with abrasive paper. If bodystopper is used, it can be mixed with cellulose thinners to form a really thin paste which is ideal for filling small holes. Repeat this spray and repair procedure until you are satisfied that the surface of the filler, and the feathered edge of the paintwork are perfect. Clean the repair area with clean water and allow to dry fully.

The repair area is now ready for final spraying. Paint spraying must be carried out in a warm, dry, windless and dust free atmosphere. This condition can be created artificially if you have access to a large indoor working area, but if you are forced to work in the open, you will have to pick your day very carefully. If you are working indoors, dousing the floor in the work area with water will help to settle the dust which would otherwise be in the atmosphere. If the repair area is confined to one body panel, mask off the surrounding panels; this will help to minimise the effects of a slight mis-match in paint colours. Bodywork fittings (eg chrome strips, door handles etc) will also need to be masked off. Use genuine masking tape and several thicknesses of newspaper for the masking operations.

Before commencing to spray, agitate the aerosol can thoroughly, then spray a test area (an old tin, or similar) until the technique is mastered. Cover the repair area with a thick coat of primer; the thickness should be built up using several thin layers of paint rather than one thick one. Using 400 grade wet-and-dry paper, rub down the surface of the primer until it is really smooth. While doing this, the work area should be thoroughly doused with water, and the wet-and-dry paper periodically rinsed in water. Allow to dry before spraying on more paint.

Spray on the top coat using Holts Dupli-Color Autospray, again building up the thickness by using several thin layers of paint. Start spraying in the centre of the repair area and then, with a single side-to-side motion, work outwards until the whole repair area and about 2 inches of the surrounding original paintwork is covered. Remove all masking material 10 to 15 minutes after spraying on the final coat of paint.

Allow the new paint at least two weeks to harden, then, using a paintwork renovator or a very fine cutting paste such as Turtle Wax New Color Back or Holts Body + Plus Rubbing Compound, blend the edges of the paint into the existing paintwork. Finally, apply wax polish.

Plastic components

With the use of more and more plastic body components by the vehicle manufacturers (eg bumpers, spoilers, and in some cases major body panels), rectification of more serious damage to such items has become a matter of either entrusting repair work to a specialist in this field, or renewing complete components. Repair of such damage by the DIY owner is not really feasible owing to the cost of the equipment and materials required for effecting such repairs. The basic technique involves making a groove along the line of the crack in the plastic using a rotary burr in a power drill. The damaged part is then welded back together by using a hot air gun to heat up and fuse a plastic filler rod into the groove. Any excess plastic is then removed and the area rubbed down to a smooth finish. It is important that a filler rod of the correct plastic is used, as body components can be made of a variety of different types (eg polycarbonate, ABS, polypropylene).

Damage of a less serious nature (abrasions, minor cracks etc) can be repaired by the DIY owner using a two-part epoxy filler repair material like Holts Body + Plus or Holts No Mix which can be used directly from the tube. Once mixed in equal proportions (or applied direct from the tube in the case of Holts No Mix), this is used in similar fashion to the bodywork filler used on metal panels. The filler is usually cured in twenty to thirty minutes, ready for sanding and painting.

If the owner is renewing a complete component himself, or if he has repaired it with epoxy filler, he will be left with the problem of finding a suitable paint for finishing which is compatible with the type of plastic used. At one time the use of a universal paint was not possible owing to the complex range of plastics encountered in body component applications. Standard paints, generally speaking, will not bond to plastic or rubber satisfactorily, but Holts Professional Spraymatch paints to match any plastic or rubber finish can be obtained from dealers. However, it is now possible to obtain a plastic body parts finishing kit which consists of a pre-primer treatment, a primer and coloured top coat. Full instructions are normally supplied with a kit, but basically the method of use is to first apply the pre-primer to the component concerned and allow it to dry for up to 30 minutes. Then the primer is applied and left to dry for about an hour before finally applying the special coloured top coat. The result is a correctly coloured component where the paint will flex with the plastic or rubber, a property that standard paint does not normally possess.

5   Major body damage – repair

Where serious damage has occurred, or large areas need renewal due to neglect, it means that completely new sections or panels will need welding in, and this is best left to professionals. If the damage is due to impact, it will also be necessary to completely check the alignment of the bodyshell structure. Due to the principle of construction, the strength and shape of the whole car can be affected by damage to one part. In such instances the services of an accident repair specialist or Renault dealer with specialist checking jigs are essential. If a body is left misaligned, it is first of all dangerous, as the car will not handle properly, and secondly uneven stresses will be imposed on the steering, engine and transmission, causing abnormal wear or complete failure. Tyre wear may also be excessive.

6   Maintenance – hinges and locks

1   Oil the hinges of the bonnet, tailgate and doors with a drop or two of light oil at regular intervals (see Routine Maintenance).
2   At the same time, lightly oil the bonnet release mechanism and all door locks.
3   Do not attempt to lubricate the steering lock.

7   Door rattles – tracing and recification

1   Check first that the door is not loose at the hinges, and that the latch is holding the door firmly in position. Check also that the door lines up with the aperture in the body. If the door is out of alignment, adjust it, as described in Sections 18 and 19 or 22 and 23.
2   If the latch is holding the door in the correct position, but the latch still rattles, the lock mechanism is worn and should be renewed.
3   Other rattles from the door could be caused by wear in the window operating mechanism, interior lock mechanism, or loose glass channels.

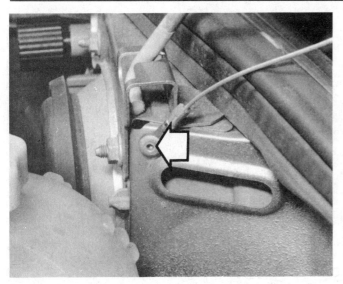

8.2 Bonnet safety wire mounting rivet

8.4 Loosening the bonnet hinge nuts

8 Bonnet – removal, refitting and adjustment

1   Open the bonnet and support it in the open position using the stay.
2   Using a suitable drill, drill the head off the rivet securing the safety wire to the front panel (photo). Tap out the remains of the rivet with a punch and remove the wire.
3   Disconnect the windscreen washer hose.
4   Mark the outline of the hinges with a soft pencil, then loosen the four retaining nuts (photo).
5   With the help of an assistant, remove the stay, unscrew the four nuts and lift the bonnet off the car.
6   Refitting is the reverse sequence of removal. Position the bonnet hinges within the outline marks made during removal, but alter its position as necessary to provide a uniform gap all round. Adjust the front height of the bonnet with shims beneath the hinges, and the rear height by re-positioning the lock up or down as necessary (refer to Section 9).

9 Bonnet lock and release cable – removal, refitting and adjustment

Bonnet lock
1   With the bonnet open remove the plastic cover, then disconnect the cable eye from the lock lever and withdraw the cable from the lock (photo).
2   Undo the two retaining bolts and remove the lock from the car.
3   Refitting is the reverse sequence of removal, but adjust the lock height so that the bonnet line is flush with the front wings and shuts securely without force. If necessary adjust the lock laterally so that the striker enters the lock recess correctly.

Release cable
4   With the bonnet open remove the plastic cover, then disconnect the cable eye from the lock lever and unclip the outer cable.
5   From inside the car unscrew the two bolts securing the release handle to the left-hand side panel under the facia. For better access remove the fusebox and surround panel (photo).
6   Unhook the cable from the handle and withdraw it through the bulkhead into the engine compartment (photo).
7   Refitting is a reversal of removal.

10 Radiator grille – removal and refitting

1   Open the bonnet then unscrew the centre top retaining bolt (photo).

9.1 Bonnet lock

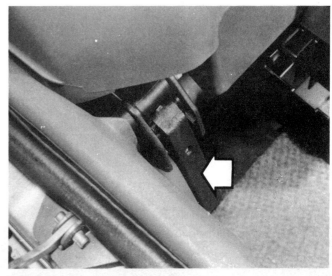

9.5 Bonnet release handle

Fig. 10.1 Bonnet lock components (Sec 9)

| 1 | Lock | 3 | Clip |
| 2 | Cable | 4 | Release handle |

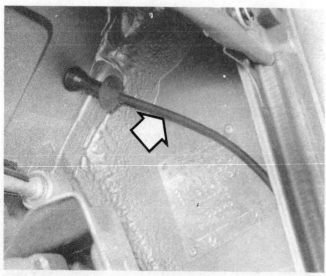

9.6 Bonnet release cable on the left-hand side of the bulkhead

10.1 Radiator grille centre top retaining bolt

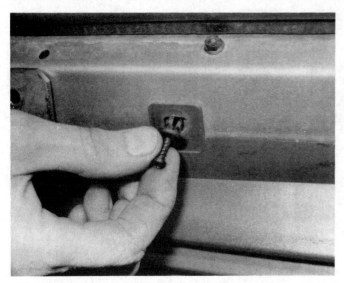

10.2 Radiator grille upper clip and screw

10.3 Releasing a radiator side clip

2   Remove the screws from the two remaining upper clips and pull out the clips (photo).
3   From inside the car release the two clips either side of the radiator and withdraw the radiator grille (photo).
4   Refitting is a reversal of removal.

11 Front wing – removal and refitting

1   Jack up the front of the car and support on axle stands. Apply the handbrake.

2   Remove the front bumper (Section 30) and the appropriate front wheel.
3   Remove the fastenings and withdraw the plastic shield from beneath the wing.
4   Unscrew the bolts securing the wing to the front door pillar and sill.
5   Using a suitable drill, drill the heads from the retaining rivets (Fig. 10.2).
6   Using a hair dryer, soften the sealant beneath the wing upper edge then withdraw the wing.
7   Clean away the old sealant.
8   Refitting is a reversal of removal, using new sealant.

12 Tailgate support struts – removal and refitting

1   With the tailgate open, unhook the parcel shelf support cords and support the tailgate in the raised position using a stout length of wood, or an assistant.
2   Remove the rear light cluster as described in Chapter 11.
3   Using a screwdriver, carefully lever out the locking retainer at the strut ball end fittings (photos).
4   Withdraw the strut from the ball pegs and remove it from the car.
5   No attempt must be made to dismantle the strut or expose it to high temperatures, as it contains gas at high pressure.
6   Refitting is a reversal of removal.

13 Tailgate – removal and refitting

1   Disconnect the support struts from the tailgate as described in the previous Section.
2   Remove the inner trim panel then disconnect the battery leads as described in Chapter 11, and disconnect the wiring for the rear screen wiper, heated rear window and rear number plate lights. If necessary the number plate terminal block can be released from the tailgate inner panel by squeezing the extension with a pair of pliers (Fig. 10.3)).
3   Disconnect the rear screen washer pipe.
4   Withdraw the wiring and pipe from the top corners of the tailgate taking care not to damage them.
5   Remove the rear headlining trim panel by prising out the centre cap and removing the screw, then disengaging the panel from the retaining clips.

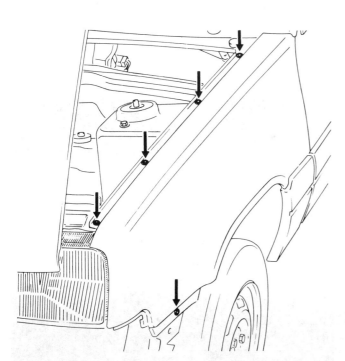

Fig. 10.2 Front wing retaining rivet locations (Sec 11)

12.3A Prising out the tailgate support strut locking retainer from the tailgate

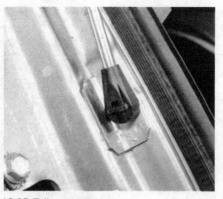

12.3B Tailgate support strut mounting on the body

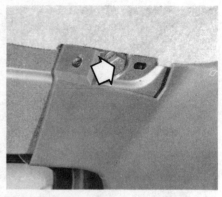

13.6 Tailgate hinge bolt

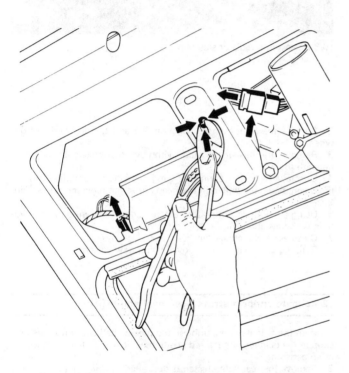

Fig. 10.3 Removing the number plate terminal block (Sec 13)

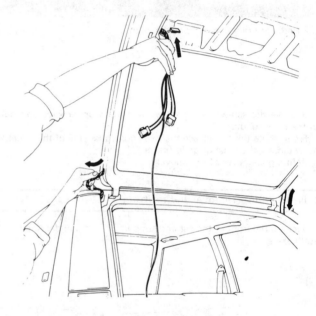

Fig. 10.4 Removing the wiring and washer pipe from the tailgate (Sec 13)

6   With the help of an assistant support the tailgate then unscrew the hinge bolts from inside the car (photo).
7   Refitting is a reversal of removal, but tape the wiring together temporarily to facilitate inserting it through the holes in the top corners of the tailgate. A length of string can be used to pull the wiring through. Adjust the lock and striker as described in Section 14.

14 Tailgate lock – removal, refitting and adjustment

1   Open the tailgate and remove the trim panel.
2   Unscrew the retaining bolts and withdraw the lock (photo). If necessary, unclip and remove the private lock.
3   Refitting is a reversal of removal, but check that the tailgate is held firmly against the weatherseal when shut. If necessary loosen the bolt and adjust the position of the striker as required (photo).

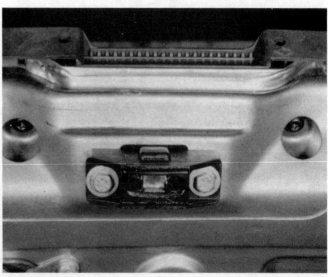

14.2 Tailgate lock

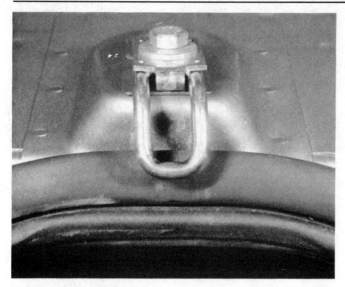

14.3 Tailgate lock striker

15 Windscreen – removal and refitting

The windscreen is bonded in place with special mastic, and special tools are required to cut free the old unit and fit the new unit together with cleaning solutions and primers. It is therefore recommended that this work be entrusted to a Renault dealer or windscreen replacement specialist.

16 Tailgate heated rear window – removal and refitting

1   Remove the rear wiper arm and blade as described in Chapter 11.
2   Remove the inner moulding from the bottom of the window by extracting the screws from the special expanding clips.
3   Disconnect the wiring at the connectors on either side of the window.
4   If the window is broken, cover the floor area with a blanket and use adhesive tape to hold the remaining fragments together.
5   Using a blunt tool push the inner lip of the rubber seal to the outside of the flange starting at one of the top corners and working downwards (Fig. 10.5). Have an assistant support it as it comes free.
6   Reverse the rubber seal from the window then thoroughly clean the edges of the tailgate aperture and also the window glass if this is to be refitted.
7   Fit a new rubber seal around the window and place a suitable length of strong cord in the body flange groove of the seal with its ends overlapping at the top centre of the window. When fitting the window with the tailgate open, the cord ends will then be at the bottom.
8   With the help of an assistant place the window in position from the outside with the cord ends inside. Insert the heating element connectors through the holes provided. Have the assistant press on the window from the outside then start pulling one end of the cord so that the seal lip locates over the inside of the flange.
9   When the top centre of the window is reached repeat the procedure for the other side until the complete inner lip is located on the flange.
10 Reconnect the wiring and refit the inner moulding, wiper arm and blade.

17 Front door interior trim panel – removal and refitting

1   Remove the external mirror quarter trim panel. Where the mirror is remotely controlled, the panel is retained by one screw on its lower

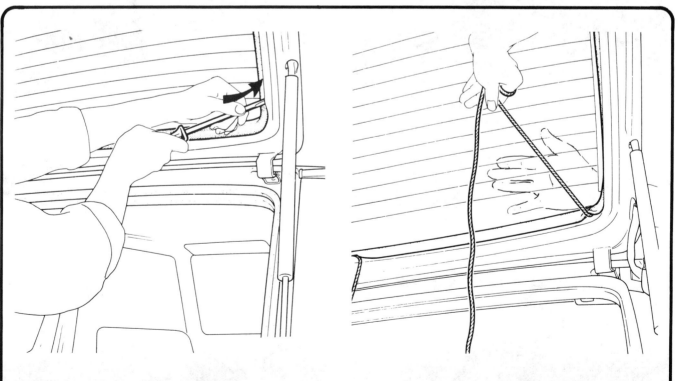

Fig. 10.5 Releasing the heated rear window rubber seal from the tailgate (Sec 16)

Fig. 10.6 Pull the cord to locate the seal lip on the tailgate flange (Sec 16)

edge and the panel must be lifted to release it from the bracket. Where a standard mirror is fitted prise out the panel to release the retaining pegs.

2   Prise out the bottom edge of the upper trim strip then lift it over the locking knob and remove it (photo).

3   Using a Torx key remove the screws and withdraw the map pocket. Also remove the bracket (photos).

4   Fully close the window on manually operated windows and note the position of the regulator handle. Pull the handle direct from the splines and remove the bezel – the handle is only a press fit on the splines (photo).

5   Remove the screw then slightly lift the interior remote door handle and withdraw the finger plate (photos).

6   Using a wide blade screwdriver release the clips securing the interior trim panel to the door. Do not lever on the panel itself otherwise the attachment may break, but position the blade close to the plastic pin of the clip (photos).

7   If the trim panel has been removed for access to the door internal components, peel back the plastic sheet as necessary (photo).

17.2 Removing the upper trim strip

17.3A Removing a map pocket retaining screw

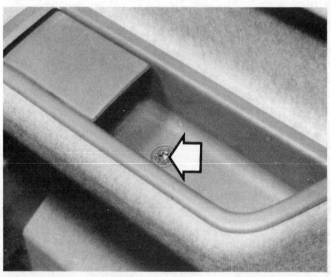

17.3B Removing the map pocket bracket

17.4 Pull the window regulator handle from the splines

17.5A Remove the screw ...

17.5B ... and withdraw the remote door handle finger plate

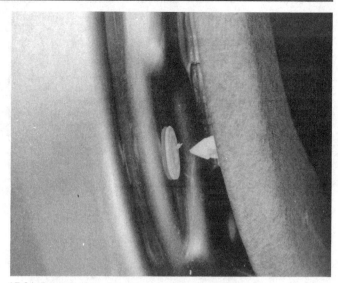

17.6A Releasing the door interior trim panel clips

17.6B Trim panel clip

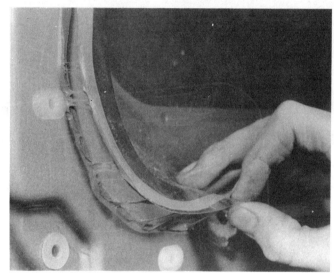

17.7 Peel back the plastic sheet

18 Front door – removal, refitting and adjustment

1   On models having electrically-operated windows, electro-mechanical door locks or door mounted speakers remove the interior trim panel, as described in Section 17, and disconnect the wiring multi-plug connectors. Remove the wiring harness from the door.

2   Release the door check strap by driving out the retaining pin with a drift (photo).

3   Support the door on blocks or with the help of an assistant.

4   Prise out the two caps covering each hinge pin, using a screwdriver (photo).

5   Using a cranked metal rod of suitable diameter as a drift, drive out the upper and lower hinge pins.

6   With the hinge pins removed, carefully lift off the door.

7   Refitting is a reversal of removal, but check that it is correctly aligned with the surrounding bodywork with an equal clearance around its edge. Adjustment is made by bending the hinges as the latter are welded in position. Only attempt to bend the hinge arm welded to the front pillar, and use a block of wood and a mallet or a suitable claw lever. Check that the striker enters the lock centrally, and if necessary loosen it with a Torx key, re-position and re-tighten (photo).

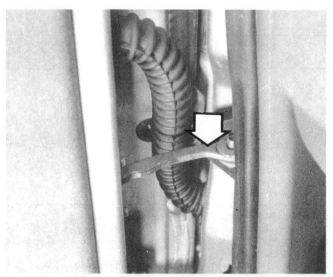

18.2 Door check strap

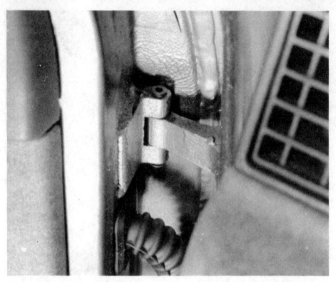

18.4 Front door hinge

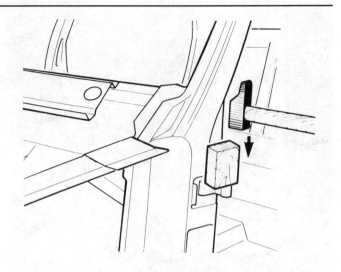

Fig. 10.7 Use a block of wood and a mallet to bend the door hinge arm (Sec 18)

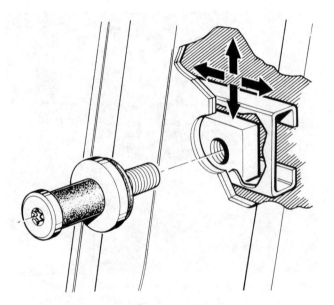

Fig. 10.8 The door striker is adjustable (Sec 18)

18.7 Front door striker

19 Front door lock and exterior handle – removal and refitting

1   Open the door and wind the window fully up.
2   Remove the interior trim panel, as described in Section 17.
3   If the car is fitted with electro-mechanical door locks, reach inside the door and disconnect the wiring connector from the lock solenoid or motor.
4   Remove the Torx screw and withdraw the remote interior handle (photo). Unhook it from the control rod.
5   Reach through the aperture and disconnect the private lock and exterior handle control rods from the lock (photo).
6   Remove the screw securing the exterior door handle to the edge of the door (three-door models) or outside (four-door models), withdraw the handle and unhook the control rod (photos).
7   Remove the lock mounting screws then withdraw the lock from the door. Disconnect the locking knob and interior door handle control rods (photos).
8   To remove the private lock pull out the retaining plate and withdraw the lock outwards together with the control rod (photos).
9   Refitting is a reversal of removal.

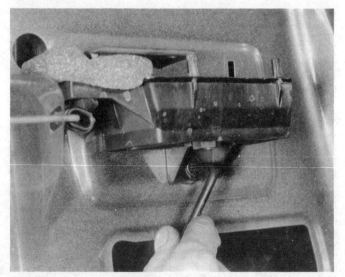

19.4 Removing the remote interior handle

19.5 Disconnect the private lock and exterior handle control rods from the locks (three-door models)

19.6A Remove the screw ...

19.6B ... and unhook the exterior door handle (three-door models)

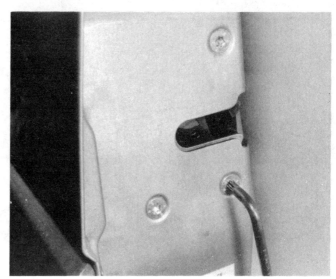

19.7A Unscrew the mounting screws ...

19.7B ... and withdraw the front door lock

19.7C Front door lock removed from the door

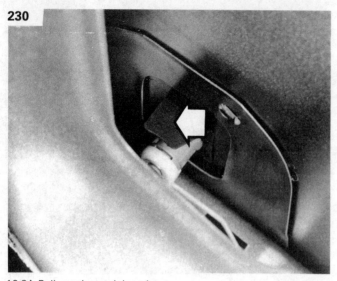

19.8A Pull out the retaining plate ...

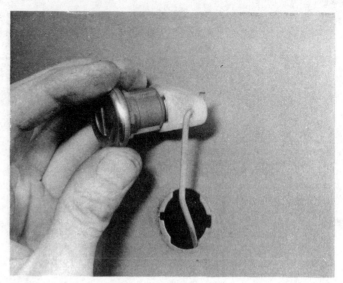

19.8B ... and withdraw the private lock

Fig. 10.9 Front door lock and solenoid on models with central locking (Sec 19)

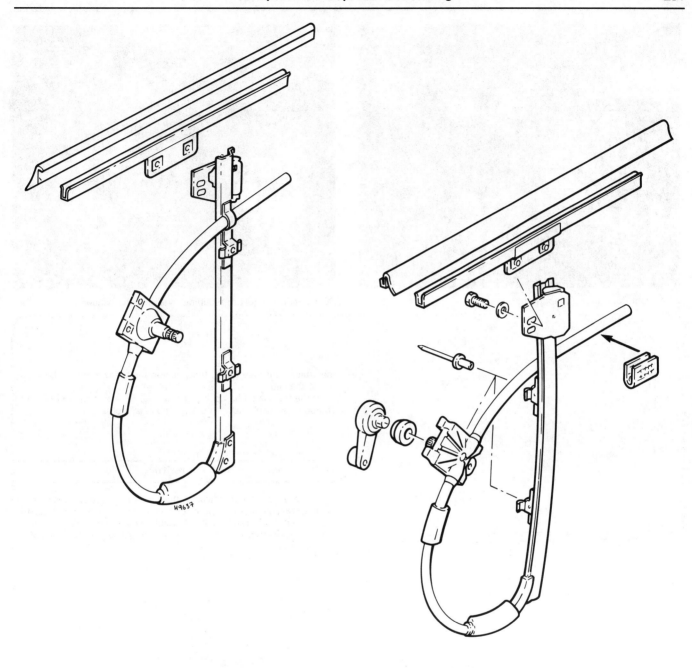

Fig. 10.10 Front door window regulator (Sec 20)

20 Front door glass and regulator – removal and refitting

1   Remove the interior trim panel as described in Section 17.
2   With the window fully down remove the inner wiper strip taking care not to break it as it is fragile.
3   Prise out the window channel and outer wiper strip.
4   Raise the window so that the front support bolt is aligned with the hole provided, then support the window and unscrew both bolts (photo).
5   Lower the regulator then lift the glass and withdraw it from the outside.
6   On models with electrically-operated windows disconnect the wiring from the motor and unscrew the motor mounting nuts.
7   Drill out the retaining rivets and withdraw the regulator mechanism through the aperture (photo).
8   Refitting is a reversal of removal, but use new pop rivets to secure

the mechanism. Centralize the glass in the fully closed position before fully tightening the support bolts. Where necessary refit the lower channel to the glass in accordance with Figs 10.11 or 10.12.

21 Rear door interior trim panel – removal and refitting

1   Prise out the bottom edge of the upper trim strip then lift it over the locking knob and remove it.
2   Fully close the window and note the position of the regulator handle. Pull the handle direct from the splines and remove the bezel – the handle is only a press fit on the splines.
3   Remove the screw then slightly lift the interior remote door handle and withdraw the finger plate.
4   Using a wide blade screwdriver release the clips securing the interior trim panel to the door. Do not lever on the panel itself otherwise

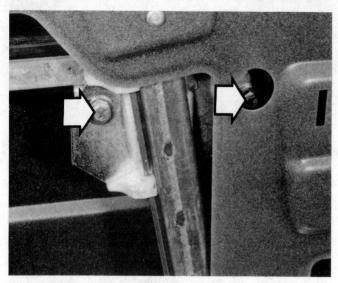

20.4 Front door glass support bolts

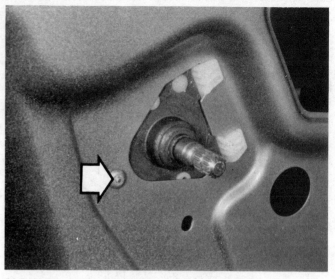

20.7 Window regulator retaining rivet near the winder

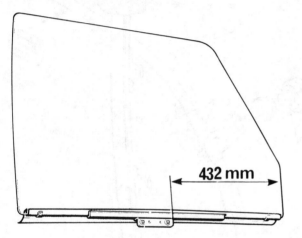

Fig. 10.11 Front door glass to channel fitting dimension on
three-door models (Sec 20)

the attachment may break, but position the blade close to the plastic
pin of the clip.
5 If the trim panel has been removed for access to the door internal
components, peel back the plastic sheet as necessary.

22 Rear door – removal and refitting

The procedure is identical to that for the front door described in
Section 18 with the exception of the reference to wiring. Note that
replacement hinges supplied by Renault are of the bolt type and in this
case, adjustment is by movement of the hinges within the limits of the
bolt holes and by the use of shims.

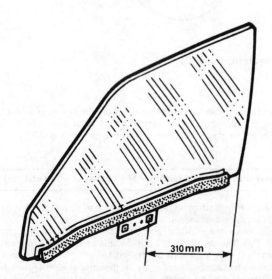

Fig. 10.12 Front door glass to channel fitting dimension on
five-door models (Sec 20)

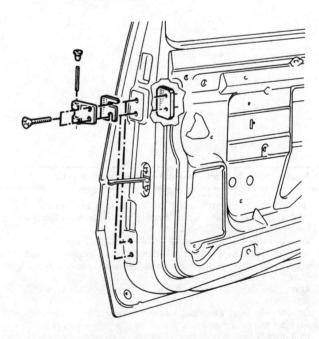

Fig. 10.13 Bolt-on type hinges for the rear doors on
five-door models (Sec 22)

23 Rear door lock and exterior handle – removal and refitting

1   Remove the interior trim panel as described in Section 21.
2   Remove the Torx screw and withdraw the remote interior handle. Unhook it from the control rod.
3   Pull out the retaining plate and release the locking knob and lever inside the panel. Also release the rod from the clip.
4   Remove the lock mounting screws then withdraw the lock assembly from inside the door.
5   To remove the exterior handle unscrew the bolt from inside the door and withdraw the handle and packing from the outside.
6   Refitting is a reversal of removal.

24 Rear door glass and regulator – removal and refitting

1   Remove the interior trim panel as described in Section 21.
2   With the window fully down remove the outer wiper strip and mouldings followed by the inner strips.
3   Unscrew the bottom bolt and top screw then withdraw the intermediate channel followed by the fixed window (if applicable) by tilting them forward.
4   Raise the window so that the support bolts are aligned with the holes provided then unscrew both bolts while supporting the window.
5   Lift the window glass, tilt it forwards and withdraw it from the outside. Recover the channel.
6   Drill out the retaining rivets and withdraw the regulator mechanism through the aperture.
7   Refitting is a reversal of removal, but where necessary refit the lower channel to the glass in accordance with Fig. 10.16.

25 Interior rear view mirror – removal and refitting

1   To remove the interior rear view mirror slide it up from the base.
2   Refitting is a reversal of removal.
3   The mirror base is bonded to the windscreen. If it becomes detached or if the windscreen is being renewed, fit the base using the following procedure.

4   Clean the inside of the windscreen and the base of the mirror with trichlorethylene or a similar solvent and allow it to air dry.
5   Apply a strip of adhesive tape to the outside of the windscreen so that its top edge is 45 mm (1.77 in) below the seal lower edge. Measure the width of the windscreen and then mark its centre on the tape. The base of the mirror should be positioned centrally, with the tape mark as a reference, and with its top edge level with the top edge of the tape.
6   Obtain a quantity of Loctite 312 from a Renault dealer and then spray the activator onto the inside of the glass in the bonding zone.
7   Allow the activator to dry, then apply the adhesive to the mirror base. Immediately place the mirror base against the glass and hold it

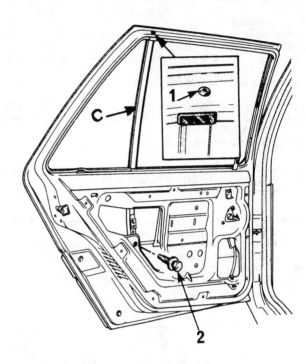

Fig. 10.14 Remove the top screw (1) and bottom bolt (2) securing the rear door glass intermediate channel (C) (Sec 24)

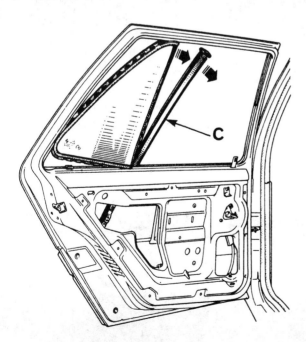

Fig. 10.15 Removing the intermediate channel (C) and fixed window (Sec 24)

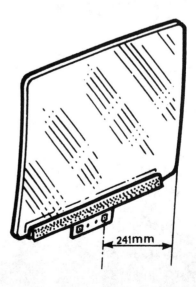

Fig. 10.16 Rear door glass to channel fitting dimension (Sec 24)

firmly for at least one minute. The adhesive will be fully set after approximately one hour.

26 Exterior rear view mirror – removal and refitting

Standard mirror

1 Prise the quarter trim panel from the inside of the front door so that the retaining pegs are released from the holes (photo).
2 Unscrew the mounting bolt and withdraw the mirror assembly from the outside of the door. Recover the collar.
3 Refitting is a reversal of removal.

Remote control mirror

4 Remove the screw from the lower edge of the quarter trim panel, lift the panel and release it from the bracket (photos).
5 Unscrew the screws securing the remote control bracket to the door.
6 Unscrew the ring nut and separate the bracket from the control knob.
7 Prise the grommet from the door then unscrew the mounting bolt and withdraw the mirror assembly, control knob and wires from the outside. Recover the collar.
8 Refitting is a reversal of removal.

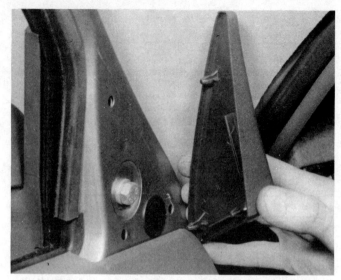

26.1 Removing the quarter trim panel from the standard exterior mirror

27 Front and rear seats – removal and refitting

Front seat

1 Adjust the seat fully forward then unscrew the Torx screws securing the seat rails at the rear (photo).
2 Adjust the seat fully back and unscrew the Torx screws securing the seat rails at the front (photo).
3 Remove the seat from the car.
4 Refitting is a reversal of removal.

Rear seat

5 Lift the cushion(s) and tilt forward then lift to release the brackets from the slots in the floor (photo).
6 Unlock the top of the backrest then unbolt the hinge brackets from the floor (photo).
7 Remove the cushion and backrest from the car.
8 Refitting is a reversal of removal.

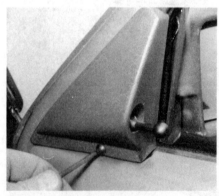

26.4A Remove the screw ...

26.4B ... and lift the quarter trim panel from the remote control exterior mirror

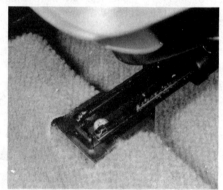

27.1 Front seat rail rear mounting

27.2 Front seat rail front mounting

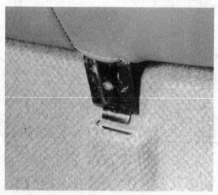

27.5 Rear seat cushion support bracket and slot

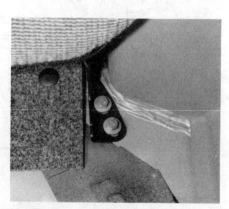

27.6 Rear seat backrest hinge bracket mounting

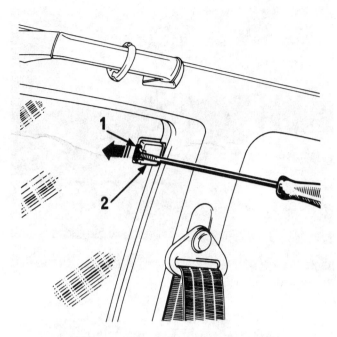

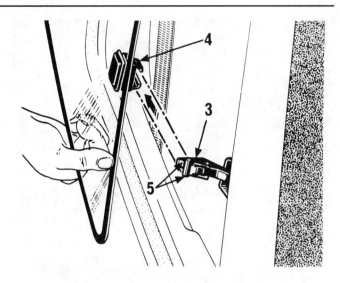

Fig. 10.18 Pull the window forwards to release the base (4) from the notches (5) on the catch (3) (Sec 28)

Fig. 10.17 Prise the retaining fork (1) from the base (2) on the opening rear quarter window (Sec 28)

28 Opening rear quarter window – removal and refitting

1   Open the window then use a screwdriver to prise the retaining forks on the hinges out to the rear.
2   Remove the hinge bases and covers together with the seals.
3   With the catch open pull the window forwards so that the base on the window is released from the notches on the catch. Withdraw the window from the car leaving the catch and hinges attached to the body. These can be removed separately if required.
4   Refitting is a reversal of removal, but make sure that the seals are fitted correctly to the bases.

29 Seat belts – removal and refitting

Front flexible stalks
1   Prise off the cap then unbolt the stalk from the floor (photo).
2   Refitting is a reversal of removal, but make sure that the stalk faces directly foward and tighten the bolt to the specified torque.

Front bolts
3   Unscrew the anchor bolt from the inner sill and, on three-door models unhook the slide rail (photos).
4   Unscrew the bolt securing the guide to the door pillar.
5   Remove the screws and prise back the sill trim sufficient to gain access to the inertia reel (photo).
6   Unscrew the bolt and withdraw the inertia reel (photos).
7   Refitting is a reversal of removal, but tighten the bolts to the specified torque.

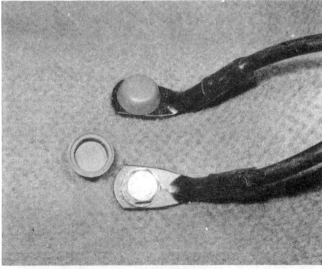

29.1 Front seat belt flexible stalk mounting

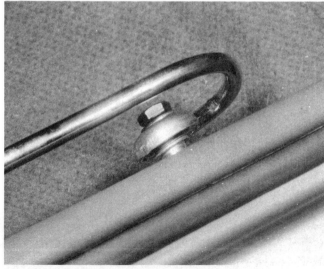

29.3A Front seat anchor bolt on the inner sill

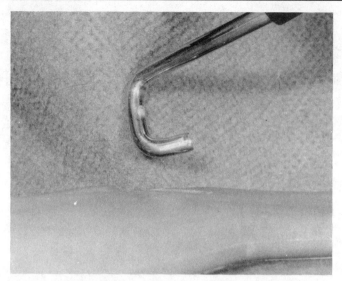

29.3B Unhook the front seat belt slide rail on three-door models

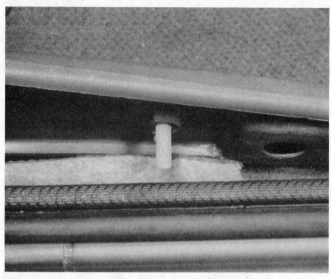

29.5 Removing the sill trim

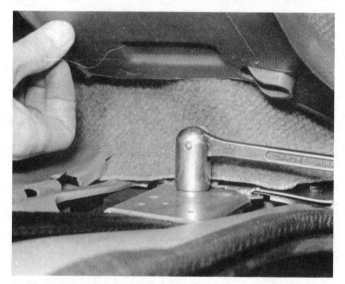

29.6A Unscrew the bolt ...

29.6B ... and withdraw the inertia reel

Rear bolts

8   Lift the rear seat cushion then unbolt the flexible stalk(s) or centre lap belt from the floor.
9   Remove the cover then unbolt the inertia reels from the side panel.
10 Remove the cover and unbolt the guide from the corner panel.
11 Refitting is a reversal of removal, but tighten the bolts to the specified torque.

30 Bumpers – removal and refitting

Front bumper

1   Where applicable remove the foglights from the front bumper as described in Chapter 11.
2   Apply the handbrake then jack up the front of the car and support on axle stands.
3   Unscrew the bolts securing the bumper to the front body frame and withdraw it from the car (photo). If necessary unbolt and remove the mounting brackets. Remove the impact blocks.
4   Refitting is a reversal of removal.

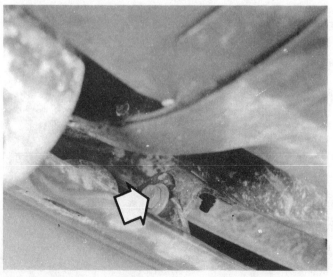

30.3 Front bumper mounting bolt

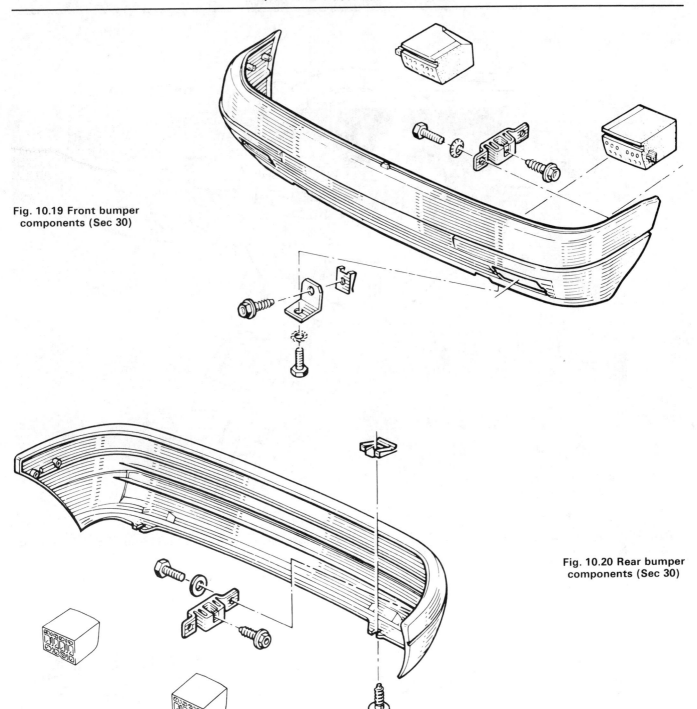

Fig. 10.19 Front bumper components (Sec 30)

Fig. 10.20 Rear bumper components (Sec 30)

Rear bumper
5   Unscrew the side and bottom mounting bolts and withdraw the bumper from the car. If necessary unbolt and remove the mounting brackets. Remove the impact blocks.
6   Refitting is a reversal of removal.

31 Roof console – removal and refitting

1   Disconnect the battery negative lead as described in Chapter 11.
2   Using a screwdriver prise out the roof console switch and light panel then disconnect the wiring multi-plug.
3   Remove the two retaining screws from the panel recess.

4   Release the console by pressing it down from the head lining then disconnect the wiring from the infra-red receiver.
5   Refitting is a reversal of removal.

32 Facia panel – removal and refitting

1   Disconnect the battery system lead as described in Chapter 11.
2   Remove the instrument panel as described in Chapter 11.
3   Where the gear lever is integral with the centre console, prise up the rubber gaiter and remove the two console retaining screws.
4   Remove the screws on either side of the console by the vents (photo).
5   Remove the choke control and knob as described in Chapter 3.

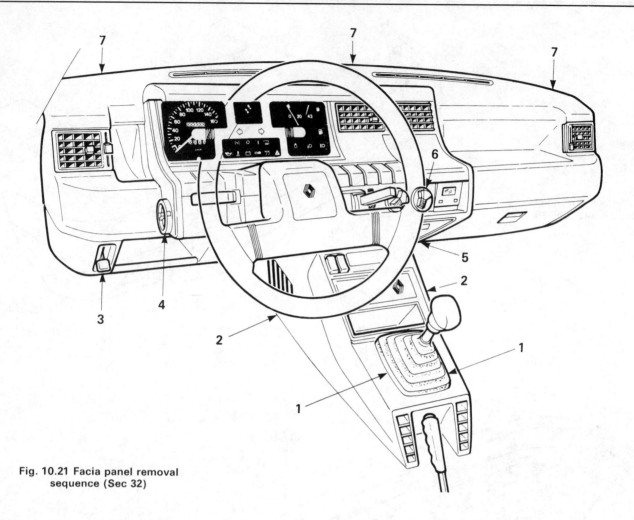

**Fig. 10.21 Facia panel removal
sequence (Sec 32)**

6   Remove the headlight level adjusting knob where fitted.
7   Lift the ashtray and unscrew the two retaining screws in the recess.
Withdraw the assembly and disconnect the wiring (photos).
8   Remove the heater controls as described in Section 35.
9   Remove the upper and lower trim panels on either side of the facia.
10 Remove the steering column as described in Chapter 9.
11 Remove the facia switches with reference to Chapter 11.

12 Unhook the centre console and disconnect the wiring as
applicable (photos).
13 Unscrew the lower facia retaining screws (photo).
14 Remove the clock or trip computer, and the fusebox as described in
Chapter 11.
15 Disconnect all remaining wiring from the facia.
16 Lift the right of the facia panel to release it from the plastic clip,

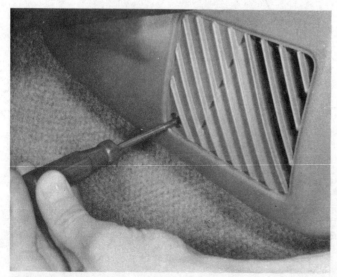

32.4 Removing the centre console retaining screws

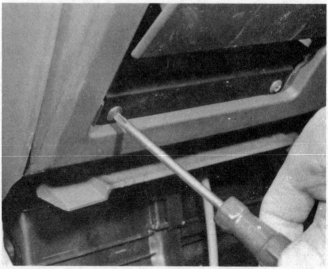

32.7A Remove the screws ...

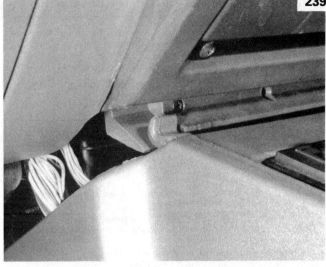

32.7B ... then withdraw the ashtray assembly and disconnect the wiring

32.12A Unhook the centre console ...

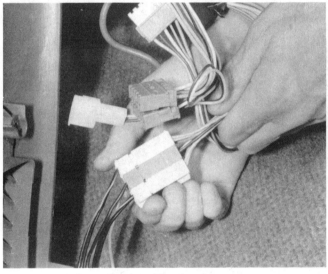

32.12B ... and disconnect the wiring

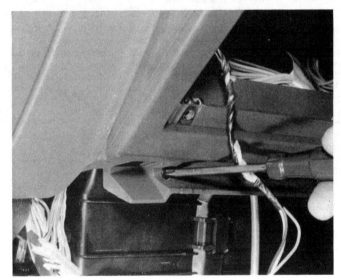

32.13 Removing the facia lower retaining screws

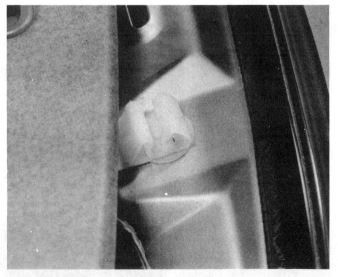

32.16 Lift the facia panel from the plastic clips

then the centre section from the centre clip and the left of the panel from the left clip (photo). If necessary use a flat blade lever to prise the panel from the clips which are located on the front edge.

17 Withdraw the facia panel from the bulkhead and remove it from the car.

18 Refitting is a reversal of removal.

33 Heater fan motor – removal and refitting

1 Disconnect the battery negative lead as described in Chapter 11.

2 Remove the plastic sheet from the plenum chamber on the bulkhead.

3 Extract the clips and withdraw the grille cover from the heater inlet (photo).

4 Pull the fan and motor direct from the casing (photo).

5 Check the condition of the motor terminals and the socket clips in the casing, and clean if necessary.

6 Refitting is a reversal of removal, but make sure that the motor terminals locate correctly in the socket clips.

34 Heater – removal and refitting

1 Remove the facia panel as described in Section 32, however there is no need to remove the heater controls, but instead depress the two clips located under the control panel and push the panel into the facia without disconnecting the cables. Carry out this after having removed the ashtray and the screw at the top of the ashtray aperture.

2 Drain the cooling system as described in Chapter 2.

3 Working in the engine compartment locate the heater hoses on the bulkhead and identify them for position (photo). Loosen the clips and disconnect them.

4 Unbolt the heater casing from the bulkhead and withdraw it together with the controls. Disconnect the wiring.

5 Release the plastic clips and carefully slide the heater matrix from the casing. Clean any debris from it by hosing or using an air line.

6 Disconnect the controls if necessary with reference to Section 35.

7 The two halves of the casing may be separated if necessary by releasing the metal clips.

8 Refitting is a reversal of removal, but refill the cooling system with reference to Chapter 2.

33.3 Showing the heater fan grille cover

33.4 The fan and motor is pulled direct from the casing

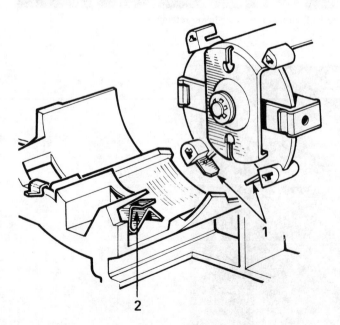

Fig. 10.22 Heater fan motor terminals (1) and socket clips (2) (Sec 33)

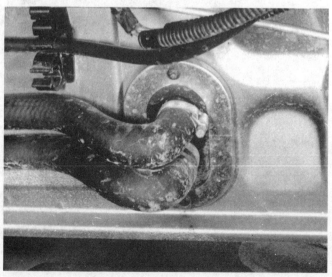

34.3 Heater hoses on the bulkhead

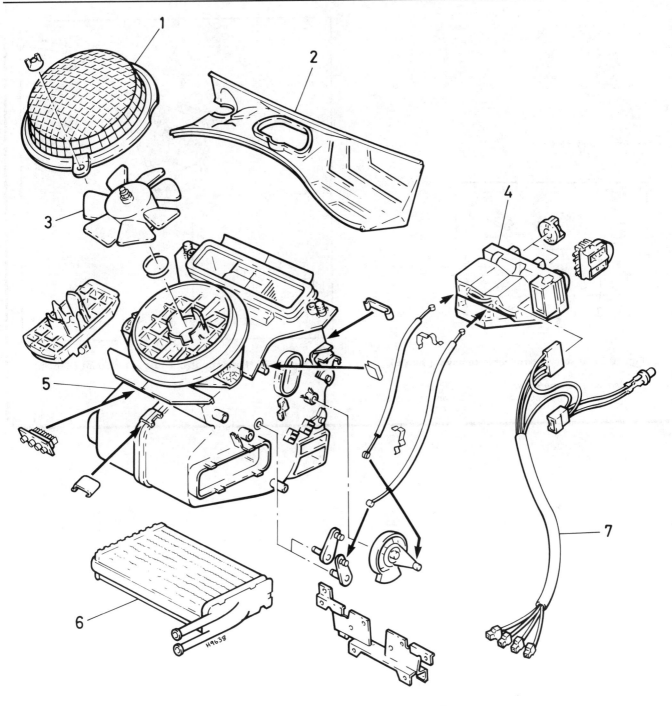

Fig. 10.23 Heater components (Sec 34)

1	Grille	4	Control panel	6	Matrix
2	Plastic cover	5	Heater casing	7	Wiring harness
3	Fan and motor				

35 Heater control cables – removal, refitting and adjustment

1 Disconnect the battery negative lead as described in Chapter 11.
2 Remove the centre console and ashtray with reference to Section 32. Remove the screw from the top of the ashtray aperture.
3 Depress the two clips located under the control panel and push the panel into the facia so that it can be removed through the ashtray aperture.

4 Unscrew the facia lower retaining screws with reference to Section 32 then lift it slightly.
5 Unclip and disconnect the control cables from the side of the heater, disconnect the wiring, and withdraw the control panel and cables from the car.
6 Refitting is a reversal of removal, but before fitting the outer cable clips, adjust the control knobs to distribute cool air as shown in Fig. 10.25 and position the levers as shown with the special dots aligned where applicable.

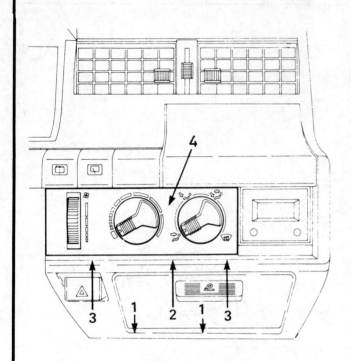

Fig. 10.24 Heater control cable removal (Sec 35)

1   Ash tray retaining screws
2   Panel retaining screw
3   Clip locations
4   Control panel

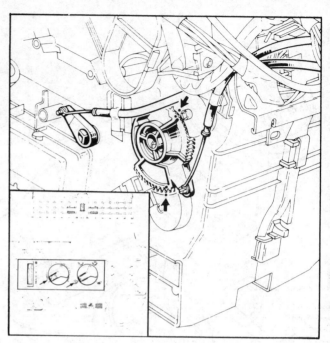

Fig. 10.25 Heater control cable adjustment (Sec 35)

Chapter 11 Electrical system

For modifications, and information applicable to later models, see Supplement at end of manual

Contents

Specifications

System type .... 12 volt, negative earth

Battery

Type .... Low maintenance or maintenance-free 'sealed for life'
Capacity .... 30, 35, 40, 50, 65 or 70 Amp hr according to model

Alternator

Type and output (at 6000 rpm):
    Ducellier 516058 .... 48 Amp
    Paris-Rhone A13N104 .... 48 Amp
    Paris-Rhone A14N87 .... 70 Amp

Starter motor

Type and current (locked pinion):
    Ducellier 534042 pre-engaged .... 350 Amp
    Ducellier 534043 pre-engaged .... 340 Amp
    Paris-Rhone D9E771 pre-engaged .... 460 Amp
    Paris-Rhone D9E76 pre-engaged .... 420 Amp

Wiper blades .... Champion X-4503 (front) and X-4103 (rear)

Bulbs (typical)

	Wattage
Headlamp:	
Standard bulb	45/40
Halogen bulb	60/55
Front foglamp	55
Front sidelight	4
Direction indicators	21
Stop/tail	21/5
Reversing lamp	21
Rear foglamp	21
Rear number plate lamp	5
Interior lamp	10
Instrument panel illumination	1.2 or 2

Torque wrench settings

	Nm	lbf ft
Battery terminal clamp – positive	5	4
Battery terminal clamp – negative	3	2
Battery retaining clamp bolt	10	7

1 General description

The electrical system is of the 12 volt negative earth type, and consists of a battery, alternator, starter motor and related electrical accessories, components and wiring.

The battery, charged by the alternator which is belt-driven from the crankshaft pulley, provides a steady amount of current for the ignition, starting, lighting and other electrical circuits. The battery may be a low maintenance type or a maintenance-free 'sealed for life' type, according to model.

The starter motor is of the pre-engaged type incorporating an integral solenoid. On starting, the solenoid moves the drive pinion into engagement with the flywheel ring gear before the starter motor is energised. Once the engine has started, a one-way clutch prevents the motor armature being driven by the engine until the pinion disengages from the flywheel.

Further details of the major electrical systems are given in the relevant Sections of this Chapter.

Caution: *Before carrying out any work on the vehicle electrical system, read through the precautions given in Safety First! at the beginning of this manual and in Section 2 of this Chapter.*

2 Electrical system – precautions

It is necessary to take extra care when working on the electrical system to avoid damage to semiconductor devices (diodes and transistors), and to avoid the risk of personal injury. In addition to the precautions given in Safety First! at the beginning of this manual, observe the following items when working on the system.

1 *Always remove rings, watches, etc before working on the electrical system.* Even with the battery disconnected, capacitive discharge could occur if a component live terminal is earthed through a metal object. This could cause a shock or nasty burn.

2 *Do not reverse the battery connections.* Components such as the alternator or any other having semiconductor circuitry could be irreparably damaged.

3 If the engine is being started using jump leads and a slave battery, connect the batteries *positive to positive* and *negative to negative*. This also applies when connecting a battery charger.

4 Never disconnect the battery earth terminals, or alternator wiring when the engine is running.

5 The battery leads and alternator wiring must be disconnected before carrying out any electric welding on the car.

3 Routine maintenance

At the intervals specified in the Routine Maintenance section in the front of the manual carry out the following procedures.

1 Check the operation of all the electrical equipment, ie wipers,

washers, lights, direction indicators, horn etc. Refer to the appropriate Sections of this Chapter if any components are found to be inoperative.

2 Visually check all accessible wiring connectors, harnesses and retaining clips for security, or any signs of chafing or damage. Rectify any problems encountered.

3 Check the alternator drivebelt for cracks, fraying or damage. Renew the belt if worn or, if satisfactory, check and adjust the belt tension. These procedures are covered in Chapter 2.

4 Check the condition of the wiper blades and if they are cracked or show signs of deterioration, renew them, as described in Section 34 of this Chapter. Check the operation of the windscreen and tailgate washers, and adjust the nozzle setting if necessary.

5 Top up the battery, on models where this is necessary, using distilled water until the tops of the cell plates are just submerged. Clean the battery terminals and case and, if necessary, check the battery condition using the procedures described in Section 4.

6 Top up the washer fluid reservoir and check the security of the pump wires and water pipes.

7 It is advisable to have the headlamp aim adjusted using optical beam setting equipment.

8 While carrying out a road test, check the operation of all the instruments and warning lights and the operation of the direction indicator self-cancelling mechanism.

4 Battery – general

1 According to model the battery may be of the low maintenance type in which the cell covers may be removed to allow periodic topping-up in the conventional way, or of the maintenance-free type which do not require topping-up. The maintenance-free battery has a sealed top cover which must not under any circumstances be removed. If the seals are broken the battery warranty will be invalidated.

2 On low maintenance batteries, periodically lift off the cover and check the electrolyte level. The tops of the cell plates should be just covered by the electrolyte. If not, add distilled or demineralized water until they are. Do not add extra water with the idea of reducing the intervals of topping-up. This will merely dilute the electrolyte and reduce charging and current retention efficiency.

3 If the electrolyte level needs an excessive amount of replenishment but no leaks are apparent, it could be due to over-charging as a result of the battery having been run down and then left to recharge from the vehicle rather than an outside source. If the battery has been heavily discharged for one reason or another, it is best to have it continuously charged at a low amperage for a period of many hours. If it is charged from the car's system under such conditions, the charging will be intermittent and greatly varied in intensity. This does not do the battery any good at all. If the battery needs topping-up frequently, even when it is known to be in good condition and not too old, then the voltage regulator should be checked to ensure that the charging output is being correctly controlled. An elderly battery, however, may need topping-up more than a new one, because it needs to take in more

charging current. Do not worry about this, provided it gives satisfactory service.

4   Keep the battery clean and dry all over by wiping it with a dry cloth. A dirty or damp top surface could cause tracking between the two terminal posts with consequent draining of power.

5   Periodically remove the battery and check the support tray clamp and battery terminal connections for signs of corrosion – usually indicated by a whitish green crystaline deposit. Wash this off with clean water to which a little ammonia or washing soda has been added. Then treat the terminals with petroleum jelly and the battery mounting with suitable protective paint to prevent further corrosive action.

6   On maintenance-free batteries access to the cells is not possible and only the overall condition of the battery can be checked using a voltmeter connected across the two terminals. On the low maintenance type a hydrometer can be used to check the condition of each individual cell. The table in the following Section gives the hydrometer readings for the various states of charge. A further check can be made when the battery is undergoing a charge. If, towards the end of the charge, when the cells should be 'gassing' (bubbling), one cell appears not to be, this indicates the cell or cells in question are probably breaking down and the life of the battery is limited.

5   Battery – charging

1   In winter when a heavy demand is placed on the battery, such as when starting from cold and using more electrical equipment, it may be necessary to have the battery fully charged from an external source. *Note that both battery leads must be disconnected before charging in order to prevent possible damage to any semiconductor electrical components.*

2   The terminals of the battery and the leads of the charger must be connected *positive to positive* and *negative to negative*.

3   Charging is best done overnight at a 'trickle' rate of 1 to 1.5 amps. Alternatively, on low maintenance batteries, a 3 to 4 amp rate can be used over a period of 4 hours or so. Check the specific gravity in the latter case and stop the charge when the reading is correct. Maintenance-free batteries should not be charged in this way due to their design and construction. It is strongly recommended that you seek the advice of a Renault dealer on the suitability of various types of charging equipment before using them on maintenance-free batteries.

4   The specific gravities for hydrometer readings on low maintenance batteries are as follows:

Fully discharged	Electrolyte temperature	Fully charged
1.098	38°C (100°F)	1.268
1.102	32°C (90°F)	1.272
1.106	27°C (80°F)	1.276
1.110	21°C (70°F)	1.280
1.114	16°C (60°F)	1.284
1.118	10°C (50°F)	1.288
1.122	4°C (40°F)	1.292
1.126	-1.5°C (30°F)	1.296

6   Battery – removal and refitting

1   The battery is located in the engine compartment on the right-hand side of the bulkhead. First check that all electrical components are switched off in order to avoid a spark occurring as the negative lead is disconnected.

2   Loosen the plastic knob on the negative terminal clamp (photo) lift the clamp and lead from the terminal and place it on the bulkhead. This is the terminal to disconnect before working on any electrical component on the car.

3   Loosen the nut on the positive terminal clamp, lift the clamp and lead from the terminal and place it on the bulkhead.

4   Unscrew the extended clamp bolt and move the clamp to one side (photo).

5   Lift the battery from the tray keeping it upright and taking care not to touch clothing.

6   Clean the battery terminals posts, clamps, tray and battery casing.

7   Refitting is a reversal of removal, but always connect the positive terminal clamp first and the negative terminal clamp last.

7   Alternator – removal and refitting

1   Disconnect the battery negative terminal.

2   Make a note of the electrical lead locations at the rear of the alternator and disconnect them (photos).

3   Slacken the alternator adjusting arm nut and bolt and the mounting nut and through-bolt, push the alternator towards the engine and slip off the drivebelt (photos).

4   Remove the alternator mounting and adjustment nuts and bolts then withdraw the alternator from the engine (photos).

5   Refitting is the reverse sequence of removal, but before tightening the adjustment and mounting bolts tension the drivebelt, as described in Chapter 2.

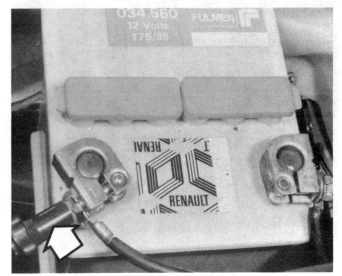

6.2 A plastic knob is provided to loosen the battery negative terminal clamp

6.4 Battery retaining clamp bolt

7.2A Wiring to the alternator regulator

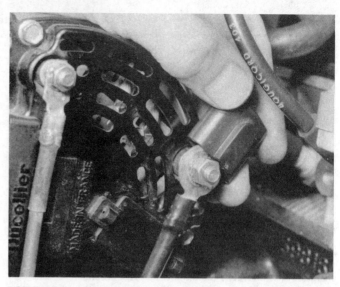

7.2B Disconnecting the alternator output lead

7.3A Loosen the alternator adjustment bolt ...

7.3B ... and push in the alternator to remove the drivebelt

7.4A Alternator mounting bolt

7.4B Alternator removed from the engine

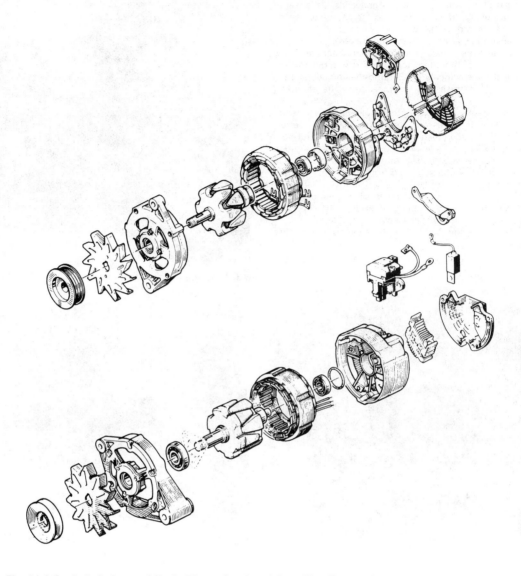

Fig. 11.1 Exploded views of Paris-Rhone (top) and Ducellier (bottom) alternators (Secs 7 to 9)

8 Alternator – fault tracing and rectification

1 If the ignition warning fails to illuminate when the ignition is switched on, first check the wiring connections at the rear of the alternator for security. If satisfactory, check that the warning lamp bulb has not blown and is secure in its holder. If the lamps stills fails to illuminate check the continuity of the warning lamp feed wire from the alternator to the bulb holder. If all is satisfactory, the alternator is at fault and should be renewed or taken to an automobile electrician for testing and repair.

2 If the ignition warning lamp illuminates when the engine is running, ensure that the drivebelt is correctly tensioned (see Chapter 2), and that the connections on the rear of the alternator are secure. If all is so far satisfactory, check the alternator brushes and commutator, as described in Section 9. If the fault still persists, the alternator should be renewed, or taken to an automobile electrician for testing and repair.

3 If the alternator output is suspect even though the warning lamp functions correctly, the regulated voltage may be checked as follows:

4 Connect a voltmeter across the battery terminals and then start the engine.

5 Increase the engine speed until the reading on the voltmeter remains steady. This should be between 13.5 and 14.8 volts.

6 Switch on as many electrical accessories as possible and check that the alternator maintains the regulated voltage at between 13.5 and 14.8 volts.

7 If the regulated voltage is not as stated, the fault may be due to a faulty diode, a severed phase or worn brushes, springs or commutator. The brushes and commutator may be attended to, as described in Section 9, but if the fault still persists the alternator should be renewed, or taken to an automobile electrician for testing and repair.

9 Alternator brushes – removal, inspection and refitting

Note: *Owing to the specialist knowledge and equipment required to test and repair an alternator accurately, it is recommended that, if the performance is suspect, the alternator be taken to an automobile electrician who will have the facilities for such work. It is, however, a relatively simple task to attend to the brush gear and this operation is described below. The work may be carried out without removing the unit from the engine.*

1 Disconnect the battery negative terminal.

2   Note the locations of the wiring connectors and leads at the rear of the alternator and disconnect them. If preferred the alternator can be completely removed to provide easier working conditions.
3   Unbolt and remove the rear cover if required (photo).
4   Undo the two small bolts or nuts securing the regulator and brush box assembly to the rear of the alternator. Lift off the regulator and brush box, disconnect the electrical leads, noting their locations, then remove the regulator and brush box assembly from the alternator (photos).
5   Check that the brushes stand proud of their holders and are free to move without sticking. If necessary clean them with a petrol-moistened cloth. Check that the brush spring pressure is equal for both brushes and gives reasonable tension. If in doubt about the condition of the brushes and springs compare them with new parts at a Renault parts dealer. The regulator can be separated from the brush box after removing the cover if necessary (photo).
6   Clean the slip rings with a petrol-moistened cloth, then check for signs of scoring, burning or severe pitting. If evident the slip rings should be attended to by an automobile electrician (photo).
7   Refitting the regulator and brush box assembly is the reverse sequence to removal.

9.3 Removing the alternator rear cover

9.4A Unscrew the retaining bolts ...

9.4B ... and withdraw the regulator and brush box

9.5 Removing the cover when separating the regulator from the brush box

9.6 Alternator slip rings

10 Starter motor – testing in the car

1   If the starter motor fails to operate, first check the condition of the battery by switching on the headlamps. If they glow brightly then gradually dim after a few seconds, the battery is in an uncharged condition.

2   If the battery is satisfactory, check the starter motor main terminal and the engine earth cable for security. Check the terminal connections on the solenoid, located on the side of the starter motor.

3   If the starter still fails to turn, use a voltmeter, or 12 volt test lamp and leads, to ensure that there is battery voltage at the solenoid main terminal (containing the cable from the battery positive terminal).

4   With the ignition switched on and the ignition key in position D check that voltage is reaching the solenoid terminal with the spade connector, and also the starter main terminal beneath the end cover.

5   If there is no voltage reaching the spade connector there is a wiring or ignition switch fault. If voltage is available, but the starter does not operate, then the starter or solenoid is likely to be at fault.

11 Starter motor – removal and refitting

1   Disconnect the battery negative terminal.

2   Remove the air cleaner as described in Chapter 3.

3   On non-Turbo models remove the protective metal shield from the starter motor by unscrewing the bolt at the cylinder block and the nut on the exhaust manifold (photos). On Turbo models disconnect the exhaust pipe flange and unbolt the retaining bracket (Fig. 11.2).

4   Disconnect the battery supply cable and solenoid feed wire from the starter solenoid terminals (photo). On Turbo models unbolt the cable support.

11.3A Starter motor shield bottom mounting

11.3B Starter motor shield top mounting

11.4 Battery supply (+) cable (1) and solenoid feed wire (2) to the starter solenoid

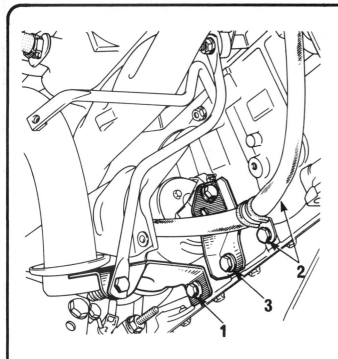

Fig. 11.2 Starter motor location on Turbo models (Sec 11)

1   Retaining bracket
2   Battery cable and support
3   Starter motor support bracket

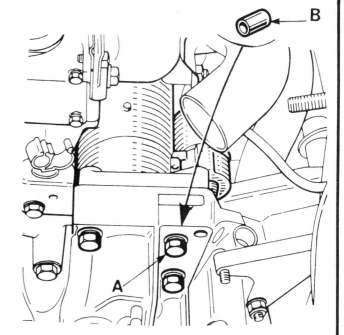

Fig. 11.3 The starter motor bolt locating dowel (B) must be positioned in hole (A) (Sec 11)

5   Undo the bolt securing the starter motor support bracket to the rear
facing side of the cylinder block.

6   Undo the three bolts securing the starter motor to the transmission
bellhousing and withdraw the starter from the engine. Note the
position of the locating dowel in the upper rear bellhousing bolt hole
and make sure that it is in place when refitting.

7   Refitting the starter motor is the reverse sequence to removal, but
tighten the bellhousing bolts before the support bracket bolt. On Turbo
models tighten the exhaust pipe flange bolts as described in Chapter 3.

12 Starter motor – overhaul

Note: *Overhaul of the starter motor is normally confined to
inspection and, if necessary, renewal of the brush gear components.
Due to the limited availability of replacement parts, any other faults
occurring on the starter usually result in renewal of the complete
motor. However, for those wishing to dismantle the starter motor, this
Section may be used as a guide. The procedure is essentially similar for
all motor types and any minor differences can be noted by referring to
the accompanying illustrations.*

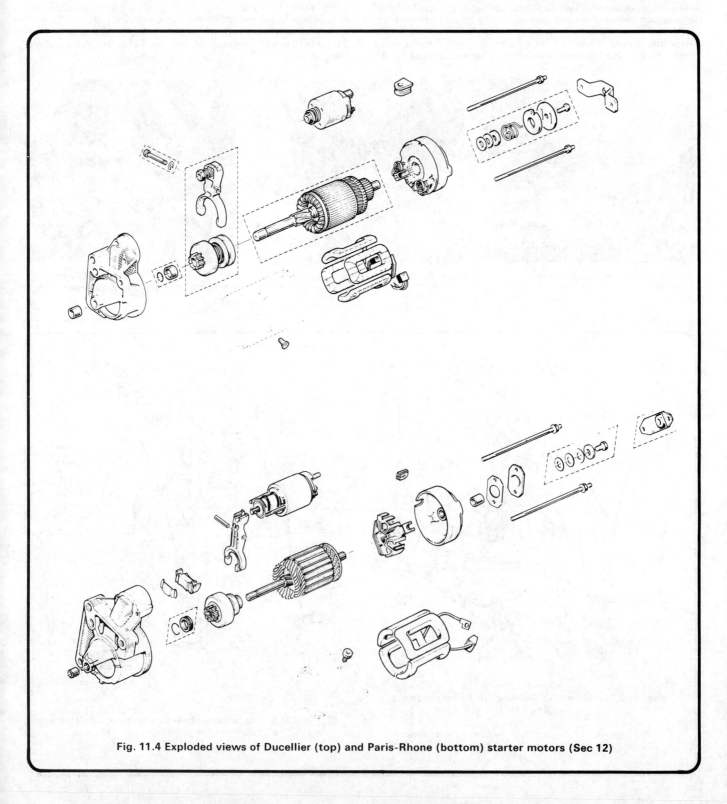

Fig. 11.4 Exploded views of Ducellier (top) and Paris-Rhone (bottom) starter motors (Sec 12)

1   Remove the starter motor from the car, as described in the previous Section.
2   Undo the two nuts and remove the mounting support bracket from the rear of the motor.
3   Undo the nut and disconnect the lead from the solenoid terminal.
4   Where fitted, remove the cap plate on the rear cover and the bolt and washers between rear cover and armature.
5   Tap out the engaging lever pivot pin from the drive end housing.
6   Undo the nuts securing the solenoid to the drive end housing.
7   Undo the through-bolts and withdraw the yoke, armature, solenoid and engaging lever as an assembly from the drive end housing.
8   Withdraw the solenoid and engaging lever, remove the rear cover with brushes, then slide the armature out of the yoke.
9   Slip the brushes out of their brush holders to release the rear cover.
10 If the pinion/clutch assembly is to be removed, drive the stop collar up the armature shaft and extract the circlip. Slide the stop collar and pinion clutch assembly off the armature.
11 With the starter motor now completely dismantled, clean all the components with paraffin or a suitable solvent and wipe dry.
12 Check that all the brushes protrude uniformly from their holders and that the springs all provide moderate tension. Check that the brushes move freely in their holders and clean them with a petrol-moistened rag if there is any tendency to stick. If in doubt about the brush length or condition, compare them with new components and renew if necessary. Note that new field brushes must be soldered to their leads.
13 Check the armature shaft for distortion and the commutator for excessive wear, scoring or burrs. If necessary, the commutator may be lightly skimmed in a lathe and then polished with fine glass paper.
14 Check the pinion/clutch assembly, drive end housing, engaging lever and solenoid for wear or damage. Make sure that the clutch permits movement in one direction only and renew the unit if necessary.

15 Accurate checking of the armature, commutator and field coil windings and insulation requires the use of special test equipment. If the starter motor was inoperative when removed from the car and the previous checks have not highlighted the problem, then it can be assumed that there is a continuity or insulation fault and the unit should be renewed.
16 If the starter is in a satisfactory condition, or if a fault has been traced and rectified, the unit can be reassembled using the reverse of the dismantling procedure.

13 Fuses and relays – general

1   The fuses and relays are located below the passenger side glovebox. Access is gained by prising open the lid. Symbols on the reverse of the lid indicate the circuits protected by the fuses, and four spare fuses are supplied together with a plastic clip to remove and fit them (photo).
2   To remove a fuse fit the clip then pull it direct from the holder. The wire within the fuse is clearly visible and it will be broken if the fuse is blown.
3   Always renew a fuse with one of an identical rating. Never renew a fuse more than once without tracing the source of the trouble. The fuse rating is stamped on top of the fuse.
4   The various relays can be removed from their respective locations by carefully pulling them upwards and out.
5   If a system controlled by a relay becomes inoperative and the relay is suspect, operate the system and if the relay is functioning it should be possible to hear it click as it is energized. If this is the case the fault lies with the components or wiring of the system. If the relay is not being energized then the relay is not receiving a main supply voltage or a switching voltage, or the relay itself is faulty.

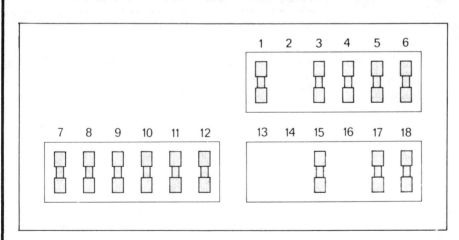

Alternative No	Amps	Function
1	–	Not used
2	–	Not used
3	20	Door locks
4	–	Not used
5	30	LH window winder
6	30	RH window winder
7	7.5	Rear foglights
8	5	RH sidelights
9	5	LH sidelights
10	10	Direction indicator lights
11	5	Windscreen wiper 'park'
12	10	Clock – interior light – infra-red remote control
13	10 or 15	Cigar lighter – windscreen wiper
14	5	Control box – (driving school car)
15	7.5	Stoplight – reverse light
16	15 or 20	Rear screen demister Rear screen wiper
17	20	Heating ventilator
18	5	Clock – car radio

Fig. 11.5 Fuse location and function chart – typical (Sec 13)

No	Amps	Function
1	15	Cigar lighter* – windscreen wipers
2	–	Unused
3	7,5	Stop switch Reversing light
4	15-20*	Heated rear screen Rear screen wiper/washer*
5	20	Heater fan
6	5	Clock-radio
7	7,5	Rear foglight*
8	5	Front RH sidelight and RH rear light control lighting

No	Amps	Function
9	5	Front LH sidelight and LH rear light
10	10	Direction indicator flasher unit
11	5	Windscreen wiper park position
12	10	Clock – interior light Infra-red remote control
13	–	Unused
14	–	Unused
15	20	Electric door locking system*
16	–	Unused
17	30	LH window winder
18	30	RH window winder

*Depending on model

13.1 Fuse and relay holder with lid open

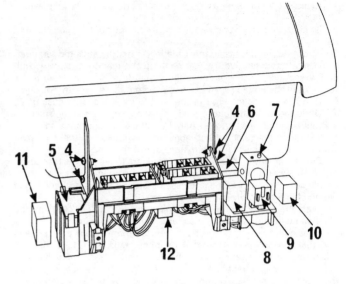

Fig. 11.6 Relay locations (Sec 13)

4 Mounting screw locations
5 Windscreen wiper timer
6 Lighting warning buzzer
7 Lock timer
8 Direction indicator flasher
   unit

9 Rear foglight relay
10 Main beam relay (not UK)
11 Dipped beam relay (not UK)
12 Rear screen wiper delay

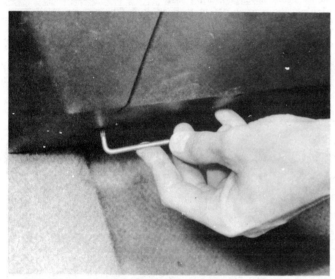

14.2A Fuse and relay holder surround removal

14.2B Fuse and relay holder with surround removed

14 Fuse and relay holder – removal and refitting

1 Disconnect the battery negative terminal.
2 Remove the surround and lid by unscrewing the two screws using a Torx key (photos).
3 Remove the mounting screws, lower the holder and disconnect the wiring.
4 Refitting is a reversal of removal.

15 Direction indicator and hazard flasher system – general

1 The flasher unit is located on the fuse and relay holder below the passenger glovebox.
2 Should the flashers become faulty in operation, check the bulbs for security and make sure that the contact surfaces are not corroded. If one bulb blows or is making a poor connection due to corrosion, the system will not flash on that side of the car.
3 If the flasher unit operates in one direction and not the other, the fault is likely to be in the bulbs, or wiring to the bulbs. If the system will not flash in either direction, operate the hazard flashers. If these function, check the appropriate fuse and renew it if blown. If the fuse is satisfactory, renew the flasher unit.

16 Instrument panel – removal and refitting

1 Disconnect the battery negative terminal.
2 Pull the visor straight up from its location over the instrument panel (photo).
3 Remove the retaining screws from the top corners (photo).
4 Lift the instrument panel to release it from the clips, and withdraw it sufficiently to gain access to the rear of the panel. Unless the panel has previously been removed it will be held firmly by the clips, and additional upwards pressure can be provided by removing the lower steering column shroud and pressing up the panel with the fingers.
5 Disconnect the speedometer cable and multi-plug connectors then withdraw the instrument panel from the facia (photos).
6 Refitting is a reversal of removal.

16.2 Removing the instrument panel visor

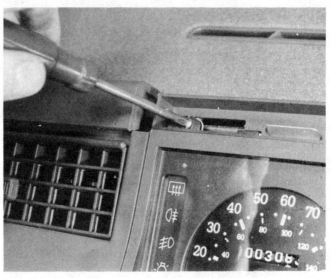

16.3 Removing the instrument panel top corner screws

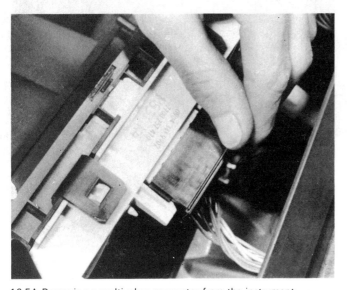

16.5A Removing a multi-plug connector from the instrument panel

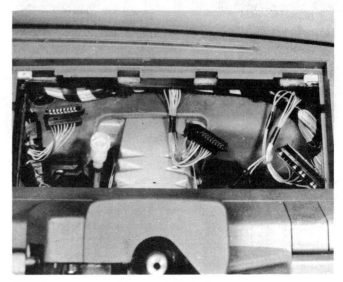

16.5B Instrument panel aperture in the facia

17 Instrument panel – dismantling and reassembly

1   Prise the plastic hooks outwards and remove the front cover (photos).
2   To remove the speedometer extract the two screws from the front and rear of the unit.
3   To remove the coolant temperature indicator extract the printed circuit nuts and the two retaining screws.
4   To remove the fuel gauge extract the printed circuit nuts and the two retaining screws.
5   To remove the tachometer extract the single rear screw and the two front screws.
6   To remove the oil level indicator first remove the tachometer then extract the printed circuit nuts and the two retaining screws.
7   Reassembly of the instrument panel is a reversal of the dismantling procedure.

18 Steering column switches – removal and refitting

1   Disconnect the battery negative terminal.
2   Remove the steering wheel and steering column lower shroud with reference to Chapter 9.
3   To remove the lighting and direction indicator switch undo the switch retaining screws using a Torx key, and the screws securing the facia to the steering column (photos). Remove the steering column upper mounting bolts and loosen the lower mounting nuts, then withdraw the switch and disconnect the wiring.
4   To remove the windscreen wiper switch undo the retaining screws, withdraw the switch and disconnect the wiring (photos).
5   Ignition switch removal is described in Chapter 12.
6   Refitting is a reversal of removal.

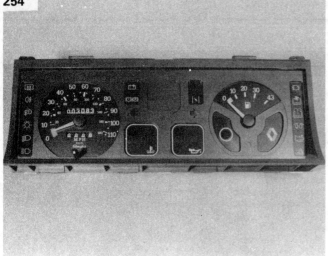

17.1A Front view of the instrument panel

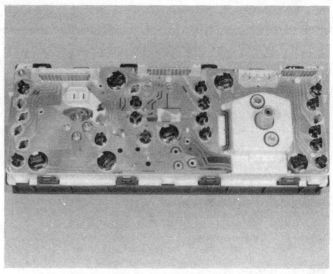

17.1B Rear view of the instrument panel

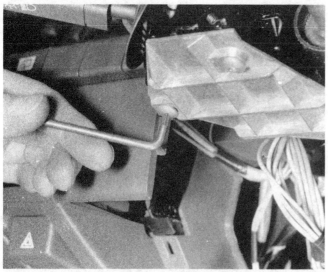

18.3A Removing the lighting and direction indicator switch retaining screws

18.3B Unscrew the facia-to-steering column lower ...

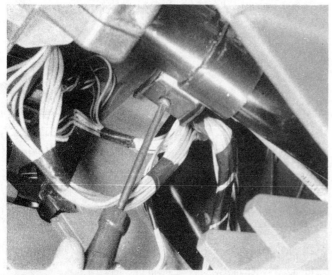

18.3C ... and upper screws

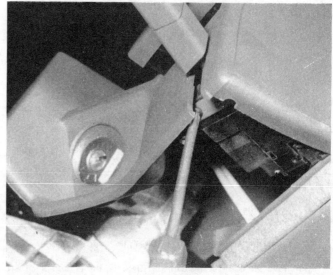

18.4A Remove the retaining screws ...

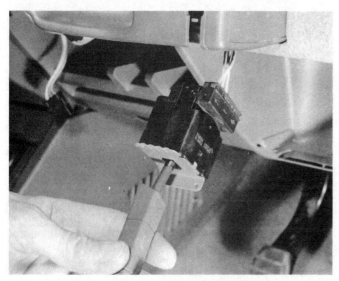

18.4B ... and withdraw the windscreen wiper switch

19 Switch (facia) – removal and refitting

1 All the facia mounted switches are held in position by plastic tags on the switch casing and the tags are designed with sloping edges to facilitate direct removal from the facia. Before removing a switch disconnect the battery negative terminal.
2 Ease out the switch then disconnect the multi-plug connector (photos). If the switch proves to be tight press it out from behind after removing the steering column lower shroud.
3 Refitting is a reversal of removal.

20 Clock/trip computer – removal and refitting

1 Disconnect the battery negative terminal.
2 Carefully ease the unit from the facia then disconnect the multi-plug connector (photo).
3 Refitting is a reversal of removal.

21 Cigarette lighter – removal and refitting

1 Disconnect the battery negative terminal.
2 Lift the ashtray lid and remove the lower retaining screws.
3 Withdraw the ashtray assembly and disconnect the wiring.
4 Unscrew the ring nut and withdraw the cigarette lighter from the ashtray.
5 Refitting is a reversal of removal.

22 Courtesy lamp pillar switches – removal and refitting

1 Disconnect the battery negative terminal.
2 Open the door and locate the front courtesy lamp switch on the door pillar.
3 Remove the retaining screw and withdraw the switch (photo).
4 Disconnect the supply wire and tie a loose knot in it to prevent it dropping into the pillar. Remove the switch.
5 Refitting is a reversal of removal.

23 Headlamp bulb – renewal

1 Open the bonnet and pull the wiring connector from the rear of the headlamp (photo).

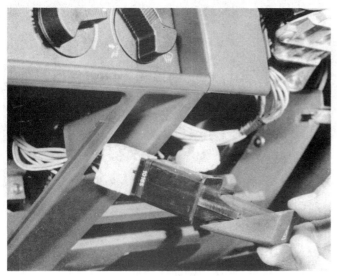

19.2A Removing the hazard warning light switch

19.2B Removing the rear window wiper/washer switch

20.2 Removing the clock

22.3 Removing the courtesy lamp pillar switch

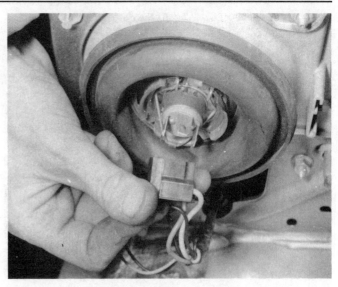

23.1 Pull off the headlamp bulb wiring connector ...

23.2 ... release the clip ...

23.3 ... and withdraw the bulb

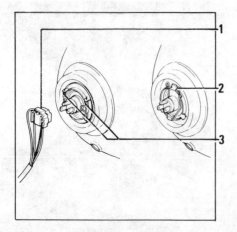

Fig. 11.7 Headlamp bulb fittings (Sec 23)

1 Wiring connector   3 Double clips for conventional bulb
2 Clip for halogen type bulb

2   If conventional bulbs are fitted, spring back the two wire retaining clips. If halogen bulbs are fitted, release the ends of the wire retaining clip and pivot the clip clear (photo).
3   The bulb can now be withdrawn from its location in the lens assembly (photo). Take care not to touch the bulb glass with your fingers; if touched, clean the bulb with methylated spirit.
4   Fit the new bulb using a reversal of the removal procedure, but make sure that the stud or tabs on the bulb support is correctly located in the lens assembly.

24 Front sidelight bulb – renewal

1   Open the bonnet and pull the wiring connector from the sidelight bulbholder on the rear of the headlamp (photo).
2   Pull the bulbholder and bulb from the grommet in the lens assembly (photo).
3   Fit the new bulb using a reversal of the removal procedure.

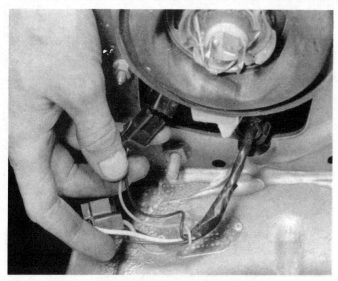

24.1 Pull off the front sidelight bulb wiring connector ...

24.2 ... and remove the bulbholder and bulb

25 Front direction indicator bulb – renewal

1   Open the bonnet and locate the wire spring positioned below the rear of the headlamp. Pull the spring rearwards to release it from the bracket then withdraw the direction indicator lamp forwards (photos).
2   Disconnect the wiring if necessary.
3   Turn the bulbholder a quarter turn anti-clockwise to release it from the lamp (photo).
4   Depress and twist the bulb to remove it from the bulbholder.
5   Fit the new bulb using a reversal of the removal procedure.

26 Front foglamp bulb – renewal

1   Undo the two screws securing the lens glass to the lamp body and carefully withdraw the lens.
2   Disconnect the two wires at the bulbholder terminals, release the retaining spring clip and lift out the bulbholder.

25.1A Release the spring ...

25.1B .. withdraw the direction indicator lamp ...

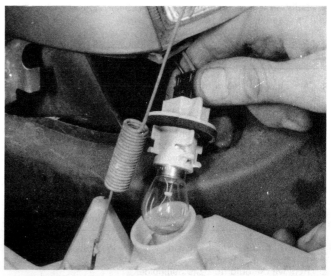

25.3 ... and remove the bulb and bulbholder

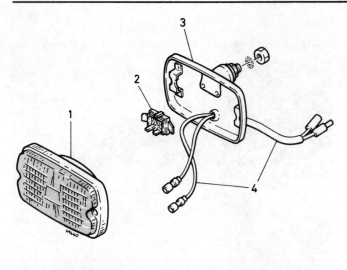

Fig. 11.8 Front foglamp components (Sec 26)

1   Bulbholder and lens   4   Wiring
2   Bulb   5   Screws
3   Lamp body

27.3A Unscrewing the four mounting nuts for the headlamp lens assembly

27.3B Headlamp lens assembly removed from the car

3   Lift and pull the bulb to remove it from the holder.
4   Refit the bulb and lens assembly using the reverse of this procedure. Ensure that the new bulb is held with a piece of cloth or tissue paper and clean the bulb glass with methylated spirit if it is touched with the fingers.

27 Headlamp lens assembly – removal and refitting

1   Remove the headlamp bulb (Section 23), sidelight bulb (Section 24) and direction indicator bulb (Section 25).
2   Remove the radiator grille as described in Chapter 10.
3   Unscrew the four mounting nuts and withdraw the headlamp lens asssembly forwards (photos).
4   Refitting is a reversal of removal, but finally adjust the headlamp aim as described in the following Section.

28 Headlamp aim – adjustment

1   Accurate adjustment of the headlamp aim can only be done using optical beam setting equipment and this work should therefore be carried out by a Renault dealer or service station with the necessary facilities. For reference, the location of the beam adjusting screws are shown in the accompanying photos (photos).
2   The headlamps incorporate a two position adjustment to compensate for 'laden' or 'unladen' conditions. On some models this is a remote control on the facia panel, but on other models a knob is provided on the rear of the headlamp lens assembly.

29 Side marker bulb (five-door models) – renewal

1   Reach up under the front wing and pull the bulbholder from the rear of the lamp.
2   Remove the bulb from the bulbholder.
3   Fit the new bulb using a reversal of the removal procedure.

Fig. 11.9 Headlamp adjuster (B) for 'laden' or 'unladen' conditions (Sec 28)

30 Rear lamp cluster bulbs – renewal

1   Open the tailgate then working through the access hole on the appropriate side of the luggage compartment unscrew the plastic knob retaining the bottom of the cluster (photo).
2   Withdraw the bottom of the cluster and lower it to release the upper tag (photo).
3   Slide the wiring connector from the terminal contacts (photo).
4   Squeeze the plastic clips together and separate the bulbholder from the lamp (photos).
5   Depress and twist the appropriate bulb to remove it (photo). The upper bulb is for the tail light and stop light, the middle bulb is for the direction indicator, and the bottom bulb is for the foglight on the left-hand side and the reversing light on the right-hand side.
6   Fit the new bulb using a reversal of the removal procedure. Check the security of the earth bolt on the body before refitting the lamp (photo).

31 Rear number plate lamp bulb – renewal

1   Prise the lamp from the tailgate using a screwdriver (photo).
2   Release the lens cover from the base (photo).
3   Remove the festoon type bulb from the spring contacts.
4   Fit the new bulb using a reversal of the removal procedure, but check the tension of the spring contacts and if necessary bend them so that they firmly contact the bulb end caps.

30.1 Unscrew the plastic knob ...

30.2 ... and release the rear lamp cluster upper tag

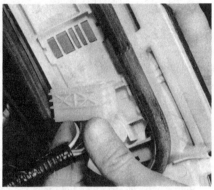

30.3 Slide the wiring connector from the terminal contacts

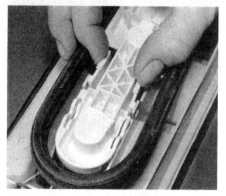

30.4A Squeeze the plastic clips ...

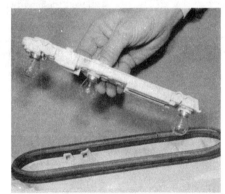

30.4B ... and remove the bulbholder

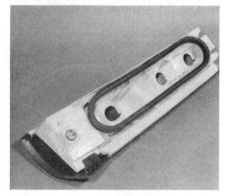

30.4C Rear lamp unit with bulbholder removed

30.5 Removing a rear lamp cluster bulb

30.6 Earth bolt positioned beneath the rear lamp unit location

31.1 Prising the rear number plate lamp from the tailgate

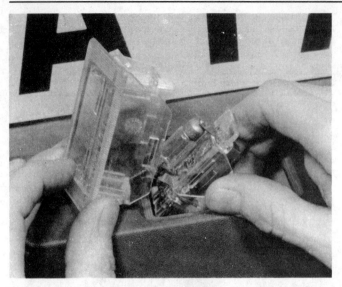

31.2 Removing the lens cover from the rear number plate lamp base

32.1 Prise off the lens cover for access to the bulbs in the roof console

32 Interior light bulb – renewal

1   Prise the lens cover from the roof console or side interior lights as applicable (photo).
2   Remove the festoon type bulb from the spring contacts.
3   Fit the new bulb making sure that it is firmly held by the spring contacts then refit the lens cover.

33 Instrument panel illumination bulbs – renewal

1   Remove the instrument panel as described in Section 16.
2   Turn the appropriate bulbholder a quarter turn to align the shoulders with the slots, then remove it from the instrument panel and extract the bulb (photos).
3   Fit the new bulb using a reversal of the removal procedure.

34 Wiper blades and arms – removal and refitting

Wiper blades
1   The wiper blades should be renewed when they no longer clean the windscreen or tailgate window effectively.
2   Lift the wiper arm away from the window.
3   Release the catch on the arm, turn the blade through 90° and withdraw the blade from the arm fork (photo).
4   Insert the new blade into the arm, making sure it locates securely.

Wiper arms
5   To remove a wiper arm, lift the hinged cover and unscrew the retaining nut (photo).
6   Using a screwdriver, carefully prise the arm off the spindle.
7   Before refitting the arm switch the wipers on and off, allowing them to return to the 'park' position.
8   Refit the arm to the spindle, with the arm and blade positioned at the bottom edge of the screen in the normal 'parked' position.
9   Refit and tighten the retaining nut and close the hinged cover.

33.2A Large type bulb removal from the instrument panel

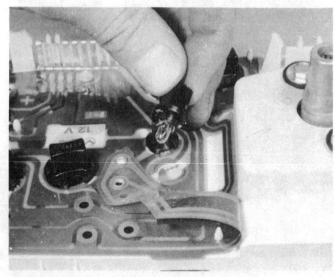

33.2B Small type bulb removal from the instrument panel

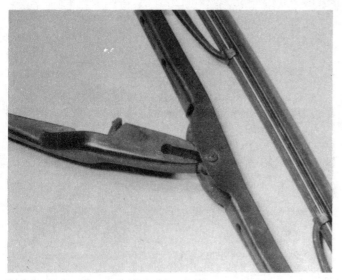

34.3 Removing the wiper blade from the arm

34.5 Lift the hinged cover for access to the wiper arm retaining nut

35 Windscreen wiper motor and linkage – removal and refitting

1 Remove the wiper arms as described in Section 34 and the washer reservoir as described in Section 37.
2 Remove the bonnet sealing rubber (photo) and the plastic cover from the bulkhead plenum chamber.
3 Disconnect the battery negative terminal.
4 At the wiper arm spindles, withdraw the rubber washers (photo), unscrew the nuts and remove the plain and rubber washers.
5 Disconnect the motor wiring multi-plug.
6 Unscrew the centre mounting bolt together with the plain and rubber washers (photo).
7 Push the spindles through their location holes then withdraw the linkage and motor as an assembly from the bulkhead.
8 Unscrew the nut securing the crank arm to the motor driveshaft and remove the arm (photo).
9 Unbolt and remove the wiper motor from the linkage centre bracket (photo).

35.2 Removing the bonnet sealing rubber

35.4 Removing the wiper arm spindle rubber washer

35.6 Wiper motor and linkage centre mounting bolt

35.8 Wiper crank arm to the motor drveshaft nut

35.9 Wiper motor mounting bolts

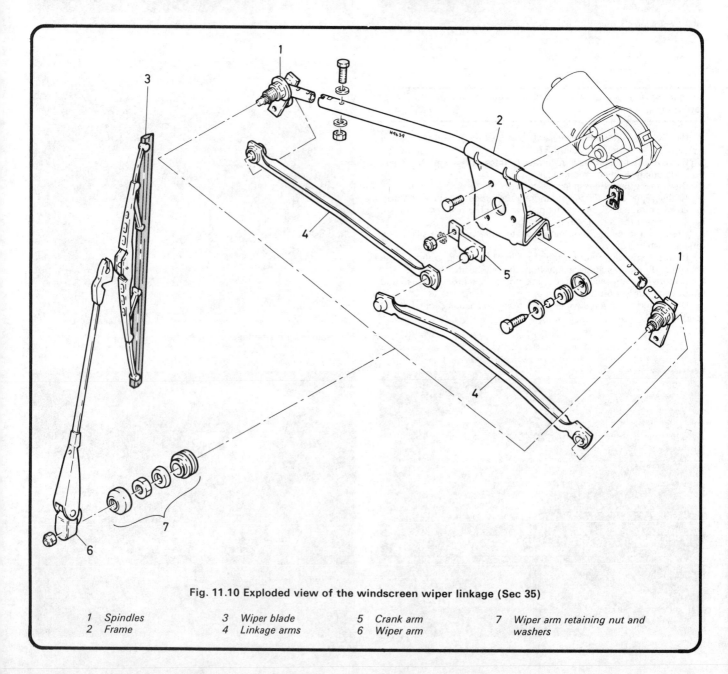

Fig. 11.10 Exploded view of the windscreen wiper linkage (Sec 35)

1	Spindles	3	Wiper blade	5	Crank arm	7	Wiper arm retaining nut and
2	Frame	4	Linkage arms	6	Wiper arm		washers

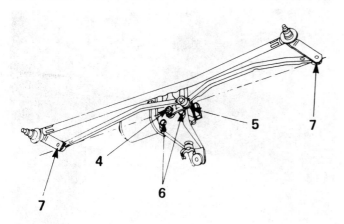

Fig. 11.11 Windscreen wiper crank arm 'parked' position (Sec 35)

4	*Nut*	6	*Motor mounting bolts*
5	*Crank arm*	7	*Spindle arm pivots*

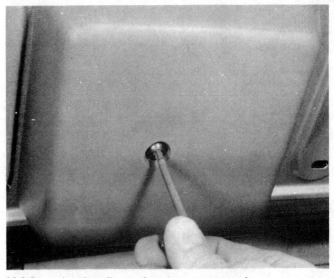

36.3 Removing the tailgate wiper motor cover panel

10 Refitting is a reversal of removal, but position the crank arm as follows. Operate the motor temporarily so that it stops at the parked position. For safety disconnect the battery negative terminal before proceeding. Fit the crank arm to the motor driveshaft in the position shown in Fig. 11.11 so that all three linkage pivots are in line.

36 Tailgate wiper motor – removal and refitting

1 Disconnect the battery negative terminal.
2 Remove the wiper arm, as described in Section 34.
3 Open the tailgate and remove the cover panel (one screw) to gain access to the motor (photo).
4 Lift off the rubber washer, then undo the nut securing the motor spindle to the tailgate. Lift off the remaining washers and spacers.
5 Disconnect the motor wiring multi-plug, undo the retaining bolts and withdraw the motor assembly from inside the tailgate (photo).
6 The motor and gearbox assembly cannot be dismantled for repair or overhaul as replacement parts are not available separately.
7 Refitting is the reverse sequence to removal.

36.5 Tailgate wiper motor and wiring multi-plug (arrowed)

37 Windscreen/tailgate washer reservoir and pumps – removal and refitting

1 Disconnect the battery negative terminal.
2 Pull the wiring connectors from the pump(s) and minimum level sender as applicable and identify them for location (photo).
3 Unscrew the mounting nut, withdraw the reservoir and disconnect the pipes noting their location (photo).
4 Pull the pump(s) from the location in the reservoir and remove the sealing grommets. Drain any remaining water.
5 Refitting is a reversal of removal, but make sure that the reservoir extension is located in the hole provided in the bulkhead bracket (photo).

38 Horn – removal and refitting

1 Either one or two horns are fitted to the body front valance behind the front bumper (photo). To remove it jack up the front of the car and support on axle stands. Apply the handbrake.
2 Disconnect the battery negative terminal then disconnect the horn supply lead.
3 Unscrew the nut securing the horn to the mounting bracket and remove it from the car.

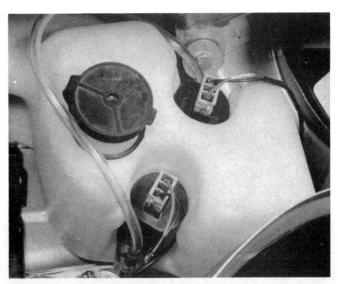

37.2 Windscreen/tailgate washer reservoir

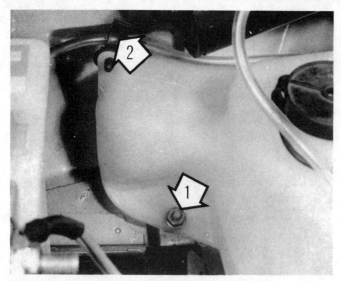

37.3 Washer reservoir mounting bolt (1) and pipe clip (2)

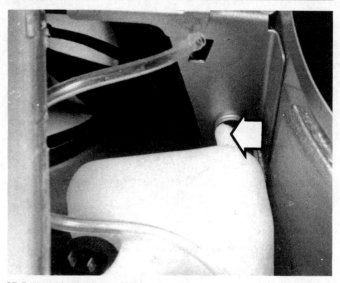

37.5 Washer reservoir location extension

38.1 Horn location behind the front bumper

4   If the horn is inoperative, check for a supply voltage to it by connecting a test bulb between the electrical lead and a good earth. With the ignition switched on, depress the horn button and the test bulb should light. If the bulb fails to light, check for a blown fuse. If the fuse is satisfactory there is a fault in the wiring or multi-function switch. If the bulb lights, the horn is faulty and the horn will have to be renewed.
5   Refitting the horn is the reverse sequence to removal.

39 Speedometer cable – removal and refitting

1   Refer to Section 17, and remove the instrument panel sufficiently to allow the speedometer cable to be disconnected.
2   Where a trip computer is fitted disconnect the sender unit from the upper and lower cable sections.
3   Release the bulkhead grommet and pull the cable through into the engine compartment.
4   Release the cable from its retaining clips in the engine compartment.
5   At the rear of the transmission, withdraw the shaped wire clip securing the cable to the transmission through the engine mounting bracket. Withdraw the cable and remove it from the engine compartment (photo).
6   Refitting is the reverse sequence of removal, but ensure that the transmission retaining clip is located as shown in Fig. 11.13.

39.5 Removing the speedometer cable

Fig. 11.12 Trip computer sender unit fitted between the upper and lower speedometer cables (Sec 39)

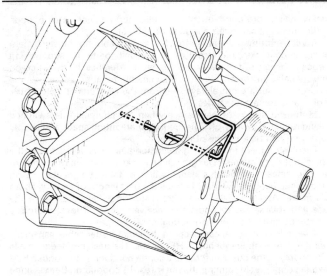

Fig. 11.13 Correct position of the speedometer cable retaining clip in the engine mounting bracket (Sec 39)

40 Engine oil level indicator – general

1   On models so equipped, a gauge is provided on the instrument panel to inform the driver of the level of oil in the sump.
2   The gauge is controlled by an electronic circuit located in the instrument panel which receives information from a sensor located in the sump. The sensor contains a high resistance wire whose thermal conductivity alters according to its depth of immersion in the oil.
3   If the engine develops a fault the following test can be carried out to isolate the component concerned.
4   Remove the sensor from the sump by disconnecting the two wires and unscrewing the unit from its mounting.
5   Using an ohmmeter, check the resistance across the sensor terminals. A reading on the ohmmeter should be shown. If not, the sensor is faulty and should be renewed.
6   If the sensor is satisfactory, remove the instrument panel, as

described in Section 17, and check the continuity of the wires from the sensor wiring connectors to the appropriate terminals in the instrument panel multi-plug. If there is no continuity, trace the wiring until the break or poor connection is found and make the necessary repair.
7   If the wiring is satisfactory the fault lies with the indicator gauge or the electronic circuit and these can only accurately be checked by substitution.
8   Refit any removed components using the reverse of the removal sequence.

41 Electro-mechanical door locks – general

1   A central door locking system may be fitted as standard equipment or optional according to model. The system enables all the doors to be locked or unlocked by locking or unlocking either of the front doors. When inside the car all the doors can be locked or unlocked by depressing the switch on the centre console.
2   A safety device consisting of an inertia switch and thermal cut-out automatically unlocks all the doors in the event of impact or heat build-up.
3   The system may also be operated by remote control using a small hand held infra-red transmitter. The transmitter signal is decoded by a receiver mounted on the roof console and this activates the electro-mechanical system to lock or unlock the doors.
4   The transmitter is powered by three 1.5 volt alkaline type batteries which have a life of approximately 12 months. The batteries can be renewed after undoing the transmitter case screw and opening the case to gain access.
5   In the event of a fault occurring in the system it is recommended that you seek the advice of a dealer as specialist knowledge and equipment are necessary for accurate fault diagnosis.

42 Radio – removal and refitting

1   Disconnect the battery negative terminal.
2   On some models it may be necessary to remove the centre console as described in Chapter 10.
3   Prise the radio from the centre console in order to release the retaining springs (photo).
4   Withdraw the radio and disconnect the aerial and wiring (photo).
5   Refitting is a reversal of removal.

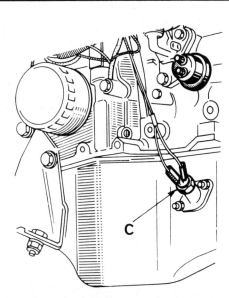

Fig. 11.14 Oil level sensor (C) located in the sump (Sec 40)

42.3 Removing the radio from the centre console

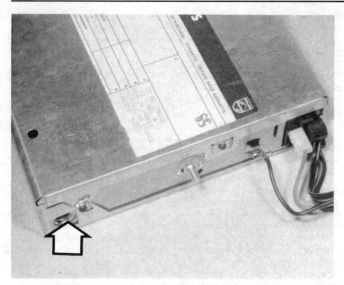

42.4 Showing radio wiring connections and aerial socket (arrowed)

43 Radio aerial and speakers – removal and refitting

1   To remove the aerial first remove the roof console. Remove the trim from the front door pillar and lower sill and pull back the carpet as necessary. With the radio removed tie string to the aerial then unscrew the mounting nut and withdraw the aerial and lead from the car. Refitting is a reversal of removal.
2   The speakers may be either mounted on the rear shelf or in the front doors. To remove the shelf type disconnect the wiring and remove the retaining screws, clips or nuts. To remove the door mounted type first remove the trim panel then drill out the rivets and disconnect the wiring (photo). Refitting is a reversal of removal using new rivets where necessary.

44 Mobile radio equipment – interference-free installation

Aerials – selection and fitting
   The choice of aerials is now very wide. It should be realised that the

quality has a profound effect on radio performance, and a poor, inefficient aerial can make suppression difficult.
   A wing-mounted aerial is regarded as probably the most efficient for signal collection, but a roof aerial is usually better for suppression purposes because it is away from most interference fields. Stick-on wire aerials are available for attachment to the inside of the windscreen, but are not always free from the interference field of the engine and some accessories.
   Motorised automatic aerials rise when the equipment is switched on and retract at switch-off. They require more fitting space and supply leads, and can be a source of trouble.
   There is no merit in choosing a very long aerial as, for example, the type about three metres in length which hooks or clips on to the rear of the car, since part of this aerial will inevitably be located in an interference field. For VHF/FM radios the best length of aerial is about one metre. Active aerials have a transistor amplifier mounted at the base and this serves to boost the received signal. The aerial rod is sometimes rather shorter than normal passive types.
   A large loss of signal can occur in the aerial feeder cable, especially over the Very High Frequency (VHF) bands. The design of feeder cable is invariably in the co-axial form, ie a centre conductor surrounded by a flexible copper braid forming the outer (earth) conductor. Between the inner and outer conductors is an insulator material which can be in solid or stranded form. Apart from insulation, its purpose is to maintain the correct spacing and concentricity. Loss of signal occurs in this insulator, the loss usually being greater in a poor quality cable. The quality of cable used is reflected in the price of the aerial with the attached feeder cable.
   The capacitance of the feeder should be within the range 65 to 75 picofarads (pF) approximately (95 to 100 pF for Japanese and American equipment), otherwise the adjustment of the car radio aerial trimmer may not be possible. An extension cable is necessary for a long run between aerial and receiver. If this adds capacitance in excess of the above limits, a connector containing a series capacitor will be required, or an extension which is labelled as 'capacity-compensated'.
   Fitting the aerial will normally involve making a $^7/_8$ in (22 mm) diameter hole in the bodywork, but read the instructions that come with the aerial kit. Once the hole position has been selected, use a centre punch to guide the drill. Use sticky masking tape around the area for this helps with marking out and drill location, and gives protection to the paintwork should the drill slip. Three methods of making the hole are in use:

(a)   Use a hole saw in the electric drill. This is, in effect, a circular hacksaw blade wrapped round a former with a centre pilot drill.
(b)   Use a tank cutter which also has cutting teeth, but is made to shear the metal by tightening with an Allen key.
(c)   The hard way of drilling out the circle is using a small drill, say $^1/_8$ in (3 mm), so that the holes overlap. The centre metal drops out and the hole is finished with round and half-round files.

   Whichever method is used, the burr is removed from the body metal and paint removed from the underside. The aerial is fitted tightly ensuring that the earth fixing, usually a serrated washer, ring or clamp, is making a solid connection. *This earth connection is important in reducing interference.* Cover any bare metal with primer paint and topcoat, and follow by underseal if desired.

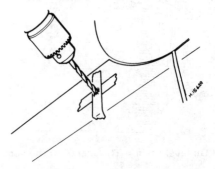

Fig. 11.15 Drilling the bodywork for aerial mounting (Sec 44)

43.2 The door mounted speaker is rivetted to the inner panel

Aerial feeder cable routing should avoid the engine compartment and areas where stress might occur, eg under the carpet where feet will be located. Roof aerials require that the headlining be pulled back and that a path is available down the door pillar. It is wise to check with the vehicle dealer whether roof aerial fitting is recommended.

Loudspeakers

Speakers should be matched to the output stage of the equipment, particularly as regards the recommended impedance. Power transistors used for driving speakers are sensitive to the loading placed on them.

Before choosing a mounting position for speakers, check whether the vehicle manufacturer has provided a location for them. Generally door-mounted speakers give good stereophonic reproduction, but not all doors are able to accept them. The next best position is the rear parcel shelf, and in this case speaker apertures can be cut into the shelf, or pod units may be mounted.

For door mounting, first remove the trim, which is often held on by 'poppers' or press studs, and then select a suitable gap in the inside door assembly. Check that the speaker would not obstruct glass or winder mechanism by winding the window up and down. A template is often provided for marking out the trim panel hole, and then the four fixing holes must be drilled through. Mark out with chalk and cut cleanly with a sharp knife or keyhole saw. Speaker leads are then threaded through the door and door pillar, if necessary drilling 10 mm diameter holes. Fit grommets in the holes and connect to the radio or tape unit correctly. Do not omit a waterproofing cover, usually supplied with door speakers. If the speaker has to be fixed into the metal of the door itself, use self-tapping screws, and if the fixing is to the door trim use self-tapping screws and flat spire nuts.

Rear shelf mounting is somewhat simpler but it is necessary to find gaps in the metalwork underneath the parcel shelf. However, remember that the speakers should be as far apart as possible to give a good stereo effect. Pod-mounted speakers can be screwed into position through the parcel shelf material, but it is worth testing for the best position. Sometimes good results are found by reflecting sound off the rear window.

Unit installation

Many vehicles have a dash panel aperture to take a radio/audio unit, a recognised international standard being 189.5 mm x 60 mm. Alternatively a console may be a feature of the car interior design and this, mounted below the dashboard, gives more room. If neither facility is available a unit may be mounted on the underside of the parcel shelf; these are frequently non-metallic and an earth wire from the case to a good earth point is necessary. A three-sided cover in the form of a cradle is obtainable from car radio dealers and this gives a professional appearance to the installation; in this case choose a position where the controls can be reached by a driver with his seat belt on.

Installation of the radio/audio unit is basically the same in all cases, and consists of offering it into the aperture after removal of the knobs (not push buttons) and the trim plate. In some cases a special mounting plate is required to which the unit is attached. It is worthwhile supporting the rear end in cases where sag or strain may occur, and it is usually possible to use a length of perforated metal strip attached between the unit and a good support point nearby. In general it is recommended that tape equipment should be installed at or nearly horizontal.

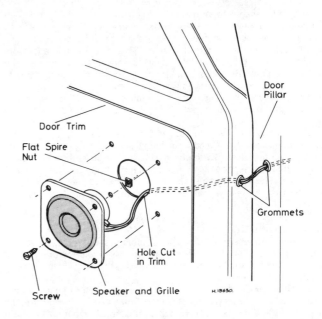

Fig. 11.16 Door-mounted speaker installation (Sec 44)

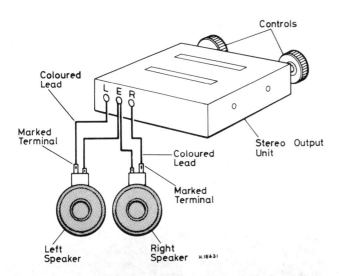

Fig. 11.17 Speaker connections must be correctly made as shown (Sec 44)

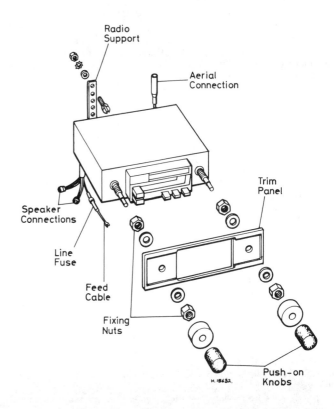

Fig. 11.18 Mounting component details for radio/cassette unit (Sec 44)

Connections to the aerial socket are simply by the standard plug terminating the aerial downlead or its extension cable. Speakers for a stereo system must be matched and correctly connected, as outlined previously.

Note: *While all work is carried out on the power side, it is wise to disconnect the battery earth lead.* Before connection is made to the vehicle electrical system, check that the polarity of the unit is correct. Most vehicles use a negative earth system, but radio/audio units often have a reversible plug to convert the set to either + or – earth. *Incorrect connection may cause serious damage.*

The power lead is often permanently connected inside the unit and terminates with one half of an in-line fuse carrier. The other half is fitted with a suitable fuse (3 or 5 amperes) and a wire which should go to a power point in the electrical system. This may be the accessory terminal on the ignition switch, giving the advantage of power feed with ignition or with the ignition key at the 'accessory' position. Power to the unit stops when the ignition key is removed. Alternatively, the lead may be taken to a live point at the fusebox with the consequence of having to remember to switch off at the unit before leaving the vehicle.

Before switching on for initial test, be sure that the speaker connections have been made, for running without load can damage the output transistors. Switch on next and tune through the bands to ensure that all sections are working, and check the tape unit if applicable. The aerial trimmer should be adjusted to give the strongest reception on a weak signal in the medium wave band, at say 200 metres.

Interference

In general, when electric current changes abruptly, unwanted electrical noise is produced. The motor vehicle is filled with electrical devices which change electric current rapidly, the most obvious being the contact breaker.

When the spark plugs operate, the sudden pulse of spark current causes the associated wiring to radiate. Since early radio transmitters used sparks as a basis of operation, it is not surprising that the car radio will pick up ignition spark noise unless steps are taken to reduce it to acceptable levels.

Interference reaches the car radio in two ways:

(a) by conduction through the wiring.
(b) by radiation to the receiving aerial.

Initial checks presuppose that the bonnet is down and fastened, the radio unit has a good earth connection (not through the aerial downlead outer), no fluorescent tubes are working near the car, the aerial trimmer has been adjusted, and the vehicle is in a position to receive radio signals, ie not in a metal-clad building.

Switch on the radio and tune it to the middle of the medium wave (MW) band off-station with the volume (gain) control set fairly high. Switch on the ignition (but do not start the engine) and wait to see if irregular clicks or hash noise occurs. Tapping the facia panel may also produce the effects. If so, this will be due to the voltage stabiliser, which is an on-off thermal switch to control instrument voltage. It is located usually on the back of the instrument panel, often attached to the speedometer. Correction is by attachment of a capacitor and, if still troublesome, chokes in the supply wires.

Switch on the engine and listen for interference on the MW band. Depending on the type of interference, the indications are as follows.

A harsh crackle that drops out abruptly at low engine speed or when the headlights are switched on is probably due to a voltage regulator.

A whine varying with engine speed is due to the dynamo or alternator. Try temporarily taking off the fan belt – if the noise goes this is confirmation.

Regular ticking or crackle that varies in rate with the engine speed is due to the ignition system. With this trouble in particular and others in general, check to see if the noise is entering the receiver from the wiring or by radiation. To do this, pull out the aerial plug, (preferably shorting out the input socket or connecting a 62 pF capacitor across it). If the noise disappears it is coming in through the aerial and is *radiation noise.* If the noise persists it is reaching the receiver through the wiring and is said to be *line-borne.*

Interference from wipers, washers, heater blowers, turn-indicators, stop lamps, etc is usually taken to the receiver by wiring, and simple treatment using capacitors and possibly chokes will solve the problem. Switch on each one in turn (wet the screen first for running wipers!)

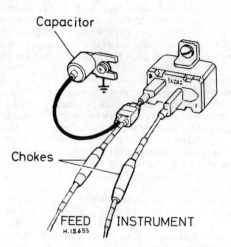

Fig. 11.19 Voltage stabiliser interference suppression (Sec 44)

and listen for possible interference with the aerial plug in place and again when removed.

Electric petrol pumps are now finding application again and give rise to an irregular clicking, often giving a burst of clicks when the ignition is on but the engine has not yet been started. It is also possible to receive whining or crackling from the pump.

Note that if most of the vehicle accessories are found to be creating interference all together, the probability is that poor aerial earthing is to blame.

Component terminal markings

Throughout the following sub-sections reference will be found to various terminal markings. These will vary depending on the manufacturer of the relevant component. If terminal markings differ from those mentioned, reference should be made to the following table, where the most commonly encountered variations are listed.

Alternator	*Alternator terminal (thick lead)*	*Exciting winding terminal*
DIN/Bosch	B+	DF
Delco Remy	+	EXC
Ducellier	+	EXC
Ford (US)	+	DF
Lucas	+	F
Marelli	+B	F

Ignition coil	*Ignition switch terminal*	*Contact breaker terminal*
DIN/Bosch	15	1
Delco Remy	+	–
Ducellier	BAT	RUP
Ford (US)	B/+	CB/–
Lucas	SW/+	–
Marelli	BAT/+B	D

Voltage regulator	*Voltage input terminal*	*Exciting winding terminal*
DIN/Bosch	B+/D+	DF
Delco Remy	BAT/+	EXC
Ducellier	BOB/BAT	EXC
Ford (US)	BAT	DF
Lucas	+/A	
Marelli		F

Suppression methods – ignition

Suppressed HT cables are supplied as original equipment by manufacturers and will meet regulations as far as interference to neighbouring equipment is concerned. It is illegal to remove such suppression unless an alternative is provided, and this may take the form of resistive spark plug caps in conjunction with plain copper HT cable. For VHF purposes, these and 'in-line' resistors may not be effective, and resistive HT cable is preferred. Check that suppressed cables are actually fitted by observing cable identity lettering, or measuring with an ohmmeter – the value of each plug lead should be 5000 to 10 000 ohms.

A 1 microfarad capacitor connected from the LT supply side of the ignition coil to a good nearby earth point will complete basic ignition interference treatment. *NEVER fit a capacitor to the coil terminal to the contact breaker – the result would be burnt out points in a short time.*

If ignition noise persists despite the treatment above, the following sequence should be followed:

(a) Check the earthing of the ignition coil; remove paint from fixing clamp.

(b) If this does not work, lift the bonnet. Should there be no change in interference level, this may indicate that the bonnet is not electrically connected to the car body. Use a proprietary braided strap across a bonnet hinge ensuring a first class electrical connection. If, however, lifting the bonnet increases the interference, then fit resistive HT cables of a higher ohms-per-metre value.

(c) If all these measures fail, it is probable that re-radiation from metallic components is taking place. Using a braided strap between metallic points, go round the vehicle systematically – try the following: engine to body, exhaust system to body, front suspension to engine and to body, steering column to body (especially French and Italian cars), gear lever to engine and to body (again especially French and Italian cars), Bowden cable to body, metal parcel shelf to body. When an offending component is located it should be bonded with the strap permanently.

(d) As a next step, the fitting of distributor suppressors to each lead at the distributor end may help.

(e) Beyond this point is involved the possible screening of the distributor and fitting resistive spark plugs, but such advanced treatment is not usually required for vehicles with entertainment equipment.

Electronic ignition systems have built-in suppression components, but this does not relieve the need for using suppressed HT leads. In some cases it is permitted to connect a capacitor on the low tension supply side of the ignition coil, but not in every case. Makers' instructions should be followed carefully, otherwise damage to the ignition semiconductors may result.

Suppression methods – generators

For older vehicles with dynamos a 1 microfarad capacitor from the D (larger) terminal to earth will usually cure dynamo whine. Alternators should be fitted with a 3 microfarad capacitor from the B + main output terminal (thick cable) to earth. Additional suppression may be obtained by the use of a filter in the supply line to the radio receiver.

It is most important that:

(a) *Capacitors are never connected to the field terminals of either a dynamo or alternator.*

(b) *Alternators must not be run without connection to the battery.*

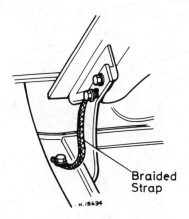

Fig. 11.20 Braided earth strap between bonnet and body (Sec 44)

Suppression methods – voltage regulators

Voltage regulators used with DC dynamos should be suppressed by connecting a 1 microfarad capacitor from the control box D terminal to earth.

Alternator regulators come in three types:

(a) *Vibrating contact regulators separate from the alternator. Used extensively on continental vehicles.*

(b) *Electronic regulators separate from the alternator.*

(c) *Electronic regulators built-in to the alternator.*

In case (a) interference may be generated on the AM and FM (VHF) bands. For some cars a replacement suppressed regulator is available. Filter boxes may be used with non-suppressed regulators. But if not available, then for AM equipment a 2 microfarad or 3 microfarad capacitor may be mounted at the voltage terminal marked D+ or B+ of the regulator. FM bands may be treated by a feed-through capacitor of 2 or 3 microfarad.

Electronic voltage regulators are not always troublesome, but where necessary, a 1 microfarad capacitor from the regulator + terminal will help.

Integral electronic voltage regulators do not normally generate much interference, but when encountered this is in combination with alternator noise. A 1 microfarad or 2 microfarad capacitor from the warning lamp (IND) terminal to earth for Lucas ACR alternators and Femsa, Delco and Bosch equivalents should cure the problem.

Suppression methods – other equipment

Wiper motors – Connect the wiper body to earth with a bonding strap. For all motors use a 7 ampere choke assembly inserted in the leads to the motor.

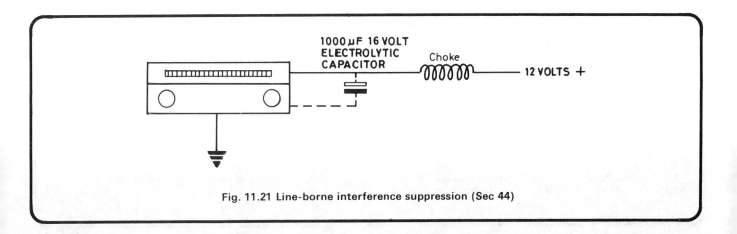

Fig. 11.21 Line-borne interference suppression (Sec 44)

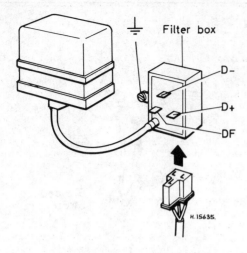

Fig. 11.22 Typical filter box for vibrating contact voltage regulator (alternator equipment) (Sec 44)

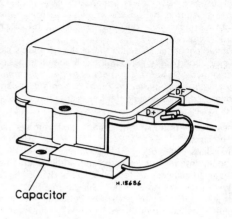

Fig. 11.23 Suppression of AM interference by vibrating contact voltage regulator (alternator equipment) (Sec 44)

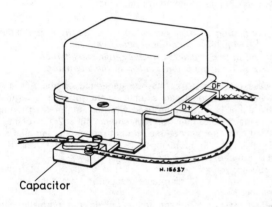

Fig. 11.24 Suppression of FM interference by vibrating contact voltage regulator (alternator equipment) (Sec 44)

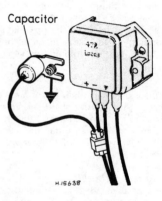

Fig. 11.25 Electronic voltage regulator suppression (Sec 44)

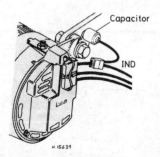

Fig. 11.26 Suppression of interference from electronic voltage regulator when integral with alternator (Sec 44)

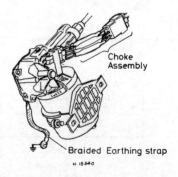

Fig. 11.27 Wiper motor suppression (Sec 44)

Heater motors – Fit 7 ampere line chokes in both leads, assisted if necessary by a 1 microfarad capacitor to earth from both leads.

Electronic tachometer – The tachometer is a possible source of ignition noise – check by disconnecting at the ignition coil CB terminal. It usually feeds from ignition coil LT pulses at the contact breaker terminal. A 3 ampere line choke should be fitted in the tachometer lead at the coil CB terminal.

Horn – A capacitor and choke combination is effective if the horn is directly connected to the 12 volt supply. The use of a relay is an alternative remedy, as this will reduce the length of the interference-carrying leads.

Electrostatic noise – Characteristics are erratic crackling at the receiver, with disappearance of symptoms in wet weather. Often shocks may be given when touching bodywork. Part of the problem is the build-up of static electricity in non-driven wheels and the acquisition of charge on the body shell. It is possible to fit spring-loaded contacts at the wheels to give good conduction between the rotary wheel parts and the vehicle frame. Changing a tyre sometimes helps – because of tyres' varying resistances. In difficult cases a trailing flex which touches the ground will cure the problem. If this is not acceptable it is worth trying conductive paint on the tyre walls.

Fuel pump – Suppression requires a 1 microfarad capacitor

between the supply wire to the pump and a nearby earth point. If this is insufficient a 7 ampere line choke connected in the supply wire near the pump is required.

Fluorescent tubes – Vehicles used for camping/caravanning frequently have fluorescent tube lighting. These tubes require a relatively high voltage for operation and this is provided by an inverter (a form of oscillator) which steps up the vehicle supply voltage. This can give rise to serious interference to radio reception, and the tubes themselves can contribute to this interference by the pulsating nature of the lamp discharge. In such situations it is important to mount the aerial as far away from a fluorescent tube as possible. The interference problem may be alleviated by screening the tube with fine wire turns spaced an inch (25 mm) apart and earthed to the chassis. Suitable chokes should be fitted in both supply wires close to the inverter.

Radio/cassette case breakthrough

Magnetic radiation from dashboard wiring may be sufficiently intense to break through the metal case of the radio/cassette player. Often this is due to a particular cable routed too close and shows up as ignition interference on AM and cassette play and/or alternator whine on cassette play.

The first point to check is that the clips and/or screws are fixing all parts of the radio/cassette case together properly. Assuming good

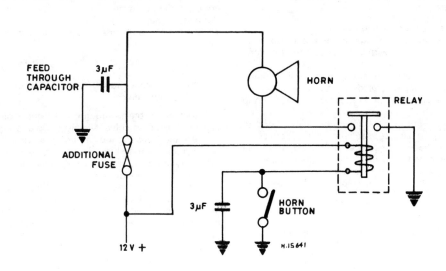

Fig. 11.28 Use of relay to reduce horn interference (Sec 44)

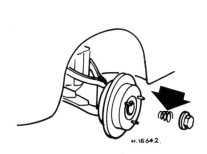

Fig. 11.29 Use of spring contacts at wheels (Sec 44)

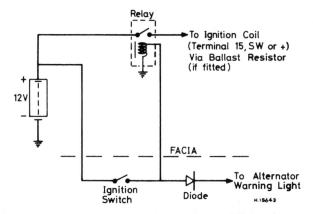

Fig. 11.30 Use of ignition coil relay to suppress case breakthrough (Sec 44)

earthing of the case, see if it is possible to re-route the offending cable – the chances of this are not good, however, in most cars.

Next release the radio/cassette player and locate it in different positions with temporary leads. If a point of low interference is found, then if possible fix the equipment in that area. This also confirms that local radiation is causing the trouble. If re-location is not feasible, fit the radio/cassette player back in the original position.

Alternator interference on cassette play is now caused by radiation from the main charging cable which goes from the battery to the output terminal of the alternator, usually via the + terminal of the starter motor relay. In some vehicles this cable is routed under the dashboard, so the solution is to provide a direct cable route. Detach the original cable from the alternator output terminal and make up a new cable of at least 6 mm² cross-sectional area to go from alternator to battery with the shortest possible route. *Remember – do not run the engine with the alternator disconnected from the battery.*

Ignition breakthrough on AM and/or cassette play can be a difficult problem. It is worth wrapping earthed foil round the offending cable run near the equipment, or making up a deflector plate well screwed down to a good earth. Another possibility is the use of a suitable relay to switch on the ignition coil. The relay should be mounted close to the ignition coil; with this arrangement the ignition coil primary current is not taken into the dashboard area and does not flow through the ignition switch. A suitable diode should be used since it is possible that at ignition switch-off the output from the warning lamp alternator terminal could hold the relay on.

Connectors for suppression components

Capacitors are usually supplied with tags on the end of the lead, while the capacitor body has a flange with a slot or hole to fit under a nut or screw with washer.

Connections to feed wires are best achieved by self-stripping connectors. These connectors employ a blade which, when squeezed down by pliers, cuts through cable insulation and makes connection to the copper conductors beneath.

Chokes sometimes come with bullet snap-in connectors fitted to the wires, and also with just bare copper wire. With connectors, suitable female cable connectors may be purchased from an auto-accessory shop together with any extra connectors required for the cable ends after being cut for the choke insertion. For chokes with bare wires, similar connectors may be employed together with insulation sleeving as required.

VHF/FM broadcasts

Reception of VHF/FM in an automobile is more prone to problems than the medium and long wavebands. Medium/long wave transmitters are capable of covering considerable distances, but VHF transmitters are restricted to line of sight, meaning ranges of 10 to 50 miles, depending upon the terrain, the effects of buildings and the transmitter power.

Because of the limited range it is necessary to retune on a long journey, and it may be better for those habitually travelling long distances or living in areas of poor provision of transmitters to use an AM radio working on medium/long wavebands.

When conditions are poor, interference can arise, and some of the suppression devices described previously fall off in performance at very high frequencies unless specifically designed for the VHF band. Available suppression devices include reactive HT cable, resistive distributor caps, screened plug caps, screened leads and resistive spark plugs.

For VHF/FM receiver installation the following points should be particularly noted:

(a) Earthing of the receiver chassis and the aerial mounting is important. Use a separate earthing wire at the radio, and scrape paint away at the aerial mounting.

(b) If possible, use a good quality roof aerial to obtain maximum height and distance from interference generating devices on the vehicle.

(c) Use of a high quality aerial downlead is important, since losses in cheap cable can be significant.

(d) The polarisation of FM transmissions may be horizontal, vertical, circular or slanted. Because of this the optimum mounting angle is at 45° to the vehicle roof.

Citizens' Band radio (CB)

In the UK, CB transmitter/receivers work within the 27 MHz and

934 MHz bands, using the FM mode. At present interest is concentrated on 27 MHz where the design and manufacture of equipment is less difficult. Maximum transmitted power is 4 watts, and 40 channels spaced 10 kHz apart within the range 27.60125 to 27.99125 MHz are available.

Aerials are the key to effective transmission and reception. Regulations limit the aerial length to 1.65 metres including the loading coil and any associated circuitry, so tuning the aerial is necessary to obtain optimum results. The choice of a CB aerial is dependent on whether it is to be permanently installed or removable, and the performance will hinge on correct tuning and the location point on the vehicle. Common practice is to clip the aerial to the roof gutter or to employ wing mounting where the aerial can be rapidly unscrewed. An alternative is to use the boot rim to render the aerial theftproof, but a popular solution is to use the 'magmount' – a type of mounting having a strong magnetic base clamping to the vehicle at any point, usually the roof.

Aerial location determines the signal distribution for both transmission and reception, but it is wise to choose a point away from the engine compartment to minimise interference from vehicle electrical equipment.

The aerial is subject to considerable wind and acceleration forces. Cheaper units will whip backwards and forwards and in so doing will alter the relationship with the metal surface of the vehicle with which it forms a ground plane aerial system. The radiation pattern will change correspondingly, giving rise to break-up of both incoming and outgoing signals.

Interference problems on the vehicle carrying CB equipment fall into two categories:

(a) Interference to nearby TV and radio receivers when transmitting.

(b) Interference to CB set reception due to electrical equipment on the vehicle.

Problems of break-through to TV and radio are not frequent, but can be difficult to solve. Mostly trouble is not detected or reported because the vehicle is moving and the symptoms rapidly disappear at the TV/radio receiver, but when the CB set is used as a base station any trouble with nearby receivers will soon result in a complaint.

It must not be assumed by the CB operator that his equipment is faultless, for much depends upon the design. Harmonics (that is, multiples) of 27 MHz may be transmitted unknowingly and these can fall into other user's bands. Where trouble of this nature occurs, low pass filters in the aerial or supply leads can help, and should be fitted in base station aerials as a matter of course. In stubborn cases it may be necessary to call for assistance from the licensing authority, or, if possible, to have the equipment checked by the manufacturers.

Interference received on the CB set from the vehicle equipment is, fortunately, not usually a severe problem. The precautions outlined previously for radio/cassette units apply, but there are some extra points worth noting.

It is common practice to use a slide-mount on CB equipment enabling the set to be easily removed for use as a base station, for example. Care must be taken that the slide mount fittings are properly earthed and that first class connection occurs between the set and slide-mount.

Vehicle manufacturers in the UK are required to provide suppression of electrical equipment to cover 40 to 250 MHz to protect TV and VHF radio bands. Such suppression appears to be adequately effective at 27 MHz, but suppression of individual items such as alternators/ dynamos, clocks, stabilisers, flashers, wiper motors, etc, may still be necessary. The suppression capacitors and chokes available from auto-electrical suppliers for entertainment receivers will usually give the required results with CB equipment.

Other vehicle radio transmitters

Besides CB radio already mentioned, a considerable increase in the use of transceivers (ie combined transmitter and receiver units) has taken place in the last decade. Previously this type of equipment was fitted mainly to military, fire, ambulance and police vehicles, but a large business radio and radio telephone usage has developed.

Generally the suppression techniques described previously will suffice, with only a few difficult cases arising. Suppression is carried out to satisfy the 'receive mode', but care must be taken to use heavy duty chokes in the equipment supply cables since the loading on 'transmit' is relatively high.

45 Fault diagnosis – electrical system

Symptom	Reason(s)
Starter fails to turn engine	Battery discharged or defective Battery terminal and/or earth leads loose Starter motor connections loose Starter solenoid faulty Starter brushes worn or sticking Starter commutator dirty or worn Starter field coils earthed
Starter turns engine very slowly	Battery discharged Starter motor connections loose Starter brushes worn or sticking
Starter noisy	Pinion or flywheel ring gear teeth badly worn Mounting bolts loose
Battery will not hold charge for more than a few days	Battery defective internally Battery terminals loose Alternator drivebelt slipping Alternator or regulator faulty Short circuit
Ignition light stays on	Alternator faulty Alternator drivebelt broken
Ignition light fails to come on	Warning bulb blown Indicator light open circuit Alternator faulty
Fuel or temperature gauge gives no reading	Wiring open circuit Sender unit faulty
Fuel or temperature gauge give maximum reading all the time	Wiring short circuit Gauge faulty
Lights inoperative	Bulb blown Fuses blown Battery discharged Switch faulty Wiring open circuit Bad connection due to corrosion
Failure of component motor	Commutator dirty or burnt Armature faulty Brushes sticking or worn Armature bearings dry or misaligned Field coils faulty Fuse blown Wiring loose or broken
Failure of an individual component	Wiring loose or broken Fuse blown Bad circuit connection Switch faulty Component faulty

	TC – TL – TS	TC – TL – TS with rear screen wiper	GTL – GTS	GTS with infra red receiver	TSE	TSE with car borne computer	Turbo
AEI ignition	11	12	11	12	17	17	20
Assisted ignition	13	15	13	15	–	–	–
Battery charge indicator	5	10	11	15	22	22	22
Brake pad wear warning light	5	8	6	9	7	7	7
Cigar lighter	8	8	13	9	18	18	18
Clock	1	1	1	12	17	17	17
Cooling fan motor	8	8	8	8	17	17	22
Direction indicator lights	1	1	2	2	3	3	21
Door locks	–	–	–	14	16	16	16
External temperature sensor	–	–	–	12	–	17	20
Feed to car radio	5	5	5	5	16	16	16
Flowmeter	–	–	–	12	–	17	20
Front foglight	–	–	–	19	19	19	19
Fuel gauge	5	8	11	12	18	17	20
Glovebox illumination	–	–	–	–	18	18	18
Handbrake	5	8	6	9	7	7	7
Hazard warning lights	1	1	2	2	3	3	21
Headlight main beam	1	1	2	2	3	3	3
Headlight dipped beam	1	1	2	2	3	3	3
Headlight wiper/washer	–	–	–	4	–	19	19
Heating	10	10	10	10	18	18	18
Horn	3	3	3	3	3	3	19
Identification plate lights + switches	10	10	13	13	18	18	18
Interior lights	10	10	10	14	16	16	16
Lights 'on' buzzer	–	–	–	–	21	21	21
Luggage compartment light	–	–	–	–	21	21	–
Minimium coolant level indicator	–	–	–	–	22	22	22
Minimum fuel level indicator	–	–	–	12	–	17	20
Minimum windscreen washer fluid level	–	–	–	–	7	7	7
Nivocode	5	8	6	9	7	7	7
Oil level probe	–	–	11	12	17	17	22
Oil pressure switch (minimum level and pressure)	5	8	11	15	17	17	22
Rear foglight	–	8	–	15	21	–	21
Rear screen defroster	1	1	6	9	7	7	7
Rear screen wiper/washer	–	6	6	9	7	7	7
Registration plate light	1	1	2	2	3	3	3
Reversing lights	–	8	8	15	22	22	21
Revolution counter	–	–	11	12	17	17	20
Sidelights	1	1	2	2	3	3	21
Speed sensor	–	–	–	12	–	17	20
Standard ignition	10	14	–	–	–	–	–
Start flap	5	10	6	9	22	22	22
Starter	5	10	11	15	22	22	22
Stop-lights	5	8	8	15	22	22	21
Temperature switch	5	10	6	9	22	22	22
Trip computer	–	–	–	12	–	17	20
Window winder	–	–	–	14	16	16	16
Windscreen wiper/washer	6	6	6	9	7	7	7

Key to wiring diagram circuits

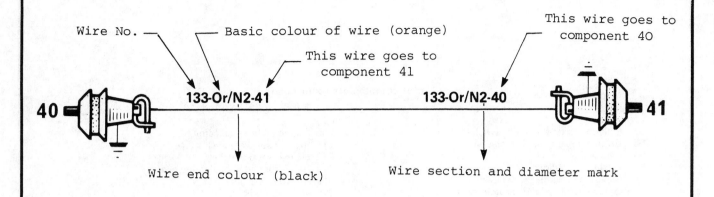

Fig. 11.31 Wire identification diagram

Wire colours

B	Blue	C	Clear	M	Brown	R	Red
Bc	White	G	Grey	N	Black	S	Salmon pink
Be	Beige	J	Yellow	Or	Orange	V	Green
						Vi	Voilet

Wire diameters

No	mm	No	mm	No	mm	No	mm
1	0.7	4	1.2 and 1.4	7	2.5	10	5.0
2	0.9	5	1.6	8	3.0	11	7.0
3	1.0	6	2.0	9	4.5	12	8.0

List of components

1	LH sidelight and/or direction indicator	27	Nivocode or ICP (pressure drop indicator)
2	RH sidelight and/or direction indicator	28	Heating-ventilating fan motor
7	LH headlight	29	Instrument panel
8	RH headlight	30	Connector No.1 – instrument panel
9	LH horn	31	Connector No.2 – instrument panel
10	RH horn	32	Connector No.3 – instrument panel
12	Alternator	33	Connector No.4 – instrument panel
13	LH front earth	34	Hazard warning lights switch
14	RH front earth	35	Rear screen demister switch
15	Starter	36	Heating fan resistances or rheostat
16	Battery	37	LH window switch
17	Engine cooling fan motor	38	RH window switch
18	Ignition coil (or mounting)	40	LH front door pillar switch
19	Distributor	41	RH front door pillar switch
20	Windscreen washer pump	42	LH window motor
21	Oil pressure switch	43	RH window motor
22	No. 1 thermal switch on radiator	45	Junction block – front harness – accessories plate
24	LH front brake	46	Junction block – front harness – accessories plate
25	RH front brake	47	Junction block – front harness – accessories plate
26	Windscreen wiper motor	52	Stoplights switch

List of components (continued)

53 Ignition-starter-anti-theft switch	209 Engine oil level indicator
55 Glove compartment illumination	211 RH rear speaker panel
56 Cigar lighter	212 LH rear speaker panel
57 Feed to car radio	214 No. 1 front additional lights relay
58 Windscreen washer/wiper switch	215 RH front foglight
59 Lights and direction indicators switch	216 LH front foglight
60 Direction indicators switch or connector	220 Junction block – ventilation compartment, harness
61 Before ignition terminal	230 Ignition starter box
64 Handbrake switch	231 Junction block – tailgate harness
65 Fuel gauge tank unit	239 No. 2 petrol pump
66 Rear screen demister	241 Horn compressor
67 Luggage compartment illumination	247 Junction block – additional lights switch harness
68 LH rear light assembly	273 Flowmeter
69 RH rear light assembly	274 Wire joint No. 1
70 Licence plate lights	276 Engine earth
71 Choke "On" warning light switch	286 Wire joint No. 2
72 Reversing lights switch	289 Wire joint No. 3
73 Rear light assembly earth	290 Wire joint No. 4
74 Flasher unit	296 Horn compressor relay
75 Heating fan switch	306 Unlocking remote control
76 Instrument panel lighting rheostat	308 No. 2 junction – rear harness
77 Diagnostic socket	319 Ignition cut-out relay
78 Rear screen wiper motor	321 AEI module
79 Rear screen washer pump	340 "Driving aid" computer
80 Junction block – front and engine harnesses	341 External temperature sensor
81 Junction block No. 1 – rear harness	342 Headlight washer solenoid valve
83 Junction block – heating wiring harness	386 Antipercolation motor fan
86 Lights reminder relay	409 Junction block – registration plate light harnesses
97 Bodyshell earth	422 Junction No. 3 – door locking/unlocking harnesses
99 Dashboard earth	423 Junction No. 4 – door locking/unlocking harnesses
106 Rear foglight switch	432 Junction RH front and dashboard harnesses
109 Speed sensor	433 Junction LH front and dashboard harnesses
110 Engine cooling fan motor relay	438 Wire joint No. 5
114 Windscreen wiper timer relay	439 Wire joint No. 6
123 Clock	440 Wire joint No. 7
129 Front foglight switch	441 Wire joint No. 8
135 LH front door lock solenoid	447 Coolant level detector
136 RH front door lock solenoid	454 Junction – headlight wiper harness
139 Centre front interior light	460 Wire joint No. 9
144 Junction block – interior lights harness	461 Wire joint No. 10
146 Temperature or thermal switch	462 Door locking timer relay
150 LH front speaker	464 Wire joint No. 11
151 RH front speaker	467 Wire joint No. 12
152 Electro-magnetic locks central switch	476 Windscreen washer fluid level detector
164 Electric petrol pump	484 Wire joint No. 13
171 Rear screen wiper/washer switch	487 Wire joint No. 14
172 Impulse generator	493 Petrol pump relay
174 RH headlight wiper motor	494 Wire joint No. 15
175 LH headlight wiper motor	518 RH front pillar earth
176 Headlight wipers timer relay	521 Antipercolation relay
184 Luggage compartment light switch	560 Antipercolation sensor
185 Glove compartment light switch	
187 Speedo drive relay (petrol pump)	

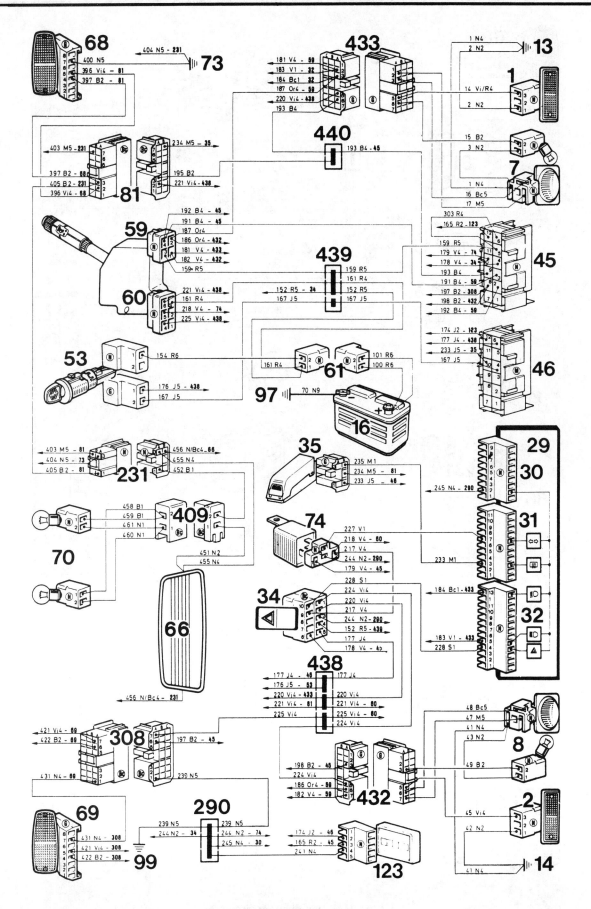

Fig. 11.32 Wiring diagram circuit 1

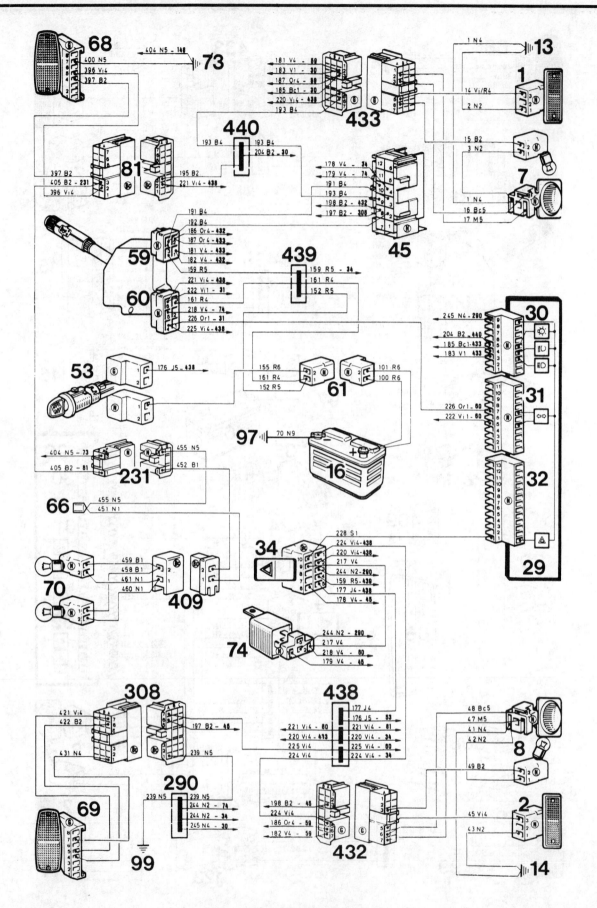

Fig. 11.32 Wiring diagram circuit 2

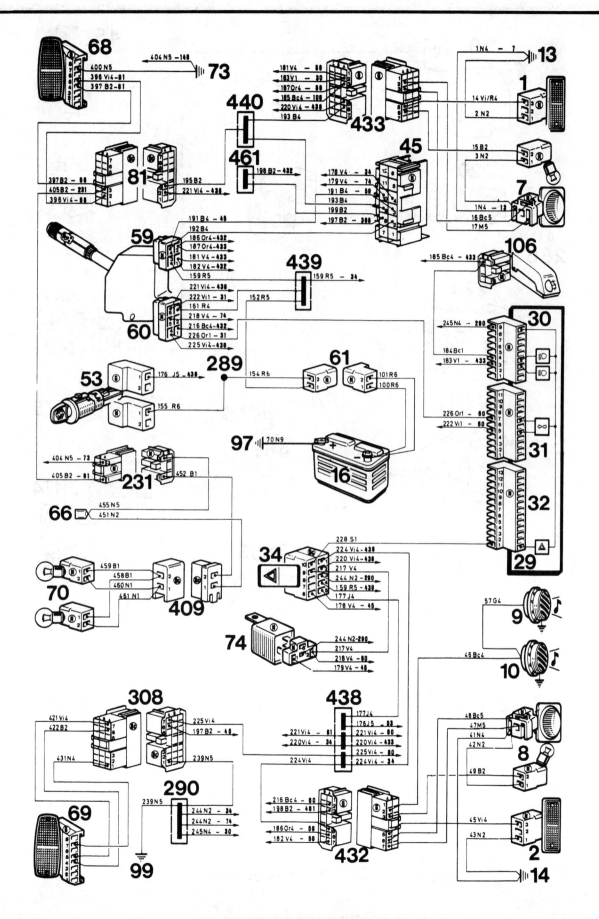

Fig. 11.32 Wiring diagram circuit 3

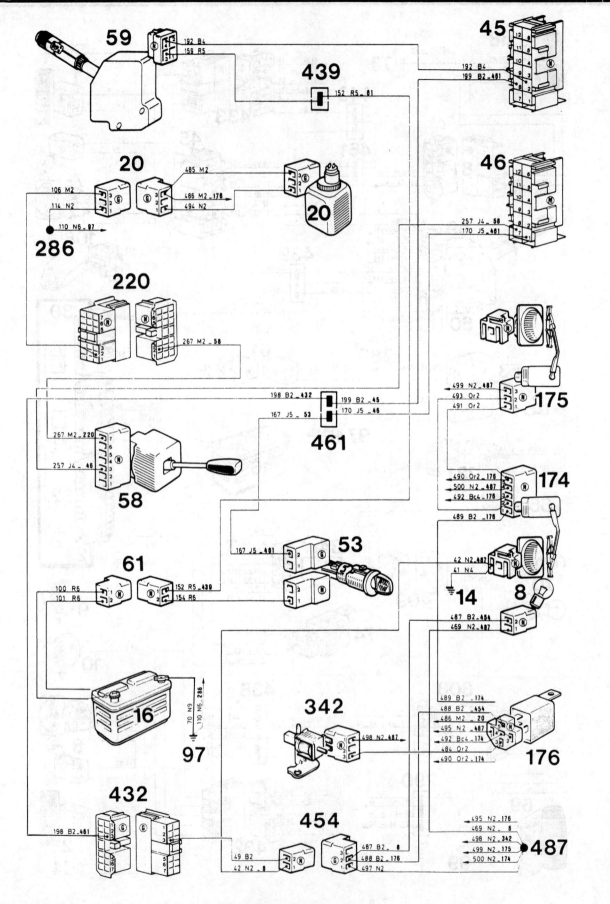

Fig. 11.32 Wiring diagram circuit 4

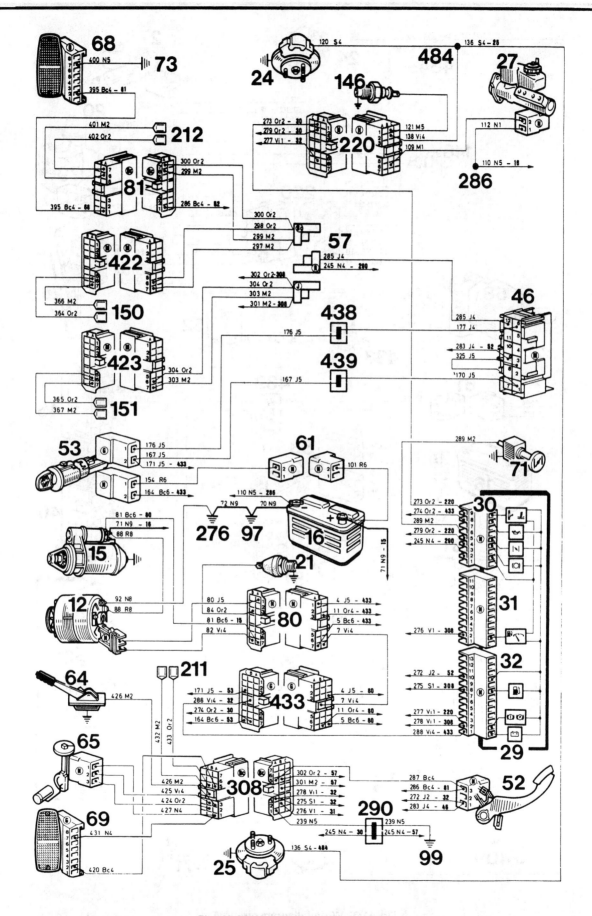

Fig. 11.32 Wiring diagram circuit 5

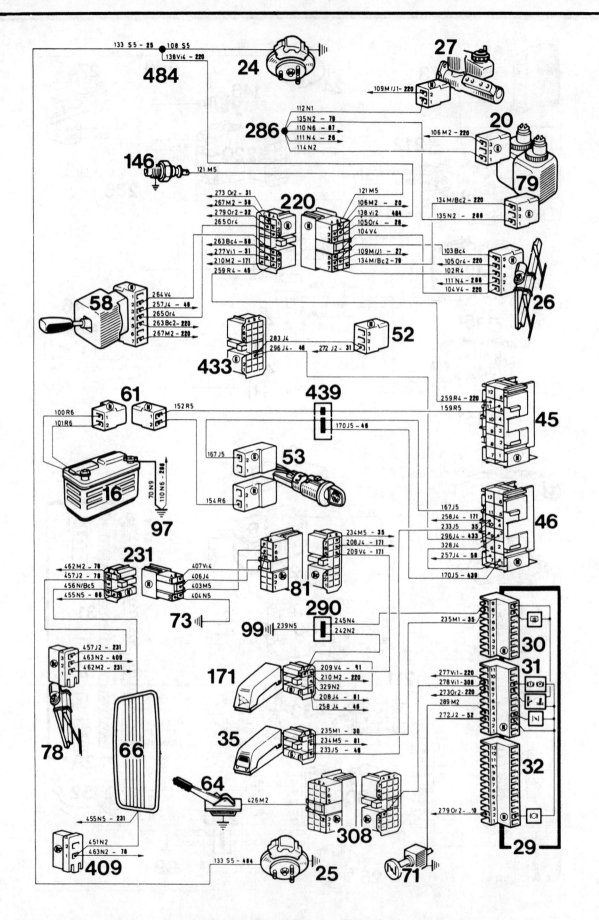

Fig. 11.32 Wiring diagram circuit 6

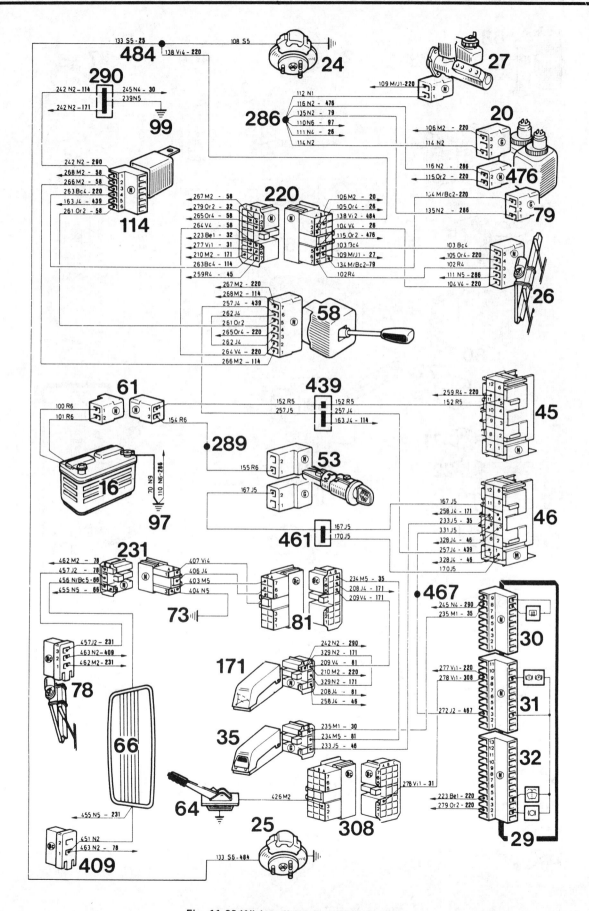

Fig. 11.32 Wiring diagram circuit 7

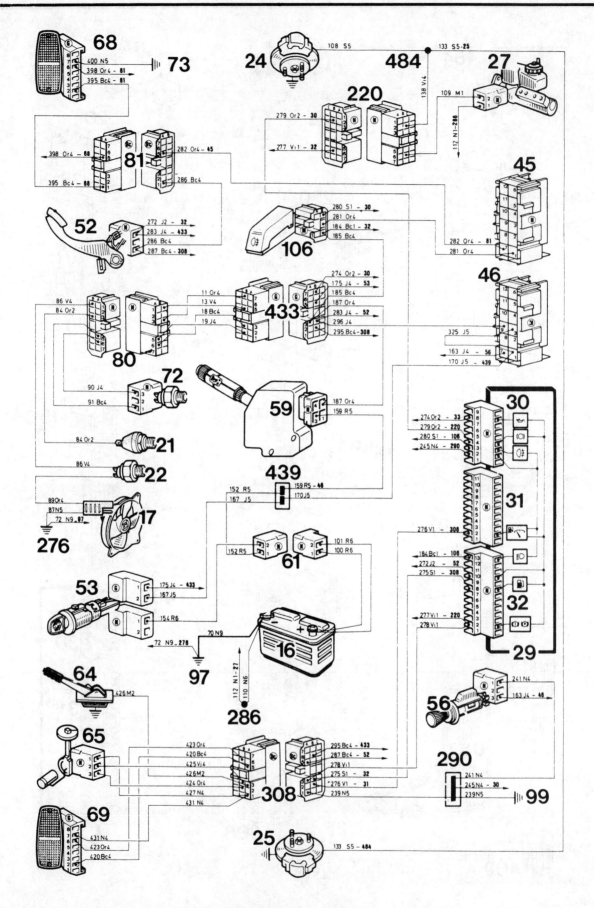

Fig. 11.32 Wiring diagram circuit 8

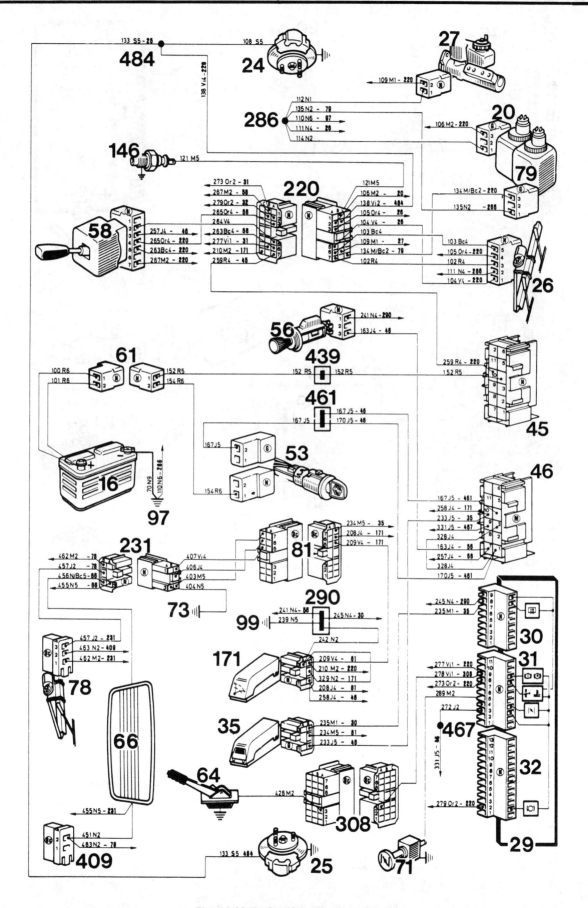

Fig. 11.32 Wiring diagram circuit 9

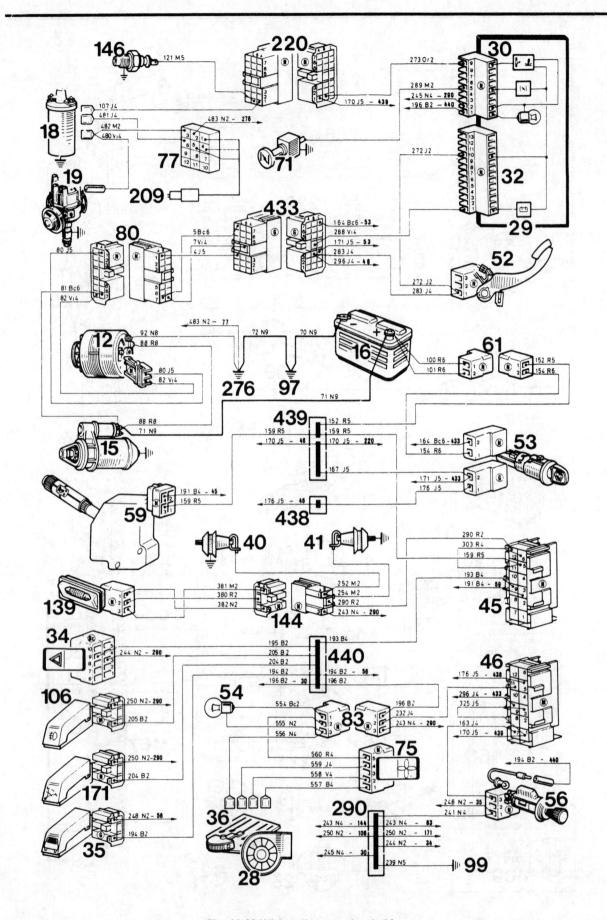

Fig. 11.32 Wiring diagram circuit 10

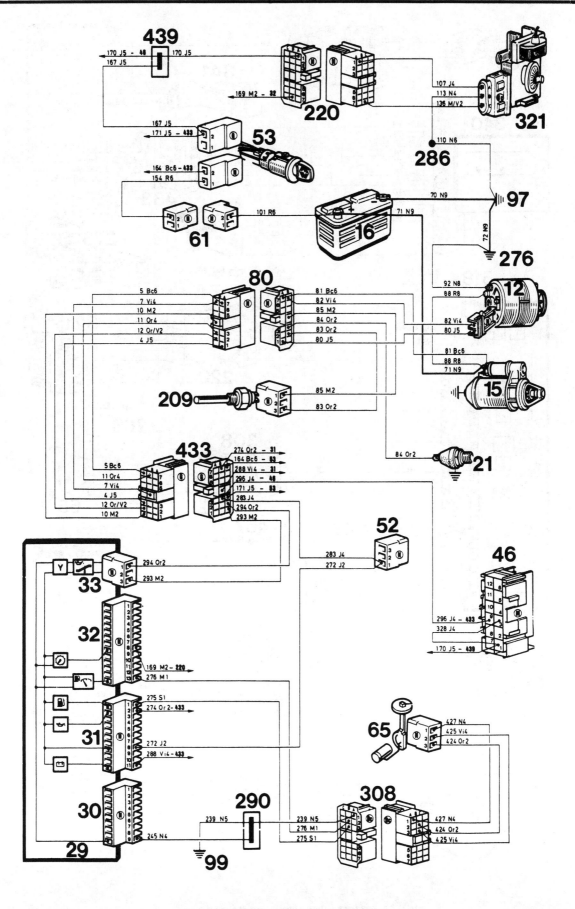

Fig. 11.32 Wiring diagram circuit 11

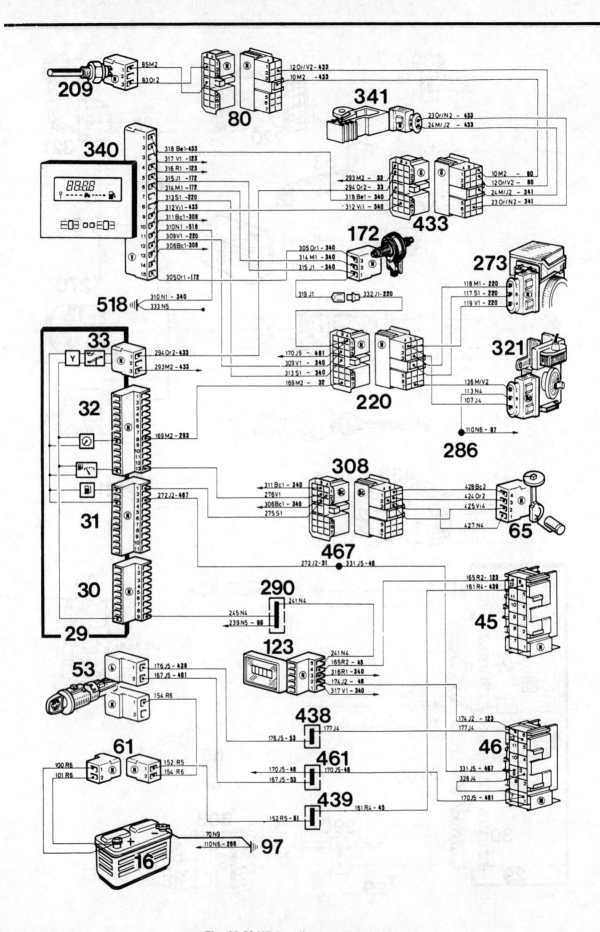

Fig. 11.32 Wiring diagram circuit 12

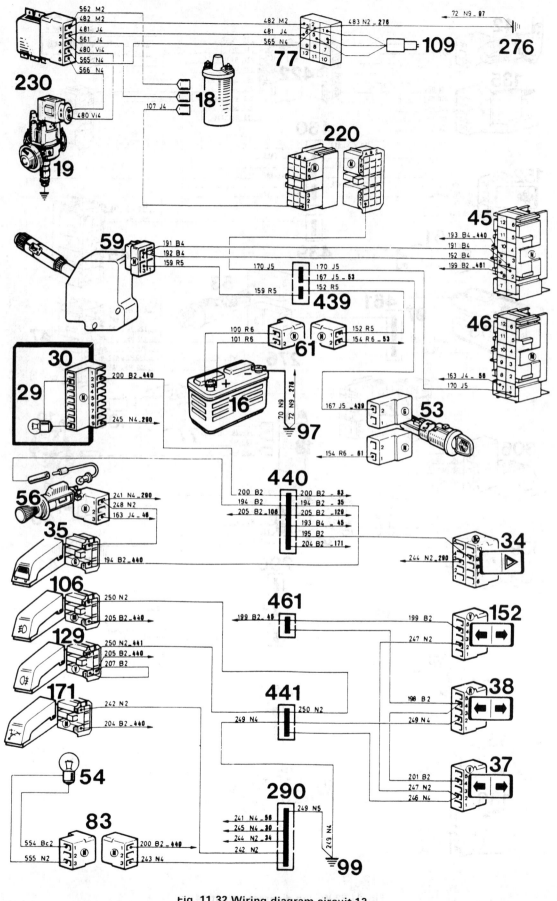

Fig. 11.32 Wiring diagram circuit 13

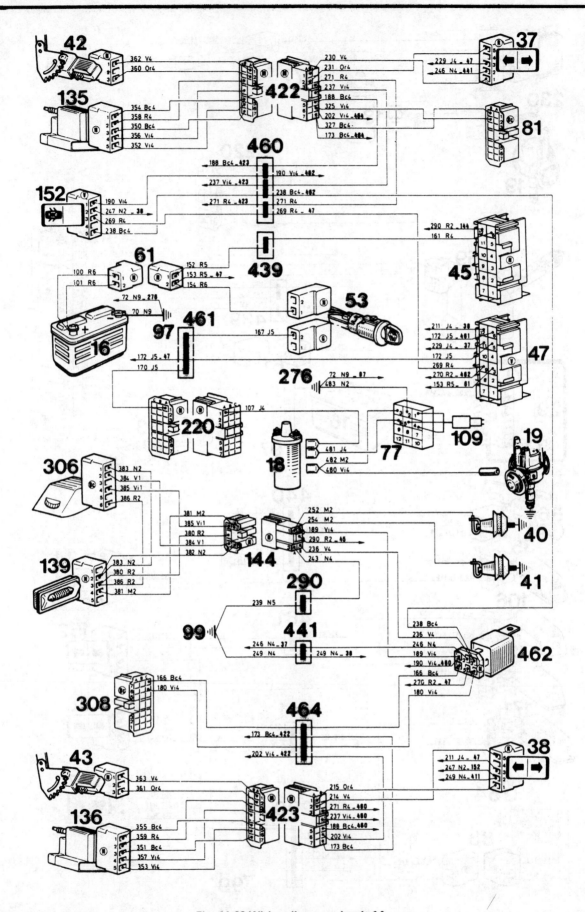

Fig. 11.32 Wiring diagram circuit 14

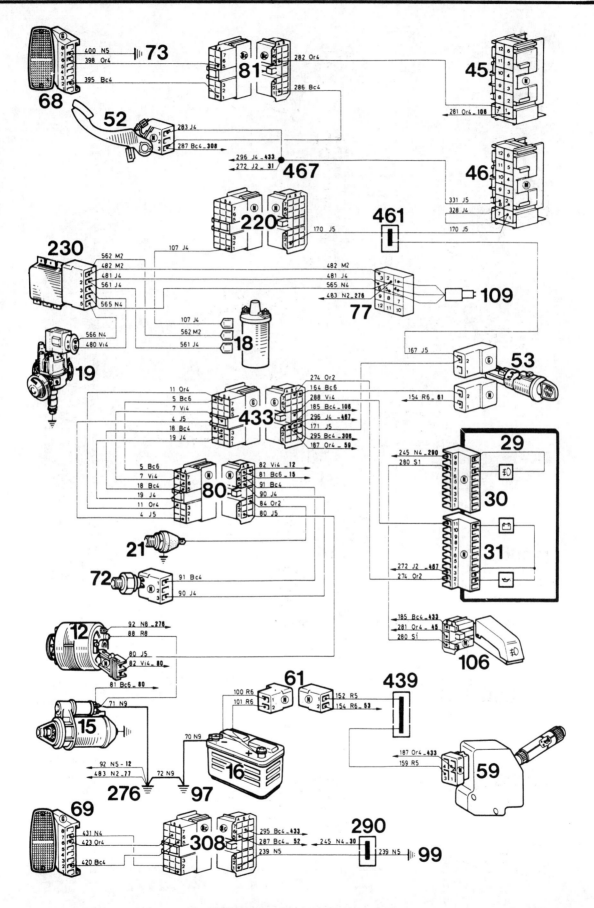

Fig. 11.32 Wiring diagram circuit 15

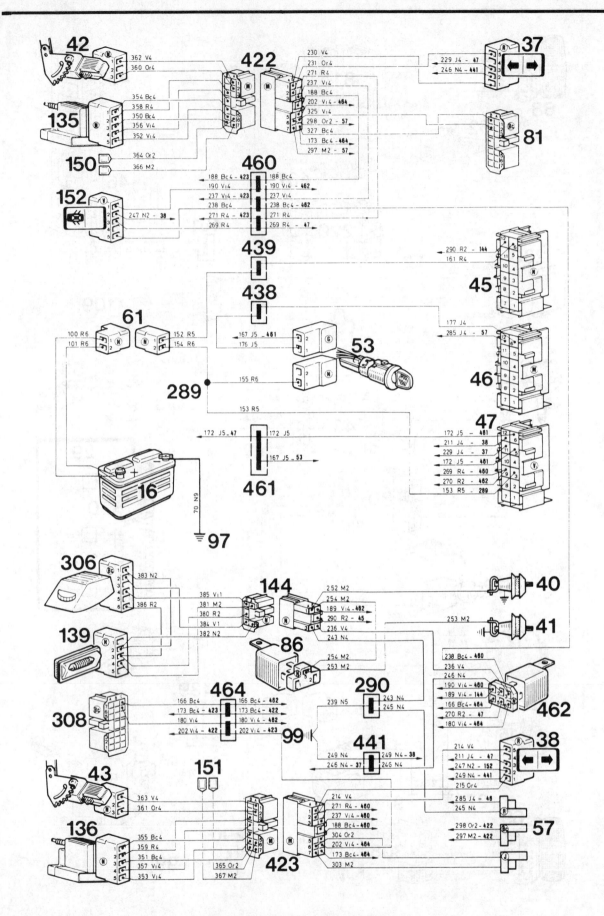

Fig. 11.32 Wiring diagram circuit 16

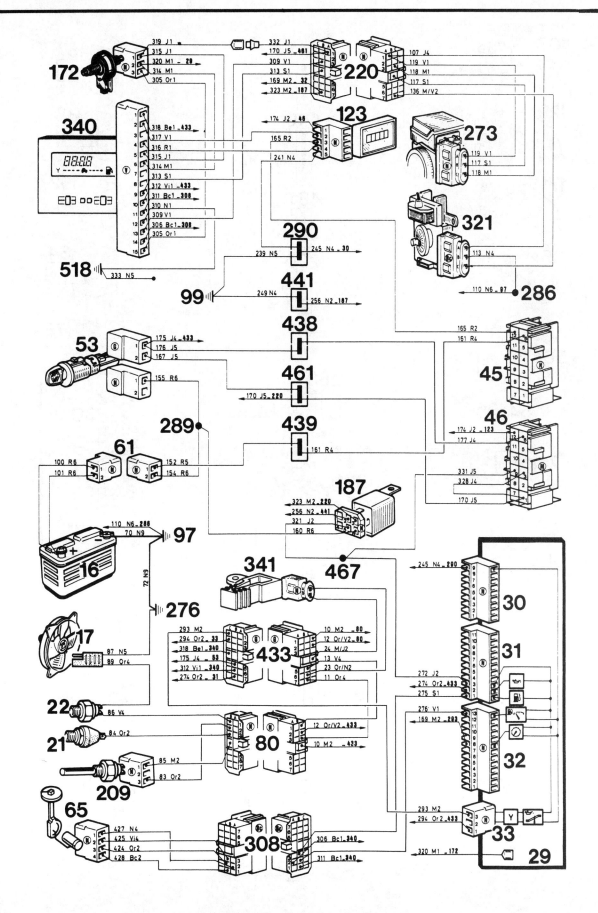

Fig. 11.32 Wiring diagram circuit 17

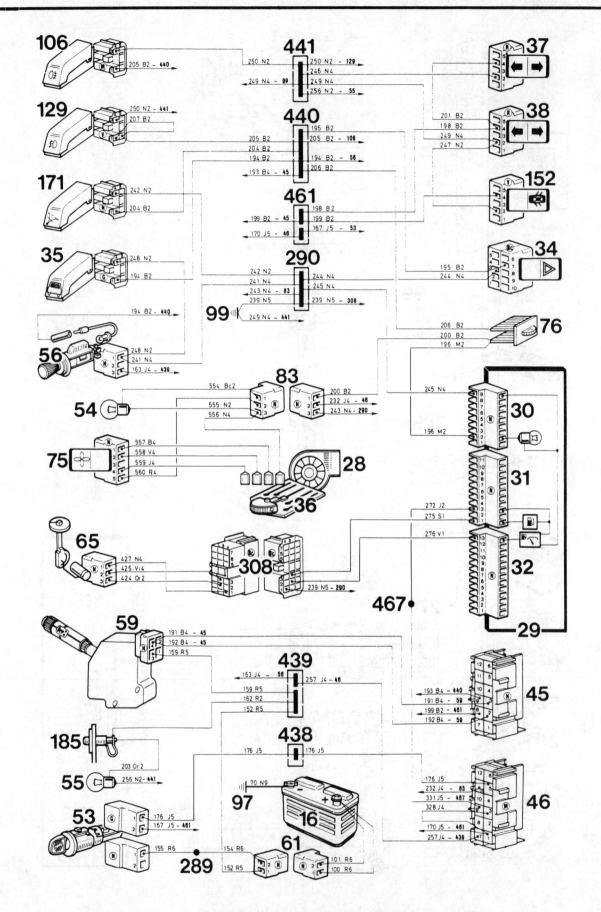

Fig. 11.32 Wiring diagram circuit 18

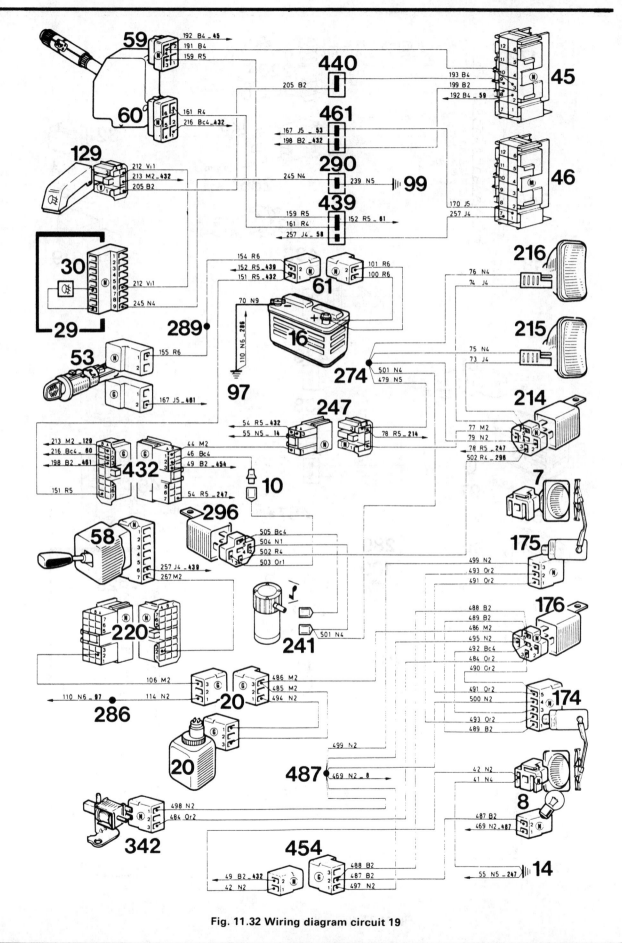

Fig. 11.32 Wiring diagram circuit 19

296

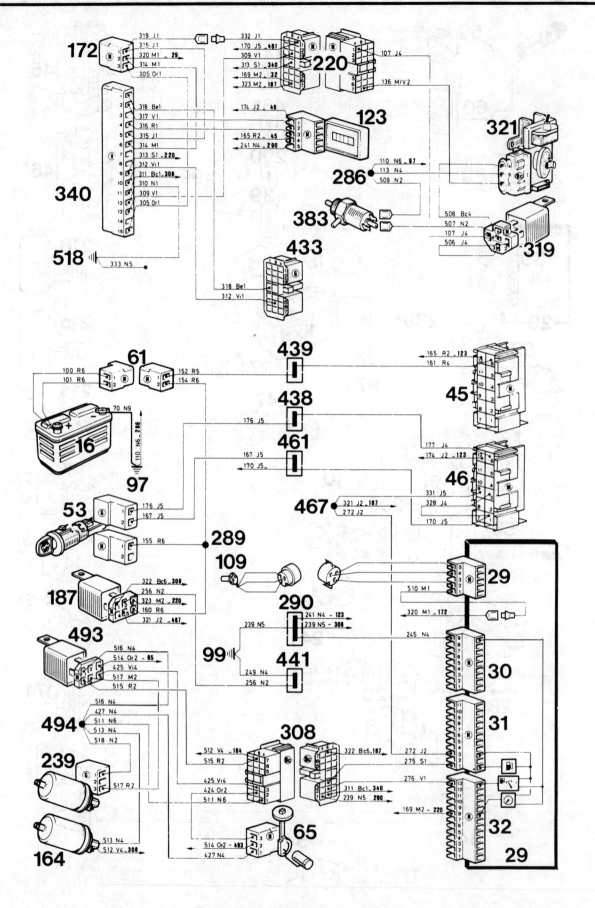

Fig. 11.32 Wiring diagram circuit 20

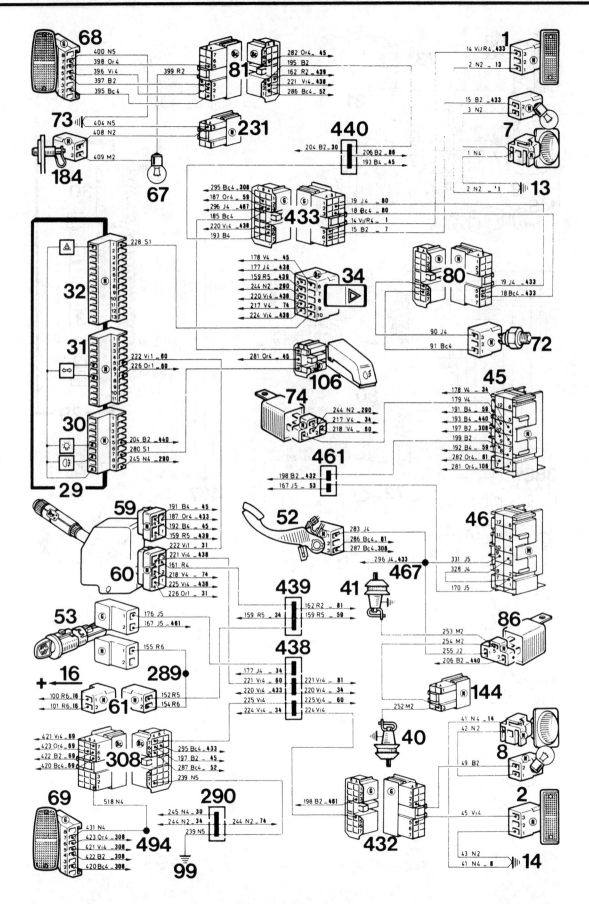

Fig. 11.32 Wiring diagram circuit 21

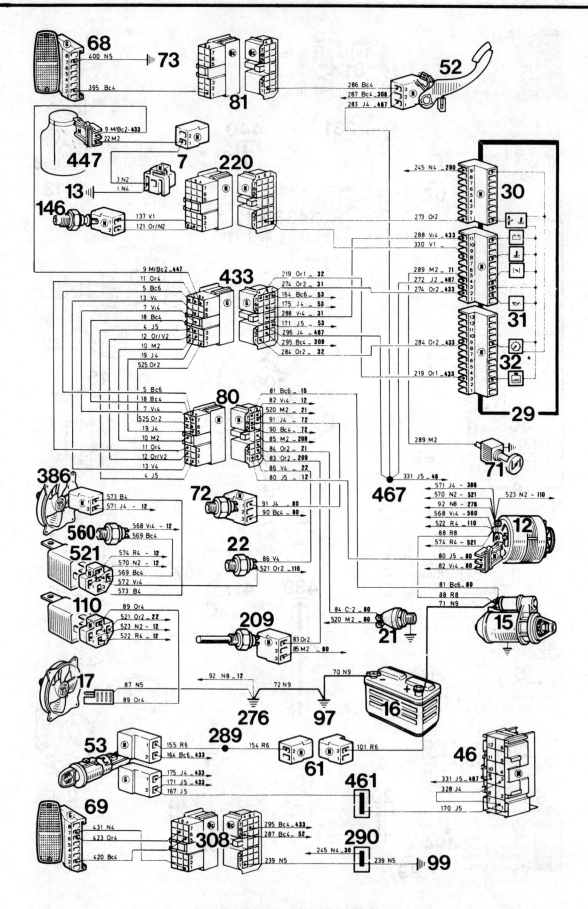

Fig. 11.32 Wiring diagram circuit 22

Chapter 12 Supplement:
Revisions and information on later models

Contents

1   Introduction

This Supplement contains information which is additional to, or a revision of, material in the first eleven Chapters. Much of it is concerned with the 1721 cc engine and associated items fitted to the GTX models introduced in 1987, but some of the information applies to all models.

The Sections in the Supplement follow the same order as the Chapters to which they relate. The Specifications are all grouped together for convenience, but they too follow Chapter order.

It is recommended that, before any operation is undertaken, reference be made to the appropriate Section(s) of the Supplement. In this way, changes to procedures or components can be noted before referring to the main Chapters.

2   Specifications

These Specifications are revisions of, or supplementary to, those at the beginning of the preceding Chapters

Engine type C1G (1237 cc)

General
Type	Four-cylinder, in-line, overhead valve
Bore	71.5 mm
Stroke	77.0 mm
Capacity	1237 cc
Compression ratio	9.2 : 1

Other data as for C1C engine (Chapter 1)

Engine type F2N (1721 cc)

General
Type	Four-cylinder, in-line, overhead cam
Bore	81.0 mm
Stroke	83.5 mm
Capacity	1721 cc
Compression ratio	10.0 : 1
Firing order	1-3-4-2 (No 1 at flywheel end)

Crankshaft
Number of main bearings	5
Main bearing journal diameter:	
New	54.795 mm
Undersize	54.545 mm
Crankpin journal diameter:	
New	48.000 mm
Undersize	47.750 mm
Crankshaft endfloat	0.07 to 0.23 mm
Thrust washer thicknesses	2.30, 2.35, 2.40, 2.45 and 2.50 mm

Connecting rods
Endfloat on crankshaft	0.22 to 0.40 mm

Under-bonnet view of a Renault 5 GTX (1721 cc) with power steering

1   Power steering fluid
    reservoir
2   Brake fluid reservoir
3   Suspension strut mounting
4   Screen washer reservoir
5   Fuel filter
6   Engine oil filler cap

7   Camshaft drivebelt cover
8   Steering fluid supply pipe
9   Alternator
10 Steering fluid high-pressure
    pipe
11 Oil filter
12 Fuel vapour separator

13 Radiator top hose
14 Engine oil dipstick
15 Oil separator
16 Cooling fan
17 Carburettor cooling duct
18 Radiator sealing cap
19 Expansion tank filler cap

20 Distributor
21 Idle speed adjusting hole
22 Air cleaner
23 Fast idle actuator vacuum
    valve
24 Battery cover

Pistons

Fitted direction	'V' or arrow on crown towards flywheel
Gudgeon pin fit:	
In piston	Hand-push
In connecting rod	Interference
Gudgeon pin length	$65.0\ ^{+0}_{-0.3}$ mm
Gudgeon pin outside diameter	21.0 mm
Piston clearance in bore	0.023 to 0.047 mm

Piston rings

Number	Three (two compression, one oil control)
Compression ring thickness:	
Top ring	1.75 mm
Second ring	2.00 mm
Oil control ring thickness	3.0 mm
End gaps	Supplied preset

Camshaft

Drive	Toothed belt
Number of bearings	5
Endfloat	0.048 to 0.133 mm

Auxiliary shaft

Bush diameter	
Inner	39.5 mm
Outer	40.5 mm
Endfloat	0.07 to 0.15 mm

Cylinder head

Height	169.5 ± 0.2 mm
Maximum permitted warp	0.05 mm
Refinishing limit	No refinishing permitted

Tappets

Diameter	$35.00\ ^{-0.00}_{-0.04}$ mm

Valves

Stem diameter	8.0 mm
Head diameter	
Inlet	38.1 mm
Exhaust	32.5 mm
Seat included angle:	
Inlet	120°
Exhaust	90°
Seat width in cylinder head	1.7 ± 0.2 mm
Valve head-to-cylinder head recess depth	0.8 to 1.1 mm

Valve guides

Outside diameter (nominal):	
Production	13.0 mm
Repair	13.3 mm
Bore diameter in cylinder head	0.1 mm less than outside diameter
Fitted height above joint face	43.0 ± 0.2 mm

Valve springs

Free height	44.9 mm

Valve timing

At theoretical clearance of 0.40 mm inlet, 0.50 mm exhaust:

Inlet opens	4° BTDC
Inlet closes	40° ABDC
Exhaust opens	40° BBDC
Exhaust closes	4° ATDC

Valve clearances (cold)

Inlet	0.20 mm (0.008 in)
Exhaust	0.40 mm (0.016 in)

Lubrication system

Oil pump:

Gear-to-body clearance	0.02 mm maximum
Gear endfloat	0.085 mm maximum

Oil pressure (at 80°C):

At 1000 rpm	2.0 bar (29 lbf/in²)
At 3000 rpm	3.5 bar (51 lbf/in²)
Oil capacity (including filter)	5.2 litres (9.2 pints) approx
Oil filter	Champion F102

Torque wrench settings

	Nm	lbf ft
Cylinder head bolts:		
Stage 1	30	22
Stage 2	37	52
Stage 3	Wait three minutes, then slacken	
Stage 4	20	15
Stage 5	Angle-tighten a further 123°	
Main bearing cap bolts	65	48
Big-end bearing cap bolts	50	37
Flywheel retaining bolts	55	41
Camshaft bearing cap bolts:		
6 mm diameter	10	7
8 mm diameter	20	15
Camshaft sprocket bolt	50	37
Idler roller bolt	20	15
Tensioner roller nut	40	30
Auxiliary shaft sprocket bolt	50	37
Crankshaft pulley bolt	95	70
Oil pump bolts:		
6 mm diameter	10	7
8 mm diameter	20	15
Sump bolts	15	11
Piston cooling jet bolts	30	22
Engine mounting nuts and bolts	40	30

Fuel and exhaust systems – non-Turbo models

Carburettor application

C1G (1237 cc engine)	Solex 32 BIS or Zenith 32 IF 2
C2J (later 1397 cc) engine:	
Manual transmission	Weber 32 DRT 21.100
Automatic transmission	Weber 32 DRT 8
F2N (1721 cc) engine	Solex 28/34 Z10 or 32/34 Z13

Carburettor data

Zenith 32 IF 2:

Type identification number	V10517
Venturi	24
Main jet	130
Idling jet	58
Air compensating jet	90 x 200
Pneumatic enrichment jet	100
Accelerator pump stroke	27 mm (1.06 in)
Accelerator pump jet	50
Accelerator pump delivery tube setting	60 mm (2.36 in)
Needle valve	1.25
Float height dimension	13.65 mm (0.537 in)
Auxiliary jet	60
Auxiliary jet tube setting	6.0 mm (0.24 in)
Defuming valve setting	2.0 mm (0.08 in)
Initial throttle opening (fast idle)	0.8 mm (0.032 in)
Idle speed	650 ± 25 rpm
CO mixture	1.5 ± 0.5%

Solex 32 BIS:

	869	**907**
Type identification number	869	907
Venturi	24	24
Main jet	115	120
Air compensating jet	155	125
Idling jet	38	42
Enrichener	52	40
Needle valve	1.3	1.3
Accelerator pump jet	40	40
Initial throttle opening (fast idle)	0.75 mm (0.03 in) or 20°	0.75 mm (0.03 in) or 20° 30'
Defuming valve setting	3 mm (0.12 in)	3 mm (0.12 in)

Carburettor data (continued)

Weber 32 DRT 21.100:

	Primary	Secondary
Venturi	23	24
Main jet	110	105
Air compensating jet	230	135
Idling jet	55	70
Emulsifier	F58	F56
Needle valve	1.75	
Float height dimension	8 mm (0.32 in)	
Float travel dimension	13 mm (0.51 in)	
Accelerator pump jet	45	
Initial throttle opening (fast idle)	0.8 mm (0.032 in)	
Pneumatic part-opening setting	3.5 mm (0.14 in)	
Defuming valve throttle opening	Not applicable	
Idling speed	700 ± 50 rpm	
CO mixture	1.5 ± 0.5%	
Fast idling speed*	1050 ± 50 rpm	

Models with power steering

Weber 32 DRT 8:

	Primary	Secondary
Venturi	23	24
Main jet	107	105
Air compensating jet	220	135
Idling jet	52	70
Emulsifier	F58	F56
Needle valve	1.75	
Float height dimension	8 mm (0.32 in)	
Float travel dimension	13 mm (0.51 in)	
Accelerator pump jet	50	
Initial throttle opening (fast idle)	0.9 mm (0.035 in)	
Pneumatic part-opening setting	3.5 mm (0.14 in)	
Defuming valve throttle opening	0.3 mm (0.012 in)	
Idling speed (in 'D')	600 ± 25 rpm	
CO mixture	1.0 ± 0.5%	
Fast idling speed*	1050 ± 50 rpm	

Models with power steering

Solex 28/34 Z10:

	Primary	Secondary
Venturi	20	27
Main jet	97.5	145
Idling jet	46 (49*)	50
Air compensating jet	200	190
Econostat	–	120
Enrichener	50	–
Accelerator pump injector	40	35
Needle valve	1.8	
Float level	33.5 mm (1.32 in)	
Initial throttle opening (fast idle)	1.0 mm (0.039 in) or 25° 30'	
Defuming valve setting	2 mm (0.08 in)	
Pneumatic part-opening setting	2.2 mm (0.09 in)	
Idling speed	800 ± 50 rpm	
Fast idling speed*	1050 ± 50 rpm	
CO mixture	1.5 ± 0.5%	

Models with power steering

Solex 32/34 Z13:

	Primary	Secondary
Venturi	24	27
Main jet	115	137.5
Idling jet	43	50
Air compensating jet	165	190
Econostat	–	120
Enrichener	50	–
Accelerator pump injector	40	35
Needle valve	1.8	
Float level	33.5 mm (1.32 in)	
Initial throttle opening (fast idle)	0.75 mm (0.03 in) or 22° 30'	
Defuming valve setting	0.3 mm (0.012 in)	
Pneumatic part-opening setting	3.5 mm (0.14 in)	
Idling speed	800 ± 50 rpm	
Fast idling speed*	1050 ± 50 rpm	
CO mixture	1.5 ± 0.5%	

Models with power steering

Air cleaner element

1237 cc models	Champion W145
1721 cc models	Champion type not available

Ignition system
General
System type:
1237 cc (C1G)	Integrated electronic system (as fitted to 1397 cc engines)
1721 cc (F2N)	As above, but with distributor rotor mounted directly on camshaft

Ignition timing (not adjustable)
At idling with vacuum pipe disconnected:
1237 cc	6° BTDC
1721 cc	7° BTDC

Spark plugs
Type:
1237 cc	Champion N9YCC or N281YC
1721 cc	Champion N7YCC or N279YC
Electrode gap	0.8 mm (0.32 in)

HT leads
1237 cc, 1721 cc models	Champion type not available

Clutch
Disc diameter
1721 cc models	200 mm (7.9 in)

Manual gearbox
Designation
1237 cc models	JB3 (5-speed) or JB4 (4-speed)
1721 cc models	JB3

Ratios – JB3
1st	3.091 : 1
2nd	1.842 : 1
3rd	1.320 : 1
4th	0.967 : 1
5th	0.758 : 1
Reverse	3.545 : 1
Final drive:	
Non-Turbo models	3.733 : 1 (56/15)
Turbo models	3.563 : 1 (57/16)

Suspension and steering
Power steering
Fluid type	Dexron type ATF (Duckhams Uni-matic or D-Matic)

Tyres
Tyre size (1721 cc models)	165/65 R13T	
Tyre pressures (bar/lbf/in²):	**Front**	**Rear**
1721 cc models	2.2/32	2.2/32
Automatic transmission models	2.1/31	2.2/32

Torque wrench setting – front suspension
	Nm	**lbf ft**
Lower suspension arm pivot - Turbo models from June 1987	90	66

General dimensions, weights and capacities
Dimensions (Renault Extra)
Length	3982 mm (156.8 in)
Width	1588 mm (62.5 in)
Height	1765 mm (69.5 in)
Wheelbase	2580 mm (101.6 in)

Weights (Renault Extra)
	Extra 1.1	**Extra 1.4**
Kerb weight	790 kg (1742 lb)	810 kg (1786 lb)
Payload (including driver)	525 kg (1157 lb)	575 kg (1268 lb)
Maximum towing weight:		
Braked	600 kg (1323 lb)	700 kg (1543 lb)
Unbraked	395 kg (871 lb)	405 kg (893 lb)
Maximum roof load	60 kg (132 lb)	60 kg (132 lb)

Weights (1721 cc models)
Kerb weight:
3-door .... 775 kg (1709 lb)
5-door .... 840 kg (1852 lb)

Capacities
Engine oil (including filter) – 1721 cc models .... 5.2 litres (9.2 pints) approx
Power steering fluid.. 1.1 litres (1.9 pints) approx
Load space – Renault Extra .... 2.6 m³ (91.8 cu ft)

---

3   Vehicle identification numbers

The list of type numbers given at the beginning of the manual has grown considerably. The details are as follows:

Prefix	Body type
B	5-door
C	3-door
F	Van 'Extra'
S	Van

Suffix	Engine code	Engine capacity
400	C1C	956 cc
401	C1E	1108 cc
402	C1J	1397 cc
403	C2J	1397 cc
405	C1J	1397 cc (Turbo)
40F	C1G	1237 cc
40G	F2N	1721 cc

---

4   Routine maintenance

Maintenance intervals – all models
1   The intervals specified in the schedule at the beginning of the manual are for vehicles working under average conditions. In adverse conditions maintenance should be more frequent. Adverse conditions include:

Operating in extreme of climate
Operation in dusty conditions (eg on unmade roads)
Predominantly short journeys
Full-time towing

Engine oil change interval – Turbo models
2   On models where the turbocharger is not water-cooled, the engine oil must be changed every 3000 miles (say 5000 km) or three months, whichever comes first.
3   On models with a water-cooled turbocharger the specified oil change interval is 6000 miles (10 000 km) or six months.
4   On all turbocharged models the oil filter must be renewed every 6000 miles (10 000 km) or six months.

Brake fluid renewal – all models
5   The renewal of brake fluid as a maintenance task is no longer specified by Renault. The reason stated is that modern fluid in a well-designed system does not deteriorate to a significant extent.
6   The conscientious DIY mechanic may prefer to continue renewing the brake fluid periodically. In any event, the fluid must be renewed when new calipers or wheel cylinders are fitted, or if the hydraulic system is drained for any other reason.

Maintenance schedule – 1721 cc models
7   The schedule at the beginning of the manual applies equally to these models, with the following additional task.
8   Renew the camshaft drivebelt every 72 000 miles (say 120 000 km). See Section 6 of this Chapter for details.

Automatic transmission models – additional maintenance
9   When the transmission fluid is renewed at the 30 000 mile (50 000 km) service, the filter screen inside the transmission must be renewed. See Section 13 of this Chapter.

Power steering – maintenance
10   Check the steering fluid level every 6000 miles (10 000 km). See Section 16.
11   On models with a separate drivebelt for the steering pump, check the tension and condition of the drivebelt at the same interval.

---

5   OHV engine

Engine splash guards – general
1   Later models are fitted with the engine splash guards (Fig. 12.1). When operations requiring access to the underside of the engine are carried out, the splash guards will need to be removed.

Engine C1G (1237 cc) – description
2   This engine was added to the range in July 1987. Mechanically it is identical to the other OHV engines described in Chapter 1.

Engine – removal and refitting (models with power steering)
3   On these models the alternator and the steering pump must be removed before engine removal. Refer to Section 16.

Engine – removal and refitting (Turbo models)
4   On Turbo models the removal of the engine alone is no longer recommended; instead, it should be removed with the gearbox.

Cylinder liners – incorrect protrusion after reassembly
5   If, after the reassembly procedure given in Chapter 1, Section 27, the liner protrusion cannot be brought into tolerance, a new set of liners should be fitted to establish if it is the liners or the cylinder block which is at fault.
6   If the new liners cannot be brought into tolerance, the cylinder block is probably at fault. Consult a Renault dealer for further guidance.

Engine/gearbox locating dowels – all models
7   The length of the dowels which locate the engine/gearbox mating areas may vary with model and year. The variation is not great – roughly 2.5 mm (0.1 in). If fitting a different engine or gearbox, therefore, make sure that the lengths of the dowels correspond to the depths of the recesses into which they fit. Obtain new dowels if necessary.

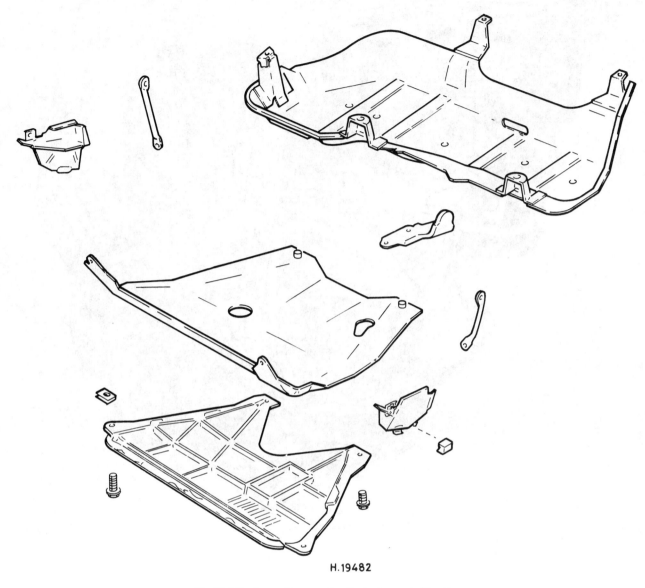

H.19482

Fig. 12.1 Engine and spare wheel splash guards (Sec 5)

---

6   OHC engine F2N (1721 cc)

PART A: GENERAL

Description

1   This engine became available in the Renault 5 range in July 1987. It is a well-proven unit of conventional design which has already been used in several larger Renault models.

2   The engine is of four-cylinder in-line overhead camshaft type. Like the overhead valve engines it is mounted transversely at the front of the car. The crankshaft runs in five shell-type main bearings, with thrust-washers fitted to No 2 main bearing to control endfloat.

3   The connecting rods are attached to the crankshaft by horizontally split shell-type big-end bearings, and to the pistons by gudgeon pins which are an interference fit in the small-end bushes. The pistons are of aluminium alloy, with three piston rings each. The crowns of the pistons are recessed to form the combustion chambers.

4   The cylinder bores are formed directly in the cylinder block. There are six possible bore sizes and pistons and bores are matched in production.

5   The overhead camshaft runs directly in the cylinder head, where it is

secured by five bearing caps. It is driven from the crankshaft by a toothed rubber belt (the camshaft drive belt). The cam lobes bear on shims carried in inverted bucket type tappets, the other ends of the tappets bearing on the valve stems. Valve clearances are determined by shim thickness. The valves are mounted vertically in the cylinder head and are each closed by a single spring.

6   The camshaft drivebelt also drives an auxiliary shaft which in turn drives the oil pump via a skew gear. The oil pump feeds oil to an externally mounted disposable filter, from where it passes to the main oil gallery and then to the crankshaft, auxiliary shaft and camshaft. Oil jets at the bottom of each bore squirt oil onto the pistons to lubricate and cool them.

7   The camshaft drives the fuel pump by means of an eccentric and a plunger. The distributor rotor is attached directly to the tail of the camshaft.

Routine maintenance

8   Refer to Chapter 1, Section 2.

9   At the intervals specified in Section 4 of this Chapter the camshaft drivebelt must be renewed. This is necessary because if the belt breaks or slips in service, extensive engine damage may occur. The operation is described later in this Section.

Fig. 12.2 Cutaway view of the 1721 cc engine (Sec 6A)

Major operations possible with the engine in the car

10   The following operations can be carried out without removing the engine:

(a)   *Removal and refitting of the camshaft drivebelt*
(b)   *Removal and refitting of the camshaft*
(c)   *Removal and refitting of the cylinder head*
(d)   *Removal and refitting of the sump*
(e)   *Removal and refitting of the oil pump*
(f)   *Renewal of the crankshaft front oil seal*
(g)   *Removal and refitting of the piston/connecting rod assemblies*
(h)   *Removal and refitting of the engine mountings*

Major operations requiring engine removal

11   The following operations can only be carried out after engine removal:

(a)   *Removal and refitting of the flywheel*
(b)   *Removal and refitting of the crankshaft and main bearings*
(c)   *Renewal of the crankshaft rear oil seal*
(d)   *Removal and refitting of the auxiliary shaft*

Valve clearances – checking and adjustment

12   This is not specified as a routine maintenance operation. It should only be necessary after component renewal, or if noise or compression loss give rise to suspicion that the clearances are incorrect. The clearances are checked with the engine cold.

13   Disconnect the battery earth lead.

14   Remove the air cleaner (Section 8).

15   Unbolt the fuel vapour separator from the front of the engine, but do not disconnect the hoses from it.

16   Remove the six nuts which secure the camshaft cover (photo). Lift

the fuel pipe cluster slightly and remove the cover and gasket.

17   Using a spanner on the crankshaft pulley bolt, turn the crankshaft until both cam lobes for No 1 cylinder (flywheel end) are pointing obliquely upwards, and the timing mark on the flywheel is aligned with the 'O' mark on the gearbox housing.

18   With the engine in this position, measure and record the clearance between the base of No 1 cylinder exhaust valve cam lobe and the tappet shim beneath it. (The exhaust valve cam lobe is the one nearest the flywheel). Insert various thicknesses of feeler blade until a firm sliding fit is obtained (photo). This thickness is the clearance for No 1 exhaust valve.

19   Repeat the measurement and recording on the second cam from the flywheel end. This gives No 1 inlet valve clearance.

20   Turn the crankshaft half a turn in the normal direction of rotation so that the cam lobes for No 3 cylinder are pointing obliquely upwards. Measure and record the clearances for these two valves. On cylinders 1 and 2 the exhaust valves are nearer the flywheel, while on cylinders 3 and 4 the inlet valves are nearer (Fig. 12.5).

21   Turn the crankshaft a further half a turn and deal with No 4 cylinder, then half a turn again for No 2.

22   Compare the clearances recorded with those given in the Specifications. If the clearances are as specified, commence reassembly. Otherwise, adjust the clearances as follows.

23   With the cam lobes in the same position as for checking, depress a tappet with a C-spanner or a stout screwdriver. Only press on the edge of the tappet. Flick the shim out of the top of the tappet with a small screwdriver and remove it with long-nosed pliers. Release the tappet.

24   The correct thickness of shim must now be calculated. First the thickness of the old shim must be known. It is engraved on the underside (photo), but ideally the actual thickness should be measured

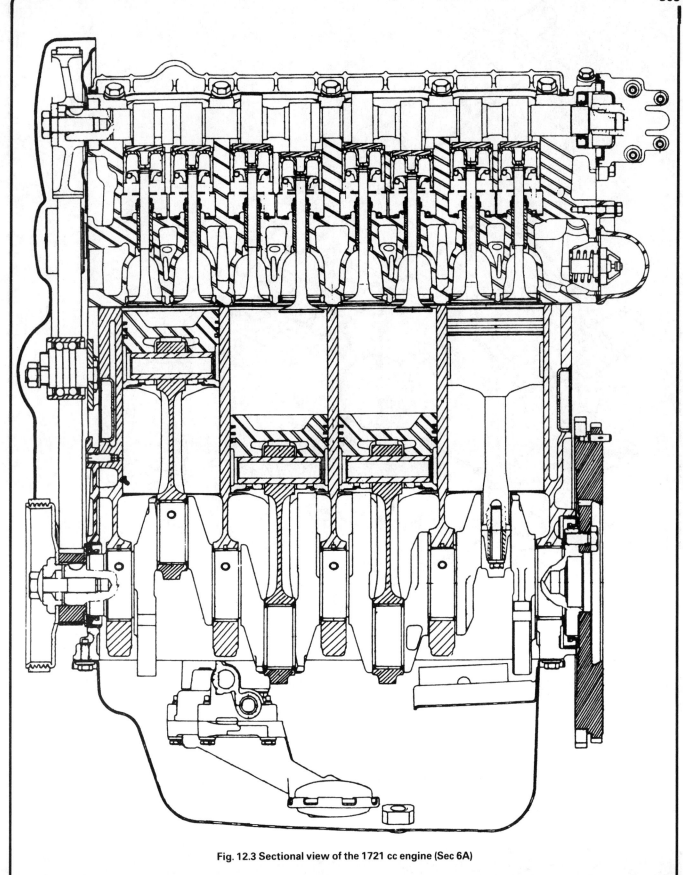

Fig. 12.3 Sectional view of the 1721 cc engine (Sec 6A)

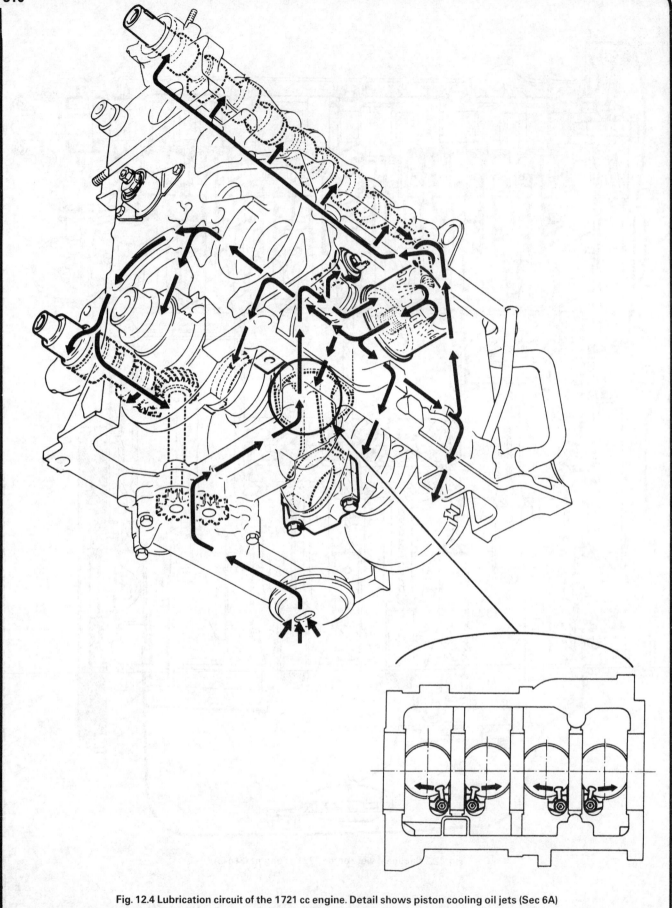

Fig. 12.4 Lubrication circuit of the 1721 cc engine. Detail shows piston cooling oil jets (Sec 6A)

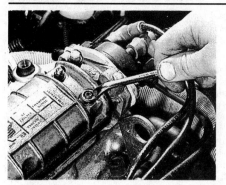

6A.16 Removing a camshaft cover nut

6A.18 Measuring a valve clearance

6A.24 Shim thickness engraved on the underside

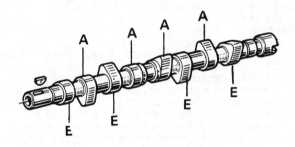

Fig. 12.5 Cam lobe identification (Sec 6A)

A Inlet   E Exhaust

using a micrometer or vernier gauge. This will take account of any wear.
25   The required shim thickness can now be calculated as shown in this example:

> *Specified clearance (A) = 0.4 mm*
> *Measured clearance (B) = 0.28 mm*
> *Original shim thickness (C) = 3.95 mm*
> *Shim thickness required = C - A + B = 3.83 mm*

The closest shim thicknesses available are 3.80 and 3.85 mm, giving clearances of 0.43 mm and 0.38 mm respectively.
26   Lubricate a new shim of the required thickness. Depress the tappet and insert the shim, marked side downwards. Release the tappet and check that the shim is properly located, and that the notches in the top of the tappet are at right-angles to the camshaft.

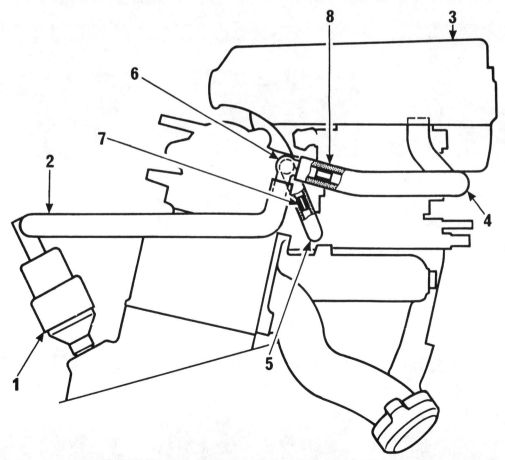

Fig. 12.6 Crankcase ventilation system – 1721 cc engine (Sec 6A)

1 Oil separator	*3 Air cleaner*	*5 Hose (to carburettor base)*	*7 Restrictor (1.7 mm)*
2 Hose	*4 Hose*	*6 3-way union*	*8 Restrictor (7 mm)*

27   Repeat the operations on the adjacent tappet, if necessary, then proceed to the other valves, each time turning the crankshaft to position the cam lobes upwards. Do not turn the crankshaft while shims are missing from tappets, as the cam lobes may jam in them.

28   When all the required shims have been fitted, turn the crankshaft through several complete turns, then check all the clearances again.

29   Refit the camshaft cover, using a new gasket if necessary, and secure it with the six nuts.

30   Refit the fuel vapour separator and the air cleaner. Reconnect the battery.

Crankcase ventilation system – description

31   The layout of the system is shown in Fig. 12.6. Its operation is as described in Chapter 1, Section 23.

32   Check the condition and security of the hoses from time to time, and make sure that the restrictors are not blocked. Blockages or leakage in the system can cause idling problems and (by raising the pressure in the crankcase) oil leaks.

PART B: REMOVAL AND DISMANTLING

Method of engine removal

1   The engine and gearbox must be removed together and separated on the bench. They are removed upwards out of the engine bay as described in the following paragraphs.

Engine – removal with gearbox

2   Jack up the front of the vehicle and support it on axle stands. Remove the front wheels. Also remove the bonnet.

3   Disconnect the battery earth lead.

4   Remove the air cleaner (see Section 8).

5   Disconnect the throttle and choke cables from the carburettor.

6   Disconnect the following items of wiring (photos):

    (a)   *Ignition coil-to-distributor HT lead*
    (b)   *Ignition unit LT and TDC sensor connectors*

    (c)   *Two multi-plugs on the left-hand inner wing*
    (d)   *Carburettor heater and idle cut-off connectors*
    (e)   *Vacuum valve electrical connectors (models with power steering)*

7   Remove the carburettor cooling duct, if fitted.

8   Disconnect the clutch cable.

9   Disconnect the vacuum hoses from the carburettor and inlet manifold, making identifying marks if necessary to aid refitting.

10   Disconnect the fuel supply hose from the fuel pump (photo), and the fuel return hose from the pipe cluster on top of the engine.

11   Unbolt the earth strap from below the fuel pump (photo).

12   Drain the engine oil, the gearbox oil and the coolant.

13   Remove the radiator (Chapter 2, Section 7).

14   On models with power steering, clamp the reservoir-to-pump hose. Disconnect the wiring from the pressure switch. Prepare for fluid spillage, then disconnect the supply hose and the high pressure pipe from the pump. Allow the high pressure pipe to drain, then move it aside. Cover the open pipes and unions to keep dirt out.

15   Disconnect the small hose from the expansion tank, and the large hose which runs from the tank to the water pump pipe. Unclip the tank and move it aside.

16   Disconnect the heater hose from the T-piece behind the distributor (photo).

17   Disconnect the temperature sensor wiring (photo).

18   Disconnect the speedometer cable from the gearbox.

19   Disconnect the track rod end balljoints and the suspension arm lower balljoints on both sides. Refer to Chapter 9 if necessary.

20   Remove the three bolts which secure the left-hand driveshaft to the gearbox. Swing the left-hand stub axle carrier outwards and disconnect the driveshaft from the gearbox.

21   Drive out the roll pin which holds the right-hand driveshaft sections together. Swing the right-hand stub axle carrier outwards and separate the driveshaft sections.

22   Unbolt the gearchange linkage at the gearbox. Be careful not to lose the spacer.

23   Remove the two nuts, springs and sleeves which secure the exhaust downpipe to the manifold. Lower the downpipe.

6B.6A Disconnecting the ignition unit multi-plugs ...

6B.6B ... two plugs on the inner wing ...

6B.6C ... and the vacuum valve connectors (power steering models)

6B.10 Disconnecting the fuel supply hose from the pump

6B.11 The nut (arrowed) which secures the earth strap

6B.16 Disconnecting the heater hose

6B.17 Disconnecting the coolant temperature sensor

6B.25 Unclipping the HT lead bracket from the lifting eye

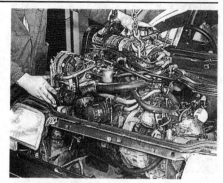
6B.28 Lifting out the engine and gearbox

6B.31 Removing the flywheel cover plate and bracing bar

6B.33 Removing an engine-to-gearbox bolt. This one has a thick spacer washer

6B.38 Removing the wheel arch splash guard

24   Disconnect the starter motor feed wire from the solenoid. Access is very poor, but an alternative procedure is to disconnect the wire at the battery, remove the bulkhead grommet and feed the wire through so that it can be removed with the engine.

25   Unclip the HT lead bracket from the left-hand lifting eye (photo).

26   Attach lifting tackle to the two lifting eyes. The chain or rope should be shorter to the right-hand eye than to the left, so that when the unit is hanging freely the engine will be slightly higher than the gearbox.

27   Take the weight of the engine/gearbox unit, then unbolt the mountings. These are positioned as follows:

   (a)   Left-hand front
   (b)   Right-hand front
   (c)   Rear centre
   (d)   Front centre (movement limiter)

28   Check that no attachments have been overlooked, then lift the engine and gearbox out of the engine bay. An assistant should guide the unit as it is lifted to make sure that nothing is trapped or fouled (photo).

Engine – separation from gearbox

29   Remove the starter motor, its heat shield and its wiring.

30   Make a TDC mark on the engine if wished – see Chapter 1, Section 8, paragraph 3.

31   Unbolt the flywheel cover plate and bracing bar from the base of the engine (photo).

32   Unbolt the TDC sensor and bracket.

33   Remove the remaining bolts which secure the engine to the gearbox (photo). Have an assistant steady the engine. Pull the gearbox off the engine, being careful not to allow the weight to hang on the input shaft.

Engine dismantling – general

34   Refer to Chapter 1, Section 9, paragraphs 1 to 9.

35   Operations which can be carried out with the engine in the car are described as if this were the case. If the engine has been removed, many of the preliminary steps can be ignored.

Ancillary components – removal

36   Refer to Chapter 1, Section 10. On models with power steering, also remove the steering pump.

Camshaft drivebelt – removal

37   Disconnect the battery negative lead.

38   Remove the right-hand front roadwheel. Also remove the splash guard in the right-hand wheel arch (photo). This will give access to the crankshaft pulley.

39   Remove the alternator/water pump drivebelt.

40   Using a spanner on the crankshaft pulley bolt turn the crankshaft until the timing marks on the camshaft sprocket and on the flywheel are aligned with the pointer on the camshaft drivebelt cover and the TDC (O) mark on the bellhousing (photos).

41   Have an assistant prevent the crankshaft turning by jamming the flywheel ring-gear teeth with a large screwdriver or a tyre lever. Slacken the crankshaft pulley bolt. Remove the bolt and the pulley (photo).

42   Check that the timing marks are still aligned. If they are not, temporarily refit the pulley and bolt and turn the crankshaft to realign them.

43   Remove the spring clip and the five Torx screws which secure the front of the camshaft drivebelt cover. Access to some of the screws is very tight, and a short cranked key will be needed to undo them. Remove the cover (photos).

44   Paint or scribe a mark on the camshaft sprocket cover in line with the timing mark on the sprocket. This will be useful for initial setting during reassembly. If the original camshaft drivebelt is to be re-used, make marks on the belt and the sprockets so that it can be refitted in exactly the same position (photo).

45   Slacken the belt tensioner nut, move the tensioner to release the belt and nip up the nut again (photo). Slide the belt off the sprockets and rollers and remove it.

6B.40A Camshaft sprocket mark aligned with pointer ...

6B.40B ... and flywheel mark aligned with 'O' line

6B.41 Removing the crankshaft pulley

6B.43A Removing the camshaft drivebelt cover clip

6B.43B Removing the camshaft drivebelt cover. The 5 screw holes are arrowed

6B.44 Mark the cover in line with the mark on the sprocket (arrowed)

6B.45 Camshaft drivebelt run – engine removed. Tensioner nut is arrowed (A) – on some engines it is in idler position (B)

6B.53 Camshaft sprocket backing plate

6B.55A Camshaft bearing cap and bolts

6B.55B Removing the No 1 (flywheel end) camshaft bearing cap

6B.56 Lifting out the camshaft

6B.57 Removing a tappet

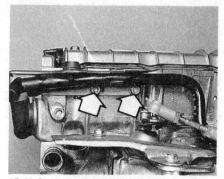

6B.68 Coolant pipe bracket bolts (arrowed)

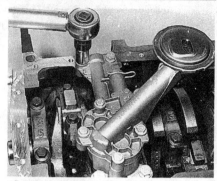

6B.86 Unbolting the oil pump

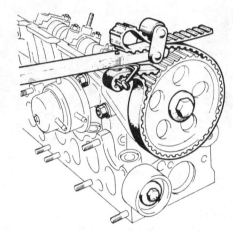

Fig. 12.7 Restraining the camshaft sprocket with an old camshaft drivebelt (Sec 6B)

Camshaft and tappets – removal

46 Remove the camshaft drivebelt as described earlier in this Section.
47 Disconnect the HT leads and remove the distributor cap and rotor arm (Section 10). Remove the rotor arm shield.
48 Remove the air cleaner (Section 8).
49 Unbolt the fuel vapour separator from the front of the engine, but do not disconnect the hoses from it.
50 Remove the six nuts which secure the camshaft cover. Lift the fuel pipe cluster slightly and remove the cover and gasket.
51 Remove the fuel pump (Section 8).
52 Prevent the camshaft sprocket from turning by gripping it with a strap wrench or with an old camshaft drivebelt (Fig. 12.7). Undo the camshaft sprocket bolt and remove the bolt and sprocket. Recover the Woodruff key if it is loose.
53 Remove the sprocket backing plate (photo).
54 Make identifying marks on the camshaft bearing caps so that they can be refitted in the same positions and the same way round.
55 Progressively slacken the bearing cap bolts until the valve spring pressure is released. Remove the bolts, and the bearing caps themselves (photos).
56 Lift out the camshaft with its oil seals (photo).
57 Remove the tappets, each with its shim (photo). Place them in a compartmented box, or on a sheet of card marked into eight sections, so that they may be refitted to their original locations. Write down the shim thicknesses – they will be needed later if any of the valve clearances are incorrect.

Cylinder head – removal

58 Disconnect the battery negative lead.
59 Drain the cooling system.

60 Remove the air cleaner (Section 8).
61 Disconnect the HT leads and remove the distributor cap.
62 Remove the camshaft drivebelt as described earlier in this Section.
63 Disconnect the wiring from the temperature sensor on the rear of the cylinder head.
64 Identify the various fuel hoses and disconnect them. Unbolt and remove the fuel vapour separator and the fuel pipe cluster.
65 Disconnect the throttle and choke cables from the carburettor.
66 Identify and disconnect the vacuum hoses from the carburettor and inlet manifold.
67 Disconnect the heater and crankcase ventilation hoses from the cylinder head.
68 Remove the two bolts which secure the coolant pipe bracket to the rear of the cylinder head (photo).
69 Disconnect the radiator top hose from the thermostat housing.
70 Remove the two nuts, springs and spacers which secure the exhaust downpipe to the manifold. Lower the downpipe.
71 Remove the six nuts which secure the camshaft cover. Remove the cover and gasket.
72 Unbolt the camshaft drivebelt backplate from the cylinder head.
73 Slacken the cylinder head bolts progressively, half a turn at a time, in the reverse of the tightening sequence (Fig. 12.10). When the tension has been released, remove the bolts.
74 Lift off the head, complete with manifolds and carburettor. If it is stuck, tap it upwards using a hammer and a block of wood. Do not try to rotate the head to free it, as it is located by two dowels. Do not try to free it by prising between the mating faces, as damage may result.
75 Remove the head gasket and clean the mating faces.

Cylinder head – dismantling

76 If not already done, remove the following components:

    (a) Carburettor and manifolds
    (b) Fuel pump
    (c) Temperature gauge sender
    (d) Camshaft and tappets
    (e) Thermostat (see Section 7)

77 Now remove the valves and associated components as described in Chapter 1, Section 13, paragraphs 2 to 5. Note however that on this engine the inlet valves are Nos 2, 4, 5 and 7, and the exhaust valves Nos 1, 3, 6 and 8.
78 Remove the oil seals from the tops of the valve guides.

Sump – removal

79 Jack up the vehicle and support it on axle stands at a height convenient for working underneath.
80 Drain the engine oil, then refit and tighten the drain plug.
81 Remove any splash guards or undertrays impeding access to the sump.
82 Unbolt and remove the flywheel cover plate and bracing bar.
83 Remove the sump-to-crankcase bolts. Tap the sump with a wooden or plastic mallet to free it, and remove it.
84 Clean the inside of the sump. Remove old jointing compound from the sump and crankcase mating faces.

6B.93 Refitting the front oil seal carrier plate. Make sure zone C is not blocked by sealant

6B.109A Oil jet and retaining bolt

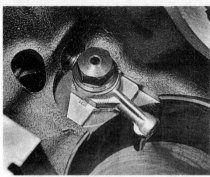

6B.109B Oil jet in position in the crankcase

6B.110 Fitting a crankshaft rear oil seal – note the piece of plastic used to protect the seal

6B.117A Removing the auxiliary shaft retaining plate ...

6B.117B ... and the auxiliary shaft itself

Oil pump – removal

85   Remove the sump as just described.

86   Remove the four bolts which secure the oil pump (photo). Withdraw the pump from its driveshaft.

Crankshaft front oil seal – renewal

87   Remove the camshaft drivebelt as described earlier in this Section. Also remove the drivebelt backplate.

88   Remove the sump.

89   Withdraw the crankshaft sprocket, preferably using a puller or by careful levering. Recover the Woodruff key.

90   Remove the bolts which secure the oil seal carrier plate to the crankcase. Remove the plate and seal.

91   Prise or tap the old oil seal out of the plate, being careful not to damage the seal housing. Remove old jointing compound from the plate and from the crankcase.

92   Fit a new seal, lips inwards, and tap it home with a tube or a piece of wood so that it is flush with the outer face of the plate.

93   Apply jointing sealant (CAF 4/60 THIXO or equivalent) to the plate mating face. Liberally lubricate the oil seal lips with clean engine oil. Make sure that the oilway in the top section of the plate is not blocked by sealant (photo).

94   Fit the oil seal carrier to the engine. Insert and tighten the retaining bolts, except for the two nearest the seal, which also secure the camshaft drivebelt backplate.

95   Refit the remaining components in the reverse order to removal. Apply a little sealant to the threads of the backplate bolts nearest the seal, as they penetrate into the crankcase. Remember that if the camshaft drivebelt has been contaminated with oil it must be renewed.

Pistons, connecting rods and big-end bearings – removal

96   Remove the sump, the oil pump and the cylinder head. If applicable, also remove the oil level sensor.

97   Turn the crankshaft to bring No 1 big-end cap (flywheel end) within reach. Make punch or paint marks on one side of the cap and the connecting rod so that they may be refitted in the same position and the same way round.

98   Remove the big-end cap bolts and withdraw the cap and shell. Push the connecting rod up the bore, recovering its shell if it is loose. Withdraw the piston and connecting rod from the top of the block.

99   Repeat the procedure on the other three pistons and rods. Keep the bearing shells with their respective caps and rods if they are to be re-used.

Engine mountings – renewal

100   Refer to Chapter 1, Section 22. The procedures are basically the same.

Flywheel – removal

101   With the engine removed, separate it from the gearbox and remove the clutch.

102   Prevent the crankshaft from turning by jamming the flywheel ring gear teeth. Slacken all the flywheel retaining bolts.

103   Remove the bolts and lift off the flywheel. Be careful, it is heavy. Obtain new bolts for reassembly.

Crankshaft and main bearings – removal

104   Remove the front oil seal carrier, the pistons and connecting rods and the flywheel. Invert the engine or place it on its side.

105   Check that the main bearing caps carry identification numbers. If not, mark them as was done for the big-end caps.

106   Remove the main bearing cap bolts. A hexagonal bit will be needed for No 1 bearing cap bolts. Withdraw the bearing caps and the bearing shell lower halves. Keep the shells with their respective caps if they are to be re-used.

107   Carefully lift out the crankshaft complete with rear oil seal.

108   Recover the thrustwashers from each side of No 2 main bearing, and the bearing shell upper halves from the crankcase. Again, identify the shell positions for refitting if necessary.

109   The cooling oil jets at the lower end of each cylinder bore may be unbolted and removed for cleaning if necessary (photos).

Crankshaft rear oil seal – renewal

110   Refer to Chapter 1, Section 21. Protect the lips of the new seal by

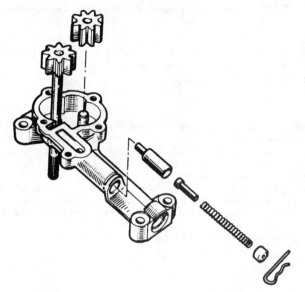

Fig. 12.8 Exploded view of the oil pump (Sec 6C)

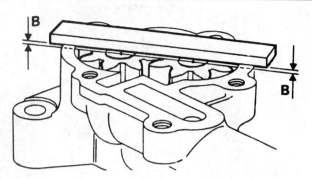

Fig. 12.9 Measuring the oil pump gear endfloat (B) (Sec 6C)

wrapping a thin piece of flexible plastic round the crankshaft (photo). Remove the plastic once the seal is fitted.

Auxiliary shaft – removal

111   With the engine removed from the vehicle, remove the camshaft drivebelt.
112   Restrain the auxiliary shaft sprocket with a strap wrench or by clamping an old camshaft drivebelt round it. Remove the sprocket bolt and washer.
113   Pull or carefully lever the sprocket off the auxiliary shaft. Recover the Woodruff key if it is loose.
114   Remove the camshaft drivebelt backplate.
115   Remove the four bolts which secure the auxiliary shaft oil seal carrier. Remove the carrier, oil seal and gasket.
116   From above the shaft remove the two bolts which secure the oil pump drivegear cover plate. Remove the plate and withdraw the drivegear using a long bolt (12 mm x 150) or a tapered piece of wood such as a chopstick.
117   Remove the two bolts and washer which secure the auxiliary shaft retaining plate. Remove the plate and lift out the shaft (photos).
118   Remove the old oil seal from the carrier. Clean the seal recess and fit a new seal, lips inwards.

PART C: EXAMINATION AND RENOVATION

Examination and renovation – general

1   Refer to Chapter 1, Section 24.

Oil pump – examination and renovation

2   Refer to Chapter 1, Section 25. Note the different construction and location of the pressure relief valve on this pump (Fig. 12.8). Note also that as well as gear-to-body clearance, the gear endfloat must be measured (Fig. 12.9). Desired values are given in the Specifications.

Crankshaft and main bearings – examination and renovation

3   Refer to Chapter 1, Section 26. The thrustwashers on this engine are fitted not to the centre bearing but to No 2.

Cylinder bores and crankcase – examination and renovation

4   The cylinder bores on this engine are formed directly in the block, as opposed to the wet liners used on the smaller engines. They must be examined for taper, ovality, scoring and scratches.
5   Examine the tops of the bores. A wear ridge will be found, marking the top limit of piston travel. The size of this ridge will give a good idea of the extent of wear. With very worn bores a high rate of oil consumption will have been experienced, accompanied by blue smoke from the exhaust.
6   For an accurate assessment of bore wear an inside dial gauge will be needed. Use this to measure the bore diameter just below the wear ridge, and again at the bottom of the bore, which is not subject to wear. If the difference between the two measurements is greater than 0.15 mm (0.006 in), this would normally be considered grounds for a rebore and new pistons.
7   Special oil control rings and pistons can be obtained if it is felt that the expense of a rebore is unjustified, but it must be said that the improvement effected by such products is sometimes short-lived.
8   If new rings or pistons are being fitted to old bores, it is essential to roughen the bore walls slightly with fine abrasive paper of a 'glaze buster' hone in an electric drill. The aim is to produce a cross-hatch pattern (not vertical).
9   The wear ridge at the top of the bore should be removed using a tool sold for the purpose, or alternatively the top piston rings may be of stepped construction ('ridge dodger' pattern). If plain rings are used and the ridge is not removed, there is a risk of the top ring hitting the ridge and breaking.
10   If a rebore is carried out, it is normal for the engineering works concerned to supply the oversize pistons required.
11   Thoroughly examine the crankcase for cracks and other damage. Probe all oilways and waterways with a piece of wire to make sure they are unobstructed.

Pistons and connecting rods – examination and renovation

12   Refer to Chapter 1, Section 28, paragraphs 1 to 6.
13   The pistons fitted in production are individually matched to their bores. If renewing a single piston, therefore, ensure that the replacement carries the same grade markings on the crown as the piston being replaced (photo).

Camshaft and tappets – examination and renovation

14   Examine the camshaft bearing surfaces and cam lobes for wear ridges, pitting or scoring. Renew the camshaft if evident.
15   Renew the oil seals at the ends of the camshaft as a matter of course. On some models the distributor rotor arm is glued to the end of the camshaft and will be broken during removal, while on other models it can be removed without damage. Lubricate the lips of the new seals before fitting them, and store the camshaft so that its weight is not resting on the seals.

6C.13 Marks on piston crown show fitting direction and grade

16   Examine the camshaft bearing surfaces in the cylinder head and bearing caps. Deep scoring or other damage means that the cylinder head must be renewed.

17   Inspect the tappet buckets and shims for scoring, pitting and wear ridges. Renew as necessary. Some scuffing and discoloration of the tappets is acceptable provided they are not actually scored.

Auxiliary shaft and bearings – examination and renovation

18   Examine the auxiliary shaft and the oil pump driveshaft for pitting, scoring or wear ridges on the bearing surfaces, and for chipping or wear of the gear teeth. Renew as necessary.

19   Examine the auxiliary shaft bearings in the cylinder block for evidence of wear. Renewal is not a DIY job and should be carried out by a Renault dealer or other specialist.

20   Renew the auxiliary shaft oil seal as a matter of course.

Camshaft drivebelt, sprockets and idlers – examination and renovation

21   Examine the belt carefully for signs of cracking, fraying or general wear, particularly at the roots of the teeth. The belt should be renewed as a matter of course at the time of major overhaul. A belt which has been contaminated with oil or grease must also be renewed.

22   Examine the sprockets for cracks, chips or burrs. They are quite fragile, and will crack or break if treated roughly. Small burrs must be removed with a fine file or an oil stone if they are in an area which will contact the belt. Cracks or chips mean that the sprockets must be renewed.

23   Spin the tensioner and idler rollers and check for roughness or shake. Renew them if necessary.

Flywheel – examination and renovation

24   Refer to Chapter 1, Section 31.

Cylinder head and pistons – decarbonising, valve grinding and renovation

25   Refer to Chapter 1, Section 32, paragraphs 1 to 10. Note however that resurfacing of this cylinder head is not permitted. If distortion exceeds the specified limit, the head must be renewed.

26   Examine the valve springs. Measure their free height and compare it with that specified. Renew the springs if they are distorted or not of the correct height, or as a matter of course if they have been in service for a high mileage.

27   Renew the valve stem oil seals as a matter of course.

PART D: REASSEMBLY AND REFITTING

Engine reassembly – general

1   Refer to Chapter 1, Section 33.

Auxiliary shaft – refitting

2   Lubricate the shaft with clean engine oil and slide it into position. Fit the retaining plate, curved edge away from the crankshaft, and secure it with the two bolts.

3   Lubricate the oil pump drivegear and refit it. Refit the cover plate, using a new O-ring, and secure it.

4   Lubricate the lips of the oil seal. Place a new gasket on the dowels on the cylinder block and refit the oil seal carrier, being careful not to damage the seal lips (photos). Fit and tighten the four bolts. (If no gasket was found during dismantling, seal the joint with CAF 4/60 THIXO sealant or equivalent.)

5   Refit the camshaft drivebelt backplate. Apply a little sealant to the two bolts nearest the crankshaft front oil seal, as they protrude into the crankcase.

6   Refit the Woodruff key (if removed) and the sprocket. Fit the bolt and washer, restrain the sprocket and tighten the bolt to the specified torque.

7   Refit the camshaft drivebelt.

Crankshaft and main bearings – refitting

8   Refit the cooling oil jets if they were removed, noting their correct positioning (see detail in Fig. 12.4).

9   Before refitting the crankshaft it is necessary to determine the

6D.4A Auxiliary shaft gasket positioned on the dowels

6D.4B Auxiliary shaft oil seal carrier

6D.11 Plain main bearing shells go in the caps

6D.12 Fit the thrustwashers to No 2 main bearing. Note that the oil grooves face outwards

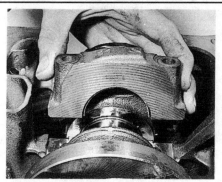

6D.15 Fitting a main bearing cap

6D.16A Checking the crankshaft endfloat using a dial gauge

6D.16B Checking crankshaft endfloat using feeler blades

6D.17 Side seal fitted to No 1 bearing cap

6D.23 Trim the seals flush with the block

thickness of No 1 bearing cap side seals. Place the cap in position without any seals and secure it with the two bolts. Insert twist drills or other rods of known diameter into the side seal grooves to establish the size of the groove. If the diameter of the largest rod which will fit is less than or equal to 5 mm (0.197 in), a side seal 5.1 mm (0.201 in) thick is needed. If the groove is larger than 5 mm, a side seal 5.3 mm (0.209 in) thick is needed. Remove the cap, obtain the necessary seals and proceed as follows.

10 Clean the backs of the bearing shells and their recesses in the crankcase and bearing caps. Clean any protective coating off new shells using white spirit or paraffin.

11 If the old bearing shells are being re-used, refit them to their original positions. If using new shells, fit the plain shells to the bearing caps (photo) and the shells with oil holes and grooves to the crankcase. Press the shells into their recesses, ensuring that the tag on each shell engages with the notch in the recess.

12 Using a little grease, stick the thrustwashers to each side of No 2 main bearing in the crankcase. The thrustwasher grooves must face outwards (photo).

13 Lubricate the lips of a new rear oil seal and fit it to the rear of the crankshaft, lips inwards. Be careful not to damage the seal lips.

14 Liberally lubricate the bearing shells in the cylinder block with clean engine oil. Lower the crankshaft into position and inject clean oil into the oilways.

15 Fit the bearing caps, with the exception of No 1, to their previously-noted positions, making sure they are the right way round (photo). Insert the bearing cap bolts and tighten them hand-tight.

16 Using a dial gauge or feeler blades, check the crankshaft endfloat while levering it back and forth (photos). Endfloat limits are given in the Specifications. If the endfloat is incorrect, the crankshaft and thrust-washers must be removed and thrustwashers of a different thickness obtained.

17 Fit the selected side seals to No 1 main bearing cap. The grooves in the seals must face outward (photo). Position the seals so that approximately 0.2 mm (0.008 in) protrudes from the cap at the crankcase mating face.

18 Apply a little sealant (CAF 4/60 THIXO or equivalent) to the crankcase mating area of the cap. Lubricate the side seals.

19 Place the retaining bolts through the holes in the cap. Lower the cap into position, making sure that the bearing shell and the side seals are not displaced, and start the bolts two or three turns into their threads. These will now serve as guide studs.

20 Push the cap firmly into place. When it is nearly home, check that the side seals are still protruding, then push it fully home and tighten the bolts hand-tight.

21 If the rear oil seal is proud of the cap, drive it in flush or recess it slightly (see Chapter 1, Section 21).

22 Tighten the main bearing cap bolts to the specified torque. Check that the crankshaft is free to turn.

23 Trim off the ends of No 1 cap side seals flush with the cylinder block face (photo).

24 Refit the remaining components in the reverse order to removal.

Flywheel – refitting

25 Clean the flywheel and crankshaft mating areas.

26 Fit the flywheel to the crankshaft. It will only fit in one position, as the bolt hole positions are not symmetrical.

27 Apply thread-locking compound to the new bolts. Fit the bolts, jam the ring gear and tighten the bolts to the specified torque.

Pistons, connecting rods and big-end bearings – refitting

28 Clean the backs of the bearing shells and the recesses in the rods and caps. Dirt here will cause tight spots and perhaps early failure. If new shells are being fitted, clean off any protective coating using white spirit or paraffin.

29 Press the shells into their correct positions in the rods and caps. Oil them liberally.

6D.30 Fitting a piston

6D.31A Fit the big-end bearing cap ...

6D.31B ... and tighten the retaining bolts

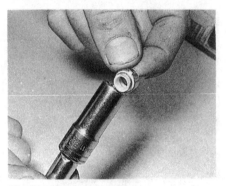

6D.41A Using a socket or tube ...

6D.41B ... fit the valve stem oil seals to the guides (arrowed)

6D.52 Tightening the cylinder head bolts using an angle gauge

30   Oil No 1 piston and its bore. Fit a ring compressor to the piston, Make sure that the piston is the right way round (arrow or 'V' mark on crown facing the flywheel end) and that No 1 crankpin is at its lowest point. Insert the piston into the bore, tapping it out of the ring compressor with a hammer handle and guiding the connecting rod onto the crankpin (photo).
31   Fit the big-end cap, making sure it is the right way round. Insert the bolts and tighten them to the specified torque (photos).
32   Check that the crankshaft turns freely, then repeat the procedure on the remaining pistons.
33   Refit the cylinder head, the oil level sensor, the oil pump and the sump, as detailed elsewhere in this Section.

Oil pump – refitting
34   Lubricate the pump with clean engine oil if it is dry.
35   Engage the pump on the driveshaft and fit it to the crankcase. Secure it with the four bolts, tightened to the specified torque.
36   Refit the sump, as detailed below.

Sump – refitting
37   Apply a bead of jointing sealant (CAF 4/60 THIXO or equivalent) to the sump mating face.

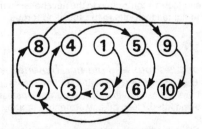

Fig. 12.10 Cylinder head bolt tightening sequence (Sec 6D)

38   Offer the sump to the engine and secure it with the bolts. Tighten the bolts in diagonal sequence to the specified torque.
39   Refit the cover plate and bracing bar, and any undertrays or splash guards which were removed.
40   Make sure the drain plug is tight, then lower the vehicle and refill the engine with oil.

Cylinder head – reassembly
41   Using a socket or box spanner, fit new oil seals to the valve guides (photos).
42   Refit the valves, springs etc as described in Chapter 1, Section 41, paragraphs 1 to 4.
43   Refit the thermostat, the tappets and camshaft, the temperature gauge sender (use some sealant on the threads), the fuel pump, the manifolds and the carburettor (using new gaskets).

Cylinder head – refitting
44   Check that the threads of the cylinder head bolts are clean. Mop any oil out of the bolt holes.
45   Check that No 1 piston is at TDC, and that the timing mark on the camshaft sprocket is aligned with the mark on the backplate.
46   Fit a new cylinder head gasket to the block, locating it over the dowels. Make sure it is the right way up.
47   Lower the cylinder head onto the block, engaging it over the dowels.
48   Lightly oil the cylinder head bolts, both on their threads and under their heads. Insert the bolts and tighten them finger-tight.
49   Following the sequence in Fig. 12.10, tighten the bolts to the torque specified for Stage 1. Repeat the sequence and tighten to the torque specified for Stage 2.
50   Wait three minutes, then progressively slacken all the bolts in the reverse of the tightening sequence. This is Stage 3.

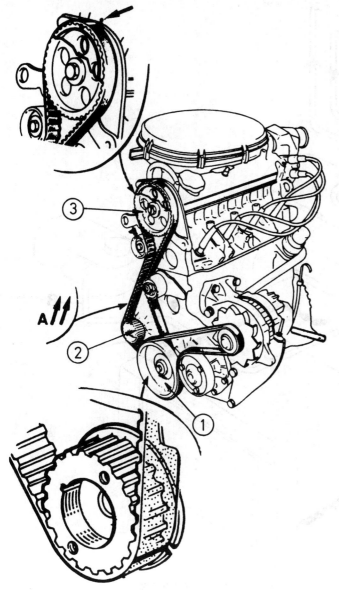

Fig. 12.11 Camshaft drivebelt run. Details show alignment of lines on belt with camshaft and crankshaft sprocket backplate marks (Sec 6D)

1 *Crankshaft pulley*	3 *Camshaft sprocket*
2 *Auxiliary shaft sprocket*	A *Arrows showing belt running direction*

51   Again following the tightening sequence, tighten the bolts to the torque specified for Stage 4.

52   Final tightening is carried out by turning each bolt through the angle specified for Stage 5. Measure the angle using a commercially-available gauge (photo), or make up a cardboard template cut to the angle required.

53   Reattach the camshaft drivebelt backplate to the cylinder head.

54   Refit the camshaft drivebelt, then check the valve clearances.

55   Refit the remaining components in the reverse order to removal, using a new camshaft cover gasket if necessary.

Camshaft and tappets – refitting

56   Oil the tappets and fit them to the bores from which they were removed. Fit the correct shim, numbered side downwards, to each tappet.

57   Oil the camshaft bearings. Place the camshaft with its oil seals onto the cylinder head. The oil seals must be positioned so that they are flush with the cylinder head faces.

58   Refit the camshaft bearing caps to their original locations, applying a little sealant to the end caps where they meet the cylinder head.

59   Apply sealant to the threads of the bearing cap bolts. Fit the bolts and tighten them progressively to the specified torque.

60   Refit the sprocket backing plate.

61   Insert the Woodruff key if it was removed. Refit the camshaft sprocket and its bolt. Restrain the sprocket and tighten the bolt to the specified torque.

62   Refit the camshaft drivebelt and check the valve clearances as described in this Section.

63   Refit the remaining components in the reverse order to removal, using a new camshaft cover gasket if necessary.

Camshaft drivebelt – refitting

64   Check that the timing mark on the flywheel is aligned with the TDC (O) line on the gearbox, and that the mark on the camshaft sprocket is aligned with the mark on the backplate.

65   Fit the belt over the sprockets and rollers. If the old belt is being refitted, observe the alignment marks made during dismantling. If a new belt is being fitted, observe the arrow showing the running direction, and the two lines on the belt which align with the mark on the camshaft sprocket and the notch in the crankshaft sprocket backplate (Fig. 12.11). The auxiliary shaft sprocket has no timing mark.

66   Slacken the tensioner nut. Move the tensioner to give roughly the correct belt tension and nip up the nut.

67   Temporarily refit the crankshaft pulley and its bolt. Turn the crankshaft through two full turns in the normal direction of rotation and check that the timing marks are still aligned. If not, the belt must be removed and the procedure recommenced.

68   Slacken the tensioner nut again. Move the tensioner to set the belt tension accurately and retighten the nut to the specified torque. Belt tension is correct when firm finger pressure, applied midway between the auxiliary shaft sprocket and the tensioner roller, will deflect the belt by 7.5 mm (0.3 in). There is a removable section in the belt cover through which the check may be made.

69   Remove the crankshaft pulley again. Refit and secure the front section of the belt cover, then refit the pulley and tighten its bolt to the specified torque. An assistant will have to jam the ring gear teeth while this is done.

70   Refit and tension the alternator/water pump drivebelt.

71   Refit the splash guard and the roadwheel. Remember to carry out final tightening of the wheel bolts after lowering the vehicle.

72   Reconnect the battery.

Engine – attachment to gearbox

73   Refit and centralise the clutch (Chapter 5, Section 2).

74   Put a smear of molybdenum grease or copper-based anti-seize compound on the gearbox input shaft splines.

75   Make sure the locating dowels are in position. Have an assistant steady the engine and offer the gearbox to it, engaging the input shaft with the clutch. Turn the crankshaft slightly if necessary to enable the splines to mate. Do not allow the weight of the gearbox to hang on the input shaft.

76   Fit and tighten the engine-to-gearbox bolts.

77   Refit the TDC sensor and bracket, the flywheel cover plate and bracing bar, and the starter motor with its wiring and heat shield.

Engine – refitting with gearbox

78   Engine and gearbox refitting is a reversal of the removal procedure described earlier in this Section. Remember to refill the engine and gearbox with oil, and the cooling system with coolant. On models with power steering, refill and bleed the system as described in Section 16.

Engine – adjustments after major overhaul

79   Refer to Chapter 1, Section 46, but ignore paragraph 4 – there is no need to retighten the cylinder head bolts on this engine.

80   After the running-in period it is advisable to change the engine oil and filter, and to check the valve clearances if new components have been fitted in this area.

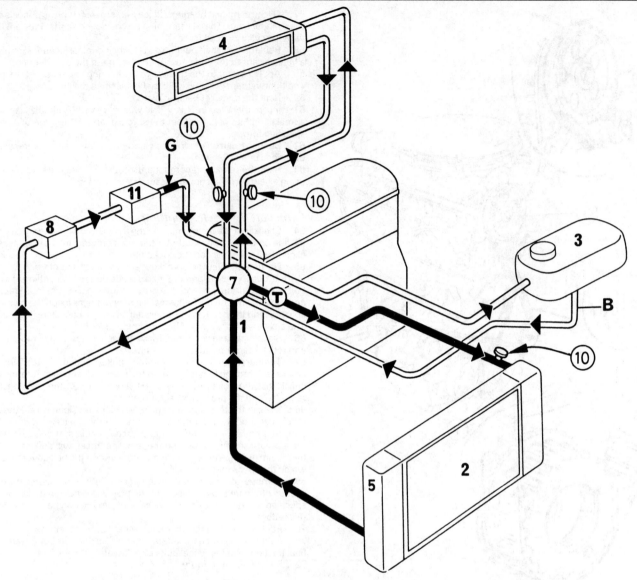

Fig. 12.12 Cooling system schematic – later Turbo models with air-cooled turbocharger (Sec 7)

1	Engine	4	Heater matrix	8	Manifold
2	Radiator	5	Temperature switch	10	Bleed screws
3	Expansion tank	7	Water pump	11	Carburettor base heater

G	Restrictor (3 mm)
T	Thermostat

7   Cooling system

Description – later Turbo models

1   The arrangement shown in Chapter 2 (Fig. 2.1) was modified to that shown in Fig. 12.12. In the new arrangement the return from the expansion tank goes to the water pump instead of to the radiator.

2   Further modifications were made with the introduction of the water-cooled turbocharger. These are shown in Figs. 12.13 and 12.14.

Description – 1721 cc models

3   The layout of the cooling system components is shown in Fig. 12.15.

Draining and refilling – 1721 cc models

4   The procedures are similar to those described in Chapter 2, Sections 3 and 5, but note the following points:

(a)   The cylinder block drain plug is on the rear face of the engine, next to the oil pressure switch (photo)

(b)   There are no bleed screws in this system

Water pump (1721 cc models) – removal and refitting

5   Disconnect the battery negative lead.

6   Drain the cooling system (Chapter 2, Section 3).

7   Remove the alternator/water pump drivebelt as described later in this Section.

8   Restrain the pulley with a strap wrench. Undo the three bolts and remove the pulley (photo).

9   Remove the nine bolts which secure the pump to the block (Fig. 12.16). Remove the pump – if it is stuck, tap it with a wooden or plastic mallet.

10   Remove the remains of the pump gasket from the mating faces.

11   Refit by reversing the removal operations, using a new gasket (photo). The gasket must be fitted dry. Adjust the drivebelt tension on completion.

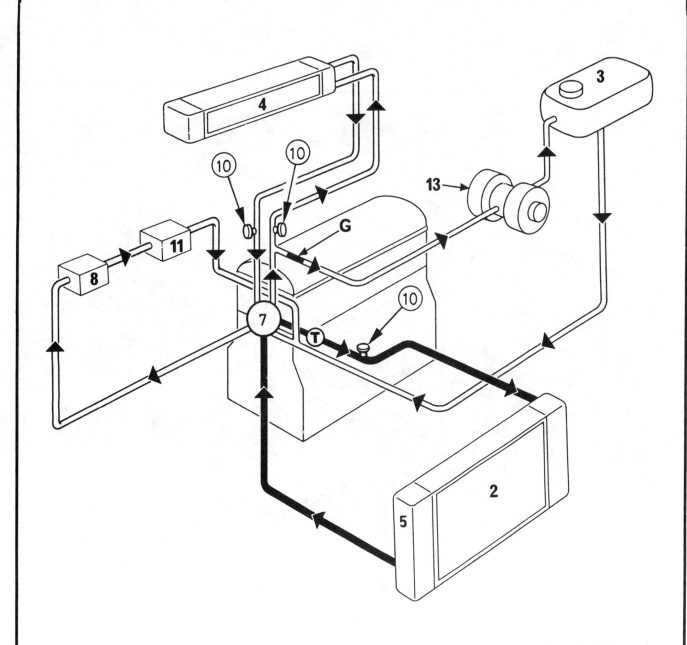

Fig. 12.13 Cooling system schematic – early arrangement for Turbo models with water-cooled turbocharger (13) (Sec 7)

For key see Fig. 12.12

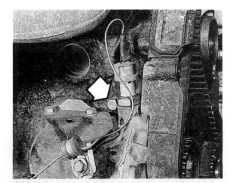

7.4 Coolant drain plug (arrowed) next to oil pressure switch on 1721 cc engine

7.8 Water pump and pulley – 1721 cc engine

7.11 Refitting the water pump

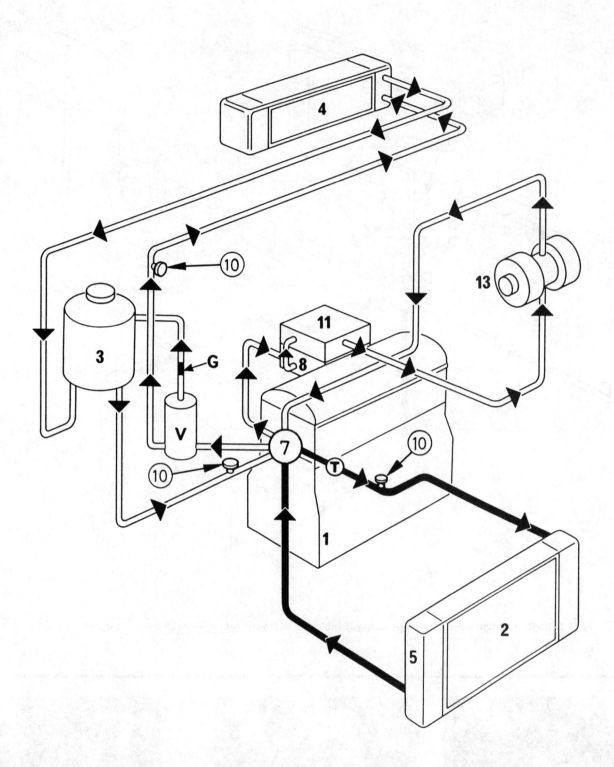

Fig. 12.14 Cooling system schematic – later arrangement for Turbo-models with water-cooled turbocharger (13) (Sec 7)

V   *Degassing unit*   *See also key to Fig. 12.12*

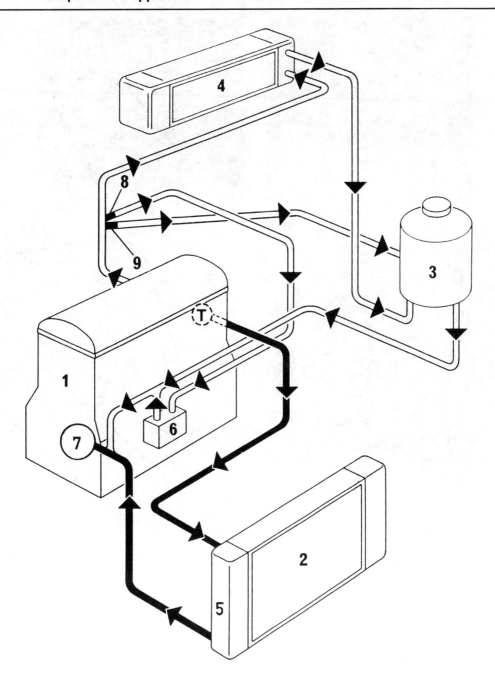

Fig. 12.15 Cooling system schematic – 1721 cc models (Sec 7)

1	Engine	4	Heater matrix	8 Restrictor (8 mm)	T Thermostat
2	Radiator	6	Oil cooler	9 Restrictor (3 mm)	For symbols see key to Fig. 12.12
3	Expansion tank				

Thermostat (1721 cc models) – removal and refitting

12   The thermostat is located in a housing on the left-hand end of the cylinder head.

13   Remove the carburettor cooling duct (if fitted).

14   Drain approximately 1 litre (nearly 2 pints) of coolant – see Chapter 2, Section 3.

15   Release the hose clip and pull the radiator top hose off the thermostat housing.

16   Remove the three bolts, withdraw the thermostat housing, and remove the thermostat and sealing ring (photo).

17   Refit by reversing the removal operations, using a new sealing ring.

Oil cooler (1721 cc models) – removal and refitting

18   The oil cooler is located between the oil filter and the cylinder block. Commence removal by removing the oil filter.

19   Drain the cooling system, or depressurise it by removing the expansion tank cap, and clamp the hoses leading to and from the cooler.

20   Disconnect the hoses from the oil cooler.

21   Undo the central nut and remove the oil cooler.

22   Refit by reversing the removal operations, using new seals and gaskets and a new oil filter.

7.16 Removing the thermostat – 1721 cc engine

7.25 Drivebelt run – 1721 cc engine with power steering. Tensioner screw is arrowed

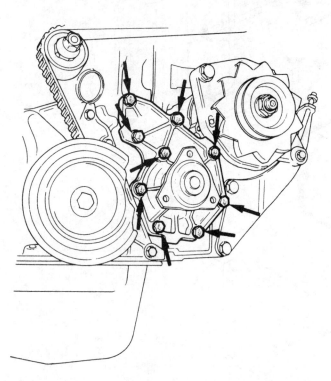

Fig. 12.16 Water pump securing bolts (arrowed) on 1721 cc model (Sec 7)

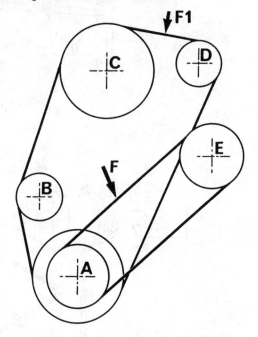

Fig. 12.17 Drivebelt runs – 1397 cc models with power steering (Sec 7)

A	Crankshaft pulley	E	Power steering pump
B	Tensioner roller		pulley
C	Water pump pulley	F	Tension checking point
D	Alternator pulley	F1	Tension checking point

Drivebelt (later models) – renewal and adjustment

23   The procedure given in Chapter 2, Section 12, still holds good, but account must be taken of the following points.
24   On 1397 cc models with power steering there are two drivebelts (Fig. 12.17). The outer belt drives the steering pump and the inner belt drives the alternator and the water pump.
25   Adjustment of belt tension on 1721 cc models is by means of an adjuster screw on the alternator slide bracket. The belt routing on such models with power steering is as shown (photo). It will be noted that the water pump is driven by the back of the belt, and that an idler roller is fitted.

8   Fuel and exhaust system – non-Turbo models

Cold start difficulties – 956 cc and 1108 cc engines

1   Check that, when the choke control lever is fully 'on', the end of the slot in the choke operating flap cam is against the eccentric spindle (Fig. 12.18). If this is not the case, check the choke cable operation and adjustment (Chapter 3, Section 11).
2   If difficulty is still experienced on the 1108 cc engine, especially after

it has been stopped for a long period, this may be due to fuel evaporating from the float chamber. The remedy, if it is felt worthwhile, is to fit an electrically-operated idle circuit cut-off solenoid, and to make sure that the defuming valve is fully closed at idle. The solenoid may be purchased from a Renault dealer.

Fuel smells in passenger compartment – Weber 32 DRT and Solex 28/34 Z10 carburettors

3   Under some conditions, fuel smells may be noticed in the passenger compartment on models fitted with the above carburettors. The smell is caused by vapour escaping from the carburettor venting system, and may be remedied as follows.
4   On the Weber 32 DRT carburettor, fit tubing between the float chamber vent and the air filter housing (Fig 12.19).
5   On the Solex carburettor, fit tubing between the float chamber vent and the left-hand wheel arch, drilling a hole in the blanking cover to accept the tubing (Fig. 12.20). The tubing must run smoothly downwards, with no kinks or bends.
6   Early versions of the Solex carburettor (before October 1987) do not have a suitable external vent, in which case the carburettor must be renewed. Consult a Renault dealer.

8.7 Three nuts and one screw which secure the air cleaner lid

8.10 Fitting a new air cleaner element

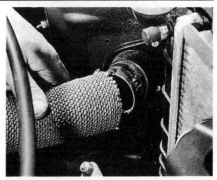

8.12 Disconnecting the cold air trunking from its intake

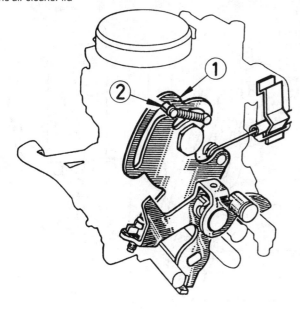

Fig. 12.18 Carburettor correctly set for cold start – no clearance between cam (1) and spindle (2) (Sec 8)

Air cleaner element (1721 cc engine) – renewal

7   Remove the screw and the three nuts from the air cleaner lid (photo).

8   Release the spring clips round the edge of the lid and remove the lid.

9   Remove the old element. Clean inside the housing and lid, being careful not to sweep debris into the carburettor.

10   Fit the new element (photo), then refit and secure the lid.

Air cleaner (1721 cc engine) – removal and refitting

11   Remove the three nuts from the air cleaner lid.

12   Release the hot and cold air pick-up trunking from the air intakes (photo).

13   Lift the air cleaner body. Disconnect the breather hose, then remove the air cleaner and trunking (photos).

14   Refit by reversing the removal operations.

Fuel pump (1721 cc engine) – removal and refitting

15   The procedure is as described in Chapter 3, Section 5, but with the following differences:

(a)   The fuel pump is mounted on the rear of the cylinder head, not on the block

(b)   The pump is secured by two nuts

(c)   There is no fuel return connection on the pump

Fuel vapour separator (all models with Solex carburettor) – general

16   A fuel vapour separator (sometimes called an anti-percolation device) is fitted to all 1721 cc models, and may also be fitted to other engines equipped with a Solex carburettor (photo). It is placed between the fuel pump and the carburettor, and prevents problems arising from fuel vaporisation when the engine is hot. Fig. 12.21 shows the fuel vapour separator and its connections.

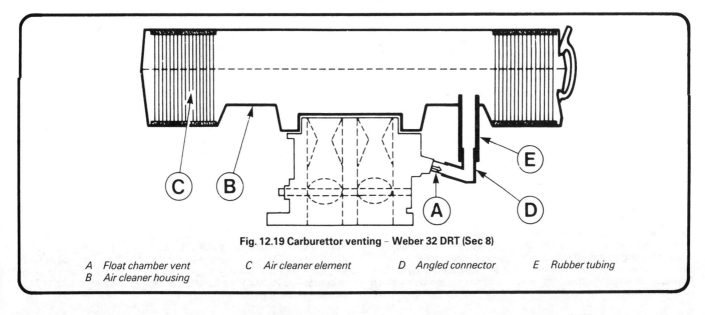

Fig. 12.19 Carburettor venting – Weber 32 DRT (Sec 8)

A   Float chamber vent
B   Air cleaner housing

C   Air cleaner element

D   Angled connector

E   Rubber tubing

8.13A Disconnect the breather hose ...

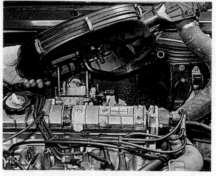
8.13B ... and remove the air cleaner

8.16 Fuel vapour separator

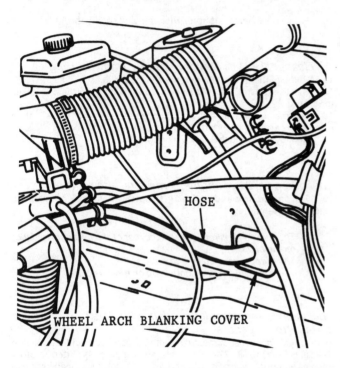

HOSE

WHEEL ARCH BLANKING COVER

Fig. 12.20 Carburettor venting hose – Solex Z10 carburettor (Sec 8)

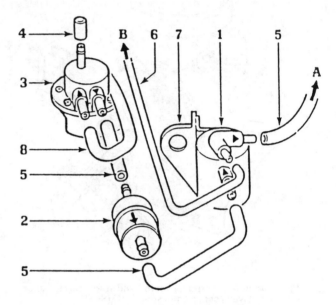

Fig. 12.21 Fuel vapour separator and associated components (OHV engine shown) (Sec 8)

1 Vapour separator	6 Fuel return hose
2 Fuel filter	7 Engine lifting eye
3 Fuel pump	8 Fuel hose (tank-to-pump)
4 Blanking stub	A To carburettor
5 Fuel hoses (to carburettor)	B To fuel tank

17   If a vapour separator is to be fitted to a model which did not originally have one, the carburettor needle valve must be changed from the 1.6 mm originally fitted to 1.3 mm. Additionally, the fuel return connection on the fuel pump must be blanked off, since this function is now carried out by the vapour separator.

18   The three hose connections to the vapour separator are inlet (from fuel pump), outlet (to carburettor) and return (to tank). Identify the hoses if they have to be disconnected for any reason.

Solex carburettor (1721 cc engine) – description

19   The Solex carburettor fitted to the 1721 cc engine is a twin throat downdraught unit, with sequential operation of the throttle valves. It is very similar in operating principles to the Weber 32 DRT described in Chapter 3, Section 14 (photos).

20   All versions of this carburettor have an idle cut-off solenoid valve which interrupts the idle mixture circuit when the ignition is switched off, so preventing running-on. If this valve is disconnected or defective, the engine will idle roughly or not at all.

21   The idle mixture circuit also incorporates an electrical heater to improve fuel vaporization when cold. This system supersedes the coolant heating of the carburettor base found on other models.

22   Later versions of the carburettor (32/34 Z13) have the opening of the secondary throttle valve controlled by a vacuum diaphragm instead of mechanically.

Carburettor cooling system (1721 cc engine) – description

23   Depending on model and year, the following system may be fitted. Its purpose is to prevent fuel vaporisation occurring in the carburettor in the minutes following engine switch-off, if when running in very hot conditions.

24   A small additional shroud is fitted to the radiator cooling fan. Trunking is fitted to the shroud and discharges under the air cleaner, so blowing air over the carburettor when the fan is turning (photo).

25   A temperature sensor adjacent to the carburettor starts the fan when necessary. The electrical feed is taken directly from the alternator live terminal, a line fuse being fitted in the feed wire (photos).

26   As with the ordinary cooling function, the fan may start after the engine has stopped, even with the ignition switched off.

Idle speed and mixture adjustment – 1721 cc engine

27   Refer to Chapter 3, Section 15, for the procedure. The locations of the idle speed and mixture screws are shown in the accompanying photos for the 28/34 Z10 carburettor, and in Fig. 12.22 for the 32/34 Z13 carburettor (photos).

8.19A Solex Z10 carburettor

1 Fast idle actuator (power steering)
2 Idle cut-off solenoid
3 Choke vacuum actuator
4 Heater

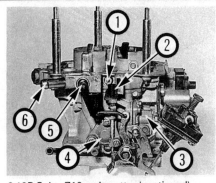

8.19B Solex Z10 carburettor (continued)

1 Idle jet
2 Idle speed adjusting screw
3 Accelerator pump
4 Enrichment device
5 Defuming valve
6 Float chamber vent

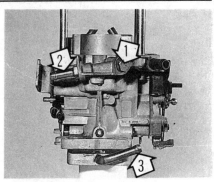

8.19C Solex Z10 carburettor (continued)

1 Fuel inlet strainer
2 Fuel inlet
3 Crankcase ventilation connection

8.19D Solex Z10 carburettor (continued)

1 Idle mixture adjustment screw
2 Fast idle adjustment screw
3 Secondary throttle stop screw (do not touch)

8.24 Carburettor cooling trunking

Solex carburettor (1721 cc engine) – removal and refitting

28   Disconnect the battery negative lead.
29   Remove the air cleaner as described in this Section.
30   Disconnect the wiring from the carburettor heater and the idle cut-off solenoid (photo).
31   Unsnap the throttle link rod balljoint (photo).
32   Disconnect the choke cable (photos).
33   Slacken the hose clip and disconnect the fuel inlet hose (photo).
34   Identify and disconnect the vacuum hoses from the carburettor (photo).
35   Disconnect the crankcase ventilation hose from the base of the carburettor (photo).
36   Remove the four Allen screws from the top of the carburettor. Recover the washers from the bases of the screws (photos).
37   Lift off the carburettor and recover the gasket from the manifold (photo).
38   Refit by reversing the removal operations, using a new gasket.

Solex carburettor (1721 cc engine) – cleaning

Note: The carburettor seen in the photographs is a Solex 28/34 Z10. The 32/34 Z13 fitted to later models is very similar, the main difference being that the secondary throttle valve is opened by a vacuum actuator instead of mechanically.

39   With the carburettor removed from the engine, thoroughly clean it externally with paraffin or a degreasing solvent.

Fig. 12.22 Idle adjustment points – Solex 32/34 Z13 (Sec 8)

A Idle speed   C Fast idle actuator (power
B Idle mixture   steering)

8.25A Carburettor temperature sensor

8.25B Line fuse for the carburettor cooling system

8.27A Adjusting the idle speed – Z10 carburettor

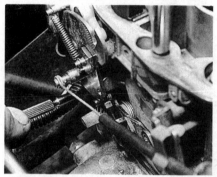

8.27B Adjusting the idle mixture – Z10 carburettor

8.30 Disconnecting the idle cut-off solenoid

8.31 Unclipping the throttle link

40   Unscrew and remove the fuel inlet strainer (photo).
41   Unscrew the idling jet from the carburettor cover (photo).
42   Remove the heater securing plate screw. Remove the plate and withdraw the roll pin with the insulator, the terminal and the heater disc (photos). Be careful with the heater disc, it is fragile.
43   Prise the defuming valve link rod out of the plastic bush (photo).
44   Remove the five screws which secure the carburettor cover. Lift off the cover with the floats and the choke vacuum actuator attached (photos).
45   Remove the float pivot pin (photo). Remove the floats, the needle valve and the gasket.
46   Remove the idle circuit filter from the carburettor body (photo).
47   Pull the accelerator pump injector assembly from the body (photo).
48   Unscrew and remove the air correction jet/emulsion tube assemblies (photo).
49   Remove the main jets from the bottom of the emulsion tube wells by unscrewing them (photos).
50   If a complete overhaul is being undertaken, remove the various diaphragm covers so that the diaphragms can be renewed.
51   Clean out any sediment from the float chamber, and blow through all passages with low-pressure compressed air.
52   Reassemble in the reverse order to dismantling, using new gaskets, O-rings etc and carrying out the adjustments described in the following paragraphs (when appropriate). Pay attention to the correct fitting of the heater components – if the insulator is misplaced, there is a risk of a short-circuit.

Solex carburettor (1721 cc engine) – overhaul adjustment
53   Refer to Chapter 3, Section 17, paragraph 1 to 4.

Float level adjustment
54   With the carburettor cover reassembled (including the gasket), invert the cover and measure the distance from the gasket to the

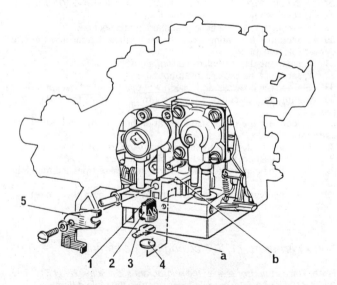

Fig. 12.23 Heater details – Solex 28/34 Z10 (Sec 8)

1	Roll pin	5	Securing plate
2	Insulator	a	Tongue
3	Terminal	b	Roll pin slot
4	Heater disc		

8.32A Disconnecting the choke control inner
cable ...

8.32B ... and unclipping the outer cable

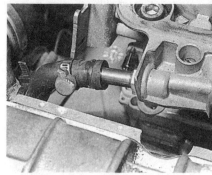

8.33 Disconnecting the fuel inlet hose

8.34 Carburettor vacuum hoses

8.35 Disconnecting the crankcase ventilation
hose

8.36A Four Allen screws (arrowed) which
secure the carburettor

8.36B Recover the washers from the bases of
the screws

8.37 Removing the carburettor

8.40 Removing the fuel inlet strainer

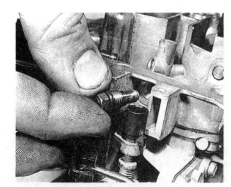

8.41 Removing the idling jet

8.42A Remove the screw and plate ...

8.42B ... and withdraw the heater assembly

8.43 Disconnecting the defuming valve link

8.44A Five screws (arrowed) which secure the cover

8.44B Removing the carburettor cover

8.45 Removing the float pivot pin

8.46 Removing the idle circuit filter

8.47 Removing the accelerator pump injector

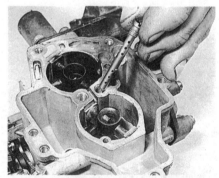

8.48 Removing an air correction jet/emulsion tube assembly

8.49A Unscrewing a main jet

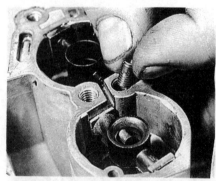

8.49B Removing a main jet from the well

8.54 Checking the float level

8.56 Fast idle adjustment screw

8.59 Fast idle actuator solenoid valve and vacuum reservoir

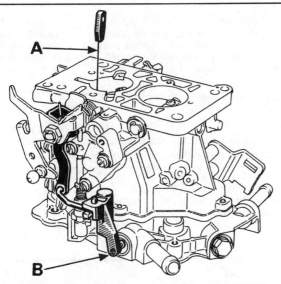

Fig. 12.24 Defuming valve adjustment – Solex 28/34 Z10 (Sec 8)

A   Gauge rod (measuring   B   Adjustment screw
     throttle valve gap)

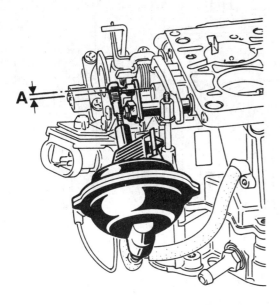

Fig. 12.26 Throttle actuator link rod adjustment – Solex 32/34 Z13 (Sec 8)

A   See text

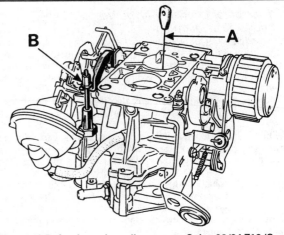

Fig. 12.25 Defuming valve adjustment – Solex 32/34 Z13 (Sec 8)

A   Gauge rod   B   Adjustment screw

furthest point of the floats (photo). The correct value is given in the Specifications. Adjust if necessary by carefully bending the float arms.

Defuming valve adjustment

55   Invert the reassembled carburettor. Open the throttle until the defuming valve just closes. In this position, the throttle valve opening should correspond to the value given in the Specifications. Adjust if necessary at the point shown (Fig. 12.24 or 12.25).

Initial throttle opening (fast idle)

56   With the carburettor still inverted, operate the choke linkage to close the choke flap. Measure the throttle valve opening, which should be as specified. Adjust if necessary by turning the screw which bears on the fast idle cam (photo).

Choke pneumatic part-opening adjustment

57   Operate the choke linkage to close the choke flap. Push the operating rod as far as it will go into the choke vacuum actuator. In this position measure the choke flap opening, which should be as specified. Adjust if necessary by means of the screw in the centre of the vacuum actuator.

Secondary throttle link adjustment (32/34 Z13 only)

58   The link rod between the throttle vacuum actuator and the secondary throttle lever should be adjusted so that there is a small amount of play ('A' in Fig. 12.26) in both the fully closed and fully open positions.

8.61 Bridging the pressure switch connector terminals with a paper clip

8.62 Adjusting the fast idle actuator

Fast idle actuator (models with power steering) – description and adjustment

59   On models with power steering, a vacuum-operated actuator raises the idle speed if the steering is turned to full lock, so preventing stalling. The vacuum feed to the actuator is via a solenoid valve which is controlled by a pressure-operated switch in the high-pressure hydraulic pipe (photo).

60   Before commencing adjustment, the engine must be at normal operating temperature and the idle speed and mixture must be correctly adjusted.

61   With the engine idling and the steering straight ahead, unplug the wiring connector from the pressure switch. Bridge the female terminals of the connector with a paper clip or a short length of stiff wire. Do not allow the bridge to touch earth (vehicle metal) (photo).

62   With the terminals bridged, idle speed should rise to the value given in the Specifications. Adjust if necessary by means of the adjusting screw on the fast idle actuator – see Fig. 12.22 or (photo).

63   When adjustment is correct, stop the engine and remake the original electrical connections.

Fuel gauge sender unit – checking

64   With the sender unit removed as described in Chapter 3, Section 8, connect an ohmmeter across terminals 1 and 3. Check that the resistance varies in an approximately linear fashion between 7 ohms with the float in the highest (full) position and 280 ohms in the lowest (empty) position.

---

9   Fuel and exhaust systems – Turbo models

Description (later models)

1   During 1986, a water-cooled turbocharger superseded the air-cooled one previously fitted. Operating principles are unchanged, and the precautions listed in Chapter 3, Section 22, still apply.

2   A schematic diagram of the later system is given in Fig. 12.27.

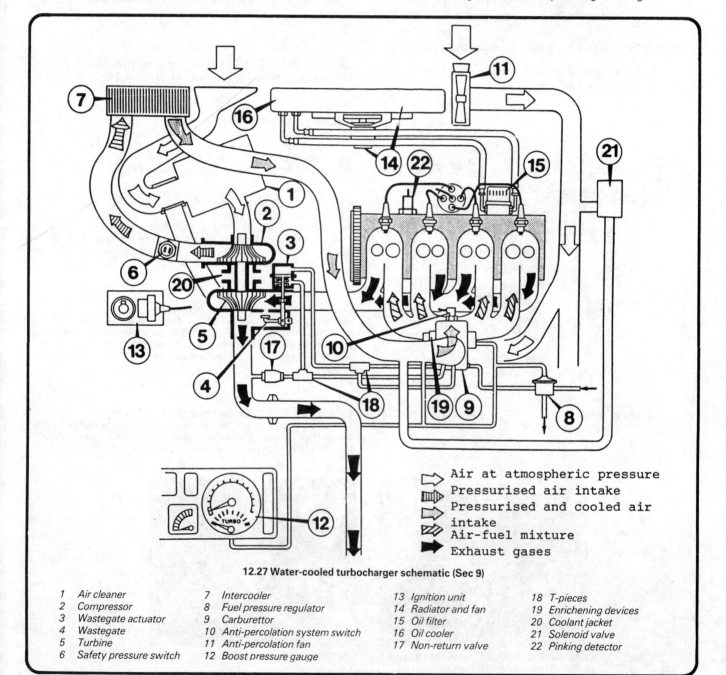

> ⇨ Air at atmospheric pressure
> ⪢ Pressurised air intake
> ⇨ Pressurised and cooled air intake
> ⬎ Air-fuel mixture
> ➤ Exhaust gases

12.27 Water-cooled turbocharger schematic (Sec 9)

1 Air cleaner	7 Intercooler	13 Ignition unit	18 T-pieces
2 Compressor	8 Fuel pressure regulator	14 Radiator and fan	19 Enrichening devices
3 Wastegate actuator	9 Carburettor	15 Oil filter	20 Coolant jacket
4 Wastegate	10 Anti-percolation system switch	16 Oil cooler	21 Solenoid valve
5 Turbine	11 Anti-percolation fan	17 Non-return valve	22 Pinking detector
6 Safety pressure switch	12 Boost pressure gauge		

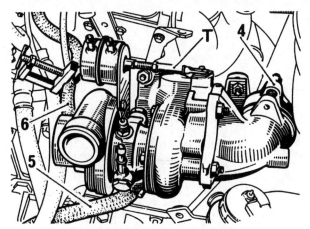

Fig. 12.28 Water-cooled turbocharger removal (Sec 9)

4 Exhaust clamp
5 Oil return pipe

6 Coolant feed hose (clamped)
T Wastegate rod (do not stress)

Turbocharger (water-cooled) – removal and refitting

3   The procedure is as described in Chapter 3, Section 27, with the following additional operations.

4   Depressurise the cooling system by removing the expansion tank cap. Clamp the turbo coolant feed hose and disconnect it. Also disconnect the output hose which connects the turbocharger to the expansion tank.

5   After refitting, release the feed hose clamp and top up the cooling system.

Auxiliary fuel tank and pump – description of operation

6   The operation of the auxiliary fuel supply should be understood in order to avoid problems after running out of fuel or after draining the main tank.

7   The auxiliary tank is at a lower level than the main tank. When filling with fuel, the fuel flows down the filler pipe into the auxiliary tank, then through the connecting pipe into the main tank. A flap at the end of the connecting pipe prevents fuel running back out of the main tank into the auxiliary tank.

8   In normal operation fuel is drawn from the main tank by the main fuel pump. When the level in the main tank falls to a certain amount, the auxiliary fuel pump runs for 40 seconds to transfer fuel from the auxiliary to the main tank. At the same time the 'low level' warning light illuminates for 5 seconds. The auxiliary pump will only operate when the engine is running or when the starter motor is cranking.

9   If the vehicle is allowed to run out of fuel, more than 10 litres (over 2 gallons) will have to be put into the filler before any appears in the main tank. If this is not possible, the engine will have to be cranked continuously on the starter for at least 60 seconds in order to energise the auxiliary pump and transfer enough fuel to the main tank.

10   To avoid a similar problem after intentional draining of the main tank, a few litres of fuel can be added via the fuel gauge sender aperture when refitting.

10   Ignition system

Description – 1721 cc models

1   The ignition system fitted to 1721 cc models is almost identical to the fully electronic system described in Chapter 4. An additional feature is the provision of an oil temperature sensor, mounted next to the oil filter. This enables the computer module to adjust the ignition timing in response to engine temperature.

2   The distributor on these models is mounted on the left-hand end of the cylinder head. The rotor arm is fitted directly to the end of the camshaft.

Distributor cap (1721 cc models) – removal and refitting

3   Disconnect the ignition coil-to-distributor HT lead from the cap.

4   Remove the three screws which secure the cap and lift off the cap (photos). If it is wished to remove the cap completely, identify the plug leads and disconnect them from the cap.

5   Refit by reversing the removal operations.

Rotor arm (1721 cc models) – removal and refitting

6   Remove the distributor cap.

7   On some models the rotor arm may now simply be pulled off (photo). On other models it is glued to the camshaft, and will almost certainly be broken during removal. The necessary adhesive should be purchased from a Renault dealer along with the new rotor arm.

8   Clean off the remains of the old adhesive, if applicable, and glue the new arm in position. If the rotor arm was not glued to the camshaft, refit it and press it home.

9   Refit the distributor cap.

Distributor types (later models) – general

10   Marelli and Femsa distributors are fitted to certain later engines in the Renault 5 range. At the time of writing little information was available on these distributors, except for ignition timing settings, which are the same as for the Ducellier distributor; see Specifications at the beginning of this Chapter or Chapter 4 (as applicable).

Transistor assistance unit (later 1108 cc C1E engines) – general

11   On later 1108 cc C1E engines, a modified transistor assistance unit is fitted which has only one wiring socket; the diagnostic socket no longer being incorporated. Therefore the information given in Section 13 of Chapter 4 regarding the bypassing of the unit is no longer applicable. The dwell angle can only be checked by a Renault dealer with access to specialised test equipment.

12   When checking or adjusting the ignition timing, note that the dynamic setting procedure remains unchanged from that described in Chapter 4, Section 8. When statically setting the ignition timing, it is not recommended that a 12 volt test lamp is connected to the distributor LT terminal due to the possible risk of damage to the transistor assistance unit. Static adjustment should be carried out by eye, with the ignition switched off, so that the contact breaker points are just opening when the appropriate flywheel notch aligns with the notch on the clutch bellhousing. This method will be sufficient to allow the engine to be started, after which the ignition timing can be accurately set dynamically.

10.4A Remove the screws ...

10.4B ... and lift off the distributor cap

10.7 Removing the rotor arm

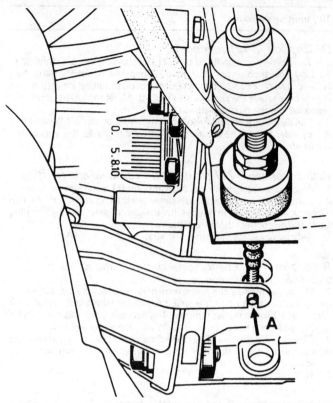

Fig. 12.29 Clutch cable trunnion greasing area (A) (Sec 11)

11   Clutch

Clutch assembly – removal and refitting (Turbo and 1721 cc models)
1   On the above models, the engine and gearbox must be removed together and then separated on the bench for access to the clutch.

Clutch release fork – later models
2   On later models the release fork spring shown in Chapter 5 is no longer fitted – the fork simply sits on the pivot stud.

Clutch cable – greasing of trunnion
3   In order that the trunnion and cable guide operate correctly and keep the clutch cable in alignment, the trunnion and cable guide should be kept coated with a general purpose lithium-based grease (Fig. 12.29).

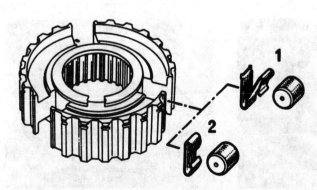

Fig. 12.31 Early (1) and later (2) types of synchro spring (Sec 12)

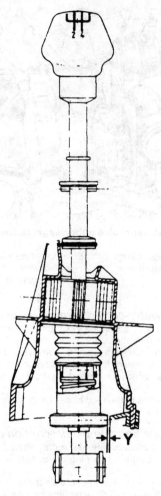

Fig. 12.30 Adjustment of later type gear lever (Sec 12)

Y   See text

12   Manual gearbox

Removal and refitting – Turbo and 1721 cc models
1   On the above models, the gearbox cannot be removed independently of the engine. The engine and gearbox must be removed together and then separated on the bench.

Gearchange mechanism (later models) – general
2   During 1989, a modified gearchange mechanism was introduced. The new mechanism incorporates a locking ring just below the gear knob which must be raised before reverse gear can be selected.
3   Accurate adjustment of the mechanism requires a special tool to be fitted to the gearchange lever on the gearbox to lock it into first gear. As a rough guide, however, adjustment is correct when with first gear selected, gap 'Y' (Fig. 12.30) is between 2 and 5 mm (0.08 and 0.20 in). Adjustment is carried out by slackening the clamp nut and bolt at the base of the gear lever and turning the selector rod one way or the other.

Synchroniser unit springs – modifications
4   Two types of synchroniser spring have been fitted (Fig. 12.31)
5   Early type springs can be used to replace later ones, provided that the same type of spring is used in any one synchro unit. However, later type springs must not be used in place of early ones.

Differential (models with electronic speedometer) – dismantling and reassembly
6   On models with an electronic speedometer, a sensor ring wheel and spring are fitted instead of a speedometer drivegear.

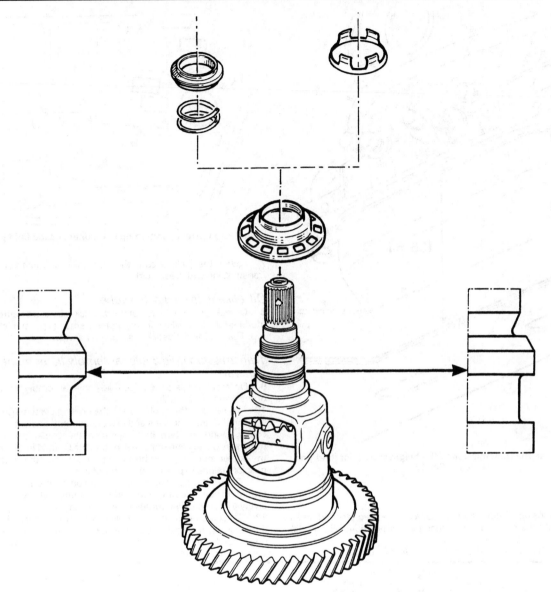

Fig. 12.32 First type (left) and second type (right) of speedometer sensor ring springs (Sec 12)

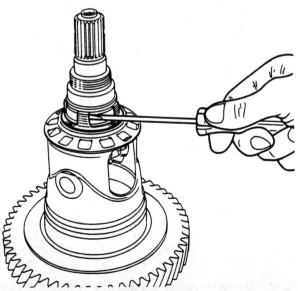

Fig. 12.33 Prising the spring tabs out of the groove (Sec 12)

7   Two types of spring have been used (Fig. 12.32). The first type of spring can be fitted in place of the second type, but not vice versa.
8   To remove the second type of spring, prise its tabs out of the groove on the differential case (Fig. 12.33). Use a new spring when reassembling, driving it home with a tube of suitable diameter and making sure that the tabs engage in the groove.

13   Automatic transmission

Filter screen renewal

1   This operation is carried out at time of routine renewal of transmission fluid. Begin by draining the fluid (Chapter 6, Section 20).
2   Remove the nut which secures the transmission mounting on the left-hand side of the vehicle.
3   Support the transmission with a jack placed under the differential housing. Raise the jack to give a clearance of approximately 135 mm (5.3 in) between the transmission fluid pan and the crossmember (Fig. 12.34).
4   Clean the fluid pan and the transmission so that no dirt will be introduced. Remove the fluid pan securing bolts. Remove the fluid pan, the filter screen and gasket.

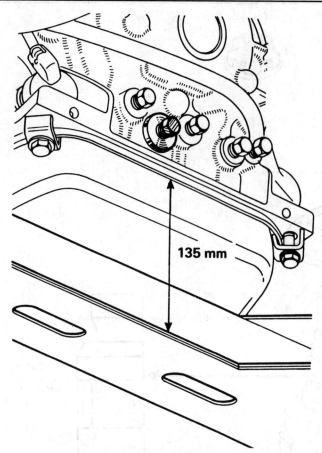

135 mm

Fig. 12.34 Raise the transmission to the height shown for fluid-pan removal (Sec 13)

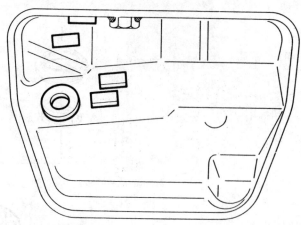

Fig. 12.35 Correct positioning of magnets inside fluid pan (Sec 13)

7   Lower the jack, secure the transmission mounting and fill the transmission with fresh fluid.

Oil leakage from dipstick tube
8   Oil leakage from the top of the dipstick tube can be cured by fitting a modified dipstick which incorporates a small expansion chamber in its top. The modified dipstick has a green handle.

Transmission fluid cooler assembly (later models) – general
9   On later models, a modified fluid cooler assembly is fitted to the top of the transmission unit.
10   To remove the cooler, drain the cooling system (Chapter 2) then slacken the retaining clips and disconnect both coolant hoses from the cooler. Undo the two bolts securing the cooler to the top of the transmission unit and remove it, noting the O-rings fitted on each side of the cooler mounting bolt holes (Fig. 12.37). Plug the cooler and transmission unions to prevent the entry of dirt.
11   On refitting, position a new O-ring on each side of the fluid cooler mounting bolt holes and tighten the mounting bolts evenly and progressively to the specified torque wrench setting.
12   On completion refill the cooling system (Chapter 2) then check and, if necessary, top up the transmission fluid level (Chapter 6). Start the engine and check the cooler for signs of fluid leakage before taking the vehicle on the road.

5   Clean the inside of the fluid pan. Remove the magnets and clean them, then refit them to the pan in their correct positions (Fig. 12.35) with the ridged faces against the pan.
6   Fit a new filter screen and gasket. then refit the fluid pan.

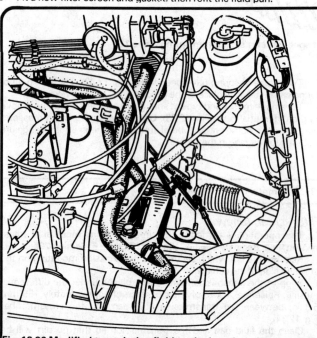

Fig. 12.36 Modified tranmission fluid cooler location – later models (Sec 13)

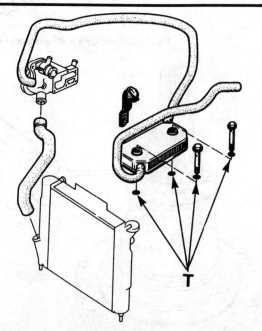

ig. 12.37 O-rings (T) must be renewed when refitting fluid cooler -- later models (Sec 13)

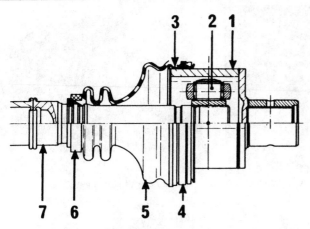

Fig. 12.38 Sectional view of later type driveshaft inboard joint
(Sec 14)

1	Yoke	5	Bellows
2	Spider	6	Clip
3	Metal cover	7	Shaft
4	Clip		

14   Driveshafts

New driveshafts – fitting

1   New driveshafts are supplied with cardboard protectors over the bellows. These protectors must be left in place until fitting is complete, then removed by hand. Do not use sharp-ended tools to remove the protectors, as there is a risk of damaging the bellows.

Driveshaft bellows – renewal (general)

2   The rubber bellows at the outboard end of each driveshaft have been superseded by bellows made of a thermoplastic material. These later bellows cannot be expanded to pass over the driveshaft yoke, so the inboard bellows will have to be removed and the driveshaft dismantled as described in Chapter 7, Section 5 or 6, or as follows in this Section.

Right-hand driveshaft inner bellows (later models) – removal

3   Two types of driveshaft joint have been used at the right-hand inner position. The first type is known as GT 62 – the bellows renewal procedure is given in Chapter 7, Section 5. The second type (Fig. 12.38) is known as RC 490, for which the bellows renewal procedure is as follows.
4   Remove the driveshaft (Chapter 7, Section 3).
5   Release the staking which secures the metal casing to the yoke.
6   Cut the bellows retaining clip. Cut open the bellows and remove as much grease as possible.
7   Remove the yoke by tapping the metal casing off it, using a brass or copper drift. Be careful that the rollers do not fall off the trunnions – they must not be interchanged.
8   Remove the circlip (if fitted) which secures the spider to the driveshaft (Fig. 12.39). Make identification marks between the spider and the shaft for use when refitting.
9   Press or pull the spider off the driveshaft – see Chapter 7, Section 5, paragraph 6.
10   Remove the bellows, metal casing and insert. Clean and examine the shaft and spider (Chapter 7, Section 5, paragraphs 8 to 10).
11   To the driveshaft fit a new retaining clip, new bellows, the insert and the metal casing.
12   Refit the spider, observing the alignment marks, and press it home.
13   Refit the securing circlip, if one was found. On versions without a circlip, secure the spider by peening the splines in three places.
14   Using the grease supplied in the repair kit, lubricate the yoke, the spider and the inside of the bellows. All the grease must be used.
15   Fit the yoke to the spider. Fit the bellows and insert to the metal casing, then slide the casing onto the yoke. Secure the casing by staking it in three places.

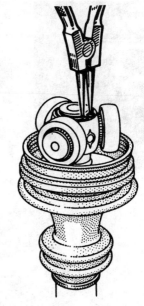

Fig. 12.39 Removing the circlip which secures the spider (Sec 14)

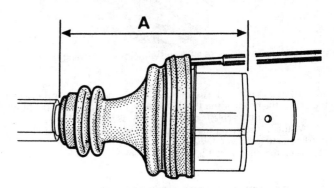

Fig. 12.40 Venting the driveshaft bellows (Sec 14)

$A = 156 \pm 1$ mm

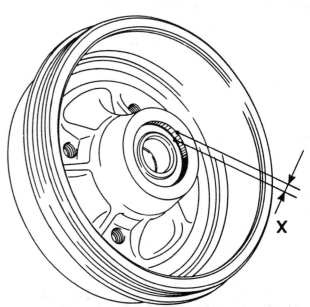

Fig. 12.41 Brake drum bearing locating area (Sec 15)

X   (early type) = 2.5 mm
X   (later type) = 4.5 mm

15.4 Later type Bendix rear brake assembly

15.7 Disconnecting the handbrake cable

15.9A Unhook the top spring ...

15.9B ... and withdraw the leading shoe

15.10 Spring and strut engagement in the trailing shoe

16   Insert a thin blunt instrument, such as a knitting needle, between the end of the bellows and the driveshaft so that air can escape. Move the joint in or out to achieve a dimension 'A' as shown in Fig. 12.40.

17   Without disturbing the joint or the bellows, remove the knitting needle and fit the new retaining clip.

18   Refit the driveshaft (Chapter 7, Section 3).

---

15   Braking system

Rear brake drum (all models) – renewal

1   Later type rear brake drums have a larger locating area for the bearing than early types (Fig. 12.41). Only later type drums are supplied as spares. If an early type drum is being replaced by a later type, proceed as follows.

2   Remove the brake backplate bolts one at a time. Discard the shakeproof washer. Apply thread-locking compound to the tapping in the suspension arm **not** to the bolt threads), then refit and tighten the bolt. This is necessary to prevent the new drum fouling the bolt heads.

Rear brake shoes (later Bendix type) – removal and refitting

3   Remove the brake drum (Chapter 8, paragraphs 1 to 10).

4   Note the initial fitted positions of the springs and the adjuster strut (photo).

5   Remove the shoe steady spring cups by depressing them and turning through 90°. Remove the cups, springs and pins.

6   Pull the shoes apart by hand and draw them off the wheel cylinder and bottom pivot. Be careful not to damage the wheel cylinder rubber boots. Allow the springs to draw the shoes together again.

7   Unhook the handbrake cable from the trailing shoe lever and remove the shoes with springs and strut (photo).

8   Remove the bottom spring.

9   Unhook the top spring from the leading shoe and withdraw it from the strut. The adjuster wheel, thread and spring will come away with the shoe (photos).

10   Unhook the springs and the strut from the trailing shoe (photo).

11   If necessary, transfer the handbrake lever from the old trailing shoe to the new one.

12   Clean the adjuster strut, paying particular attention to the wheel

and threads. Note that left-hand and right-hand struts are not interchangeable – they are marked 'G' (gauche) and 'D' (droit) respectively (photo).

13   Reassemble the shoes, strut and springs (photo).

14   Engage the handbrake cable in the lever. Pull the shoes apart and fit the assembly to the backplate, again being careful not to damage the wheel cylinder.

15   Refit the steady pins, springs and cups.

16   Turn the adjuster wheel to expand or contract the strut until the brake drum will just pass over the shoes.

17   Refit the brake drum (Chapter 8, Section 6, paragraph 26 onwards).

Rear brakes (later Bendix type) – correction of noise or drag

18   If rear brake drag or noise is a problem on models fitted with the later type Bendix brakes, renew the handbrake return spring and the adjuster strut bracket (Fig. 12.42). The latest versions of both these components have been modified – later springs are yellow or green where the early ones were white. Later brackets are green where the early ones were yellow.

19   When excessive heating has occurred as a result of drag, it is advisable to renew the wheel cylinder and/or hub bearings – consult a Renault dealer for further advice.

Rear wheel cylinder (later models) – overhaul

20   On models where the rear wheel cylinder incorporates a pressure regulating valve, the cylinder cannot be overhauled. In case of leakage or other malfunction it must be renewed.

Master cylinder (1721 cc models) – removal and refitting

21   On these models the master cylinder reservoir is remote from the cylinder itself. Commence removal by clamping the reservoir-to-master cylinder hoses (or by emptying the reservoir) and disconnect the hoses from the cylinder. Be careful not to spill brake fluid on the paintwork.

22   The procedure is now as described in Chapter 8, Section 13.

Pressure regulating valve (later models) – description

23   On most later models the pressure regulating function is carried out by a valve incorporated in each rear wheel cylinder (photo).

24   The combined wheel cylinder/regulating valve assembly cannot be repaired. If either part malfunctions it must be renewed.

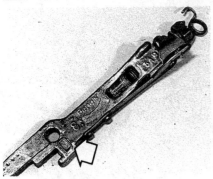

15.12 Right-hand adjuster strut is marked 'D' (arrowed)

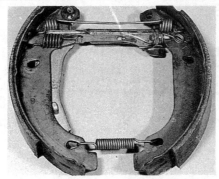

15.13 Shoes, springs and strut reassembled

15.23 Rear wheel cylinder/pressure regulating valve components

Handbrake – adjustment

25   When carrying out the handbrake adjustment procedure in Chapter 8, Section 19, it is imperative that there is no tension in the handbrake cable at the start of proceedings.

26   Adjustment of the handbrake with tension in the cable will result in faulty operation of the automatic adjuster and excessive footbrake pedal travel.

27   Under no circumstances should these symptoms be remedied by further adjustment of the handbrake, which will only make matters worse.

28   The handbrake is not a 'wear take-up' system, and should only need adjusting after the brake linings, handbrake cables or handbrake lever have been renewed.

Erratic servo operation – Turbo models

29   Lack of servo effort of Turbo models, especially when the engine is cold, may be due to the non-return valve in the inlet manifold jamming. Renew this valve before suspecting a fault in the servo itself.

---

16   Suspension and steering

Front suspension strut (later Turbo models) – dismantling and reassembly

1   On Turbo models from June 1987, a modified strut with an inclined top mounting is fitted.

2   Dismantling and reassembly are still as described in Chapter 9, Section 6, but on reassembly the dimension to which the spring must be compressed is 400 mm (15.8 in).

Rear suspension bushes (enclosed bar rear axle) – modification

3   The plastic bushes fitted originally have been superseded by needle roller races. Some suspension arm dimensions have changed slightly at the same time.

4   The new races are not a direct replacement for the old bushes, but special kits of parts are available.

5   A press and various special mandrels are needed for the fitting of the races and their tracks. The operation should therefore be carried out by a Renault dealer or a suitable workshop.

Power steering – description

6   Available on certain models, power steering reduces the effort required to turn the steering wheel by means of hydraulic assistance. Hydraulic pressure is produced by a pump, belt-driven from the crankshaft pulley, and is applied to one side or the other of a hydraulic ram inside the steering gear. The direction and amount of assistance is determined by a rotary valve on the steering gear pinion shaft.

7   If power assistance is lost for any reason, the vehicle can still be steered but considerably more effort will be required.

8   To prevent the engine stalling under sudden load from the steering pump at idle (for example when parking) a pressure-sensitive switch in the steering hydraulic system operates a fast idle device on the carburettor. Adjustment of this system is covered in Section 8.

Power steering – maintenance

9   Routine maintenance is confined to inspecting the pipes, hoses and

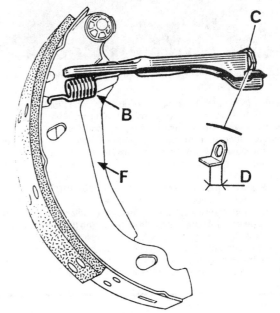

Fig. 12.42 To cure brake drag or noise, renew the spring (B) and the bracket (C) (Sec 15)

D (early type) = 12 mm
D (modified type) = 10 mm
F Handbrake lever

16.9 Topping-up the power steering fluid

16.11 Disconnecting the high-pressure pipe from the steering pump

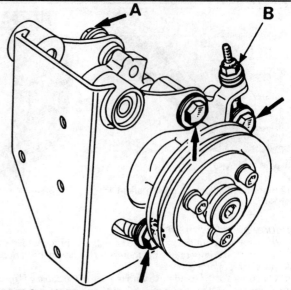

Fig. 12.43 Steering pump mounting bolts (arrowed) – 1397 cc model (Sec 16)

A   Pivot bolt   B   Belt tension adjuster

unions in the system for leaks, and checking the fluid level in the reservoir. The fluid level should be between the two lines on the reservoir. Top up if necessary with the specified grade of automatic transmission fluid (photo). Be careful not to introduce dirt into the system, and do not overfill. Frequent need for topping-up must be due to a leak, which should be investigated.

Power steering pump – removal and refitting

10   Remove the drivebelt(s) and the alternator.
11   Clamp the reservoir-to-pump hose, then disconnect the high-pressure pipe and the supply hose from the pump (photo). Be prepared for fluid spillage.
12   Undo the mounting bolts (Fig. 12.43) and remove the pump.
13   Refit by reversing the removal operations. Tension the drive-belt(s), then bleed the steering hydraulic circuit as follows.

Power steering circuit – bleeding

14   This procedure is only required after component renewal, or if the fluid level has become very low due to leakage.
15   Top up the reservoir to the maximum level line with the specified fluid. Turn the steering wheel from lock to lock and top up further if required.
16   Start the engine and again turn the steering from lock to lock. Stop the engine and top up the reservoir again to the maximum line.

Power steering gear – removal and refitting

17   Refer to Chapter 9, Section 26, but note the following additional operations.

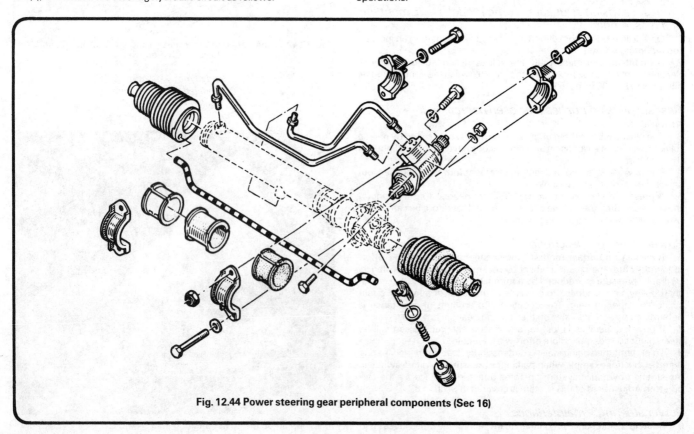

Fig. 12.44 Power steering gear peripheral components (Sec 16)

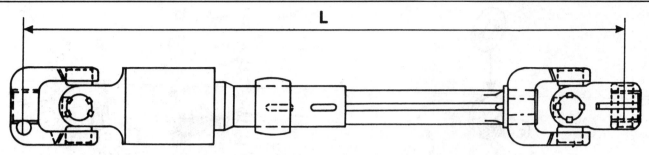

Fig. 12.45 Steering column intermediate shaft length – models with power steering (Sec 16)

L = 401 mm ± 1 mm (RHD) or 381 ± 1 mm (LHD)

18   On 1397 cc models, disconnect the gearchange linkage from the gearbox or the selector linkage from the automatic transmission.
19   On all models, clamp both hoses at the steering fluid reservoir. Disconnect the fluid supply and return pipes from the steering gear and remove them. Be prepared for fluid spillage.
20   After unbolting the steering gear from its mountings but before removing it, remove the pipes which connect the ram with the rotary valve. Plug the openings to keep dirt out.
21   After refitting, bleed the steering hydraulic circuit as previously described.

Power steering gear – overhaul
22   Overhaul of the power steering gear should be left to specialists. Purchase of a new or reconditioned unit is probably the most satisfactory course of action.

Steering column intermediate shaft length – power steering
23   On models with power steering, the intermediate shaft checking dimension is as shown (Fig. 12.45).

---

17   Bodywork and fittings

Front door interior trim panel (later models) – removal and refitting
1   On later models a plastic sheet is not fitted inside the door. A bead of sealant round the edge of the trim panel is used instead. This sealant must be cut using a sharp knife when removing the panel, and fresh sealant used during reassembly.

Door hinges (later models) – modification
2   The type of door hinge shown in Chapter 10, Section 18, has been replaced by that shown here (Fig. 12.46). The hinge pin is removed not by driving it out, but by unscrewing it.
3   A door with the new hinge can be fitted to an old hinge mount if the pin hole is drilled out to accept the new bushes.

Door striker – adjustment
4   In addition to the adjustment given in Chapter 10, Section 18, the door striker is also adjustable fore-and-aft by using shims under the door striker.

5   The shims should be placed between the thrustwasher and the plastic washer, and be of such thickness that the door lock bolt engages as near to the centre of the door striker as possible (Fig. 12.47).

Steering lock/ignition switch (all models) – removal and refitting
6   Disconnect the battery negative lead.
7   Remove the steering column lower shroud.
8   Remove the two nuts and two bolts which secure the steering column brackets, and the two Torx screws which secure the facia to the column. Lower the column slightly.
9   Follow the ignition switch wiring back behind the facia and disconnect it.
10   Remove the lock securing screw (photo).
11   Insert the ignition key and turn it to position 'G'. Depress the retaining lugs and withdraw the lock/switch assembly (photos).
12   Refit by reversing the removal operations.

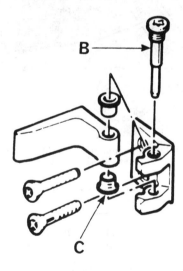

Fig. 12.46 Later type door hinge (Sec 17)

B   Hinge pin   C   Bush

17.10 Steering lock securing screw

17.11A Depress the lugs (arrowed) ...

17.11B ... and withdraw the lock and switch

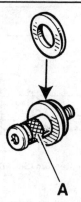

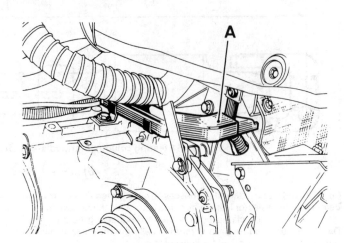

**Fig. 12.47 Adjust door striker so that lock bolt engages in area A
(Sec 17)**

Fig. 12.48 Wiring harness heat shield (A) (Sec 18)

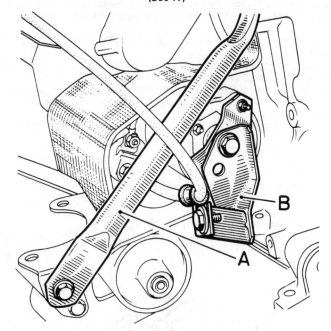

**Fig. 12.49 Exhaust downpipe mounting bar (A) and starter support
bracket (B) (Sec 18)**

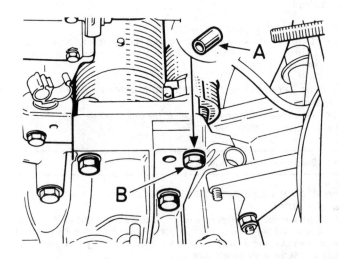

Fig. 12.50 Centring dowel (A) must be in place on bolt (B) (Sec 18)

18   Electrical system

Starter motor (Turbo models) – removal and refitting
Note: *The procedure given here is in clarification of that given in Chapter
11, Section 11.*
1   Remove the hoses for the air scoop and air filter.
2   Remove the air filter.
3   Remove the turbo heat shield.
4   Refer to Fig. 12.48 and remove the electrical harness heat shield.
5   Undo and remove the bolts securing the starter, and the starter
support bracket from the rear of the starter.
6   Remove the exhaust downpipe mounting bar (Fig. 12.49).
7   Disconnect the starter electrical connections and withdraw the
starter from behind the front right-hand roadwheel.
8   Refitting is a reversal of this procedure, but make sure the centering
dowel is still in place in the starter securing bolt hole (Fig. 12.50).
9   The turbo heat shield must be refitted.

Headlamp dim-dip system – general
10   Most UK market models covered by this manual will be fitted with
the 'dim-dip' headlamp system required by current legislation. This
system causes the headlamp dipped beams to illuminate at reduced
intensity if the sidelights and the ignition are both switched on.
11   A circuit diagram of the system is given in Fig. 12.51. The resistor is
mounted in the right-hand scuttle (photo).

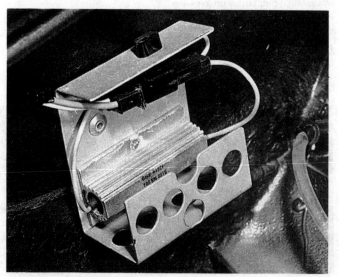

18.11 Dim-dip resistor

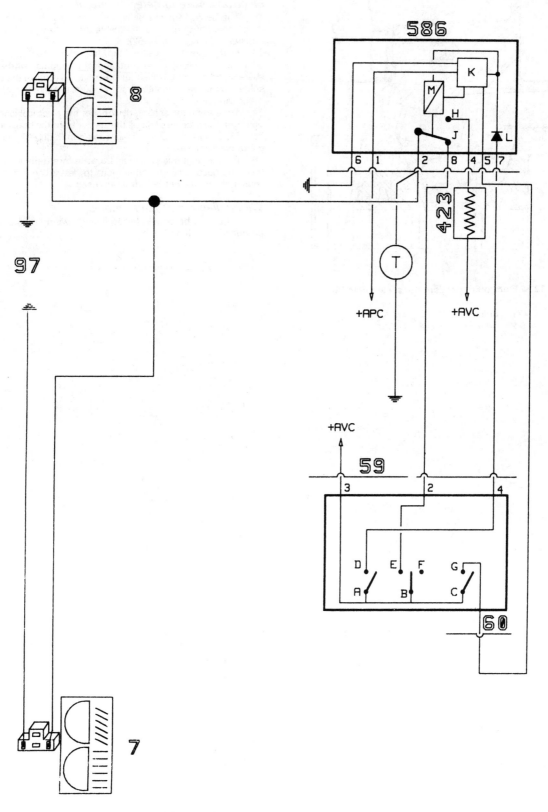

Fig. 12.51 Dim-dip headlamp circuit (Sec 18)

7   LH headlamp unit
8   RH headlamp unit

59   Headlamp and direction
     indicator control unit
60   Dipswitch

97   Body earth
423 Dipped beam headlamp
     intensity reducing resistor

586 Dipped beam headlamp
     intensity reducing relay

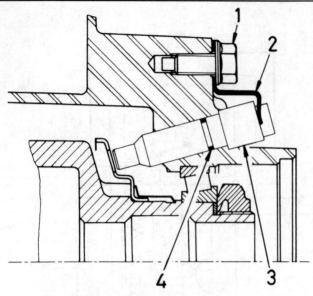

Fig. 12.52 Electronic speedometer sensor (Sec 18)

1	Bolt	3	Sensor
2	Retainer	4	O-ring

Electronic speedometer – general

12   The sensor for the electronic speedometer is mounted in the differential housing, as for the cable-driven type, and is secured by a retainer and a bolt (Fig. 12.52).

13   In the event of malfunction, first check that the sensor wiring connector is making good contact. If the condition of the connector is suspect, cut the wires on either side of it and remake the connection by soldering the wires, matching the colours. Insulate the joints from each other with tape.

14   To remove the sensor, disconnect the electrical lead, remove the bolt from the retainer and pull the sensor from the housing.

15   Make sure the O-ring is in good condition, and lubricate it with gearbox oil before refitting.

16   Further fault tracing should be done by a Renault dealer, who will have the necessary test equipment to determine if a fault lies in the sensor, the wiring or the instrument itself.

Wiring diagrams – later models

17   It has not been possible to include wiring diagrams for models produced after June 1987.

Index